WRITTEN BY
ANTONY JOHNSTON

DEAD SPACE™

Producers — Cate Latchford
            Chuck Beaver
EP — Steve Papoutsis
Art Director — Ian Milham
Production Designer — Ben Wanat

Special thanks to:
  Erika Peterson
  Frank Gibeau
  John Riccietello
  Matt Bendett
  Nick Earl

www.deadspace.com

LETTERING BY Rus Wooton

DEAD SPACE™
ISBN: 9781781165515

Published by Titan Books,
A division of Titan Publishing Group Ltd.,
144 Southwark St., London, SE1 0UP

A CIP catalogue record for this title is available from the British Library.

First edition: February 2013

10 9 8 7 6 5 4 3 2

Printed in China.

What did you think of this book? We love to hear from our readers. Please email us
at: readerfeedback@titanmail.com, or write to us at the above address.

To receive advance information, news, competitions, and exclusive offers online,
please sign up for the Titan newsletter on our website: www.titanbooks.com

DEAD SPACE

TITAN BOOKS

CONTENTS

BRAM

Abraham 'Bram' Howard Neumann was born on Mars. His father, whom he idolized, was a cop. Immediately upon leaving school, Bram joined the Martian police to follow in the old man's footsteps. Bram was a beat cop during the infamous independence riots in Mars Capita, the planet's largest city-state. The violence and depths of human behavior he witnessed there led him to try out for Homicide, to get off the streets as much as anything.

He succeeded, but the celebration was tinged with sadness, as his father died shortly after of heart failure. Bram threw himself into work to cope with his grief, and quickly established himself as a tenacious, intuitive cop, dedicated to his work.

Unfortunately, the long hours and stress of the department ruined his marriage. Bram had married Joanna back when he was just a beat cop, and she was unable to cope with a husband who was now constantly on call, always late home, and "too busy" to start a family. Seeking solace, she turned to Unitology, which was slowly growing in numbers throughout the Mars colonies. The religion soon dominated her life, but Bram was – perhaps willingly – blind to its effects on his wife. Eventually they fought when Joanna insisted on hosting a Unitologist group at their apartment, and Bram moved out.

It was at this point that a new commander took over the Capita Homicide division: a stuffy, middle-management suit whom Bram quickly discovered was also a Unitologist. During a particularly heated argument over the department's lack of resources, Bram punched his commander's lights out and resigned. For a day, he was headline news on Mars.

Perhaps as a result of such a high-profile exit from the department, Bram was contacted soon after by an old Homicide partner, now retired and working for CEC's P-Sec division. He knew they were looking for new hires and recommended the job to Bram as an easy life after the stress of being a murder investigator. Bram didn't need persuading – right then, he would have taken a janitoring job so long as it was off-planet. He eagerly accepted to get as far away from Mars, his wife and Unitology as possible.

But to his surprise, Bram found he enjoyed the work. It was sociable, low-stress and paid well enough that he soon became comfortable and had trouble remembering what it was he'd ever liked about being a Homicide detective. He soon rose to Sergeant and transferred to Commander James' squad, where he met and partnered with Detective Cortez.

Though Bram was estranged from Joanna, they were still legally married. He continued to have occasional correspondence with her, and strained irregular visits to see her on Mars. In his heart, he hoped that she would see sense and leave the Church with nothing hurt besides her pride. But that day never came, and one year ago Bram discovered that Joanna had given the Church of Unitology their entire joint life savings, including money he'd put aside since working for CEC. As Joanna was still officially his wife, the Church insisted this 'donation' was legal, and the Mars courts dismissed Bram's complaints. Bram filed for divorce immediately, and it was granted six months ago. He has since developed a casual relationship with Marla Janssen.

CORTEZ

Vera Maria Alejandra Cortez was born on Earth to a poor family in the central American sector, the youngest of five sisters. When she was twelve, her father was killed by street muggers, and her mother turned to Unitology for comfort. Soon the whole family were devout, and Vera has been a believer ever since.

Vera joined the local police as soon as she was old enough, but experienced so much sexual harassment and gender discrimination on the job that she quit and moved to the United States, finding work as a private security guard. Bored with the unsociable work, she applied to CEC for work in P-Sec and was taken on as a standard security officer.

Her diligence and perseverance paid off, and within a few years, Vera was made a Detective. She is intensely proud that she got there through hard work and merit, and brooks no disrespect from the multitude of veteran ex-cops that work for P-Sec.

In private, Vera credits her success to her Unitologist beliefs, but while she doesn't deny her faith, she also doesn't shout about it. Most of her colleagues have no idea how devout she really is.

MARLA

Marla Loren Janssen was born in the Scandinavian sector of Earth, but when she was just ten years old her father took a job on Mars and moved his family there. Already somewhat bookish, Marla became a recluse in this literally alien environment. She spent all her spare time and money on computer tech, an area that she excelled in at school, along with math and physics.

When she was thirteen, Marla's parents became suspicious that their daughter seemed to have a lot more money than her weekend should have been paying her. Their investigations unfortunately led to involvement by the police, and within weeks Marla became the youngest person on Mars to ever be arrested for 'Grade 1' hacking. She has been taking orders and payment from anonymous clients on the net, hacking into the central government's database to alter records for these clients.

Three years in Mars juvenile prison put Marla on the straight and narrow. She was released, and her record sealed, on her sixteenth birthday and promptly began working in the Mars shipyards as a systems designer and QA officer. While there, she met Bram Neumann, while he was on leave to visit his wife. He told Marla she could earn more and have an easier life with P-Sec, whom he just happened to know were looking for a new control op on Commander James' squad.

Marla followed up on the lead, and within days she was offered the job. Marla has since worked on two colonies with James' squad. Since his divorce, she and Neumann have developed a casual relationship.

DEAD SPACE
CHARACTER PROFILES

NATALIA

Natalia Raisa Deshyanov was born in Earth's North Asia sector, to a large extended family of engineers and laborers going back generations. She spent her childhood stargazing, and would often act out fantasies of living on Mars with her cousins.

Unlike most children, Natalia's fascination with the stars never faded, and while serving out her apprenticeship as an engineer, she continually applied for spacebound jobs. It was the Mars Capita riots that would eventually grant her wish, as post-revolution the fledgling city-state desperately needed good engineers to repair and rebuild its infrastructure. Natalia successfully applied, and was taken on by a general engineering contractor. Forty-eight relatives turned out to bid her goodbye as she boarded the shuttle at Baikonur, and Natalia never looked back.

Later, seeing that the Mars rebuilding was nearing completion and her job would soon be redundant, Natalia jumped before she was pushed. She found a new line of work in Mars' orbiting shipyards, working for a CEC subsidiary. She soon garnered a position within CEC itself as a supervisor.

Natalia has lived and worked her whole life around engineers and laborers, and is completely comfortable working in a predominantly male environment. She gives as good as she gets, and can drink half of her own team under the table.

ABBOTT

Deakin St. John Abbott was born on Mars, a second-genner whose parents were both first-gen Mars natives. An unremarkable early life and education was tempered by his aptitude for mechanics and engineering, which led him to a career in those fields. He came to specialize in 'hostile terrain' vehicles, and was working for the Martian police's vehicle and engineering division during the Mars Capita riots.

Deakin's wife Tina, a civilian and housewife, was killed in those same riots by police fire into a crowded street. Disillusioned with life and the world, Abbott sought solace in Unitology. The Church only deepened his growing distrust of government and its officials, even Mars Capita's new 'idealist' administration.

Soon, Unitology became Deakin's life, and he began lay preaching while continuing to work as an engineer, though he no longer accepted work on state contracts.

Deakin was slowly becoming persona non grata on Mars, and he began looking for a way off the planet. At the same time, a former colleague from his work with the police contacted him. Now working for CEC, his old colleague headhunted Deakin for the company, and he jumped at the chance to escape his bad memories.

Deakin worked his way up to become a supervisor in the VTM (Vehicular Transport & Mechanical) division of CEC's colony operations, and he continues to preach the gospel of Unitology.

SCIARELLO

Thomas Olivier Sciarello was born to a comfortable family life in the United States sector of Earth. Tom's father was a surgeon, and his mother a general practitioner. It was expected that his older brother Carlos would follow in their footsteps, but instead Carlos went off the rails and has spent a lifetime in and out of jail for petty crimes.

Feeling the weight of responsibility, Tom took up the mantle instead, and plunged headfirst into a comfortable career and family life. He married young, had two children, and ran a successful surgery on Earth for many years.

Then his parents both died within a month of each other, and Tom's life fell apart. The loss had a much greater impact than anyone could have foreseen. Within six months he had divorced his wife, closed his surgery and joined a small extraterrestrial mining company as their fleet doctor. Unfortunately, he rapidly discovered that life in space freaked him the hell out.

Tom cast around for a position on Mars, but instead found an opening with CEC, who were looking for good doctors to head up colony surgeries. Grateful for any job that would only require a bare minimum of space travel, he took it.

Ten years later, Tom has presided over three successful planetcrack colonies and was recently promoted to CMO (Chief Medical Officer). He has never remarried.

CARTHUSIA

Hanford Peter George la Salle Carthusia was born into a wealthy family of bankers and executives in the pan-European sector of Earth. His family has been a respected pillar of the Church of Scientology for three generations, and Hanford's generation is no exception. Almost all family members are Vested, and at least one is known to be an Overseer.

Hanford worked in a variety of family-owned businesses in energy, manufacturing and distribution, working his way through middle management with a genuine skill for strategy and protecting the bottom line. Eventually he was promoted, and went on to prove he had equal skills in the boardroom.

Through his family connections, Hanford came to the attention of several prominent Unitologists within the higher echelons of CEC, and was headhunted at their behest. His family gave their blessing, seeing it as an opportunity to increase their influence both in business and the Church. He joined CEC as an assistant project manager and quickly rose to become an overall project manager, with full jurisdiction over his assigned mining colony.

He has presided over four planetcracks to date, and it is widely expected within the company that he will rise to executive level and work exclusively from CEC HQ on Earth. Hanford's wife and three children, who reside on Earth under the aegis of his powerful extended family, look forward to that day.

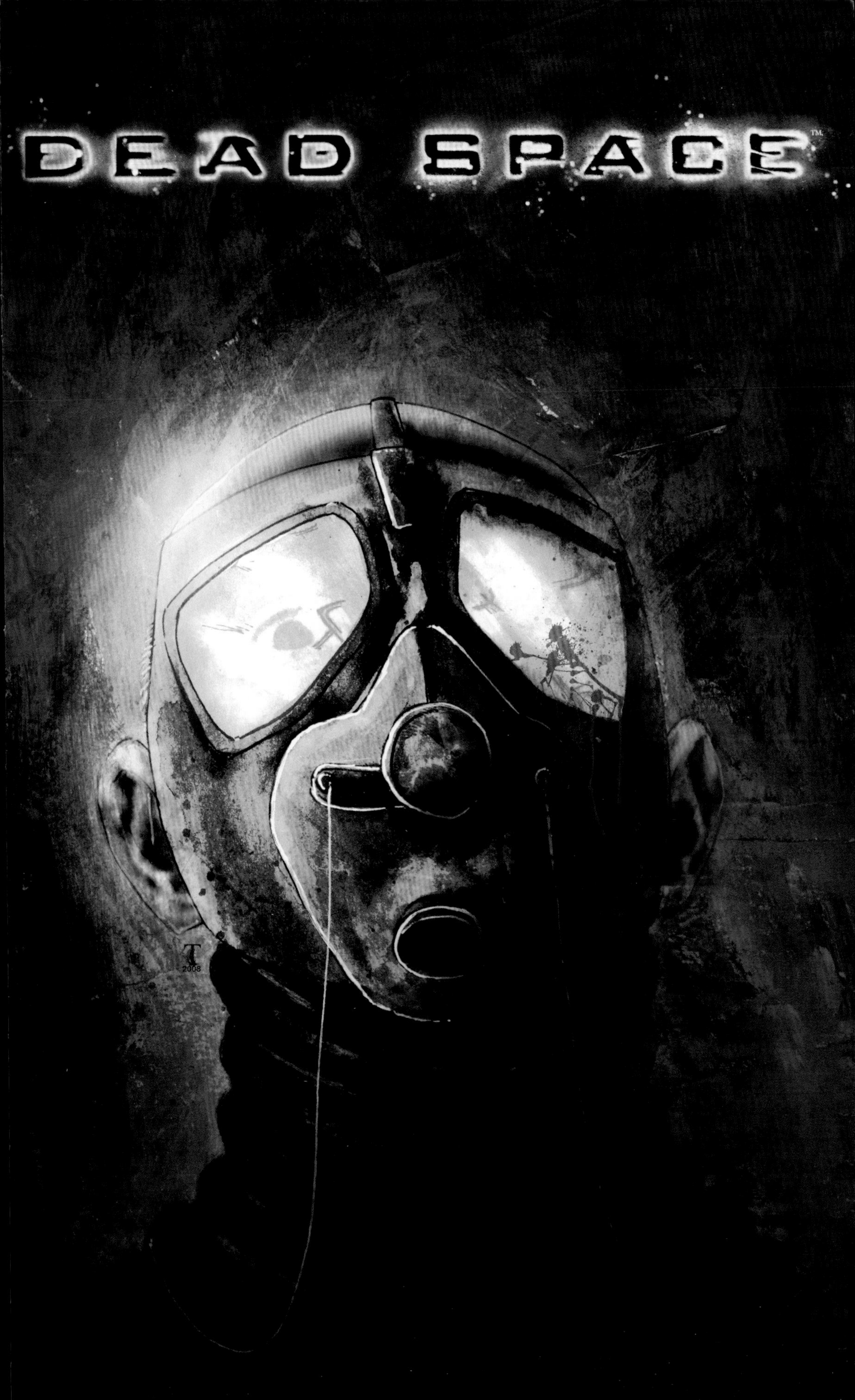
DEAD SPACE™

VOLUME 1

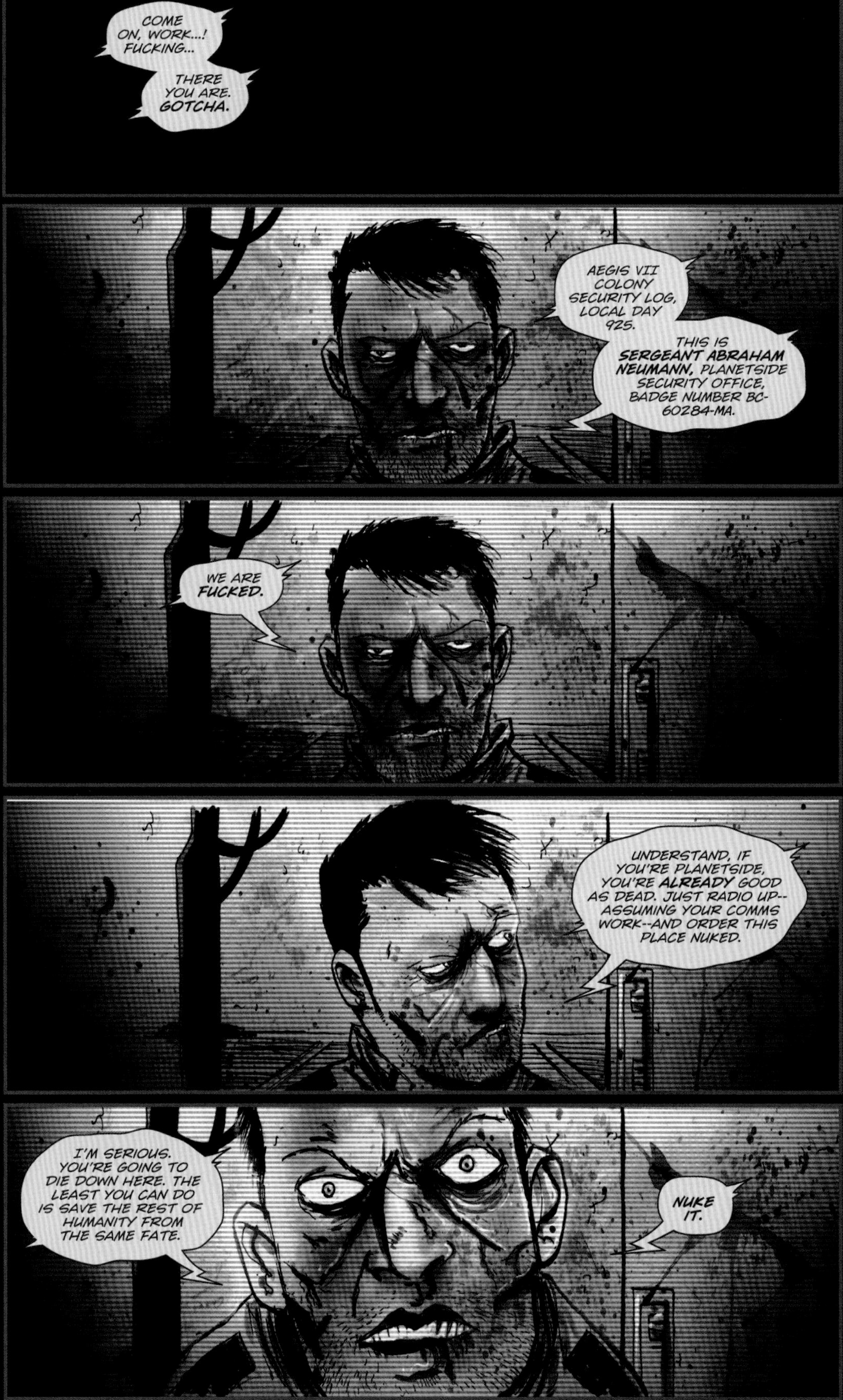
COME ON, WORK...! FUCKING...
THERE YOU ARE. GOTCHA.
AEGIS VII COLONY SECURITY LOG, LOCAL DAY 925.
THIS IS SERGEANT ABRAHAM NEUMANN, PLANETSIDE SECURITY OFFICE, BADGE NUMBER BC-60284-MA.
WE ARE FUCKED.
UNDERSTAND, IF YOU'RE PLANETSIDE, YOU'RE ALREADY GOOD AS DEAD. JUST RADIO UP--ASSUMING YOUR COMMS WORK--AND ORDER THIS PLACE NUKED.
I'M SERIOUS. YOU'RE GOING TO DIE DOWN HERE. THE LEAST YOU CAN DO IS SAVE THE REST OF HUMANITY FROM THE SAME FATE.
NUKE IT.

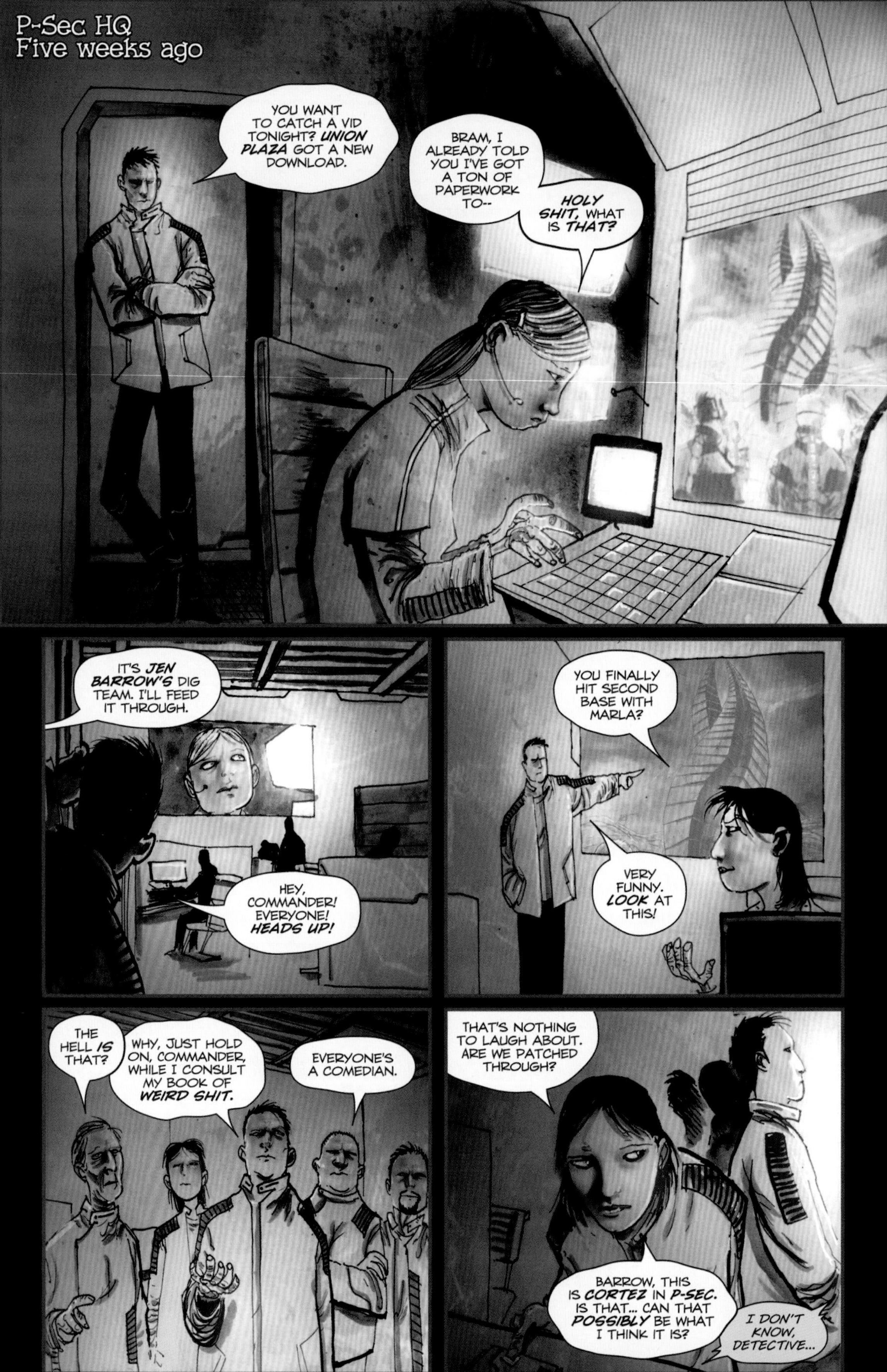
P-Sec HQ
Five weeks ago
YOU WANT TO CATCH A VID TONIGHT? UNION PLAZA GOT A NEW DOWNLOAD.
BRAM, I ALREADY TOLD YOU I'VE GOT A TON OF PAPERWORK TO--
HOLY SHIT, WHAT IS THAT?
IT'S JEN BARROW'S DIG TEAM. I'LL FEED IT THROUGH.
HEY, COMMANDER! EVERYONE! HEADS UP!
YOU FINALLY HIT SECOND BASE WITH MARLA?
VERY FUNNY. LOOK AT THIS!
THE HELL IS THAT?
WHY, JUST HOLD ON, COMMANDER, WHILE I CONSULT MY BOOK OF WEIRD SHIT.
EVERYONE'S A COMEDIAN.
THAT'S NOTHING TO LAUGH ABOUT. ARE WE PATCHED THROUGH?
BARROW, THIS IS CORTEZ IN P-SEC. IS THAT... CAN THAT POSSIBLY BE WHAT I THINK IT IS?
I DON'T KNOW, DETECTIVE...

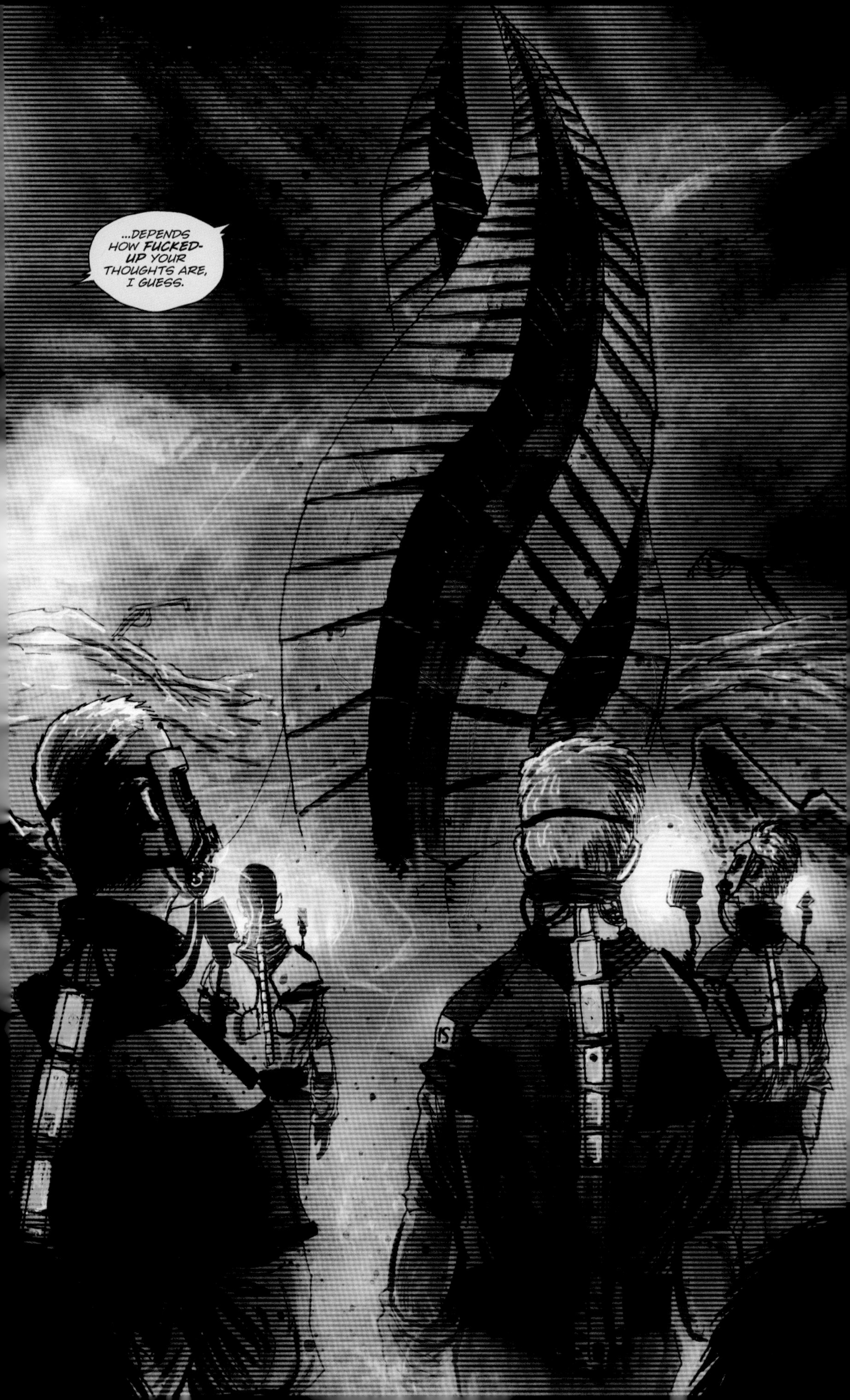
...DEPENDS HOW **FUCKED-UP** YOUR THOUGHTS ARE, I GUESS.

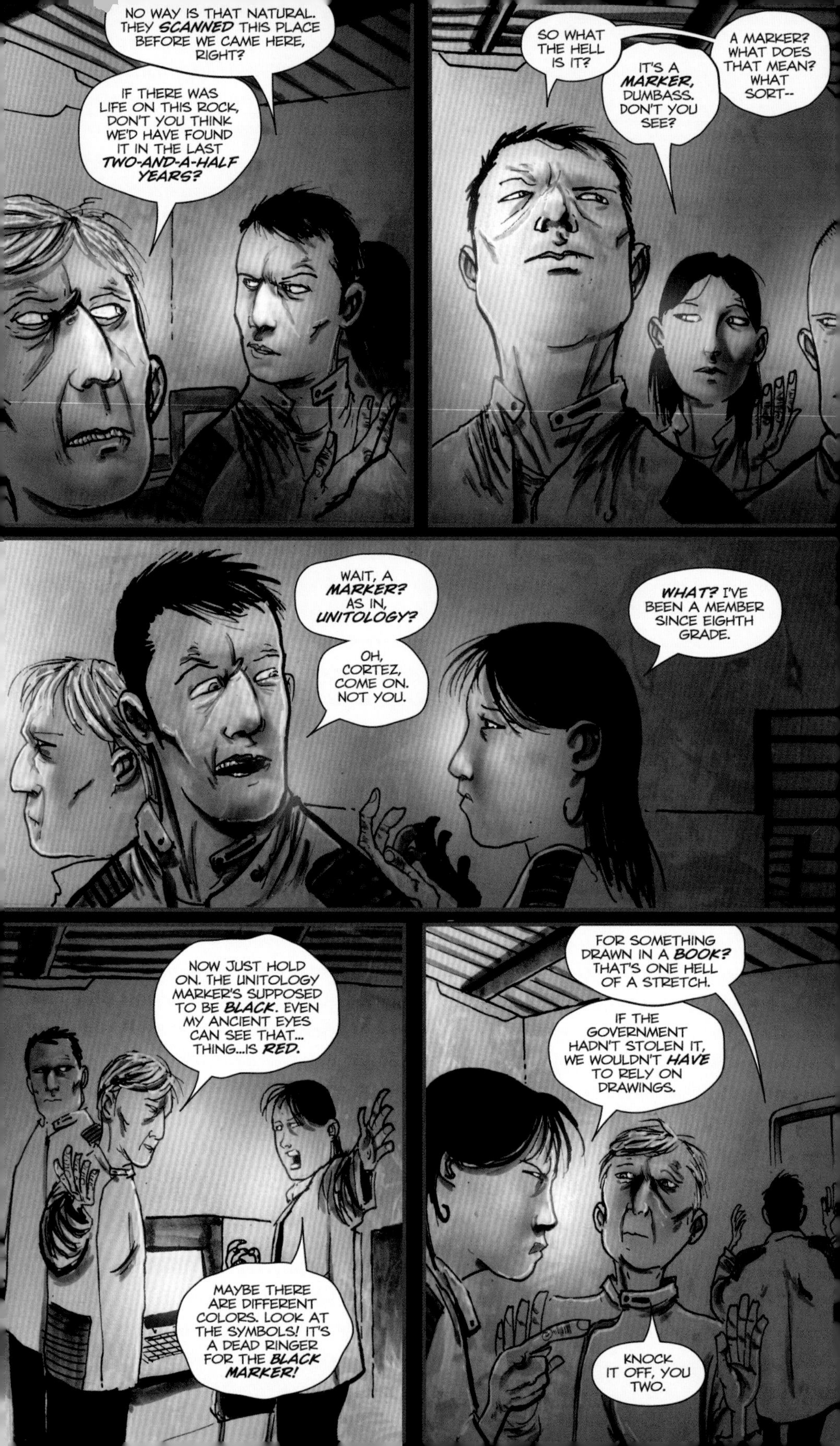
NO WAY IS THAT NATURAL. THEY SCANNED THIS PLACE BEFORE WE CAME HERE, RIGHT?
IF THERE WAS LIFE ON THIS ROCK, DON'T YOU THINK WE'D HAVE FOUND IT IN THE LAST TWO-AND-A-HALF YEARS?
SO WHAT THE HELL IS IT?
IT'S A MARKER, DUMBASS. DON'T YOU SEE?
A MARKER? WHAT DOES THAT MEAN? WHAT SORT--
WAIT, A MARKER? AS IN, UNITOLOGY?
OH, CORTEZ, COME ON. NOT YOU.
WHAT? I'VE BEEN A MEMBER SINCE EIGHTH GRADE.
NOW JUST HOLD ON. THE UNITOLOGY MARKER'S SUPPOSED TO BE BLACK. EVEN MY ANCIENT EYES CAN SEE THAT... THING...IS RED.
MAYBE THERE ARE DIFFERENT COLORS. LOOK AT THE SYMBOLS! IT'S A DEAD RINGER FOR THE BLACK MARKER!
FOR SOMETHING DRAWN IN A BOOK? THAT'S ONE HELL OF A STRETCH.
IF THE GOVERNMENT HADN'T STOLEN IT, WE WOULDN'T HAVE TO RELY ON DRAWINGS.
KNOCK IT OFF, YOU TWO.

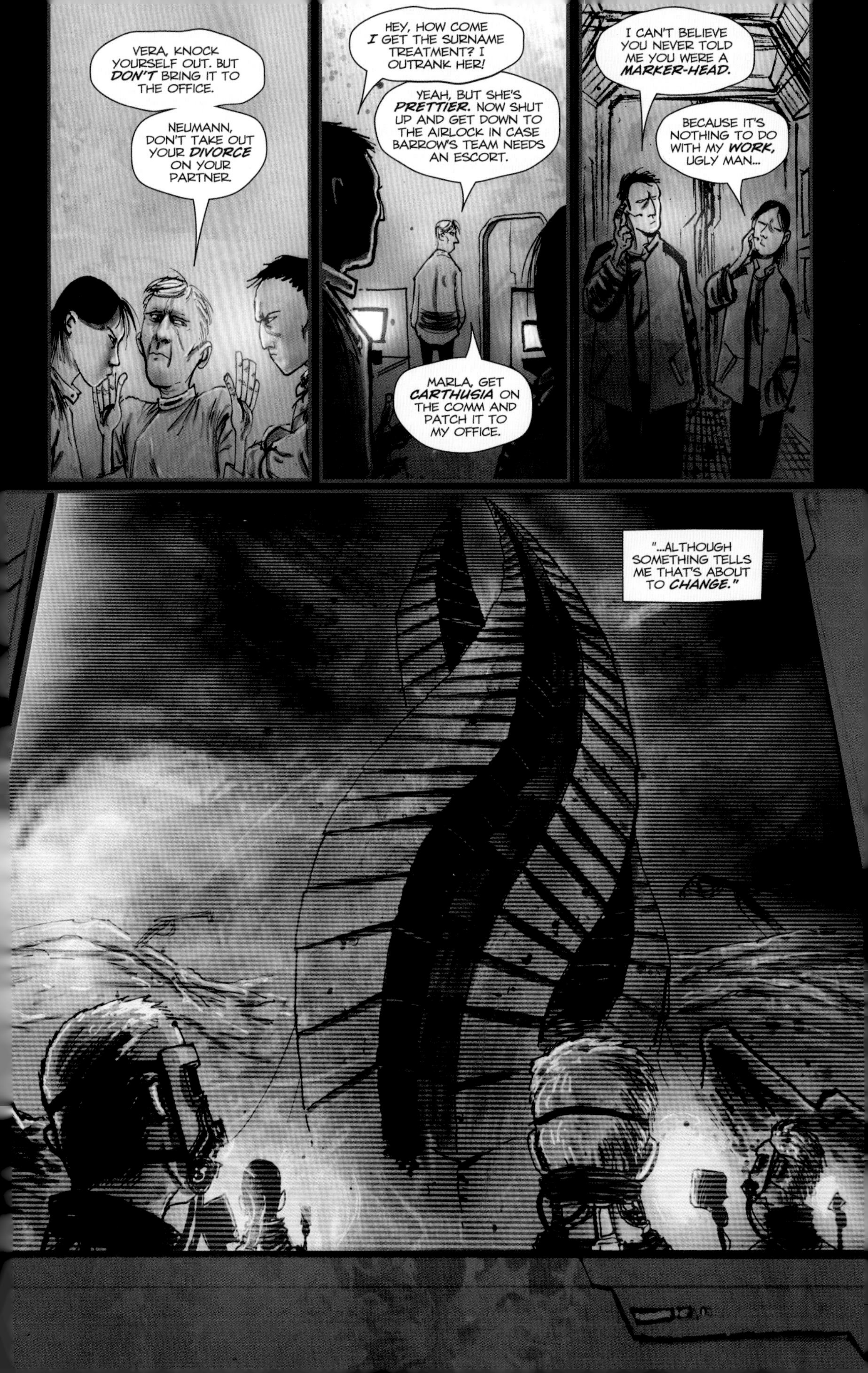
VERA, KNOCK YOURSELF OUT. BUT DON'T BRING IT TO THE OFFICE.
NEUMANN, DON'T TAKE OUT YOUR DIVORCE ON YOUR PARTNER.
HEY, HOW COME I GET THE SURNAME TREATMENT? I OUTRANK HER!
YEAH, BUT SHE'S PRETTIER. NOW SHUT UP AND GET DOWN TO THE AIRLOCK IN CASE BARROW'S TEAM NEEDS AN ESCORT.
MARLA, GET CARTHUSIA ON THE COMM AND PATCH IT TO MY OFFICE.
I CAN'T BELIEVE YOU NEVER TOLD ME YOU WERE A MARKER-HEAD.
BECAUSE IT'S NOTHING TO DO WITH MY WORK, UGLY MAN...
"...ALTHOUGH SOMETHING TELLS ME THAT'S ABOUT TO CHANGE."

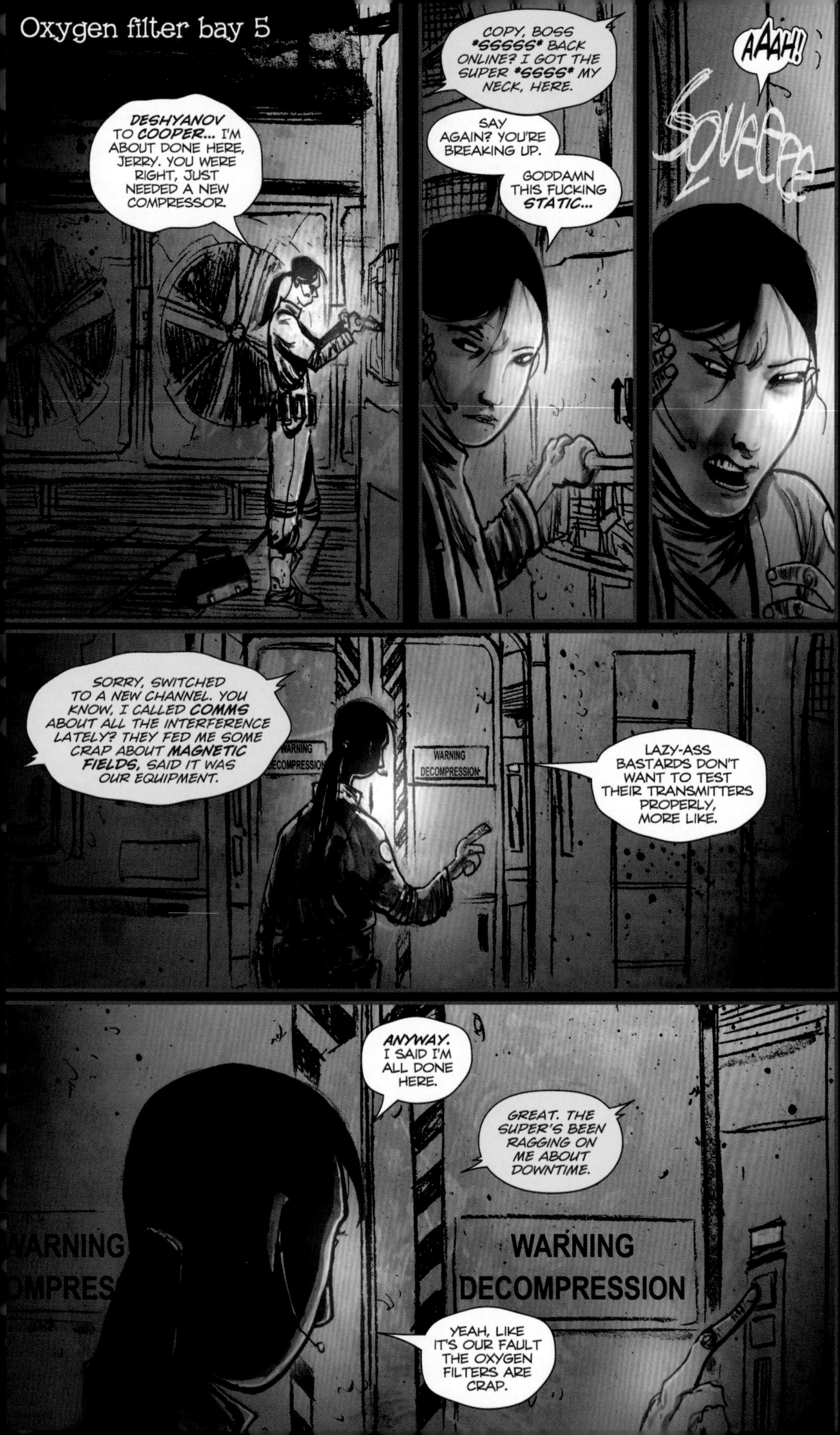
Oxygen filter bay 5
DESHYANOV TO COOPER... I'M ABOUT DONE HERE, JERRY. YOU WERE RIGHT, JUST NEEDED A NEW COMPRESSOR.
COPY, BOSS *SSSSS* BACK ONLINE? I GOT THE SUPER *SSSS* MY NECK, HERE.
SAY AGAIN? YOU'RE BREAKING UP.
GODDAMN THIS FUCKING STATIC...
AAAH!!
SQUEEEE
SORRY, SWITCHED TO A NEW CHANNEL. YOU KNOW, I CALLED COMMS ABOUT ALL THE INTERFERENCE LATELY? THEY FED ME SOME CRAP ABOUT MAGNETIC FIELDS, SAID IT WAS OUR EQUIPMENT.
WARNING DECOMPRESSION
WARNING DECOMPRESSION
LAZY-ASS BASTARDS DON'T WANT TO TEST THEIR TRANSMITTERS PROPERLY, MORE LIKE.
ANYWAY. I SAID I'M ALL DONE HERE.
GREAT. THE SUPER'S BEEN RAGGING ON ME ABOUT DOWNTIME.
WARNING DECOMPRESSION
YEAH, LIKE IT'S OUR FAULT THE OXYGEN FILTERS ARE CRAP.

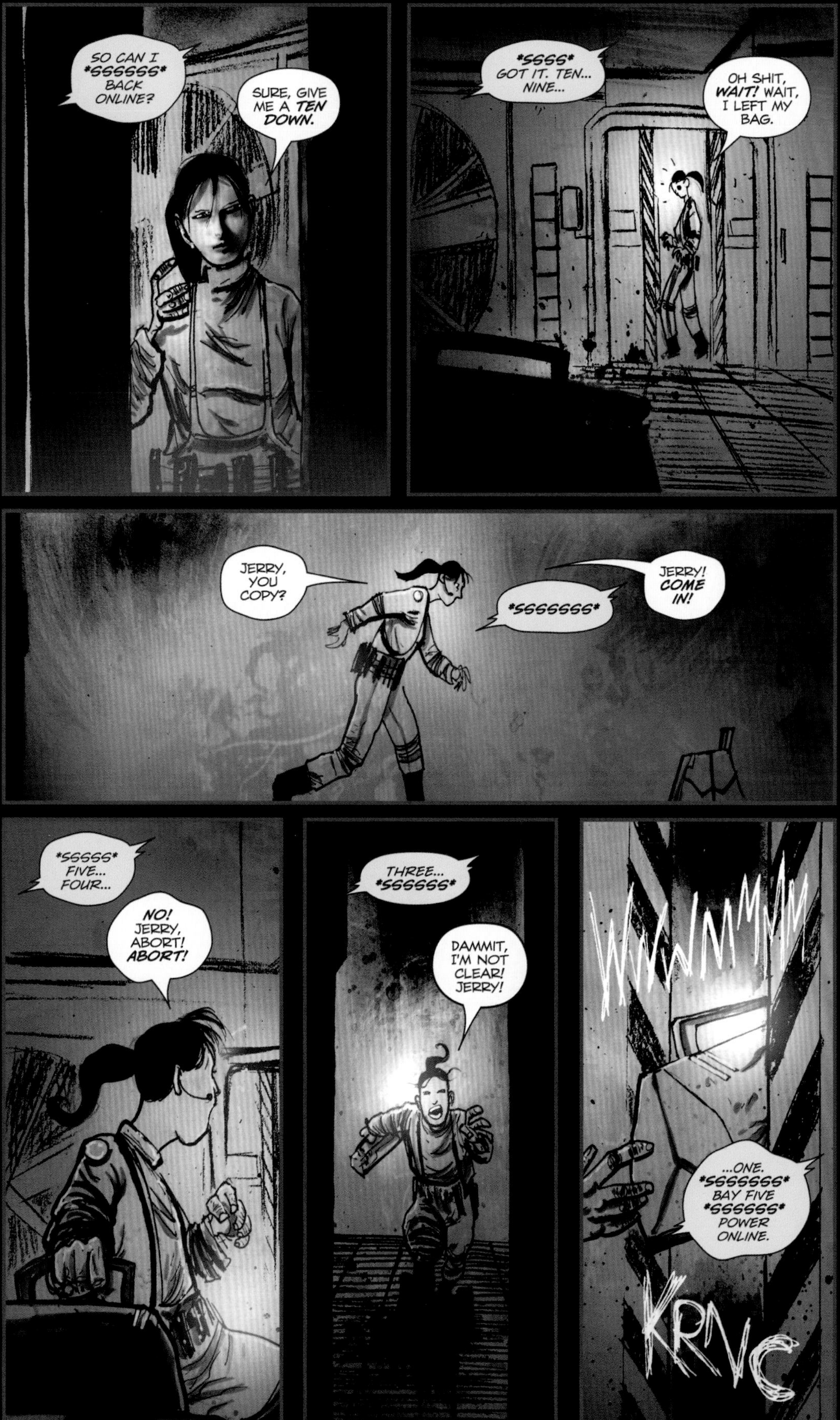
SO CAN I *SSSSSS* BACK ONLINE?
SURE, GIVE ME A TEN DOWN.
SSSS GOT IT. TEN... NINE...
OH SHIT, WAIT! WAIT, I LEFT MY BAG.
JERRY, YOU COPY?
SSSSSSS
JERRY! COME IN!
SSSSS FIVE... FOUR...
NO! JERRY, ABORT! ABORT!
THREE... *SSSSSS*
DAMMIT, I'M NOT CLEAR! JERRY!
WWMMM
...ONE. *SSSSSSS* BAY FIVE *SSSSSS* POWER ONLINE.
KRNC

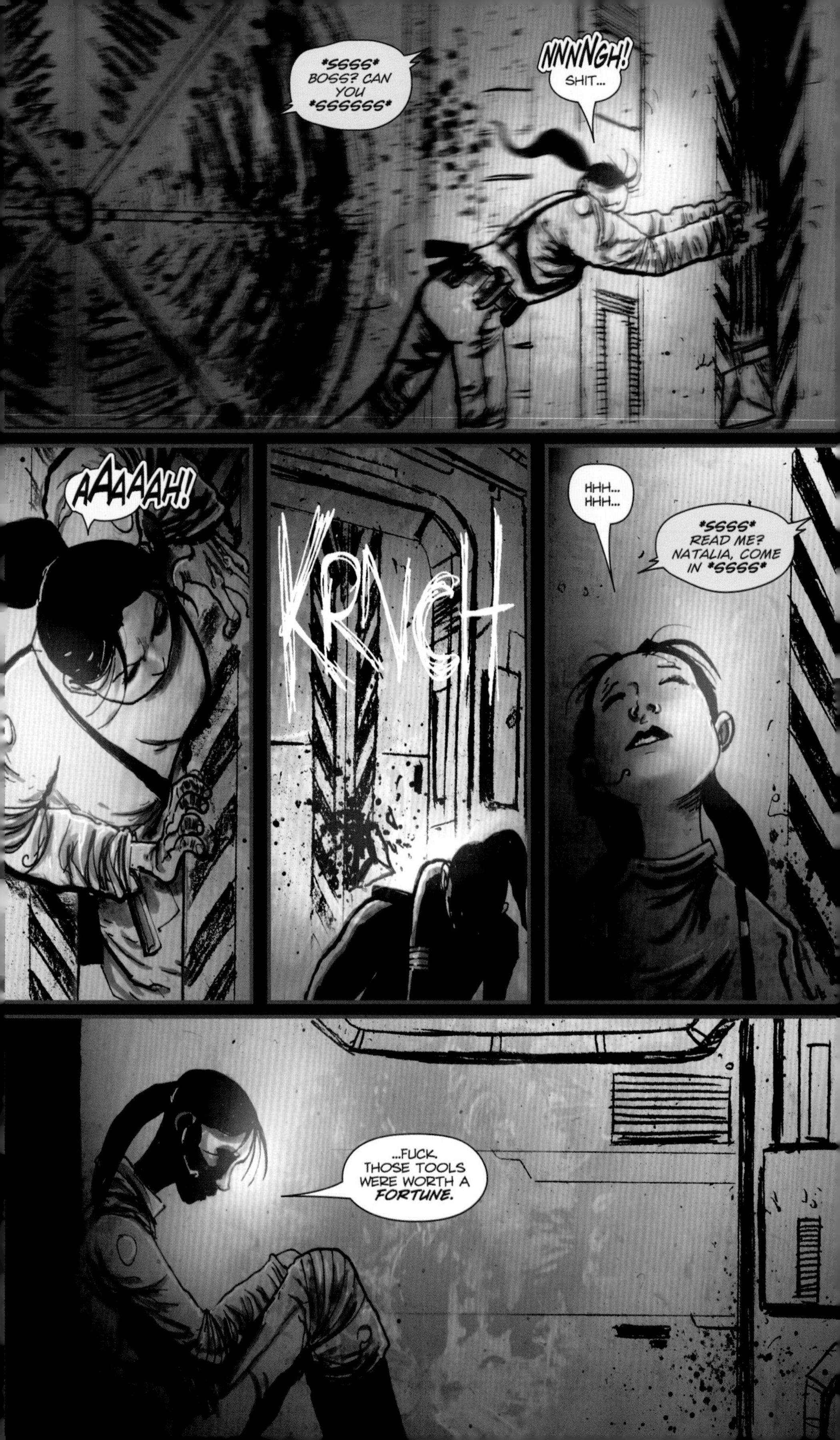
SSSS BOSS? CAN YOU *SSSSSS*
NNNNGH! SHIT...
AAAAAH!
KRNCH
HHH... HHH...
SSSS READ ME? NATALIA, COME IN *SSSS*
...FUCK. THOSE TOOLS WERE WORTH A FORTUNE.

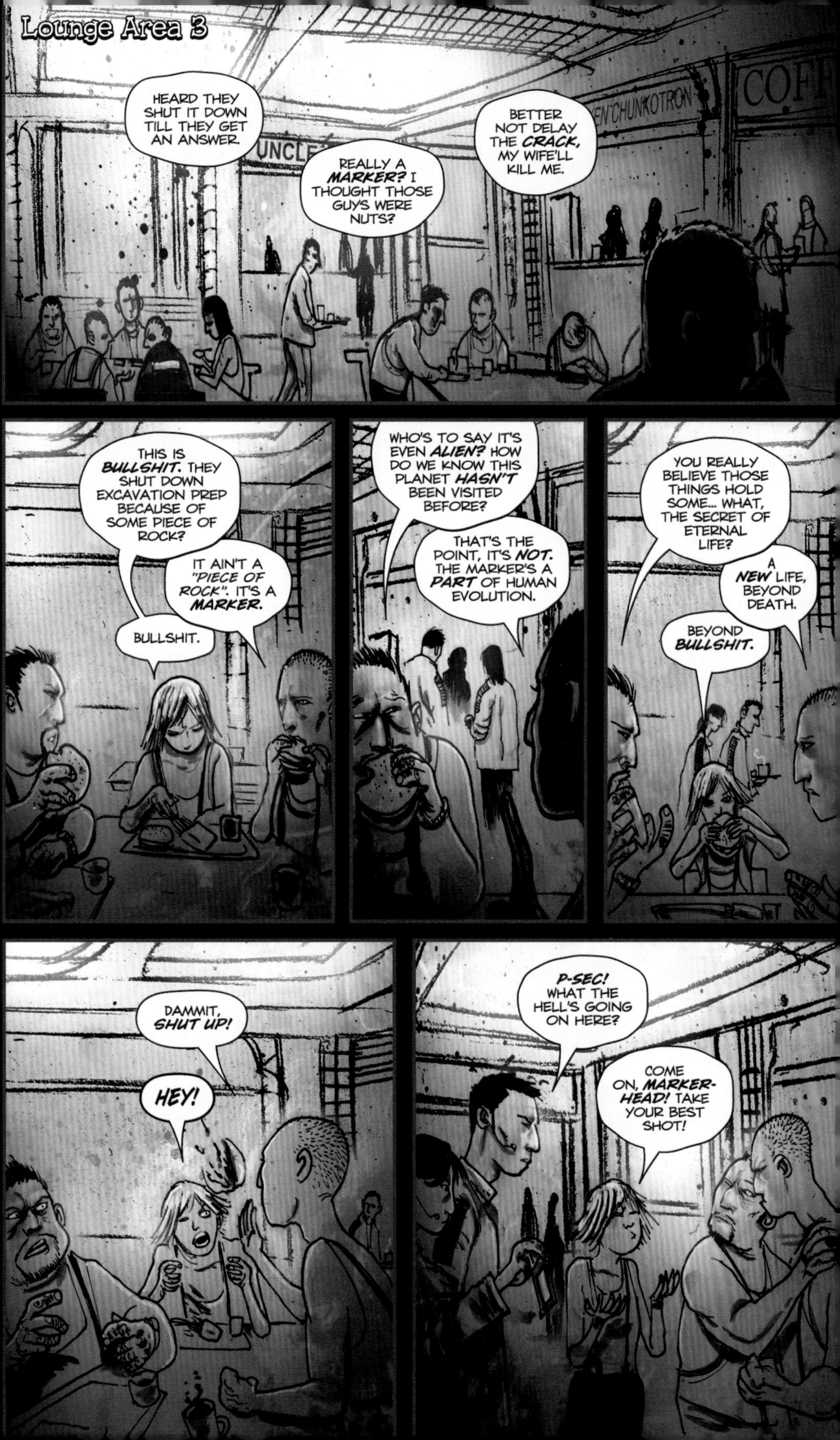
Lounge Area 3
HEARD THEY SHUT IT DOWN TILL THEY GET AN ANSWER.
REALLY A MARKER? I THOUGHT THOSE GUYS WERE NUTS?
BETTER NOT DELAY THE CRACK, MY WIFE'LL KILL ME.
THIS IS BULLSHIT. THEY SHUT DOWN EXCAVATION PREP BECAUSE OF SOME PIECE OF ROCK?
IT AIN'T A "PIECE OF ROCK". IT'S A MARKER.
BULLSHIT.
WHO'S TO SAY IT'S EVEN ALIEN? HOW DO WE KNOW THIS PLANET HASN'T BEEN VISITED BEFORE?
THAT'S THE POINT, IT'S NOT. THE MARKER'S A PART OF HUMAN EVOLUTION.
YOU REALLY BELIEVE THOSE THINGS HOLD SOME... WHAT, THE SECRET OF ETERNAL LIFE?
A NEW LIFE, BEYOND DEATH.
BEYOND BULLSHIT.
DAMMIT, SHUT UP!
HEY!
P-SEC! WHAT THE HELL'S GOING ON HERE?
COME ON, MARKER-HEAD! TAKE YOUR BEST SHOT!

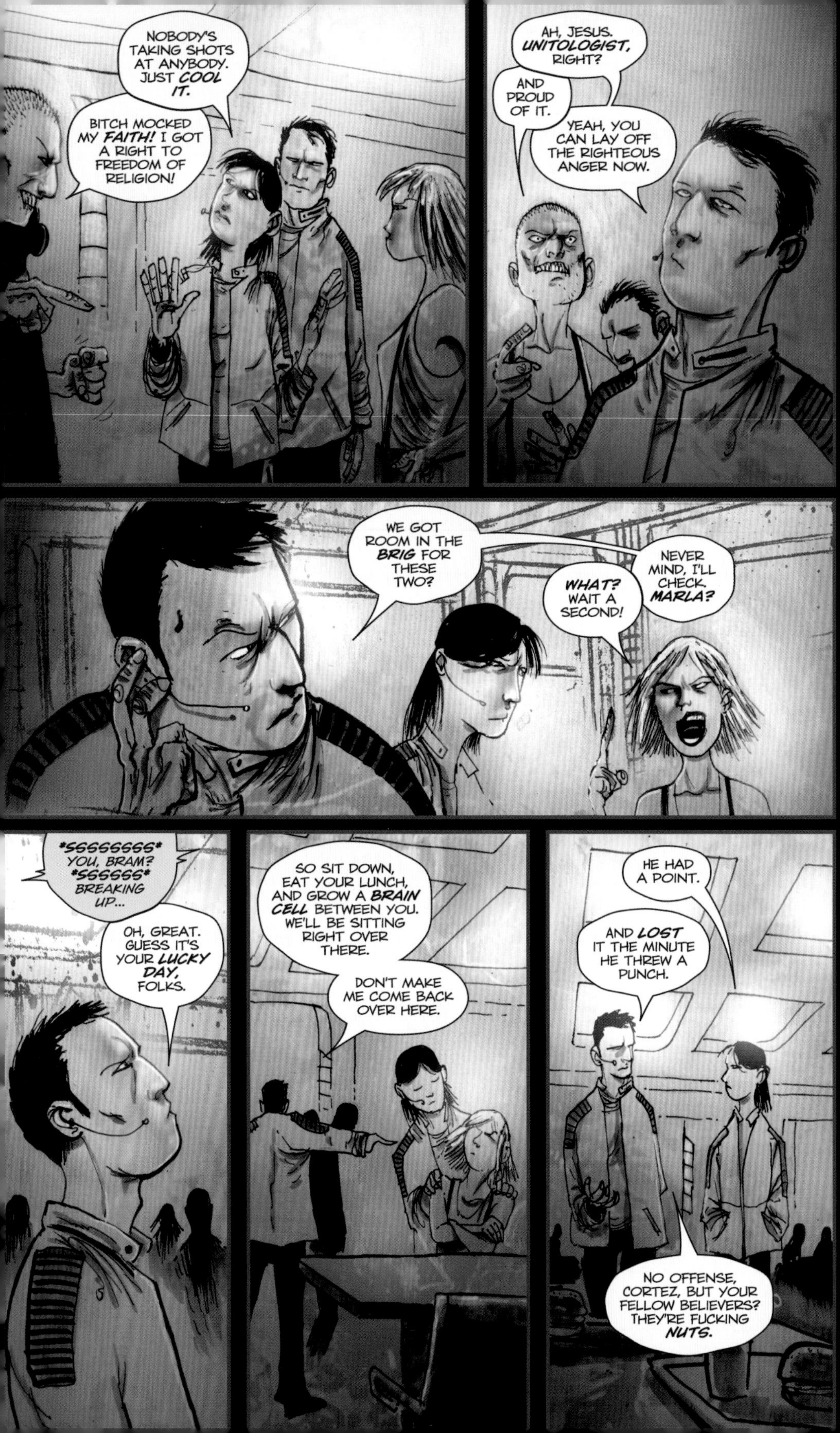
NOBODY'S TAKING SHOTS AT ANYBODY. JUST COOL IT.
BITCH MOCKED MY FAITH! I GOT A RIGHT TO FREEDOM OF RELIGION!
AH, JESUS. UNITOLOGIST, RIGHT?
AND PROUD OF IT.
YEAH, YOU CAN LAY OFF THE RIGHTEOUS ANGER NOW.
WE GOT ROOM IN THE BRIG FOR THESE TWO?
WHAT? WAIT A SECOND!
NEVER MIND, I'LL CHECK. MARLA?
SSSSSSSS YOU, BRAM? *SSSSSS* BREAKING UP...
OH, GREAT. GUESS IT'S YOUR LUCKY DAY, FOLKS.
SO SIT DOWN, EAT YOUR LUNCH, AND GROW A BRAIN CELL BETWEEN YOU. WE'LL BE SITTING RIGHT OVER THERE.
DON'T MAKE ME COME BACK OVER HERE.
HE HAD A POINT.
AND LOST IT THE MINUTE HE THREW A PUNCH.
NO OFFENSE, CORTEZ, BUT YOUR FELLOW BELIEVERS? THEY'RE FUCKING NUTS.

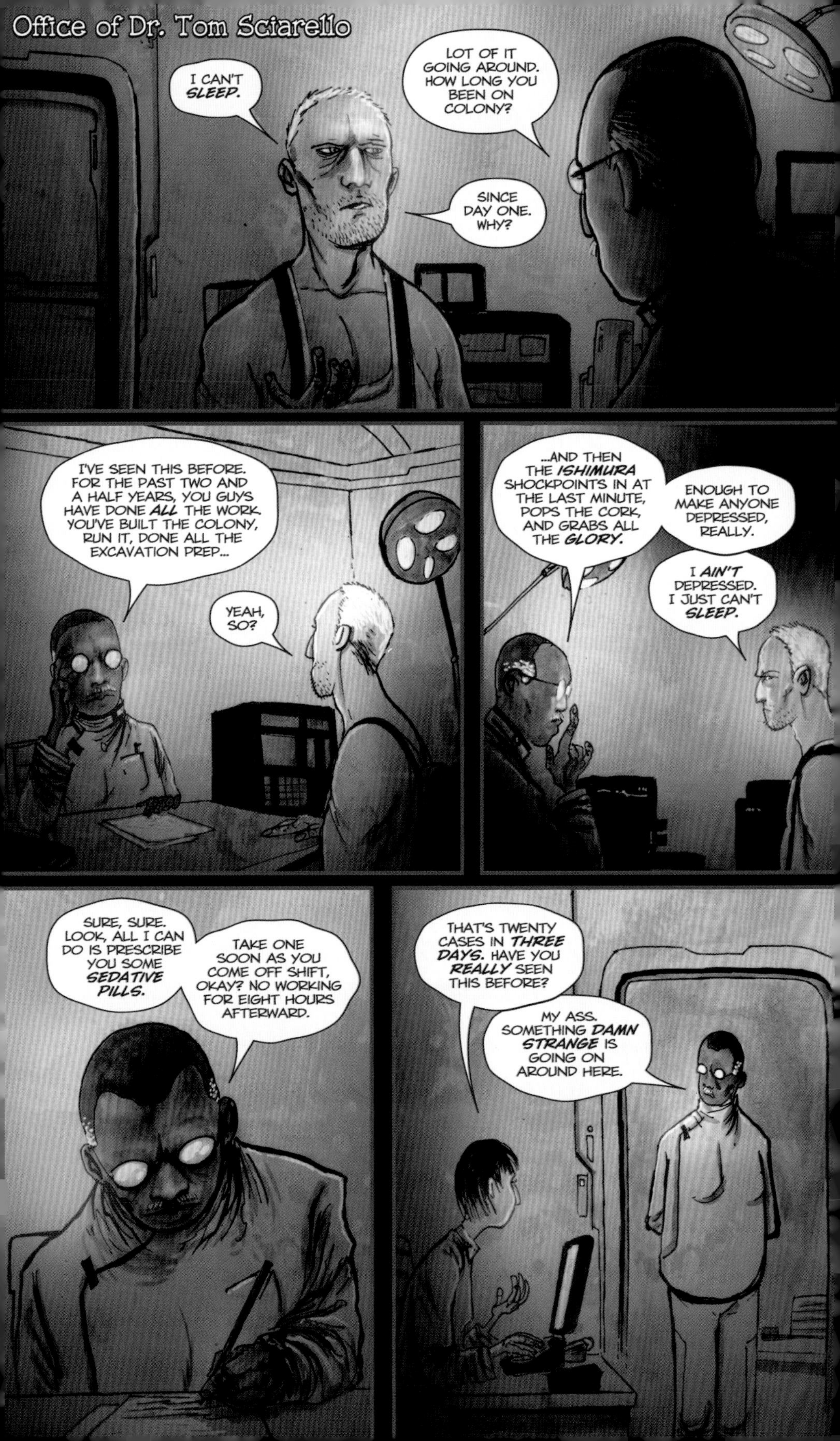
Office of Dr. Tom Sciarello
I CAN'T SLEEP.
LOT OF IT GOING AROUND. HOW LONG YOU BEEN ON COLONY?
SINCE DAY ONE. WHY?
I'VE SEEN THIS BEFORE. FOR THE PAST TWO AND A HALF YEARS, YOU GUYS HAVE DONE ALL THE WORK. YOU'VE BUILT THE COLONY, RUN IT, DONE ALL THE EXCAVATION PREP...
YEAH, SO?
...AND THEN THE ISHIMURA SHOCKPOINTS IN AT THE LAST MINUTE, POPS THE CORK, AND GRABS ALL THE GLORY.
ENOUGH TO MAKE ANYONE DEPRESSED, REALLY.
I AIN'T DEPRESSED. I JUST CAN'T SLEEP.
SURE, SURE. LOOK, ALL I CAN DO IS PRESCRIBE YOU SOME SEDATIVE PILLS.
TAKE ONE SOON AS YOU COME OFF SHIFT, OKAY? NO WORKING FOR EIGHT HOURS AFTERWARD.
THAT'S TWENTY CASES IN THREE DAYS. HAVE YOU REALLY SEEN THIS BEFORE?
MY ASS. SOMETHING DAMN STRANGE IS GOING ON AROUND HERE.

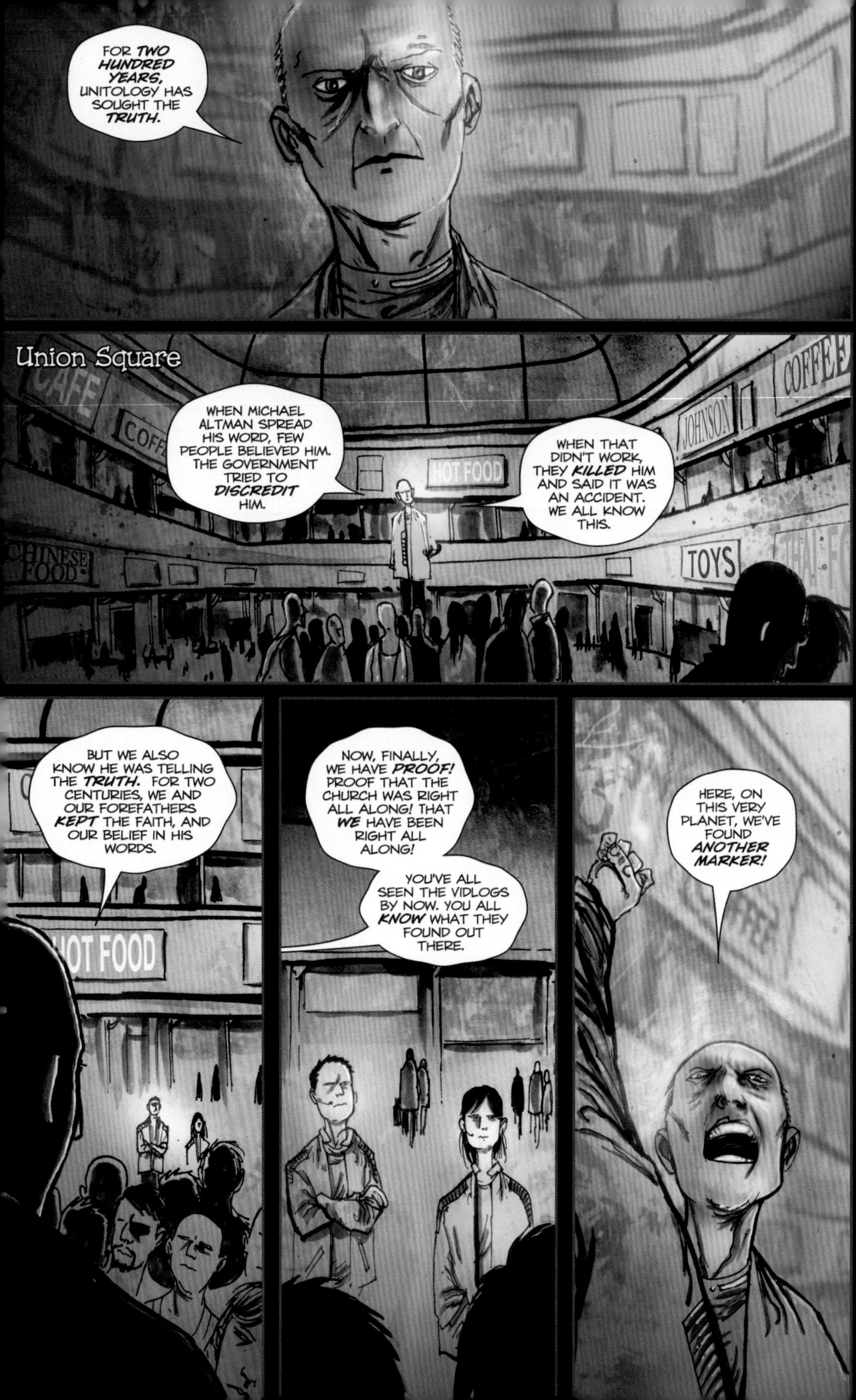
FOR TWO HUNDRED YEARS, UNITOLOGY HAS SOUGHT THE TRUTH.
Union Square
CAFE
COFFEE
JOHNSON
HOT FOOD
CHINESE FOOD
TOYS
WHEN MICHAEL ALTMAN SPREAD HIS WORD, FEW PEOPLE BELIEVED HIM. THE GOVERNMENT TRIED TO DISCREDIT HIM.
WHEN THAT DIDN'T WORK, THEY KILLED HIM AND SAID IT WAS AN ACCIDENT. WE ALL KNOW THIS.
BUT WE ALSO KNOW HE WAS TELLING THE TRUTH. FOR TWO CENTURIES, WE AND OUR FOREFATHERS KEPT THE FAITH, AND OUR BELIEF IN HIS WORDS.
HOT FOOD
NOW, FINALLY, WE HAVE PROOF! PROOF THAT THE CHURCH WAS RIGHT ALL ALONG! THAT WE HAVE BEEN RIGHT ALL ALONG!
YOU'VE ALL SEEN THE VIDLOGS BY NOW. YOU ALL KNOW WHAT THEY FOUND OUT THERE.
HERE, ON THIS VERY PLANET, WE'VE FOUND ANOTHER MARKER!

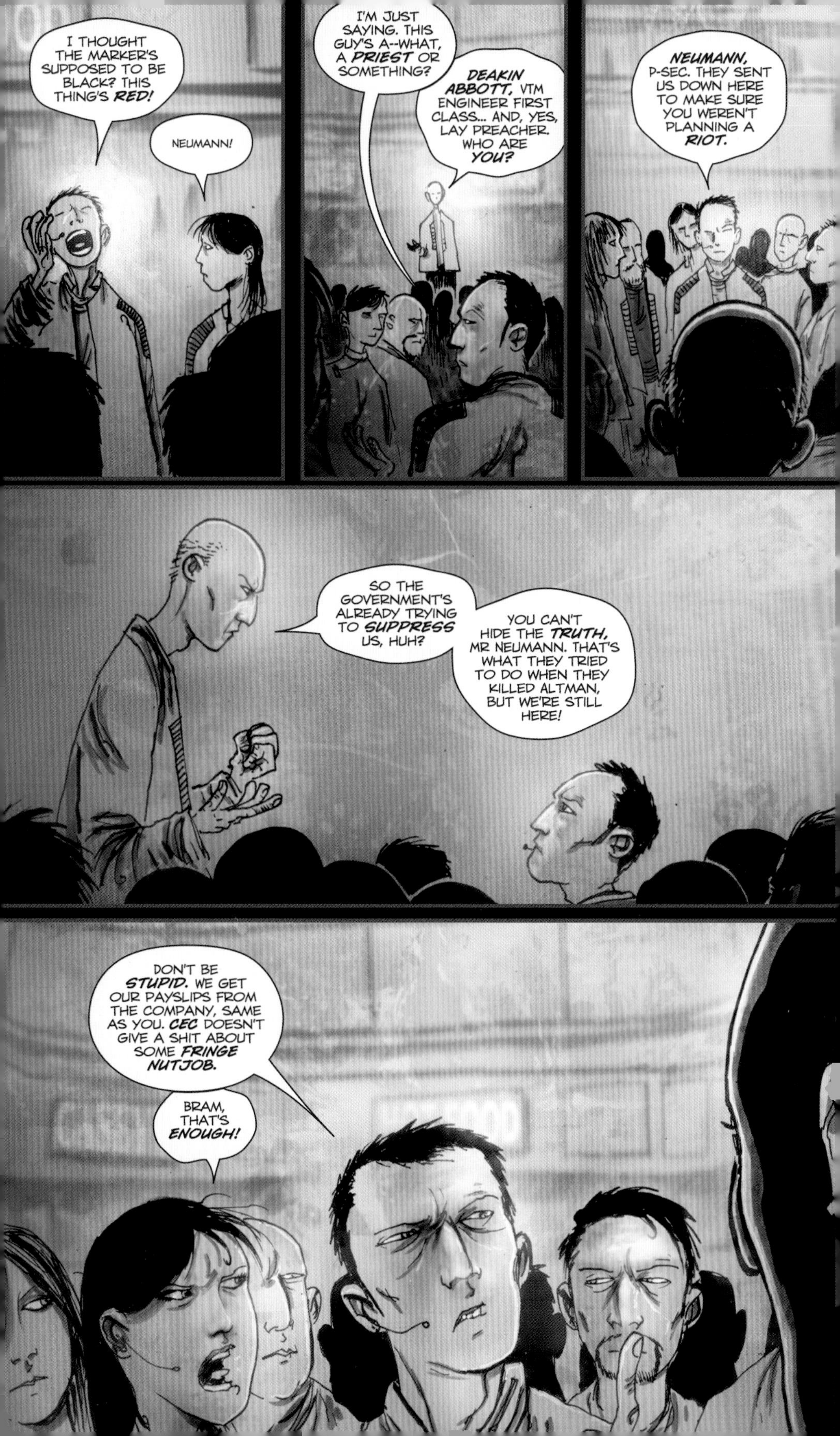

I THOUGHT THE MARKER'S SUPPOSED TO BE BLACK? THIS THING'S RED!
NEUMANN!
I'M JUST SAYING. THIS GUY'S A--WHAT, A PRIEST OR SOMETHING?
DEAKIN ABBOTT, VTM ENGINEER FIRST CLASS... AND, YES, LAY PREACHER. WHO ARE YOU?
NEUMANN, P-SEC. THEY SENT US DOWN HERE TO MAKE SURE YOU WEREN'T PLANNING A RIOT.
SO THE GOVERNMENT'S ALREADY TRYING TO SUPPRESS US, HUH?
YOU CAN'T HIDE THE TRUTH, MR NEUMANN. THAT'S WHAT THEY TRIED TO DO WHEN THEY KILLED ALTMAN, BUT WE'RE STILL HERE!
DON'T BE STUPID. WE GET OUR PAYSLIPS FROM THE COMPANY, SAME AS YOU. CEC DOESN'T GIVE A SHIT ABOUT SOME FRINGE NUTJOB.
BRAM, THAT'S ENOUGH!

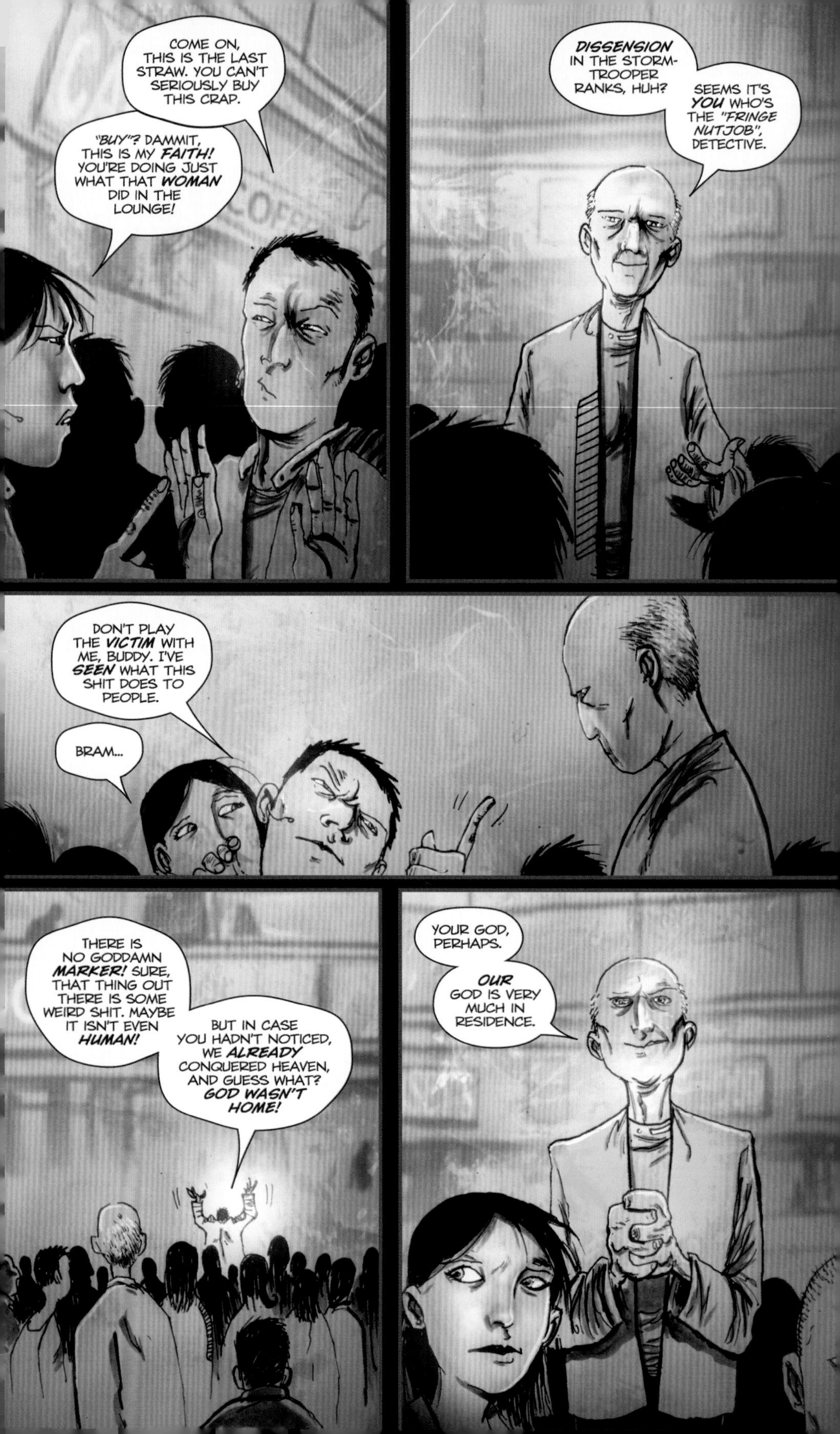
COME ON, THIS IS THE LAST STRAW. YOU CAN'T SERIOUSLY BUY THIS CRAP.
"BUY"? DAMMIT, THIS IS MY FAITH! YOU'RE DOING JUST WHAT THAT WOMAN DID IN THE LOUNGE!
DISSENSION IN THE STORM-TROOPER RANKS, HUH?
SEEMS IT'S YOU WHO'S THE "FRINGE NUTJOB", DETECTIVE.
DON'T PLAY THE VICTIM WITH ME, BUDDY. I'VE SEEN WHAT THIS SHIT DOES TO PEOPLE.
BRAM...
THERE IS NO GODDAMN MARKER! SURE, THAT THING OUT THERE IS SOME WEIRD SHIT. MAYBE IT ISN'T EVEN HUMAN!
BUT IN CASE YOU HADN'T NOTICED, WE ALREADY CONQUERED HEAVEN, AND GUESS WHAT? GOD WASN'T HOME!
YOUR GOD, PERHAPS.
OUR GOD IS VERY MUCH IN RESIDENCE.

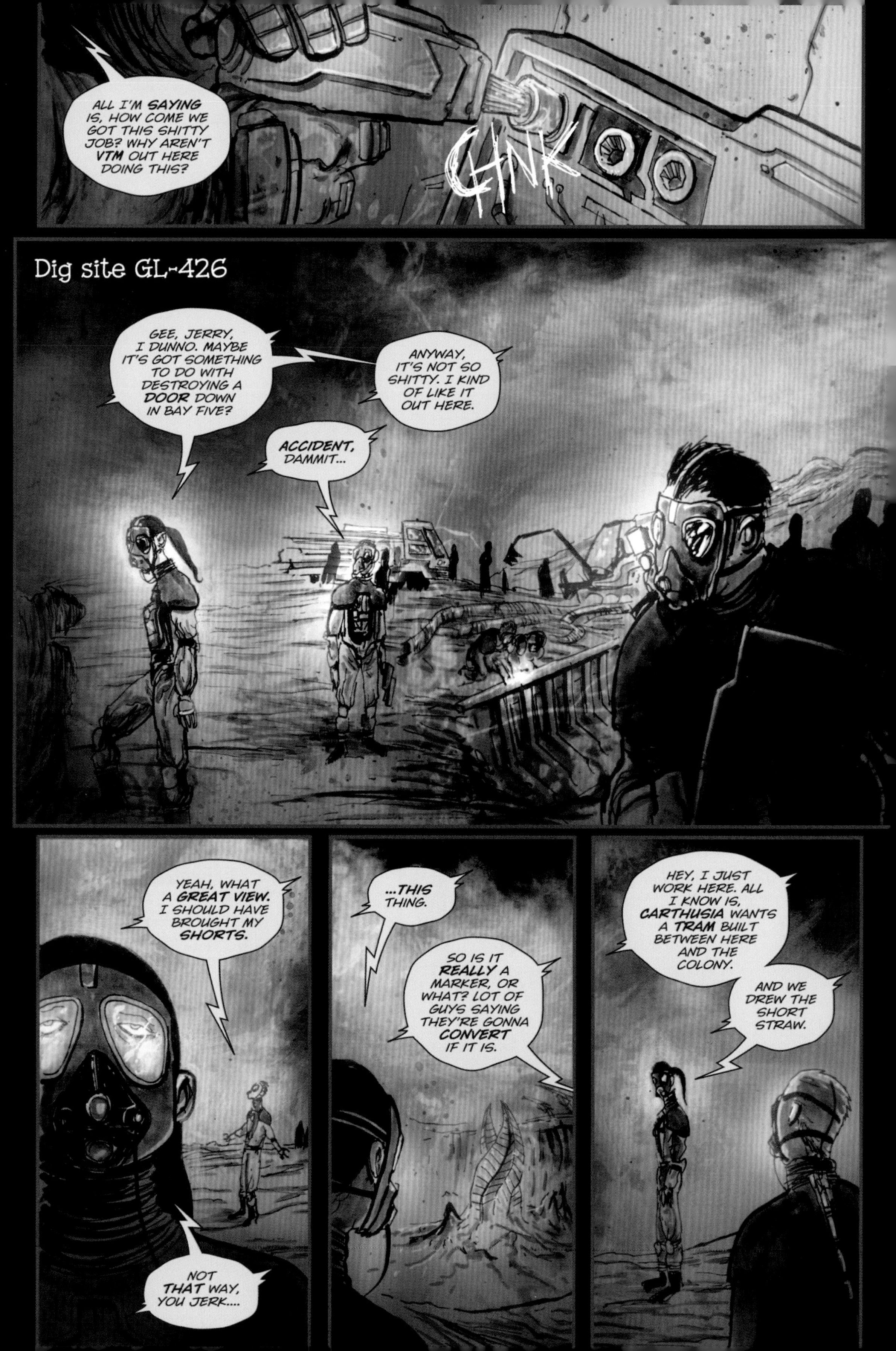
ALL I'M SAYING IS, HOW COME WE GOT THIS SHITTY JOB? WHY AREN'T VTM OUT HERE DOING THIS?
CHNK
Dig site GL-426
GEE, JERRY, I DUNNO. MAYBE IT'S GOT SOMETHING TO DO WITH DESTROYING A DOOR DOWN IN BAY FIVE?
ANYWAY, IT'S NOT SO SHITTY. I KIND OF LIKE IT OUT HERE.
ACCIDENT, DAMMIT...
YEAH, WHAT A GREAT VIEW. I SHOULD HAVE BROUGHT MY SHORTS.
NOT THAT WAY, YOU JERK....
...THIS THING.
SO IS IT REALLY A MARKER, OR WHAT? LOT OF GUYS SAYING THEY'RE GONNA CONVERT IF IT IS.
HEY, I JUST WORK HERE. ALL I KNOW IS, CARTHUSIA WANTS A TRAM BUILT BETWEEN HERE AND THE COLONY.
AND WE DREW THE SHORT STRAW.

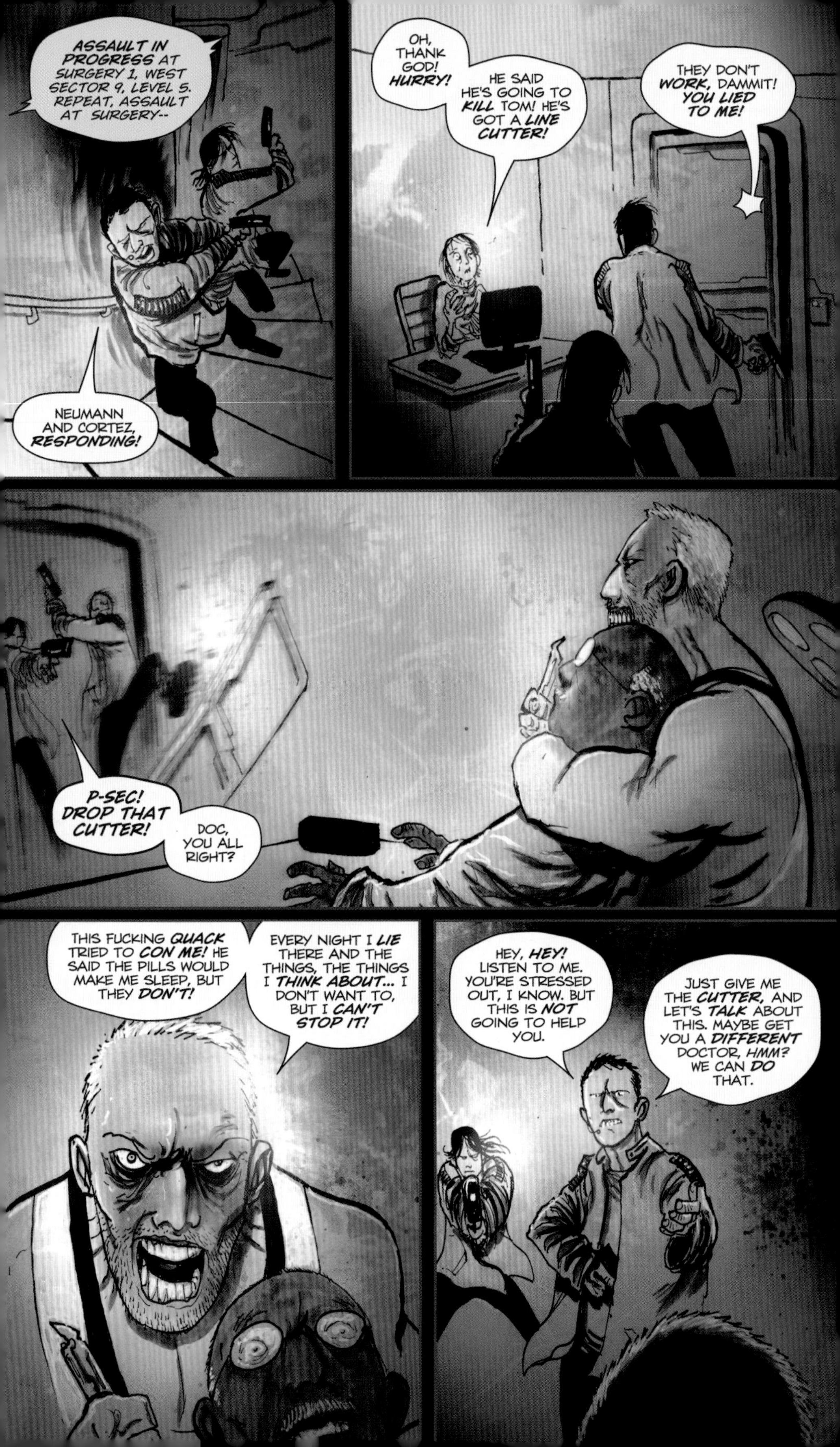
ASSAULT IN PROGRESS AT SURGERY 1, WEST SECTOR 9, LEVEL 5. REPEAT, ASSAULT AT SURGERY--
NEUMANN AND CORTEZ, RESPONDING!
OH, THANK GOD! HURRY!
HE SAID HE'S GOING TO KILL TOM! HE'S GOT A LINE CUTTER!
THEY DON'T WORK, DAMMIT! YOU LIED TO ME!
P-SEC! DROP THAT CUTTER!
DOC, YOU ALL RIGHT?
THIS FUCKING QUACK TRIED TO CON ME! HE SAID THE PILLS WOULD MAKE ME SLEEP, BUT THEY DON'T!
EVERY NIGHT I LIE THERE AND THE THINGS, THE THINGS I THINK ABOUT... I DON'T WANT TO, BUT I CAN'T STOP IT!
HEY, HEY! LISTEN TO ME. YOU'RE STRESSED OUT, I KNOW. BUT THIS IS NOT GOING TO HELP YOU.
JUST GIVE ME THE CUTTER, AND LET'S TALK ABOUT THIS. MAYBE GET YOU A DIFFERENT DOCTOR, HMM? WE CAN DO THAT.

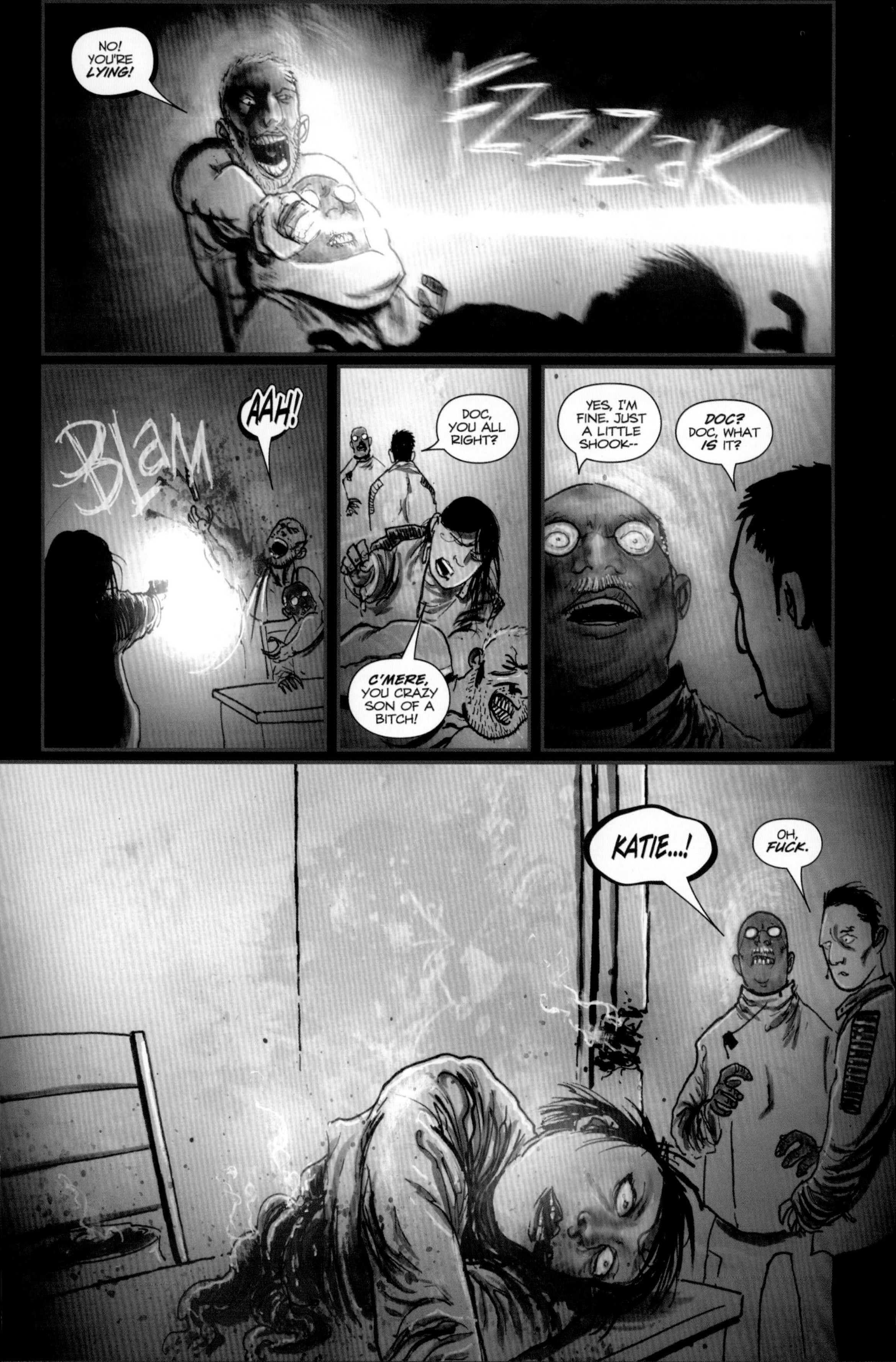
NO! YOU'RE *LYING!*
BLAM
AAH!
DOC, YOU ALL RIGHT?
C'MERE, YOU CRAZY SON OF A BITCH!
YES, I'M FINE. JUST A LITTLE SHOOK--
DOC? DOC, WHAT *IS* IT?
KATIE...!
OH, *FUCK.*

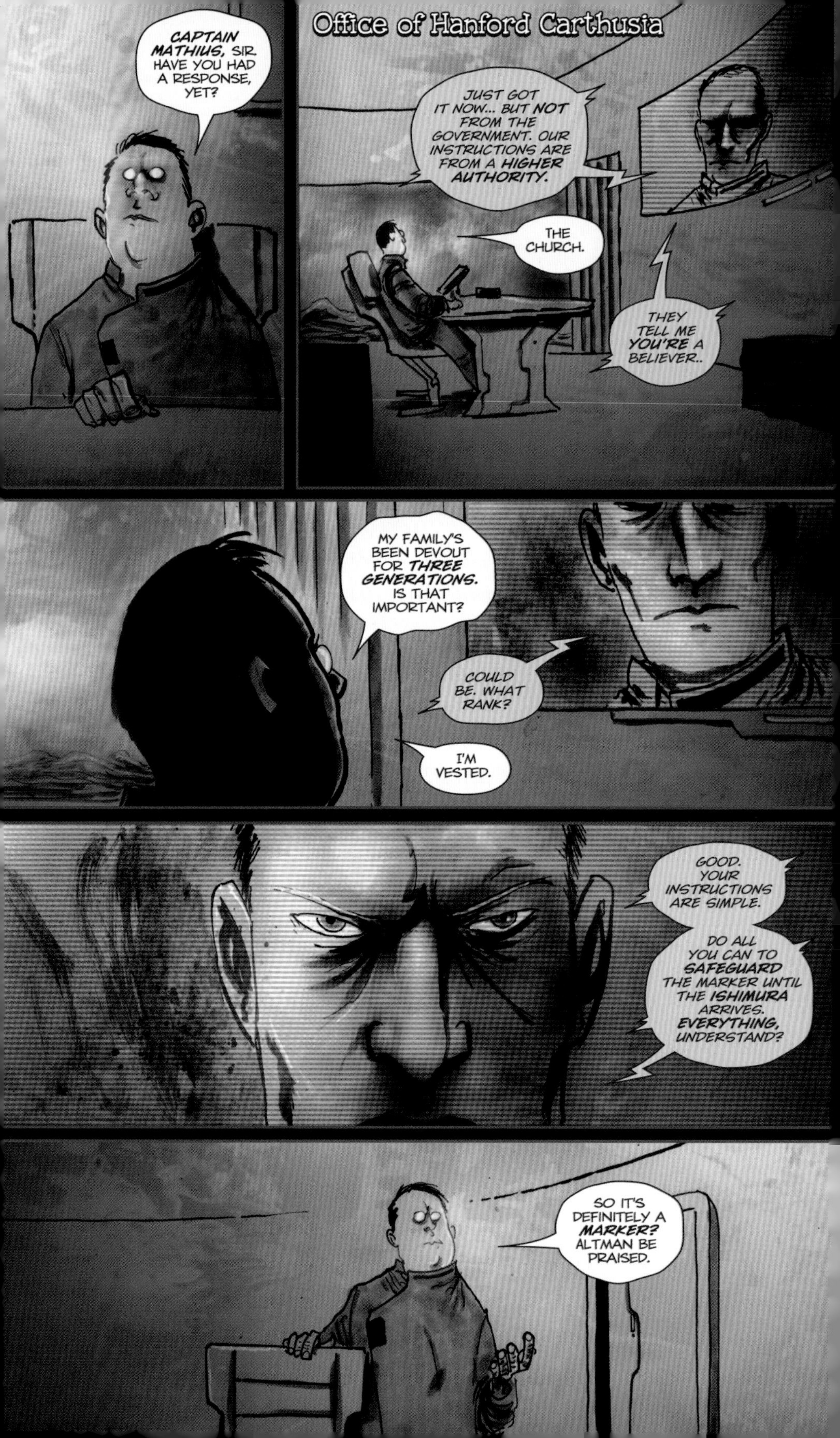
Office of Hanford Carthusia
CAPTAIN MATHIUS, SIR. HAVE YOU HAD A RESPONSE, YET?
JUST GOT IT NOW... BUT NOT FROM THE GOVERNMENT. OUR INSTRUCTIONS ARE FROM A HIGHER AUTHORITY.
THE CHURCH.
THEY TELL ME YOU'RE A BELIEVER..
MY FAMILY'S BEEN DEVOUT FOR THREE GENERATIONS. IS THAT IMPORTANT?
COULD BE. WHAT RANK?
I'M VESTED.
GOOD. YOUR INSTRUCTIONS ARE SIMPLE.
DO ALL YOU CAN TO SAFEGUARD THE MARKER UNTIL THE ISHIMURA ARRIVES. EVERYTHING, UNDERSTAND?
SO IT'S DEFINITELY A MARKER? ALTMAN BE PRAISED.

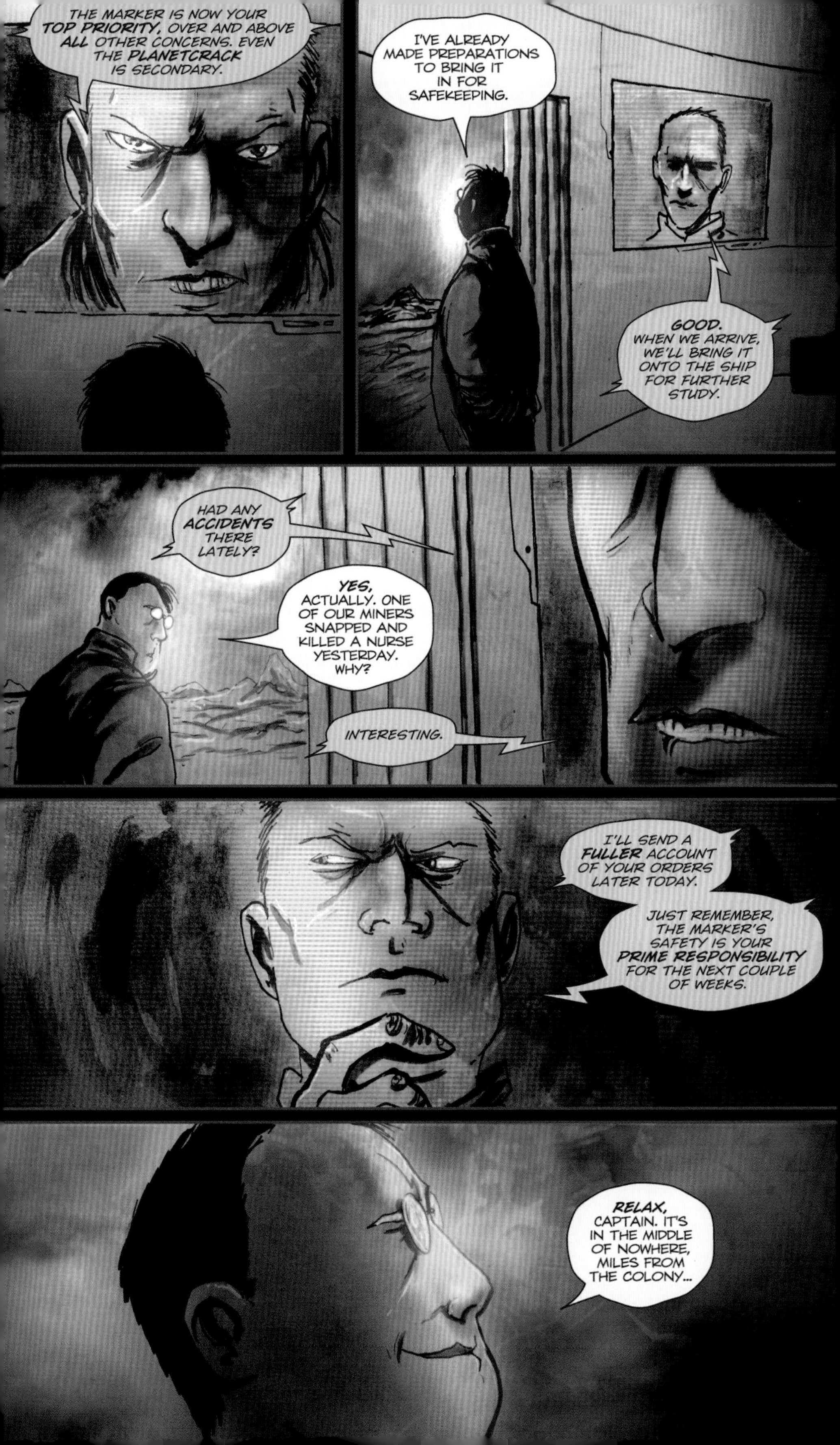
THE MARKER IS NOW YOUR TOP PRIORITY, OVER AND ABOVE ALL OTHER CONCERNS. EVEN THE PLANETCRACK IS SECONDARY.
I'VE ALREADY MADE PREPARATIONS TO BRING IT IN FOR SAFEKEEPING.
GOOD. WHEN WE ARRIVE, WE'LL BRING IT ONTO THE SHIP FOR FURTHER STUDY.
HAD ANY ACCIDENTS THERE LATELY?
YES, ACTUALLY. ONE OF OUR MINERS SNAPPED AND KILLED A NURSE YESTERDAY. WHY?
INTERESTING.
I'LL SEND A FULLER ACCOUNT OF YOUR ORDERS LATER TODAY.
JUST REMEMBER, THE MARKER'S SAFETY IS YOUR PRIME RESPONSIBILITY FOR THE NEXT COUPLE OF WEEKS.
RELAX, CAPTAIN. IT'S IN THE MIDDLE OF NOWHERE, MILES FROM THE COLONY...

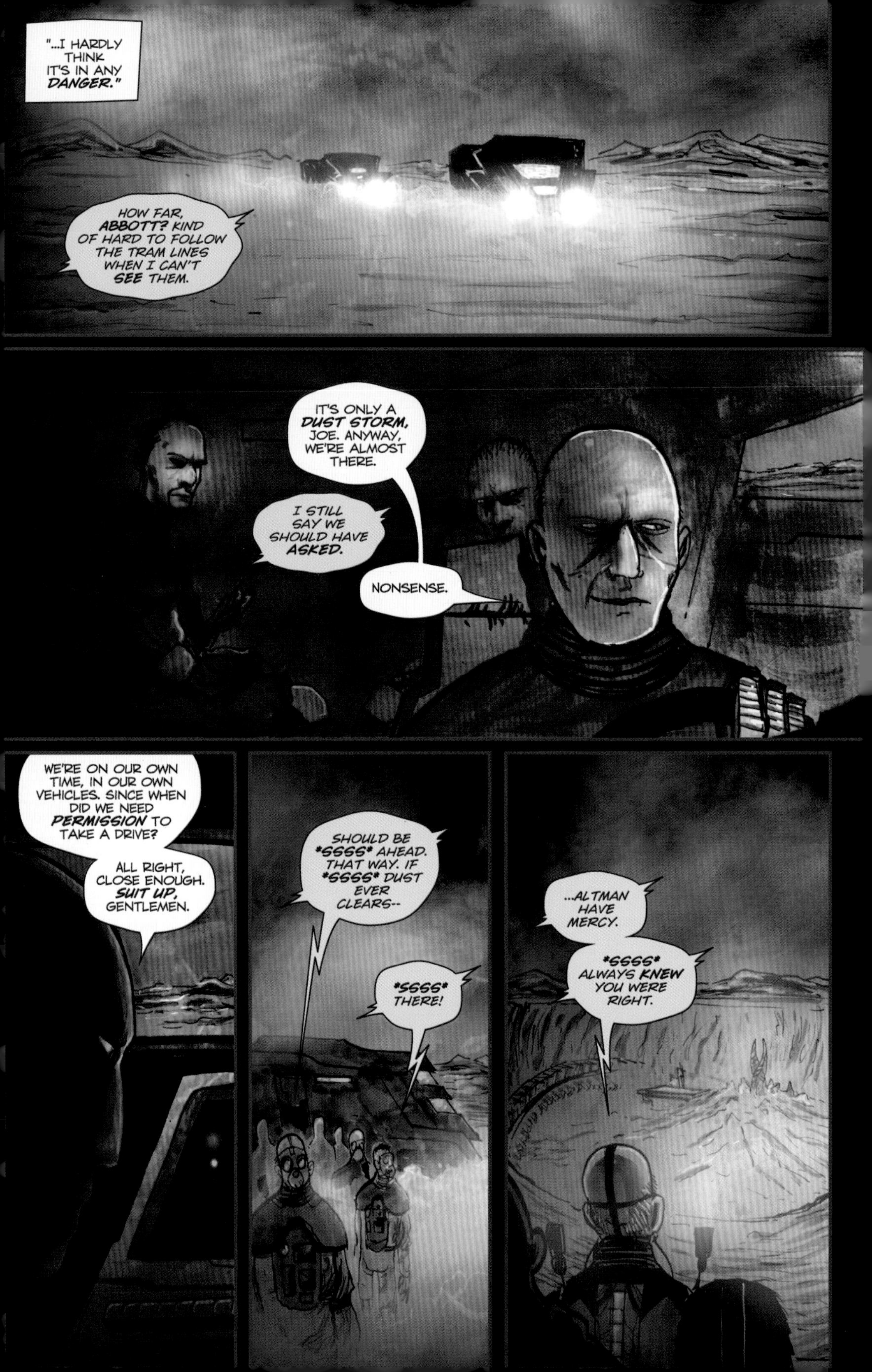
"...I HARDLY THINK IT'S IN ANY DANGER."
HOW FAR, ABBOTT? KIND OF HARD TO FOLLOW THE TRAM LINES WHEN I CAN'T SEE THEM.
IT'S ONLY A DUST STORM, JOE. ANYWAY, WE'RE ALMOST THERE.
I STILL SAY WE SHOULD HAVE ASKED.
NONSENSE.
WE'RE ON OUR OWN TIME, IN OUR OWN VEHICLES. SINCE WHEN DID WE NEED PERMISSION TO TAKE A DRIVE?
ALL RIGHT, CLOSE ENOUGH. SUIT UP, GENTLEMEN.
SHOULD BE *SSSS* AHEAD. THAT WAY. IF *SSSS* DUST EVER CLEARS--
SSSS THERE!
...ALTMAN HAVE MERCY.
SSSS ALWAYS KNEW YOU WERE RIGHT.

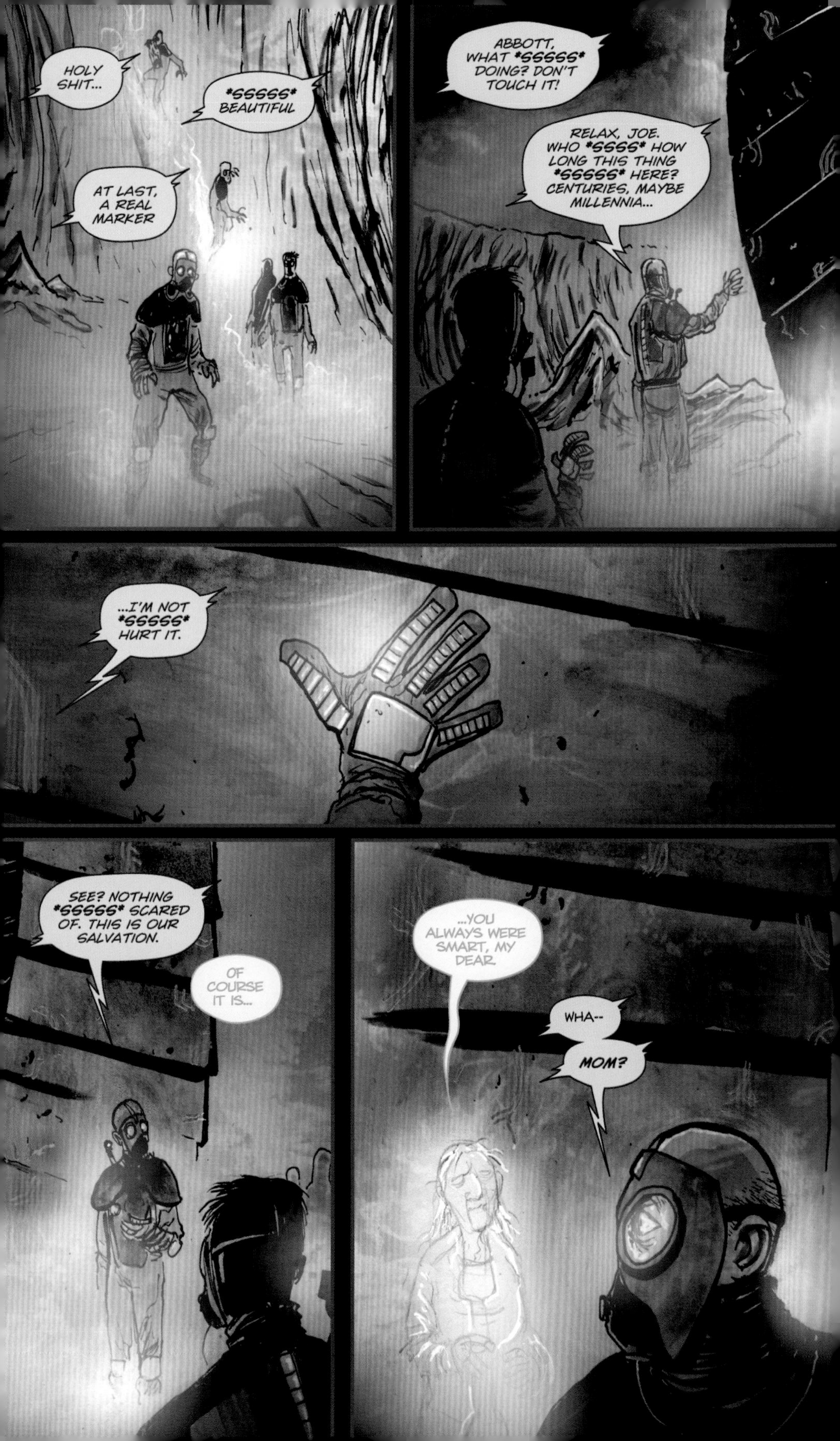
HOLY SHIT...
SSSSS BEAUTIFUL
AT LAST, A REAL MARKER
ABBOTT, WHAT *SSSSS* DOING? DON'T TOUCH IT!
RELAX, JOE. WHO *SSSS* HOW LONG THIS THING *SSSSS* HERE? CENTURIES, MAYBE MILLENNIA...
...I'M NOT *SSSSS* HURT IT.
SEE? NOTHING *SSSSS* SCARED OF. THIS IS OUR SALVATION.
OF COURSE IT IS...
...YOU ALWAYS WERE SMART, MY DEAR
WHA--
MOM?

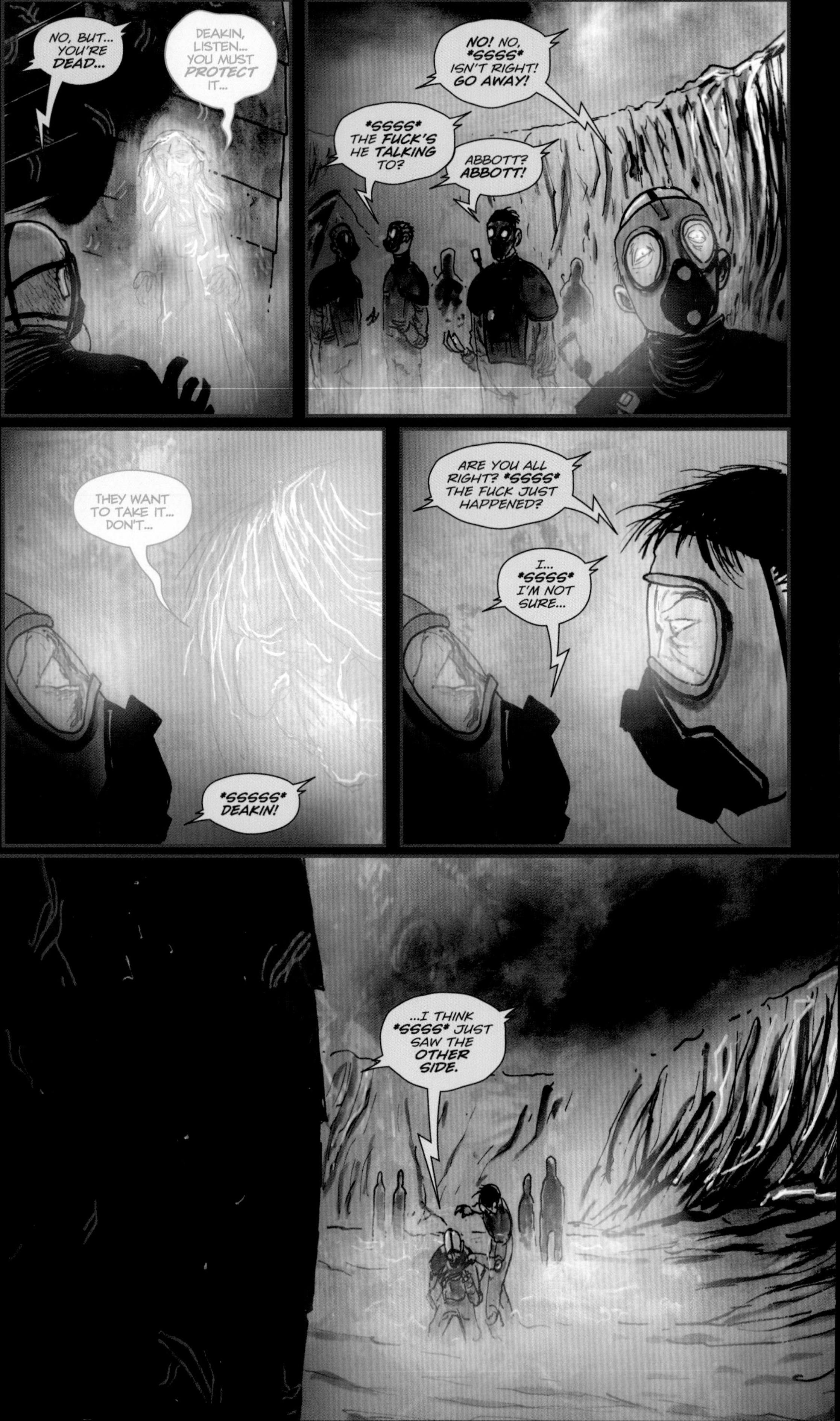
NO, BUT... YOU'RE DEAD...
DEAKIN, LISTEN... YOU MUST PROTECT IT...
NO! NO, *SSSS* ISN'T RIGHT! GO AWAY!
SSSS THE FUCK'S HE TALKING TO?
ABBOTT? ABBOTT!
THEY WANT TO TAKE IT... DON'T...
SSSSS DEAKIN!
ARE YOU ALL RIGHT? *SSSS* THE FUCK JUST HAPPENED?
I... *SSSS* I'M NOT SURE...
...I THINK *SSSS* JUST SAW THE OTHER SIDE.

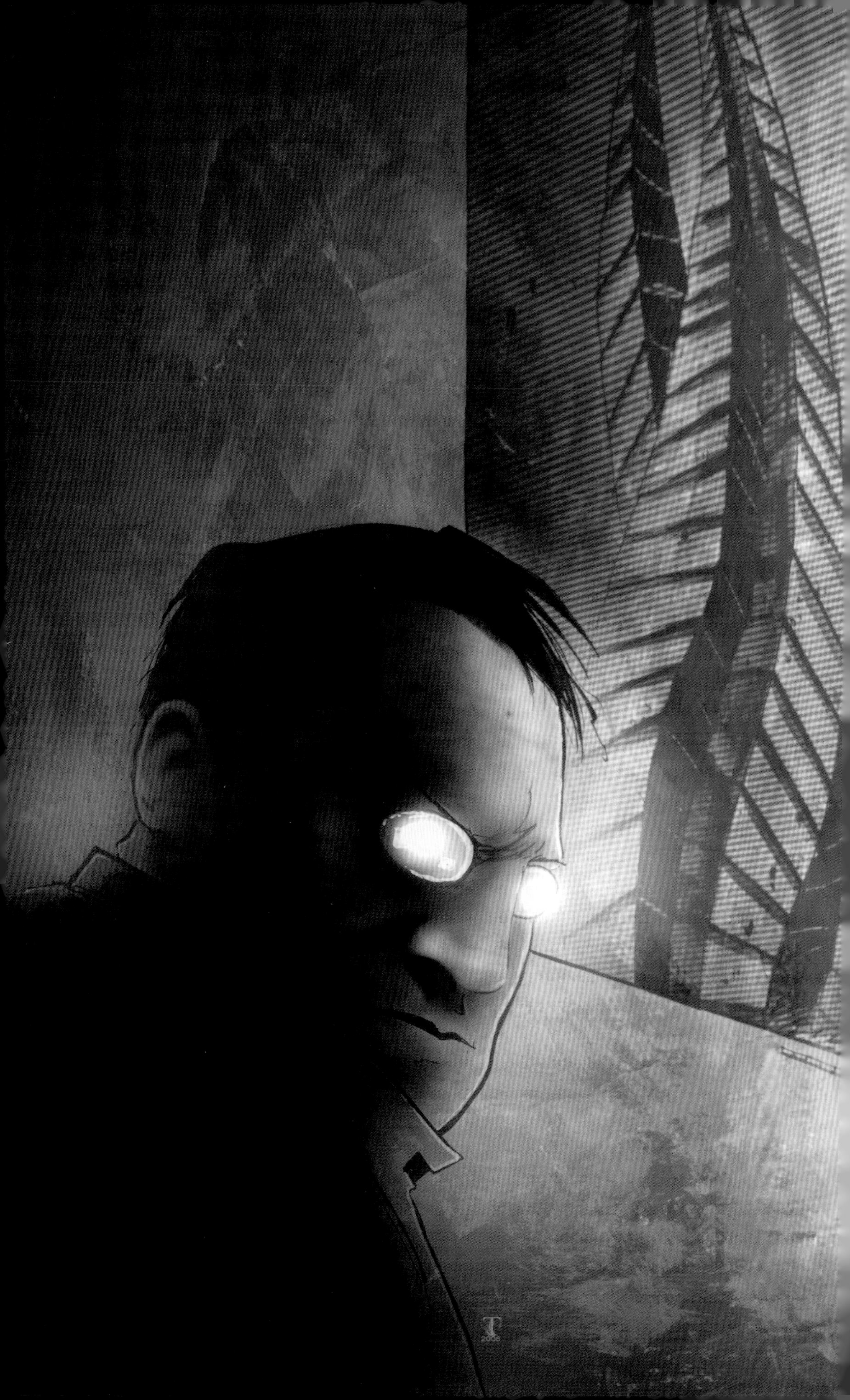

VOLUME 2

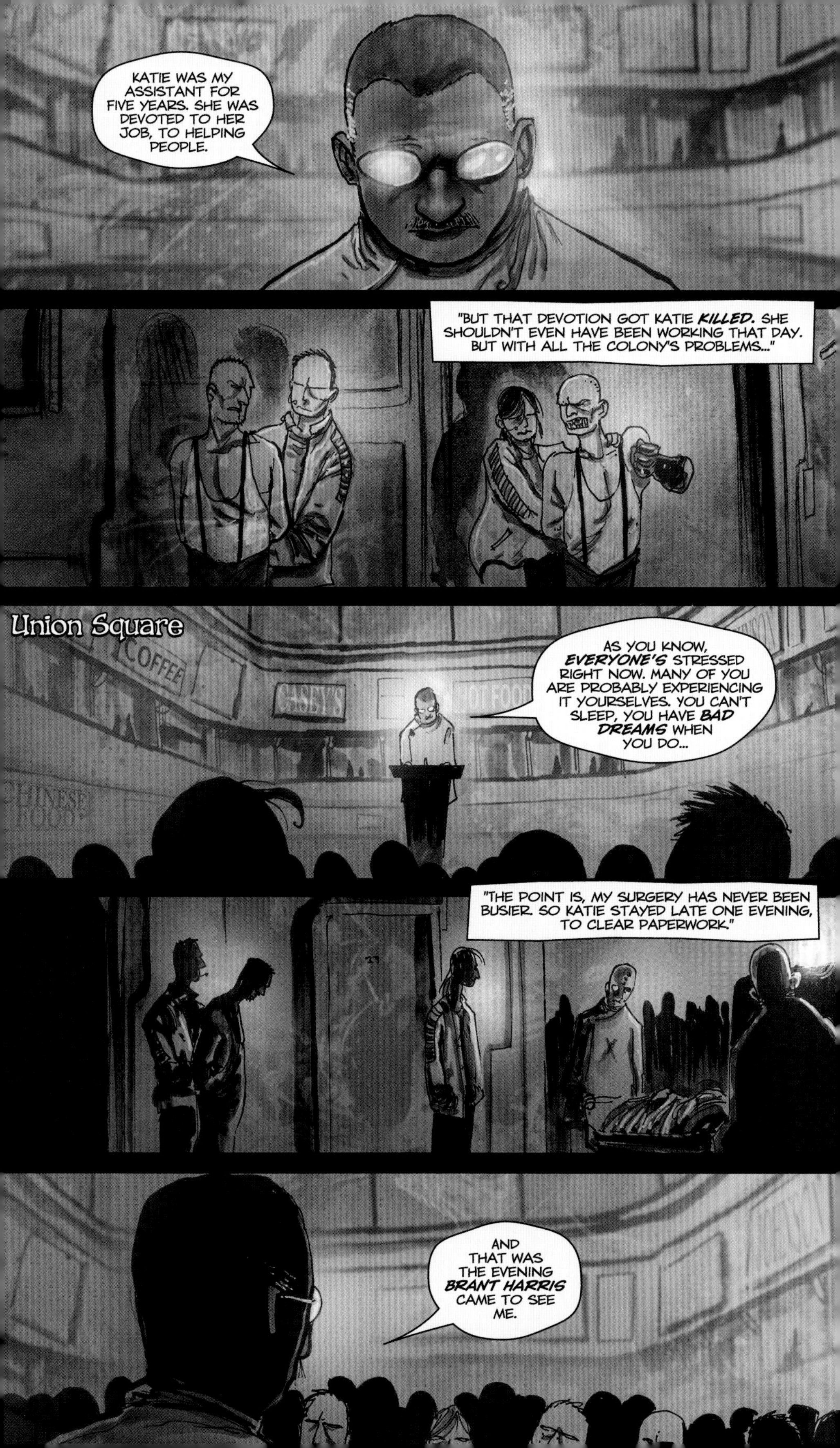
KATIE WAS MY ASSISTANT FOR FIVE YEARS. SHE WAS DEVOTED TO HER JOB, TO HELPING PEOPLE.
"BUT THAT DEVOTION GOT KATIE KILLED. SHE SHOULDN'T EVEN HAVE BEEN WORKING THAT DAY. BUT WITH ALL THE COLONY'S PROBLEMS..."
Union Square
COFFEE
CASEY'S
HOT FOOD
CHINESE FOOD
AS YOU KNOW, EVERYONE'S STRESSED RIGHT NOW. MANY OF YOU ARE PROBABLY EXPERIENCING IT YOURSELVES. YOU CAN'T SLEEP, YOU HAVE BAD DREAMS WHEN YOU DO...
"THE POINT IS, MY SURGERY HAS NEVER BEEN BUSIER. SO KATIE STAYED LATE ONE EVENING, TO CLEAR PAPERWORK."
AND THAT WAS THE EVENING BRANT HARRIS CAME TO SEE ME.

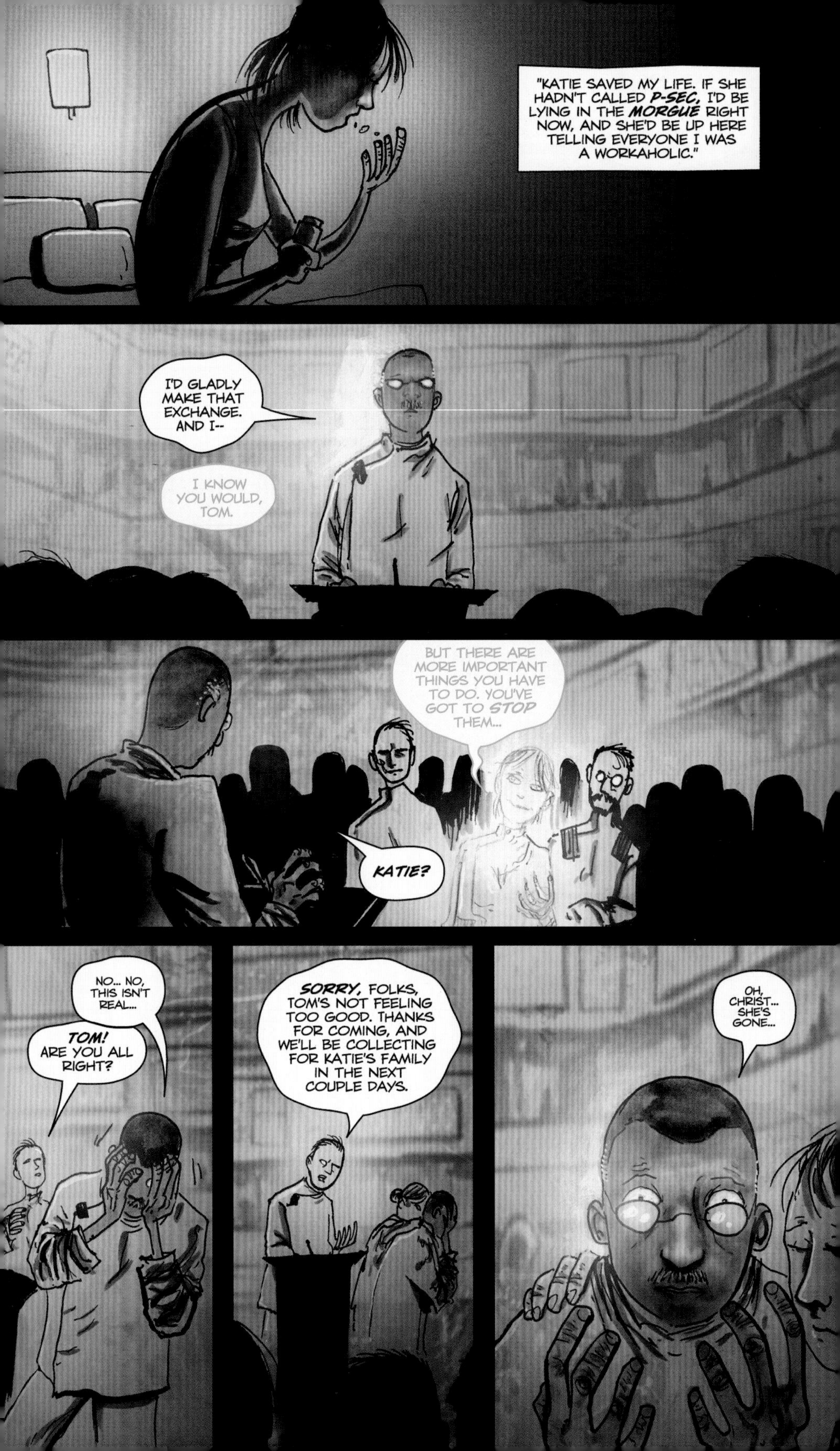
"KATIE SAVED MY LIFE. IF SHE HADN'T CALLED P-SEC, I'D BE LYING IN THE MORGUE RIGHT NOW, AND SHE'D BE UP HERE TELLING EVERYONE I WAS A WORKAHOLIC."
I'D GLADLY MAKE THAT EXCHANGE. AND I--
I KNOW YOU WOULD, TOM.
BUT THERE ARE MORE IMPORTANT THINGS YOU HAVE TO DO. YOU'VE GOT TO STOP THEM...
KATIE?
NO... NO, THIS ISN'T REAL...
TOM! ARE YOU ALL RIGHT?
SORRY, FOLKS, TOM'S NOT FEELING TOO GOOD. THANKS FOR COMING, AND WE'LL BE COLLECTING FOR KATIE'S FAMILY IN THE NEXT COUPLE DAYS.
OH, CHRIST... SHE'S GONE...

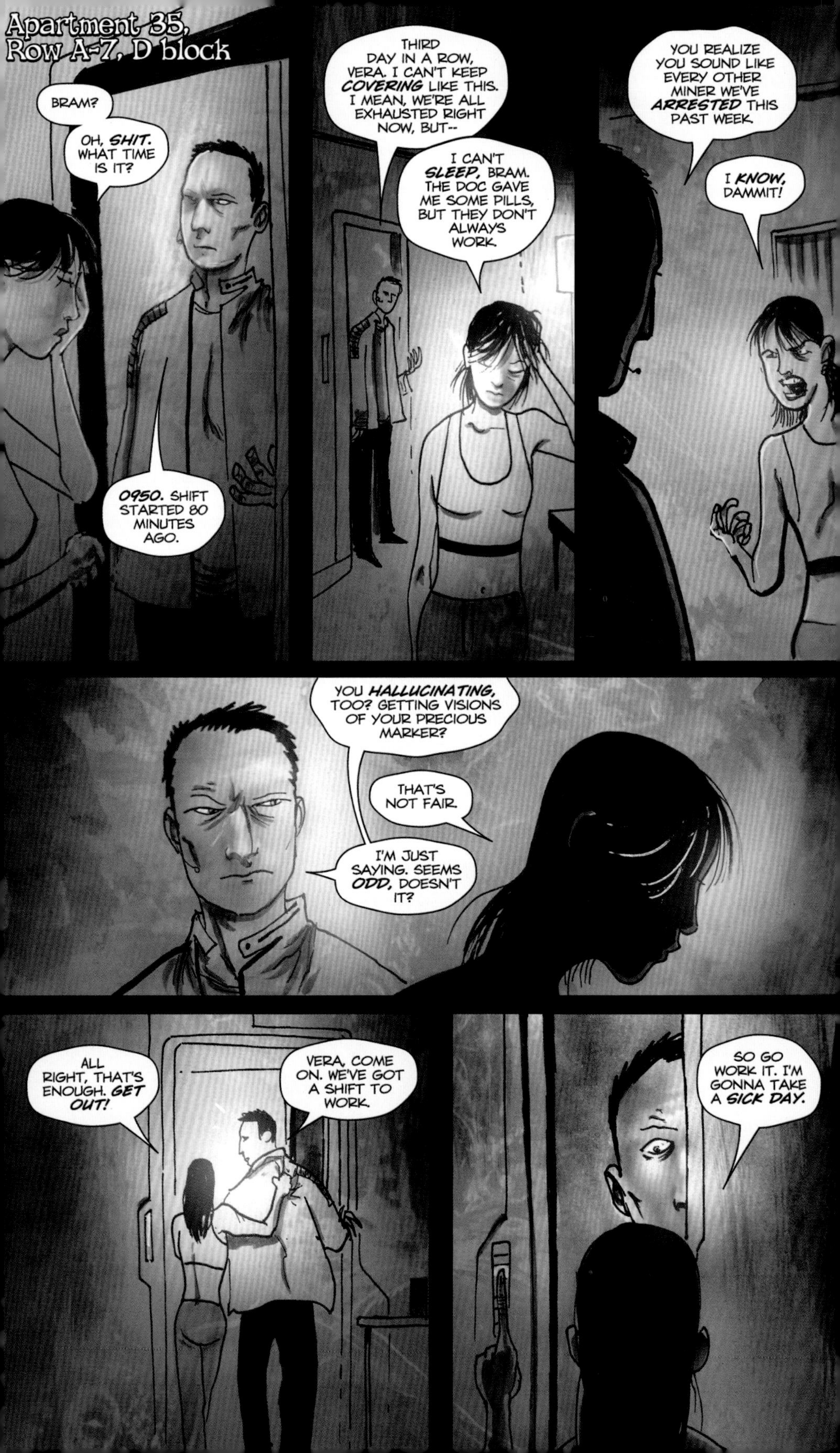
Apartment 35, Row A-7, D block
BRAM?
OH, SHIT. WHAT TIME IS IT?
0950. SHIFT STARTED 80 MINUTES AGO.
THIRD DAY IN A ROW, VERA. I CAN'T KEEP COVERING LIKE THIS. I MEAN, WE'RE ALL EXHAUSTED RIGHT NOW, BUT--
I CAN'T SLEEP, BRAM. THE DOC GAVE ME SOME PILLS, BUT THEY DON'T ALWAYS WORK.
YOU REALIZE YOU SOUND LIKE EVERY OTHER MINER WE'VE ARRESTED THIS PAST WEEK.
I KNOW, DAMMIT!
YOU HALLUCINATING, TOO? GETTING VISIONS OF YOUR PRECIOUS MARKER?
THAT'S NOT FAIR.
I'M JUST SAYING. SEEMS ODD, DOESN'T IT?
ALL RIGHT, THAT'S ENOUGH. GET OUT!
VERA, COME ON. WE'VE GOT A SHIFT TO WORK.
SO GO WORK IT. I'M GONNA TAKE A SICK DAY.

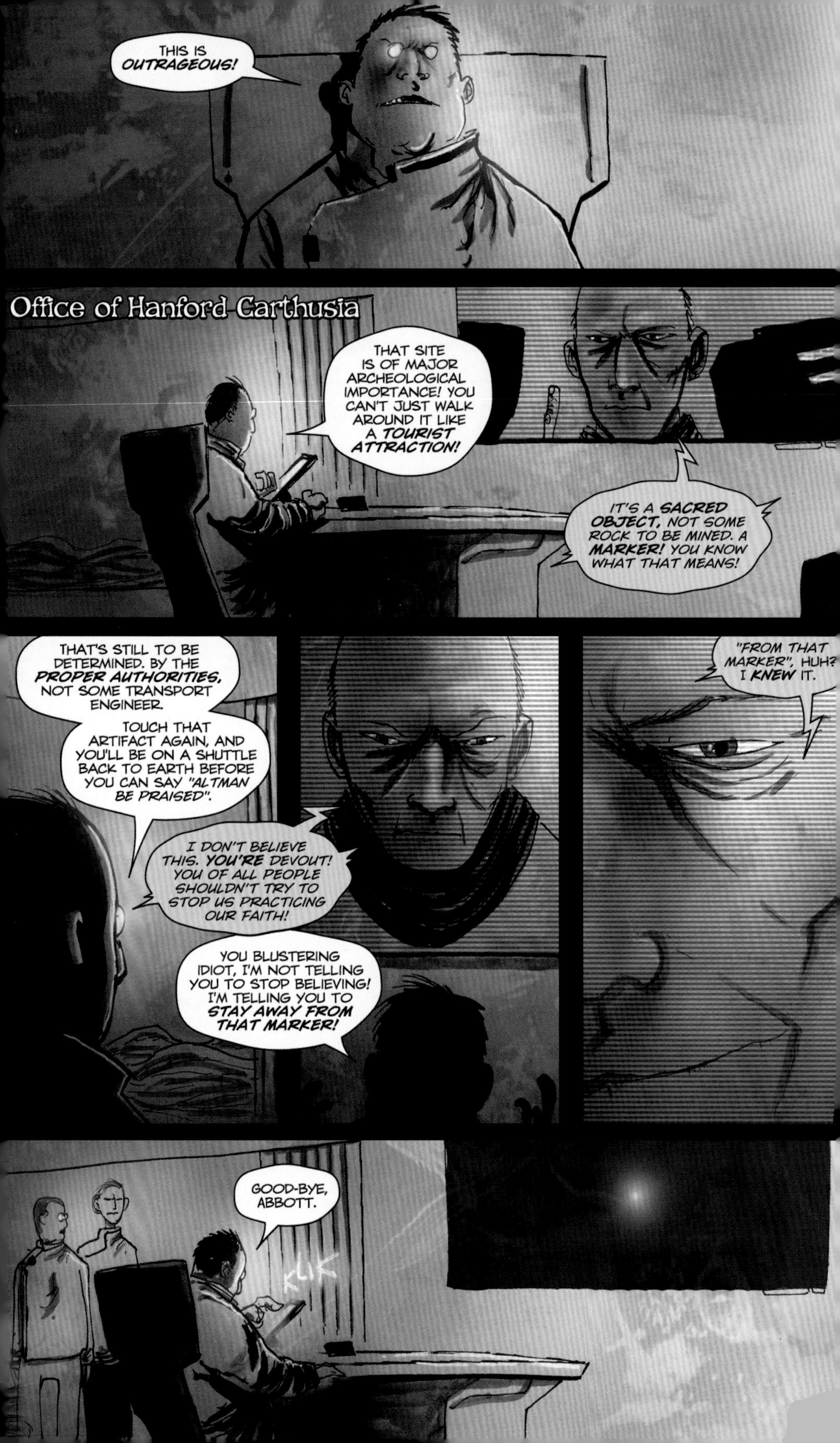
THIS IS OUTRAGEOUS!
Office of Hanford Carthusia
THAT SITE IS OF MAJOR ARCHEOLOGICAL IMPORTANCE! YOU CAN'T JUST WALK AROUND IT LIKE A TOURIST ATTRACTION!
IT'S A SACRED OBJECT, NOT SOME ROCK TO BE MINED. A MARKER! YOU KNOW WHAT THAT MEANS!
THAT'S STILL TO BE DETERMINED. BY THE PROPER AUTHORITIES, NOT SOME TRANSPORT ENGINEER.
TOUCH THAT ARTIFACT AGAIN, AND YOU'LL BE ON A SHUTTLE BACK TO EARTH BEFORE YOU CAN SAY "ALTMAN BE PRAISED".
I DON'T BELIEVE THIS. YOU'RE DEVOUT! YOU OF ALL PEOPLE SHOULDN'T TRY TO STOP US PRACTICING OUR FAITH!
YOU BLUSTERING IDIOT, I'M NOT TELLING YOU TO STOP BELIEVING! I'M TELLING YOU TO STAY AWAY FROM THAT MARKER!
"FROM THAT MARKER", HUH? I KNEW IT.
GOOD-BYE, ABBOTT.
KLIK

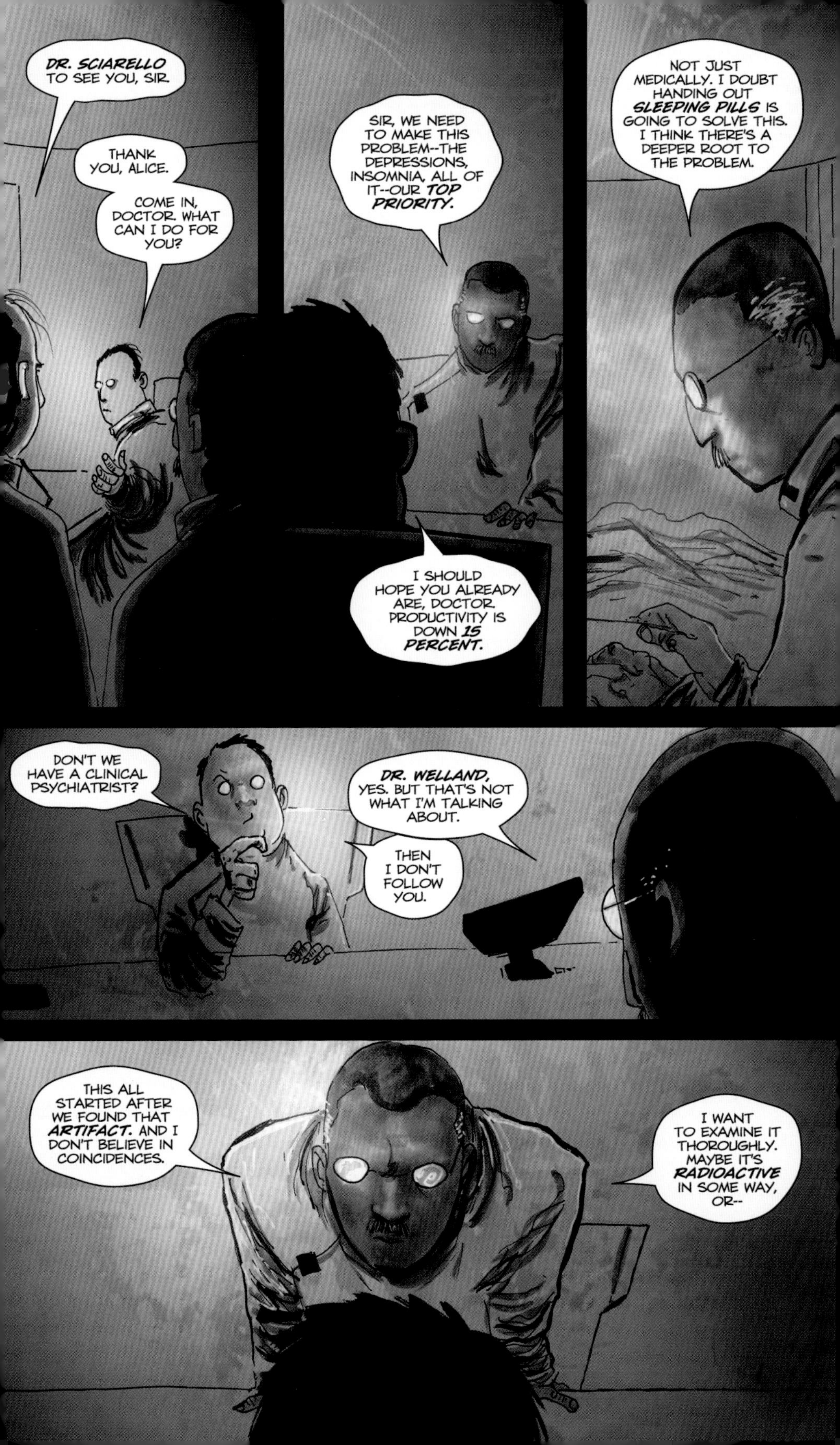
DR. SCIARELLO TO SEE YOU, SIR.
THANK YOU, ALICE.
COME IN, DOCTOR. WHAT CAN I DO FOR YOU?
SIR, WE NEED TO MAKE THIS PROBLEM--THE DEPRESSIONS, INSOMNIA, ALL OF IT--OUR TOP PRIORITY.
I SHOULD HOPE YOU ALREADY ARE, DOCTOR. PRODUCTIVITY IS DOWN 15 PERCENT.
NOT JUST MEDICALLY. I DOUBT HANDING OUT SLEEPING PILLS IS GOING TO SOLVE THIS. I THINK THERE'S A DEEPER ROOT TO THE PROBLEM.
DON'T WE HAVE A CLINICAL PSYCHIATRIST?
DR. WELLAND, YES. BUT THAT'S NOT WHAT I'M TALKING ABOUT.
THEN I DON'T FOLLOW YOU.
THIS ALL STARTED AFTER WE FOUND THAT ARTIFACT. AND I DON'T BELIEVE IN COINCIDENCES.
I WANT TO EXAMINE IT THOROUGHLY. MAYBE IT'S RADIOACTIVE IN SOME WAY, OR--

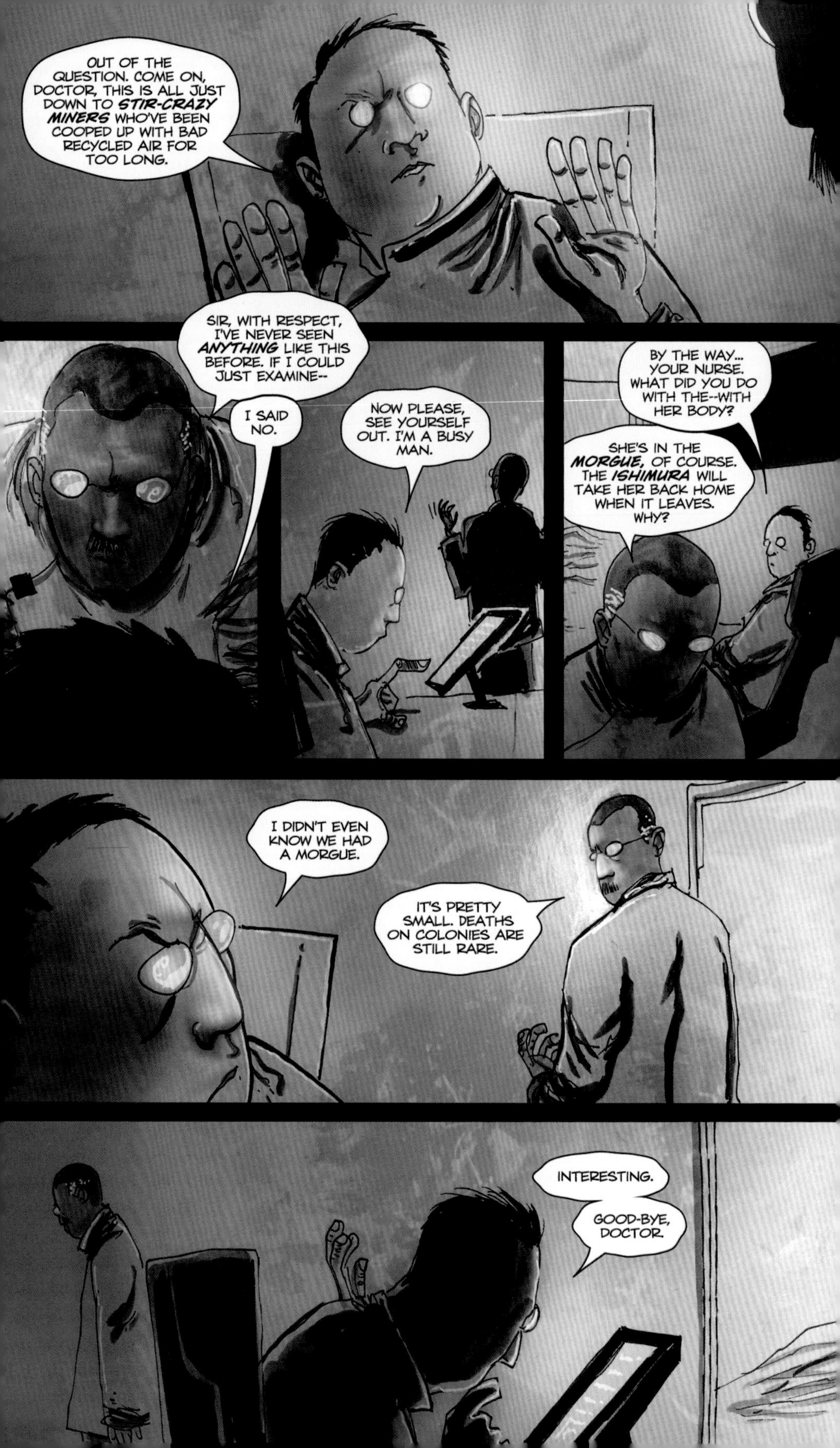
OUT OF THE QUESTION. COME ON, DOCTOR, THIS IS ALL JUST DOWN TO **STIR-CRAZY MINERS** WHO'VE BEEN COOPED UP WITH BAD RECYCLED AIR FOR TOO LONG.
SIR, WITH RESPECT, I'VE NEVER SEEN **ANYTHING** LIKE THIS BEFORE. IF I COULD JUST EXAMINE--
I SAID NO.
NOW PLEASE, SEE YOURSELF OUT. I'M A BUSY MAN.
BY THE WAY... YOUR NURSE. WHAT DID YOU DO WITH THE--WITH HER BODY?
SHE'S IN THE **MORGUE,** OF COURSE. THE **ISHIMURA** WILL TAKE HER BACK HOME WHEN IT LEAVES. WHY?
I DIDN'T EVEN KNOW WE HAD A MORGUE.
IT'S PRETTY SMALL. DEATHS ON COLONIES ARE STILL RARE.
INTERESTING.
GOOD-BYE, DOCTOR.

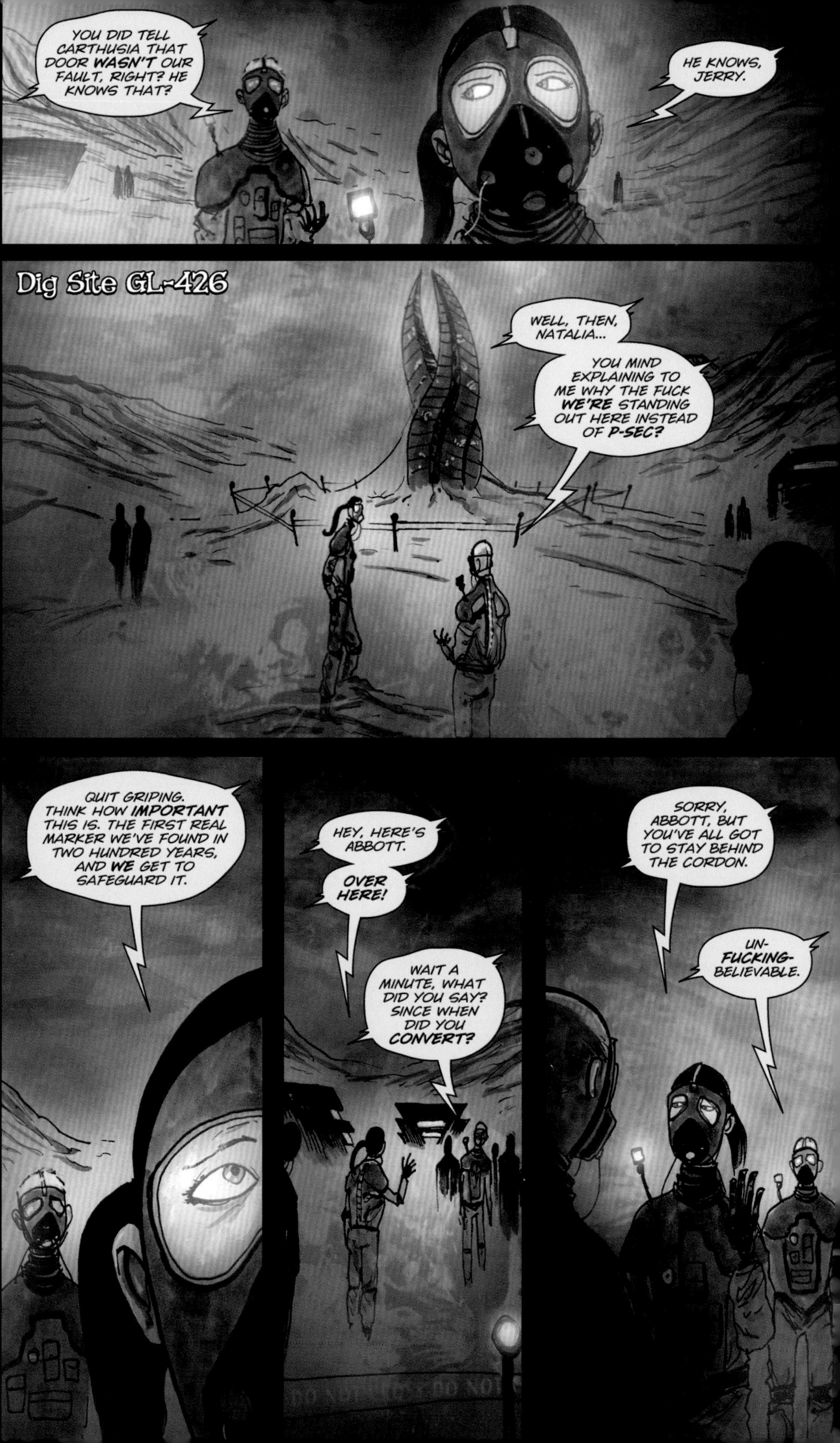
YOU DID TELL CARTHUSIA THAT DOOR WASN'T OUR FAULT, RIGHT? HE KNOWS THAT?
HE KNOWS, JERRY.
Dig Site GL-426
WELL, THEN, NATALIA...
YOU MIND EXPLAINING TO ME WHY THE FUCK WE'RE STANDING OUT HERE INSTEAD OF P-SEC?
QUIT GRIPING. THINK HOW IMPORTANT THIS IS. THE FIRST REAL MARKER WE'VE FOUND IN TWO HUNDRED YEARS, AND WE GET TO SAFEGUARD IT.
HEY, HERE'S ABBOTT.
OVER HERE!
WAIT A MINUTE, WHAT DID YOU SAY? SINCE WHEN DID YOU CONVERT?
SORRY, ABBOTT, BUT YOU'VE ALL GOT TO STAY BEHIND THE CORDON.
UN-FUCKING-BELIEVABLE.

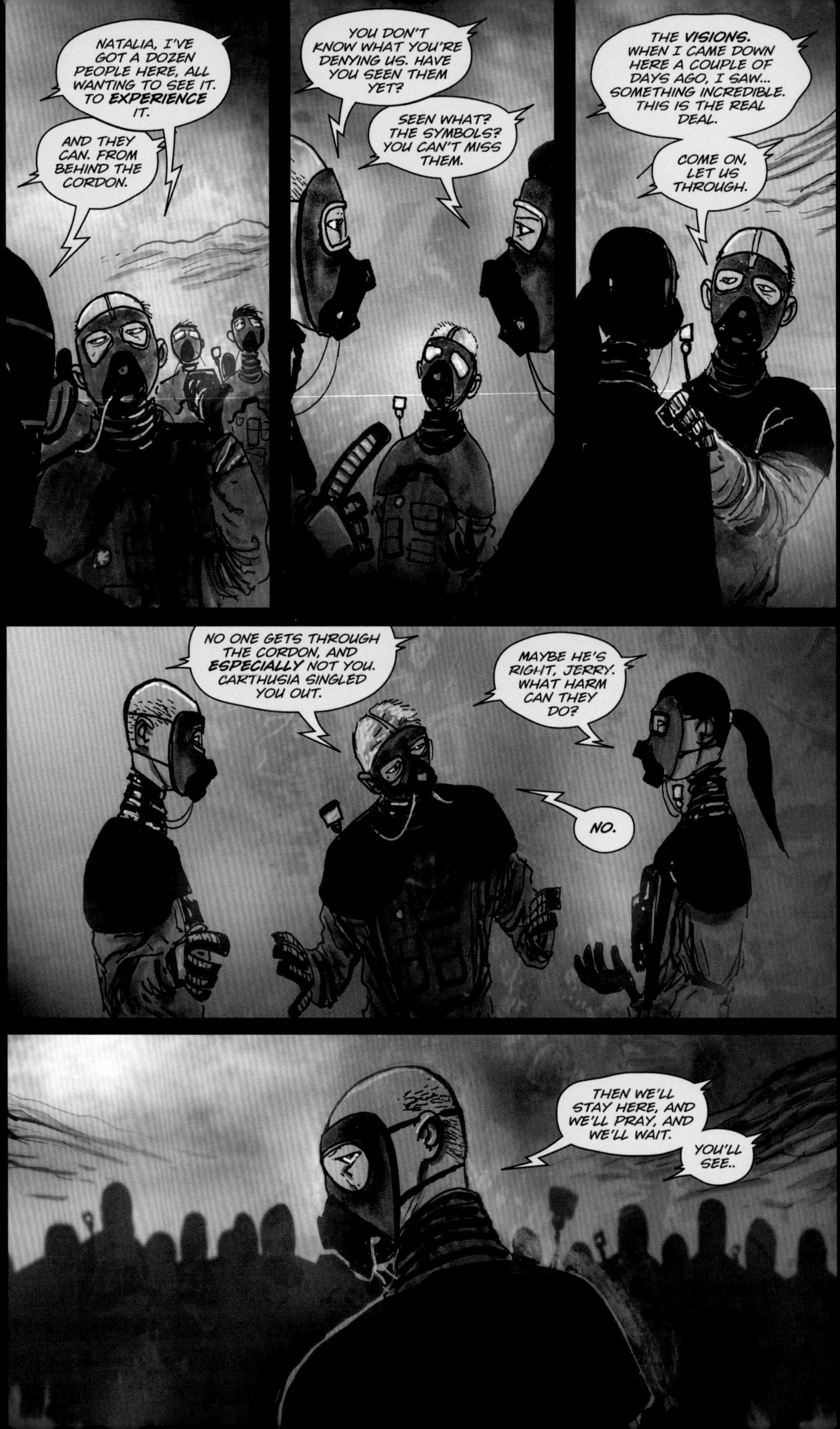
NATALIA, I'VE GOT A DOZEN PEOPLE HERE, ALL WANTING TO SEE IT. TO EXPERIENCE IT.
AND THEY CAN. FROM BEHIND THE CORDON.
YOU DON'T KNOW WHAT YOU'RE DENYING US. HAVE YOU SEEN THEM YET?
SEEN WHAT? THE SYMBOLS? YOU CAN'T MISS THEM.
THE VISIONS. WHEN I CAME DOWN HERE A COUPLE OF DAYS AGO, I SAW... SOMETHING INCREDIBLE. THIS IS THE REAL DEAL.
COME ON, LET US THROUGH.
NO ONE GETS THROUGH THE CORDON, AND ESPECIALLY NOT YOU. CARTHUSIA SINGLED YOU OUT.
MAYBE HE'S RIGHT, JERRY. WHAT HARM CAN THEY DO?
NO.
THEN WE'LL STAY HERE, AND WE'LL PRAY, AND WE'LL WAIT.
YOU'LL SEE..

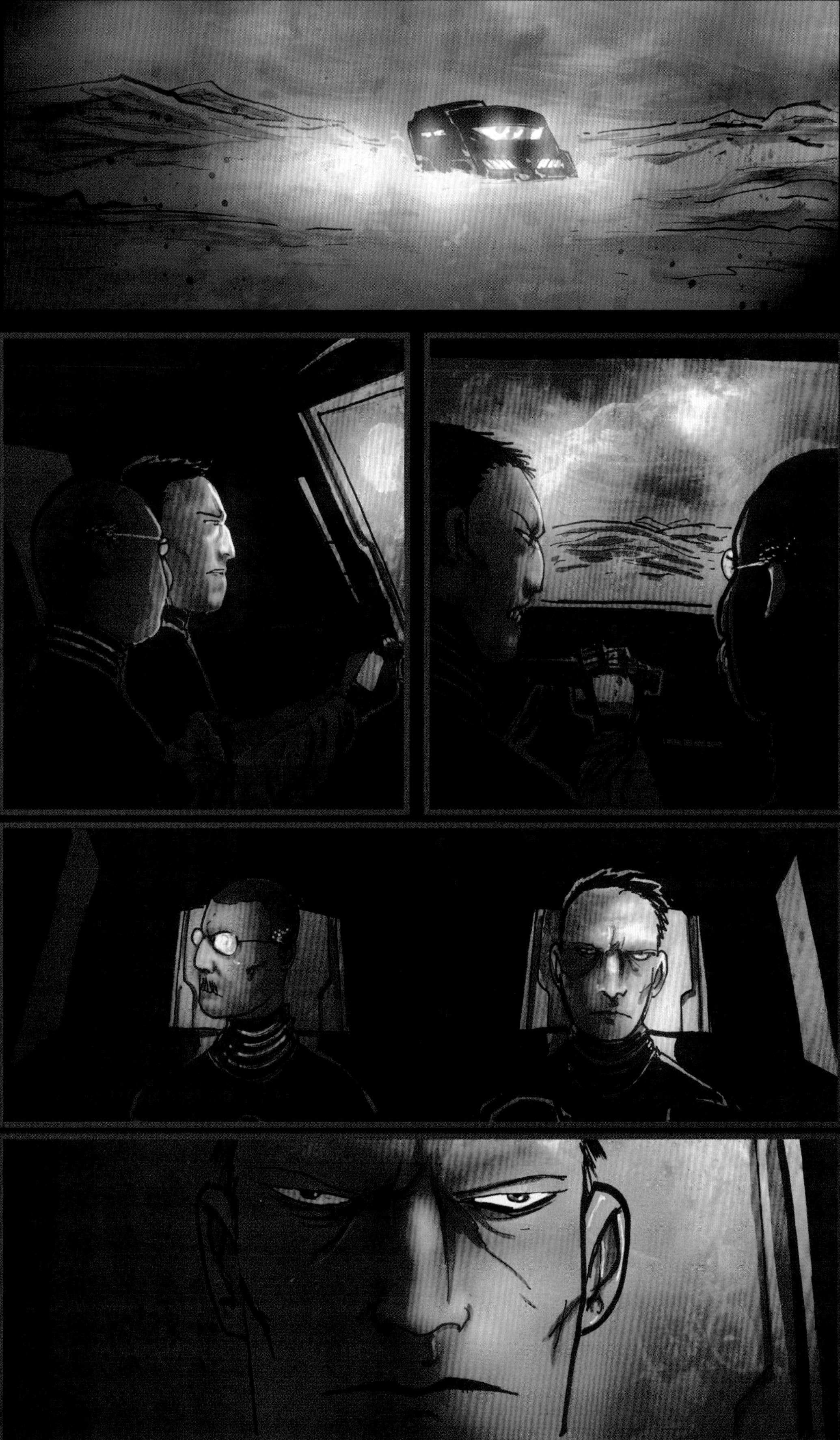

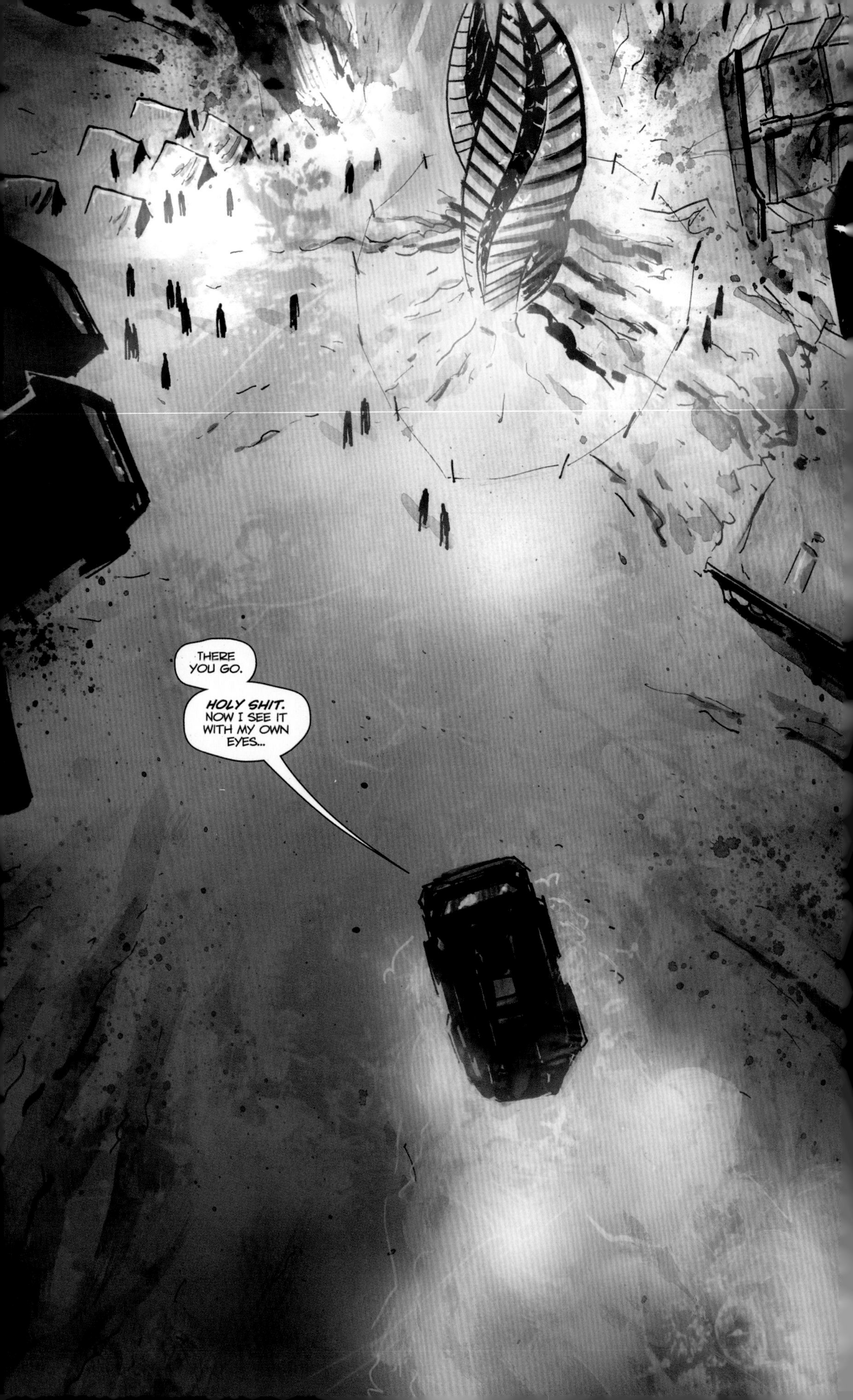
THERE YOU GO.
HOLY SHIT. NOW I SEE IT WITH MY OWN EYES...

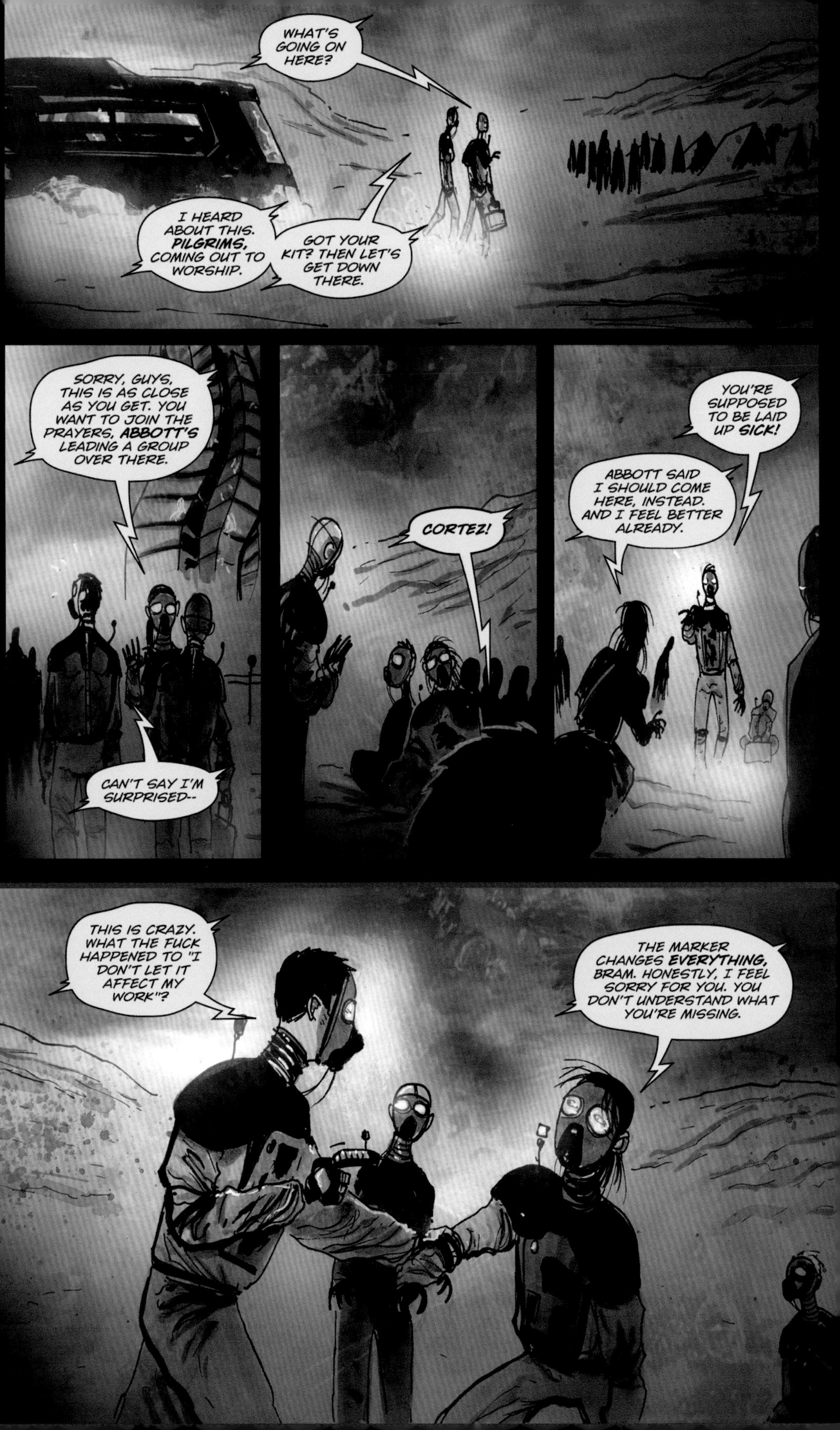
WHAT'S GOING ON HERE?
I HEARD ABOUT THIS. PILGRIMS, COMING OUT TO WORSHIP.
GOT YOUR KIT? THEN LET'S GET DOWN THERE.
SORRY, GUYS, THIS IS AS CLOSE AS YOU GET. YOU WANT TO JOIN THE PRAYERS, ABBOTT'S LEADING A GROUP OVER THERE.
CAN'T SAY I'M SURPRISED--
CORTEZ!
YOU'RE SUPPOSED TO BE LAID UP SICK!
ABBOTT SAID I SHOULD COME HERE, INSTEAD. AND I FEEL BETTER ALREADY.
THIS IS CRAZY. WHAT THE FUCK HAPPENED TO "I DON'T LET IT AFFECT MY WORK"?
THE MARKER CHANGES EVERYTHING, BRAM. HONESTLY, I FEEL SORRY FOR YOU. YOU DON'T UNDERSTAND WHAT YOU'RE MISSING.

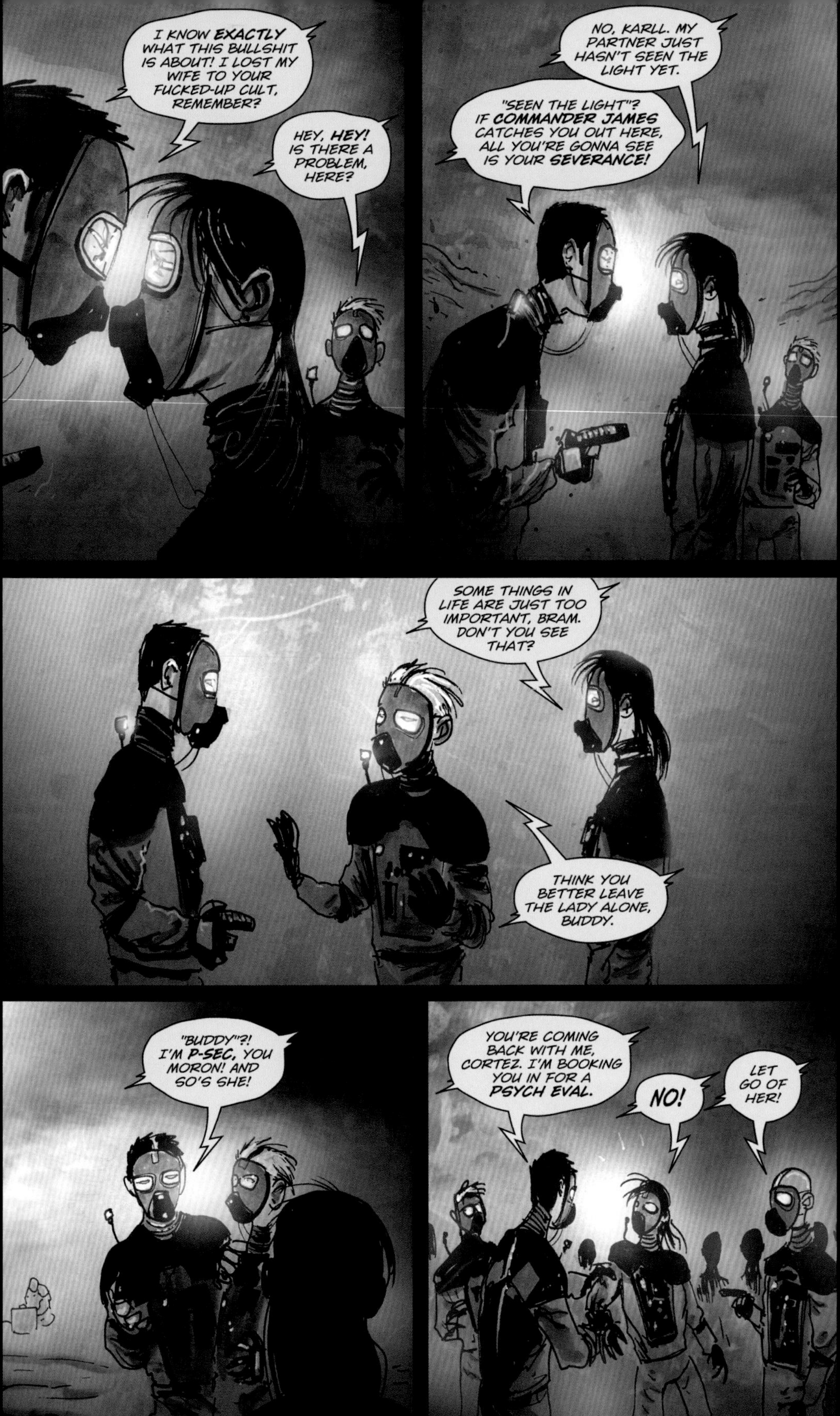

I KNOW **EXACTLY** WHAT THIS BULLSHIT IS ABOUT! I LOST MY WIFE TO YOUR FUCKED-UP CULT, REMEMBER?
HEY, **HEY!** IS THERE A PROBLEM, HERE?
NO, KARLL. MY PARTNER JUST HASN'T SEEN THE LIGHT YET.
"SEEN THE LIGHT"? IF **COMMANDER JAMES** CATCHES YOU OUT HERE, ALL YOU'RE GONNA SEE IS YOUR **SEVERANCE!**
SOME THINGS IN LIFE ARE JUST TOO IMPORTANT, BRAM. DON'T YOU SEE THAT?
THINK YOU BETTER LEAVE THE LADY ALONE, BUDDY.
"BUDDY"?! I'M **P-SEC,** YOU MORON! AND SO'S SHE!
YOU'RE COMING BACK WITH ME, CORTEZ. I'M BOOKING YOU IN FOR A **PSYCH EVAL.**
NO!
LET GO OF HER!

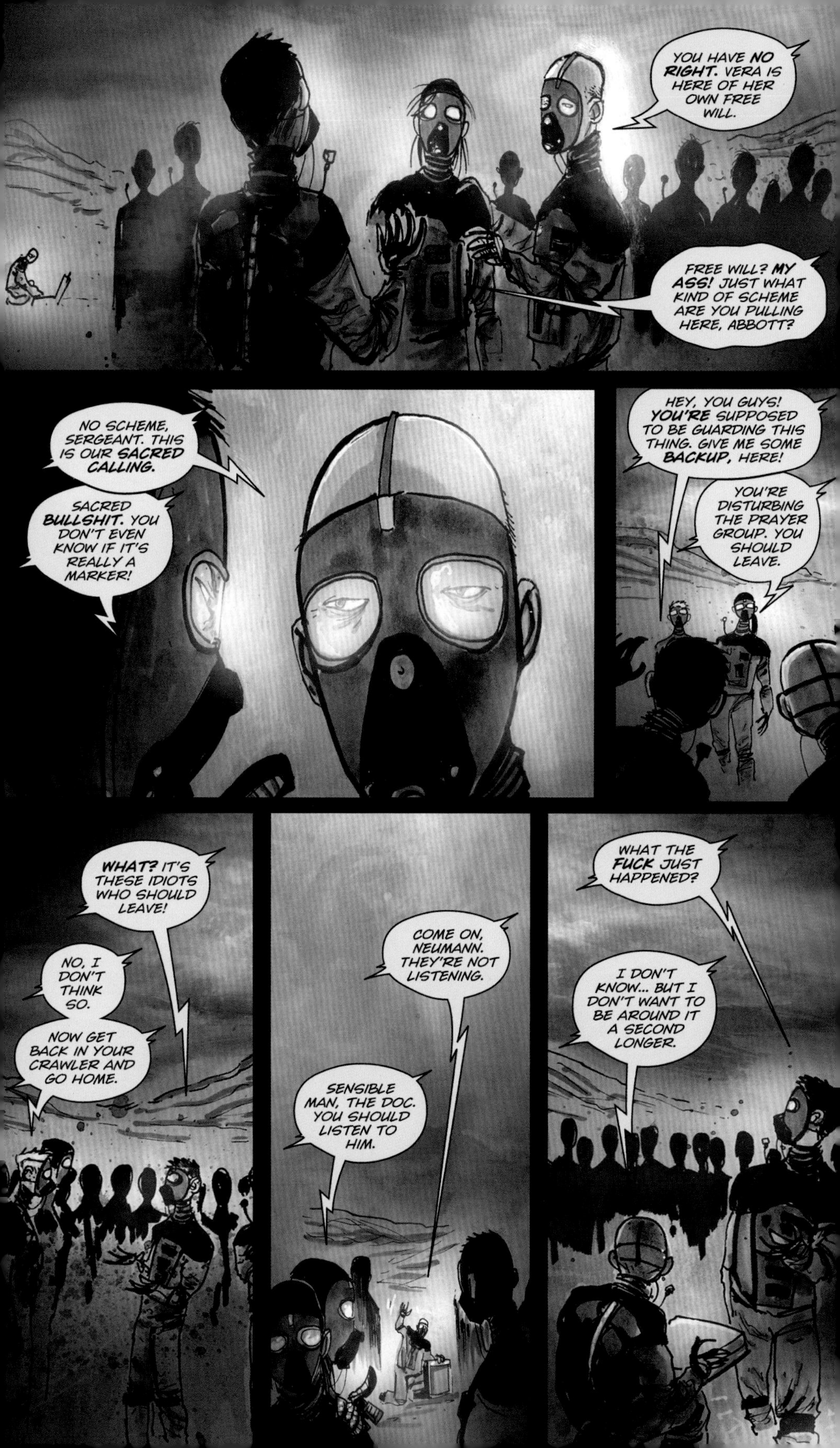

YOU HAVE NO RIGHT. VERA IS HERE OF HER OWN FREE WILL.
FREE WILL? MY ASS! JUST WHAT KIND OF SCHEME ARE YOU PULLING HERE, ABBOTT?
NO SCHEME, SERGEANT. THIS IS OUR SACRED CALLING.
SACRED BULLSHIT. YOU DON'T EVEN KNOW IF IT'S REALLY A MARKER!
HEY, YOU GUYS! YOU'RE SUPPOSED TO BE GUARDING THIS THING. GIVE ME SOME BACKUP, HERE!
YOU'RE DISTURBING THE PRAYER GROUP. YOU SHOULD LEAVE.
WHAT? IT'S THESE IDIOTS WHO SHOULD LEAVE!
NO, I DON'T THINK SO.
NOW GET BACK IN YOUR CRAWLER AND GO HOME.
COME ON, NEUMANN. THEY'RE NOT LISTENING.
SENSIBLE MAN, THE DOC. YOU SHOULD LISTEN TO HIM.
WHAT THE FUCK JUST HAPPENED?
I DON'T KNOW... BUT I DON'T WANT TO BE AROUND IT A SECOND LONGER.

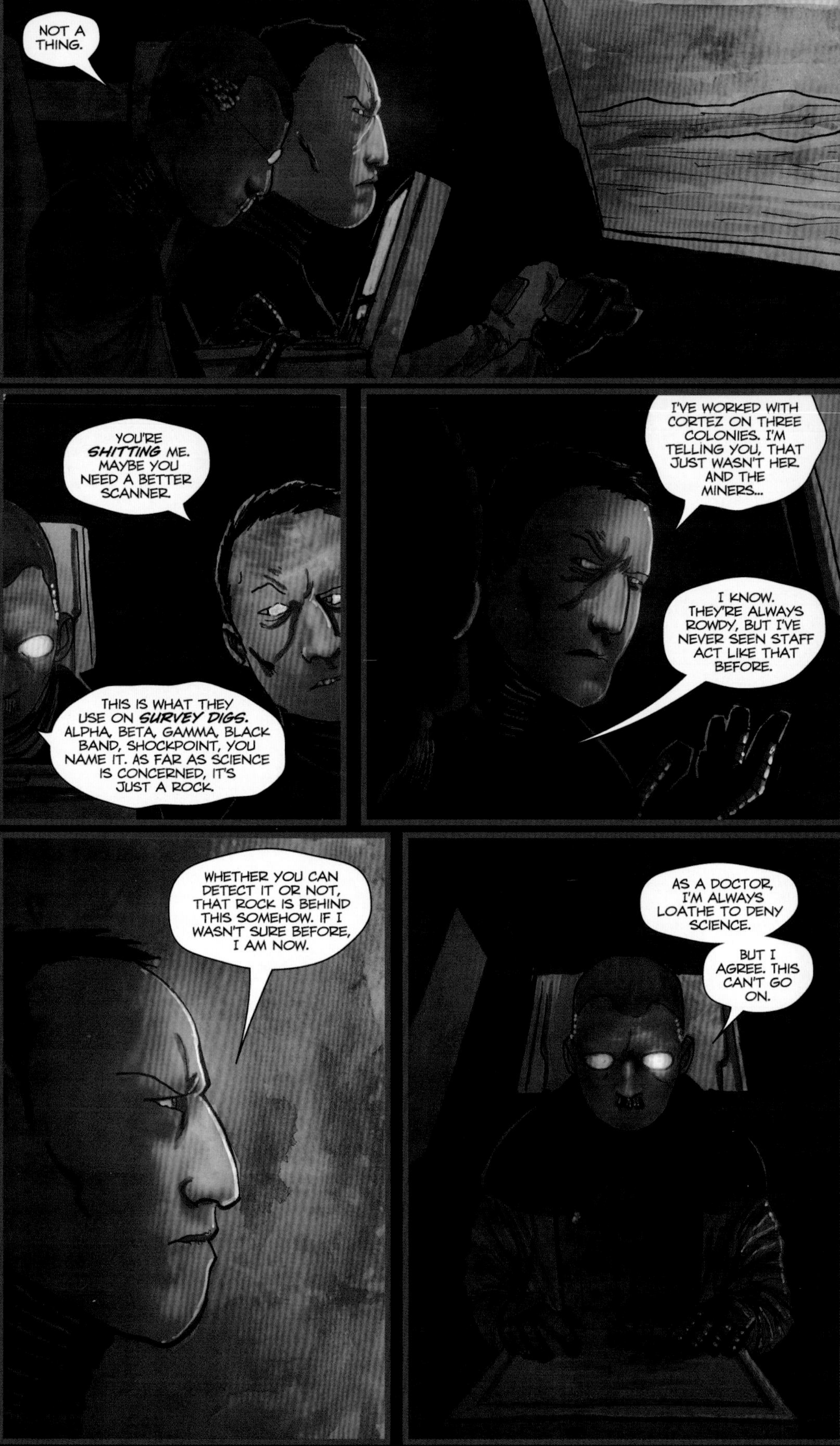
NOT A THING.
YOU'RE SHITTING ME. MAYBE YOU NEED A BETTER SCANNER.
THIS IS WHAT THEY USE ON SURVEY DIGS. ALPHA, BETA, GAMMA, BLACK BAND, SHOCKPOINT, YOU NAME IT. AS FAR AS SCIENCE IS CONCERNED, IT'S JUST A ROCK.
I'VE WORKED WITH CORTEZ ON THREE COLONIES. I'M TELLING YOU, THAT JUST WASN'T HER. AND THE MINERS...
I KNOW. THEY'RE ALWAYS ROWDY, BUT I'VE NEVER SEEN STAFF ACT LIKE THAT BEFORE.
WHETHER YOU CAN DETECT IT OR NOT, THAT ROCK IS BEHIND THIS SOMEHOW. IF I WASN'T SURE BEFORE, I AM NOW.
AS A DOCTOR, I'M ALWAYS LOATHE TO DENY SCIENCE.
BUT I AGREE. THIS CAN'T GO ON.

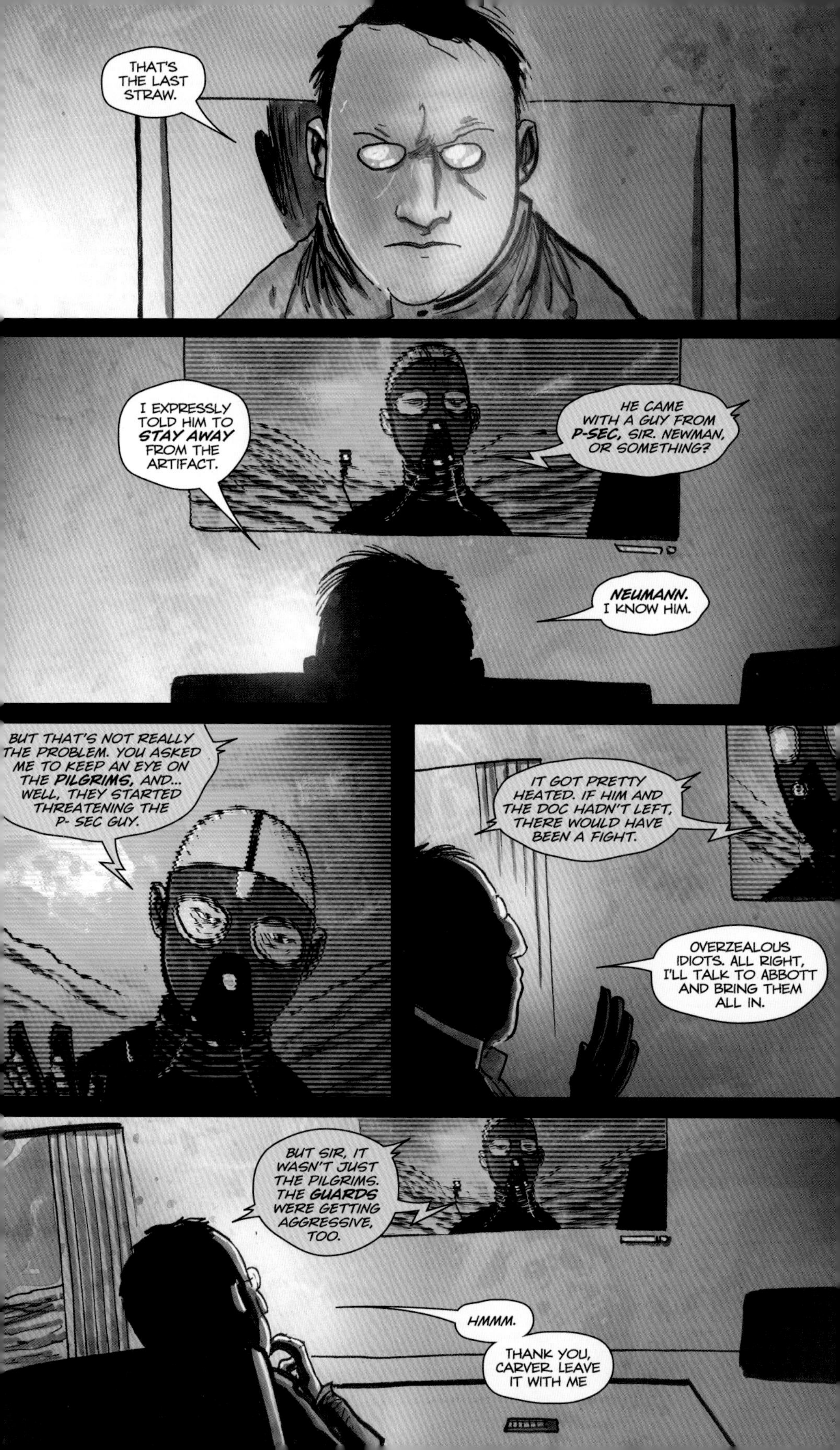
THAT'S THE LAST STRAW.
I EXPRESSLY TOLD HIM TO STAY AWAY FROM THE ARTIFACT.
HE CAME WITH A GUY FROM P-SEC, SIR. NEWMAN, OR SOMETHING?
NEUMANN. I KNOW HIM.
BUT THAT'S NOT REALLY THE PROBLEM. YOU ASKED ME TO KEEP AN EYE ON THE PILGRIMS, AND... WELL, THEY STARTED THREATENING THE P- SEC GUY.
IT GOT PRETTY HEATED. IF HIM AND THE DOC HADN'T LEFT, THERE WOULD HAVE BEEN A FIGHT.
OVERZEALOUS IDIOTS. ALL RIGHT, I'LL TALK TO ABBOTT AND BRING THEM ALL IN.
BUT SIR, IT WASN'T JUST THE PILGRIMS. THE GUARDS WERE GETTING AGGRESSIVE, TOO.
HMMM.
THANK YOU, CARVER. LEAVE IT WITH ME

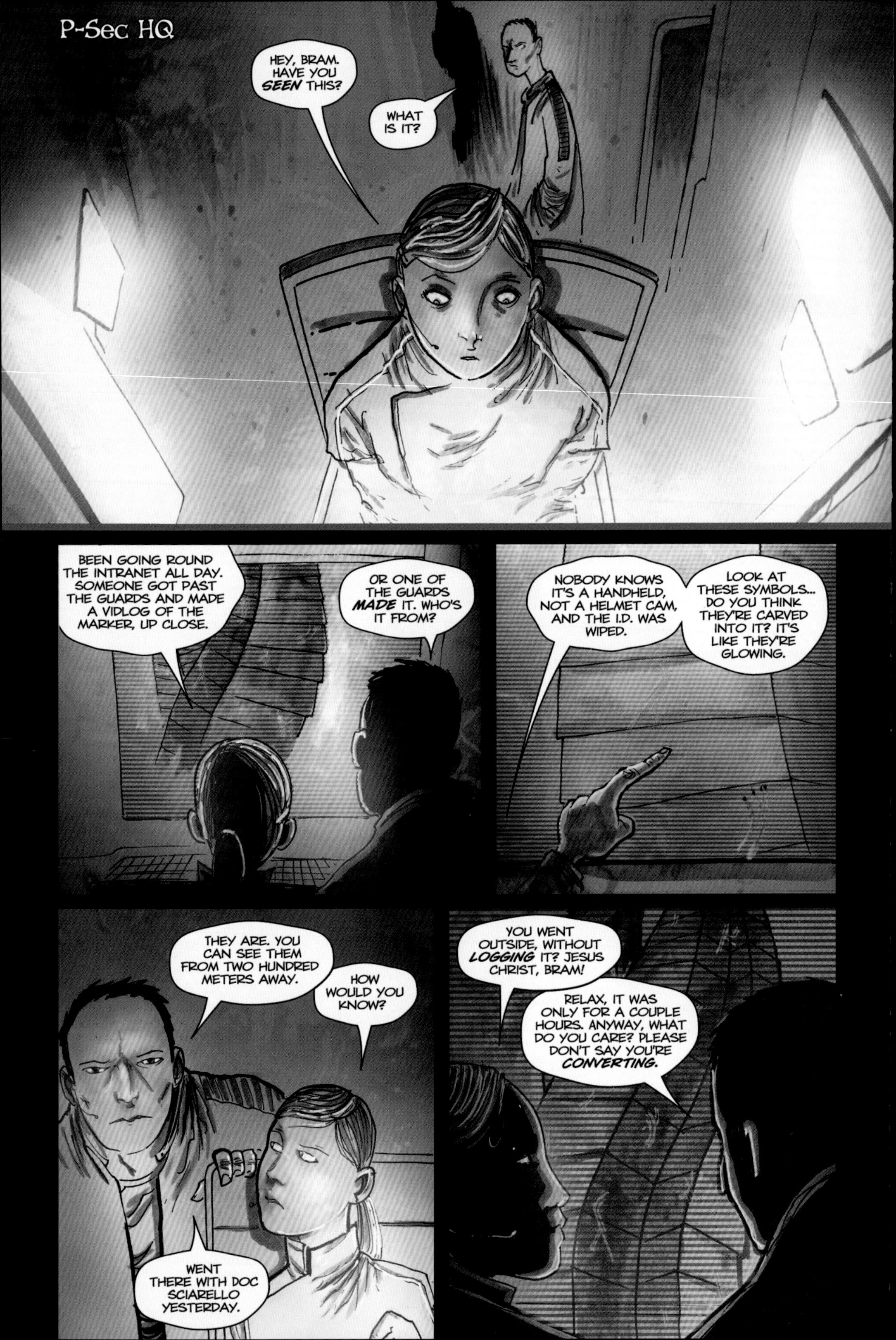
P-Sec HQ
HEY, BRAM. HAVE YOU SEEN THIS?
WHAT IS IT?
BEEN GOING ROUND THE INTRANET ALL DAY. SOMEONE GOT PAST THE GUARDS AND MADE A VIDLOG OF THE MARKER, UP CLOSE.
OR ONE OF THE GUARDS MADE IT. WHO'S IT FROM?
NOBODY KNOWS IT'S A HANDHELD, NOT A HELMET CAM, AND THE I.D. WAS WIPED.
LOOK AT THESE SYMBOLS... DO YOU THINK THEY'RE CARVED INTO IT? IT'S LIKE THEY'RE GLOWING.
THEY ARE. YOU CAN SEE THEM FROM TWO HUNDRED METERS AWAY.
HOW WOULD YOU KNOW?
WENT THERE WITH DOC SCIARELLO YESTERDAY.
YOU WENT OUTSIDE, WITHOUT LOGGING IT? JESUS CHRIST, BRAM!
RELAX, IT WAS ONLY FOR A COUPLE HOURS. ANYWAY, WHAT DO YOU CARE? PLEASE DON'T SAY YOU'RE CONVERTING.

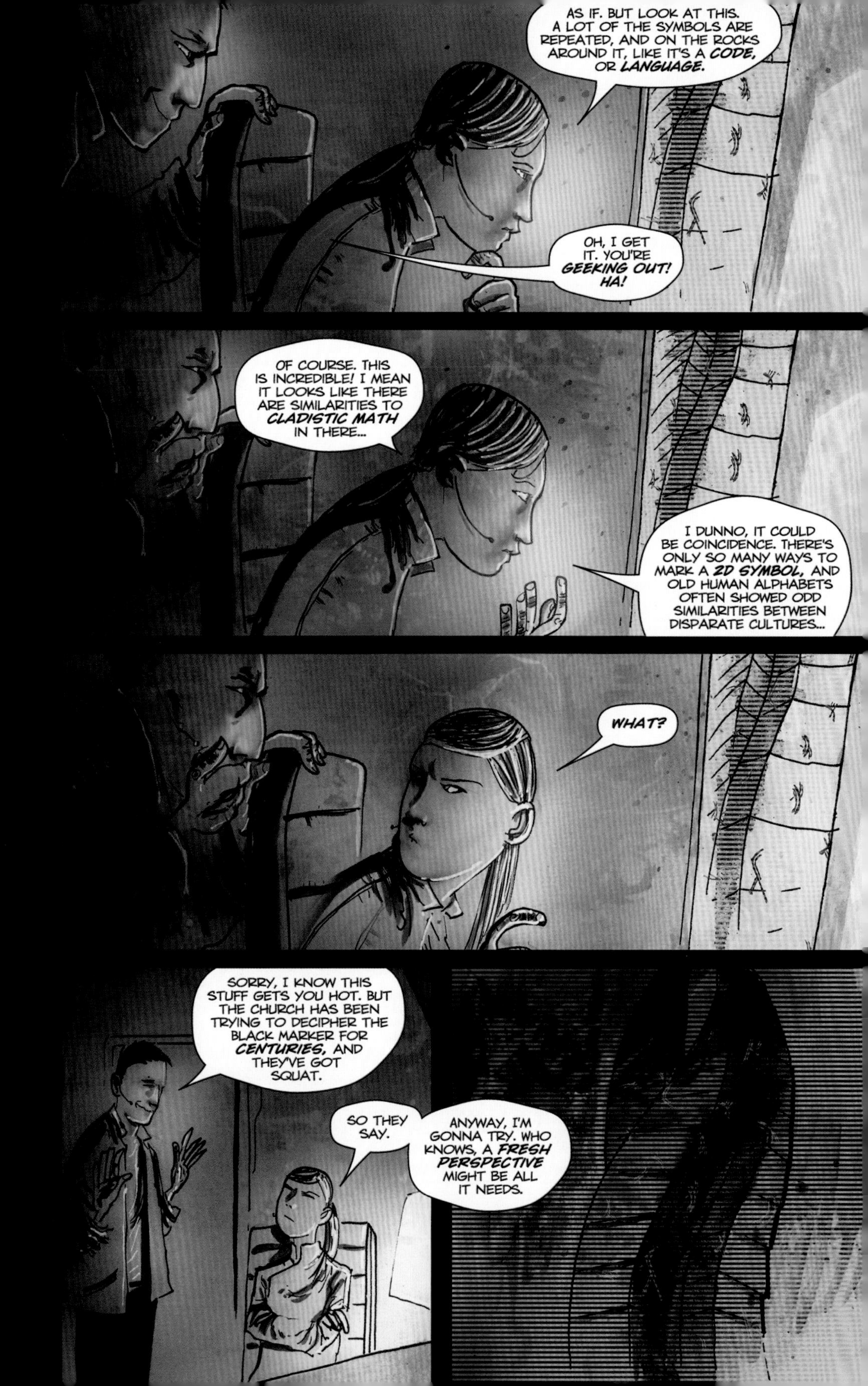
AS IF. BUT LOOK AT THIS. A LOT OF THE SYMBOLS ARE REPEATED, AND ON THE ROCKS AROUND IT, LIKE IT'S A CODE, OR LANGUAGE.
OH, I GET IT. YOU'RE GEEKING OUT! HA!
OF COURSE. THIS IS INCREDIBLE! I MEAN IT LOOKS LIKE THERE ARE SIMILARITIES TO CLADISTIC MATH IN THERE...
I DUNNO, IT COULD BE COINCIDENCE. THERE'S ONLY SO MANY WAYS TO MARK A 2D SYMBOL, AND OLD HUMAN ALPHABETS OFTEN SHOWED ODD SIMILARITIES BETWEEN DISPARATE CULTURES...
WHAT?
SORRY, I KNOW THIS STUFF GETS YOU HOT. BUT THE CHURCH HAS BEEN TRYING TO DECIPHER THE BLACK MARKER FOR CENTURIES, AND THEY'VE GOT SQUAT.
SO THEY SAY.
ANYWAY, I'M GONNA TRY. WHO KNOWS, A FRESH PERSPECTIVE MIGHT BE ALL IT NEEDS.

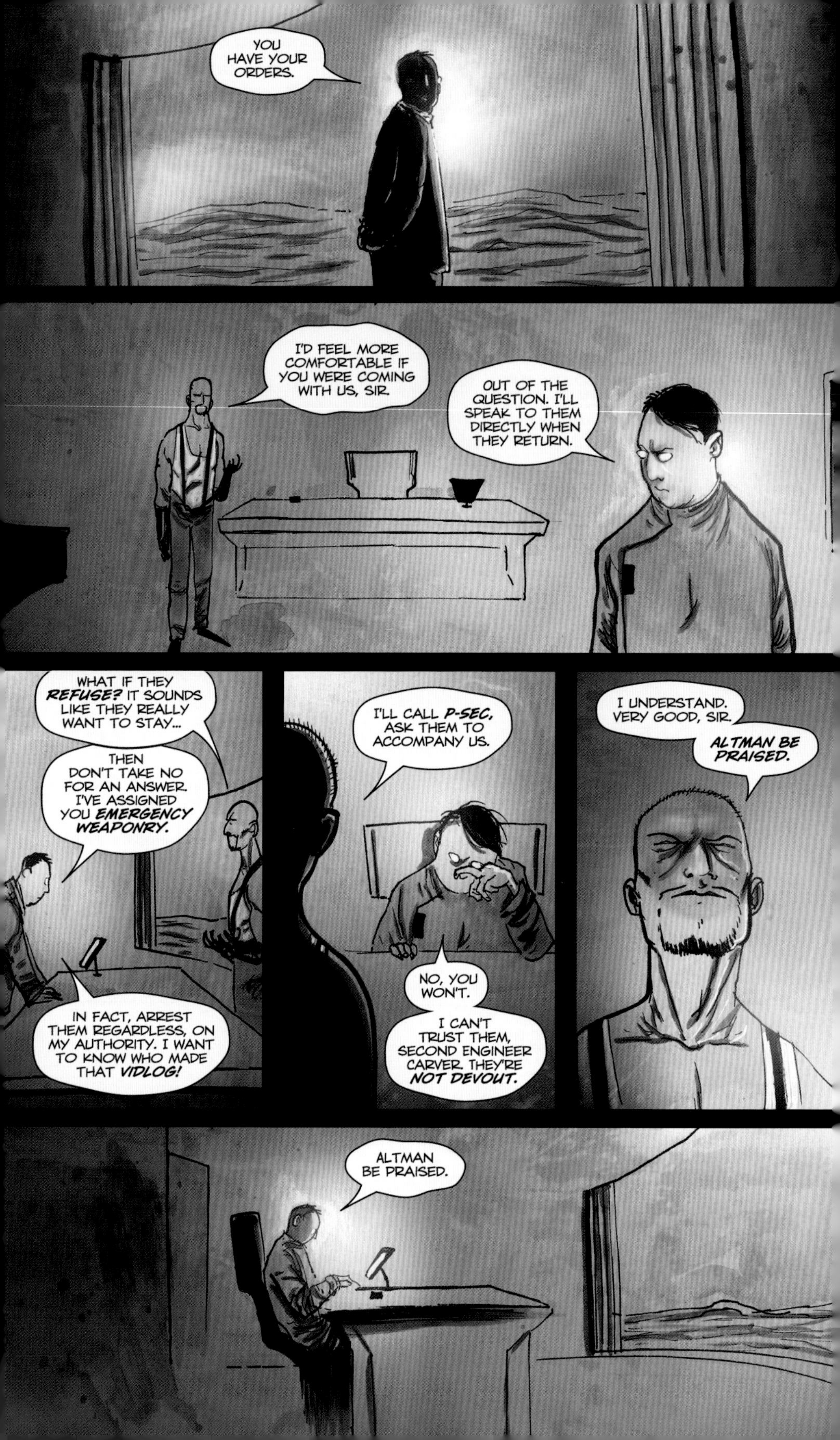
YOU HAVE YOUR ORDERS.
I'D FEEL MORE COMFORTABLE IF YOU WERE COMING WITH US, SIR.
OUT OF THE QUESTION. I'LL SPEAK TO THEM DIRECTLY WHEN THEY RETURN.
WHAT IF THEY REFUSE? IT SOUNDS LIKE THEY REALLY WANT TO STAY...
THEN DON'T TAKE NO FOR AN ANSWER. I'VE ASSIGNED YOU EMERGENCY WEAPONRY.
IN FACT, ARREST THEM REGARDLESS, ON MY AUTHORITY. I WANT TO KNOW WHO MADE THAT VIDLOG!
I'LL CALL P-SEC, ASK THEM TO ACCOMPANY US.
NO, YOU WON'T.
I CAN'T TRUST THEM, SECOND ENGINEER CARVER. THEY'RE NOT DEVOUT.
I UNDERSTAND. VERY GOOD, SIR.
ALTMAN BE PRAISED.
ALTMAN BE PRAISED.

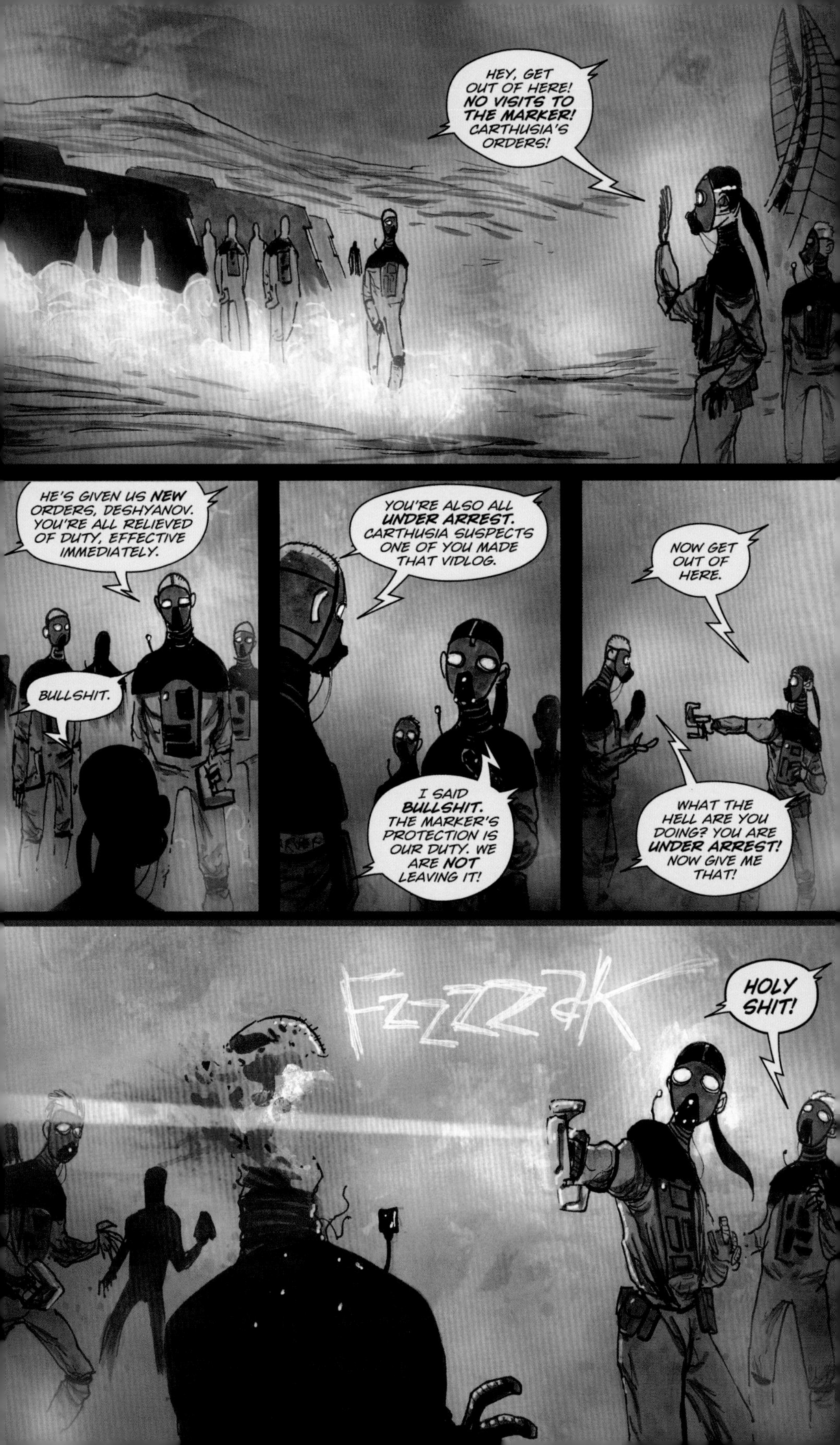
HEY, GET OUT OF HERE! NO VISITS TO THE MARKER! CARTHUSIA'S ORDERS!
HE'S GIVEN US NEW ORDERS, DESHYANOV. YOU'RE ALL RELIEVED OF DUTY, EFFECTIVE IMMEDIATELY.
BULLSHIT.
YOU'RE ALSO ALL UNDER ARREST. CARTHUSIA SUSPECTS ONE OF YOU MADE THAT VIDLOG.
I SAID BULLSHIT. THE MARKER'S PROTECTION IS OUR DUTY. WE ARE NOT LEAVING IT!
NOW GET OUT OF HERE.
WHAT THE HELL ARE YOU DOING? YOU ARE UNDER ARREST! NOW GIVE ME THAT!
FZZZZZK
HOLY SHIT!

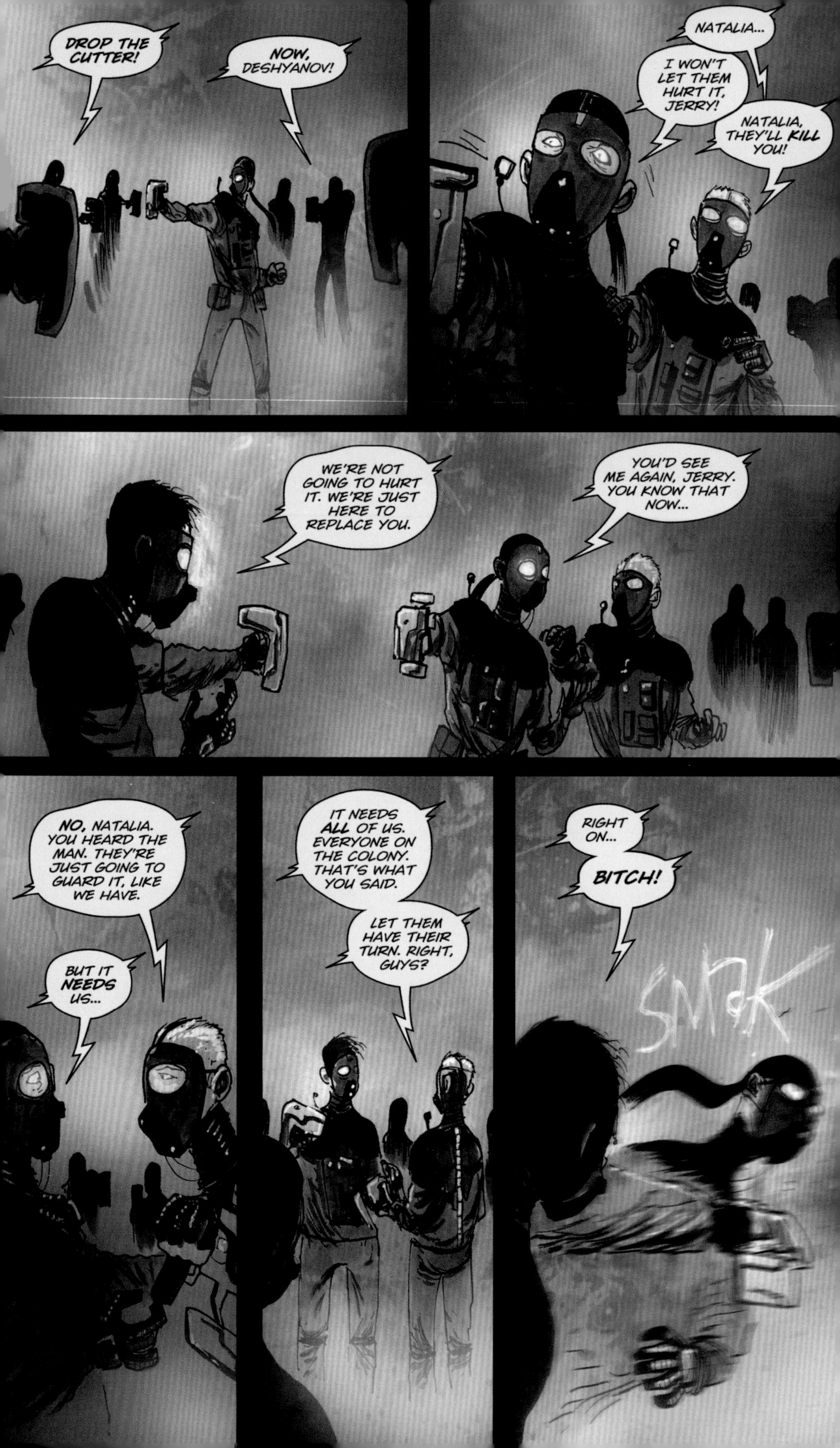
DROP THE CUTTER!
NOW, DESHYANOV!
NATALIA...
I WON'T LET THEM HURT IT, JERRY!
NATALIA, THEY'LL **KILL** YOU!
WE'RE NOT GOING TO HURT IT. WE'RE JUST HERE TO REPLACE YOU.
YOU'D SEE ME AGAIN, JERRY. YOU KNOW THAT NOW...
NO, NATALIA. YOU HEARD THE MAN. THEY'RE JUST GOING TO GUARD IT, LIKE WE HAVE.
BUT IT **NEEDS** US...
IT NEEDS **ALL** OF US. EVERYONE ON THE COLONY. THAT'S WHAT YOU SAID.
LET THEM HAVE THEIR TURN. RIGHT, GUYS?
RIGHT ON...
BITCH!
SMAK

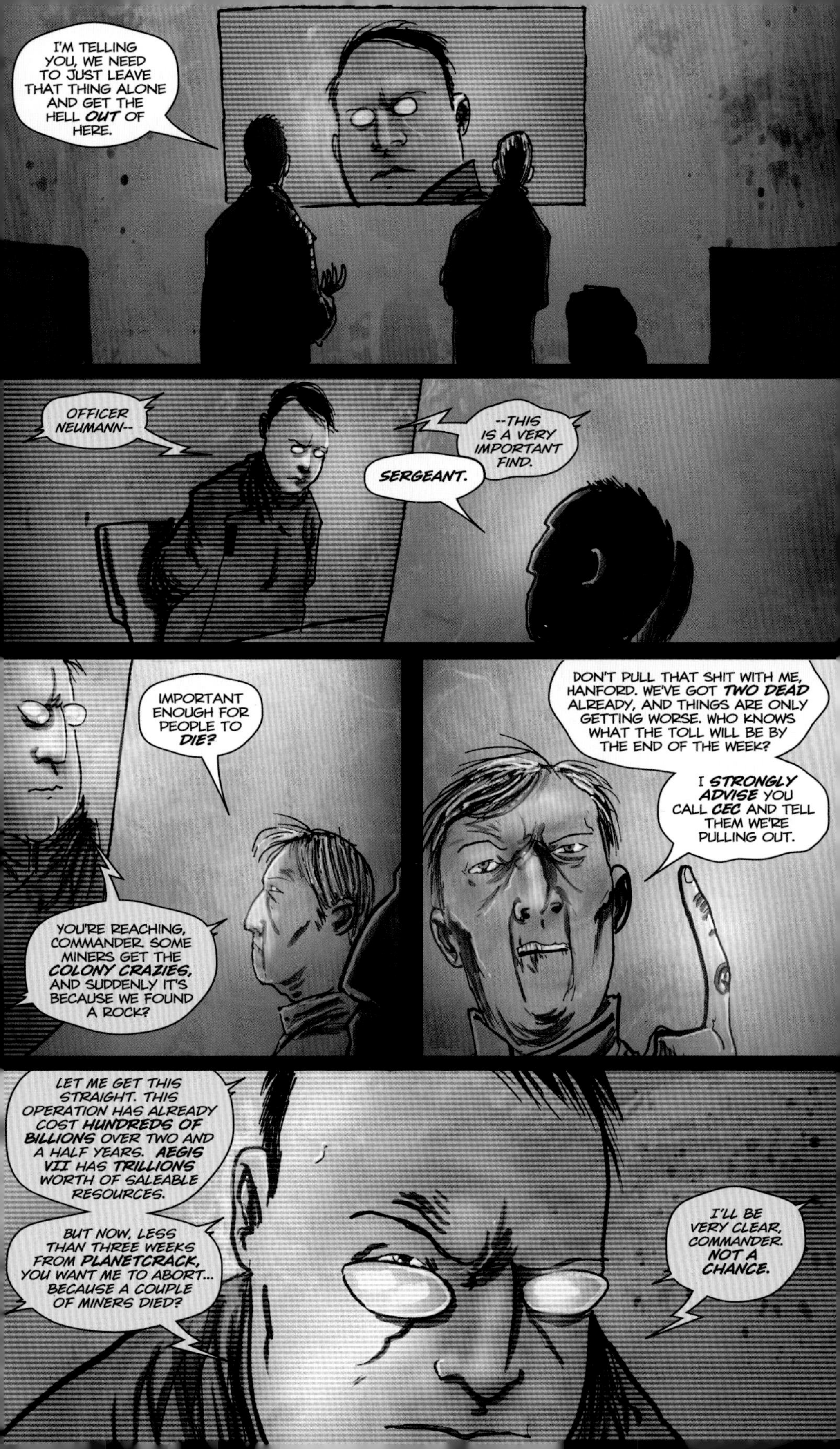
I'M TELLING YOU, WE NEED TO JUST LEAVE THAT THING ALONE AND GET THE HELL OUT OF HERE.
OFFICER NEUMANN--
SERGEANT.
--THIS IS A VERY IMPORTANT FIND.
IMPORTANT ENOUGH FOR PEOPLE TO DIE?
YOU'RE REACHING, COMMANDER. SOME MINERS GET THE COLONY CRAZIES, AND SUDDENLY IT'S BECAUSE WE FOUND A ROCK?
DON'T PULL THAT SHIT WITH ME, HANFORD. WE'VE GOT TWO DEAD ALREADY, AND THINGS ARE ONLY GETTING WORSE. WHO KNOWS WHAT THE TOLL WILL BE BY THE END OF THE WEEK?
I STRONGLY ADVISE YOU CALL CEC AND TELL THEM WE'RE PULLING OUT.
LET ME GET THIS STRAIGHT. THIS OPERATION HAS ALREADY COST HUNDREDS OF BILLIONS OVER TWO AND A HALF YEARS. AEGIS VII HAS TRILLIONS WORTH OF SALEABLE RESOURCES.
BUT NOW, LESS THAN THREE WEEKS FROM PLANETCRACK, YOU WANT ME TO ABORT... BECAUSE A COUPLE OF MINERS DIED?
I'LL BE VERY CLEAR, COMMANDER. NOT A CHANCE.

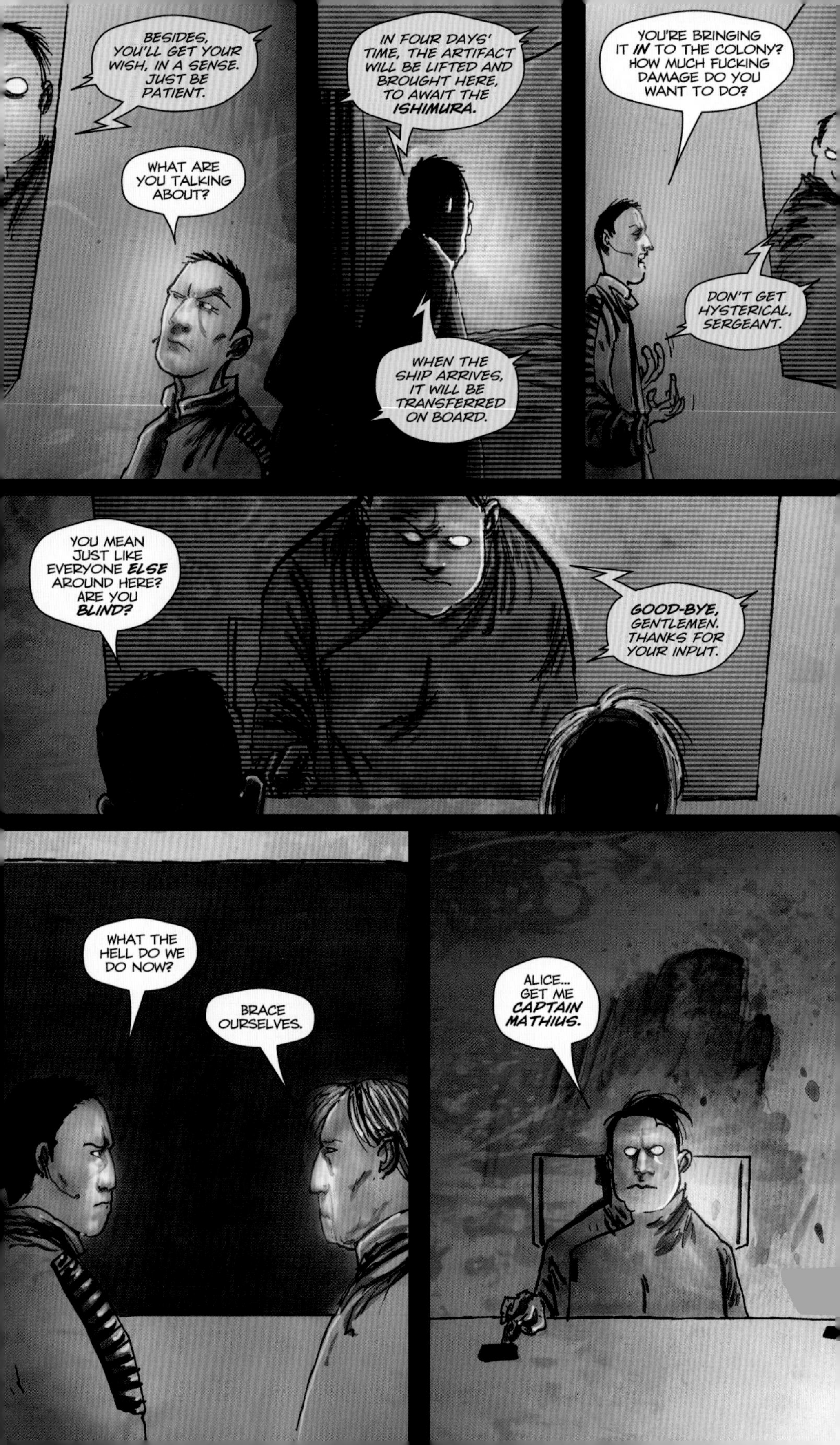
BESIDES, YOU'LL GET YOUR WISH, IN A SENSE. JUST BE PATIENT.
WHAT ARE YOU TALKING ABOUT?
IN FOUR DAYS' TIME, THE ARTIFACT WILL BE LIFTED AND BROUGHT HERE, TO AWAIT THE ISHIMURA.
WHEN THE SHIP ARRIVES, IT WILL BE TRANSFERRED ON BOARD.
YOU'RE BRINGING IT IN TO THE COLONY? HOW MUCH FUCKING DAMAGE DO YOU WANT TO DO?
DON'T GET HYSTERICAL, SERGEANT.
YOU MEAN JUST LIKE EVERYONE ELSE AROUND HERE? ARE YOU BLIND?
GOOD-BYE, GENTLEMEN. THANKS FOR YOUR INPUT.
WHAT THE HELL DO WE DO NOW?
BRACE OURSELVES.
ALICE... GET ME CAPTAIN MATHIUS.

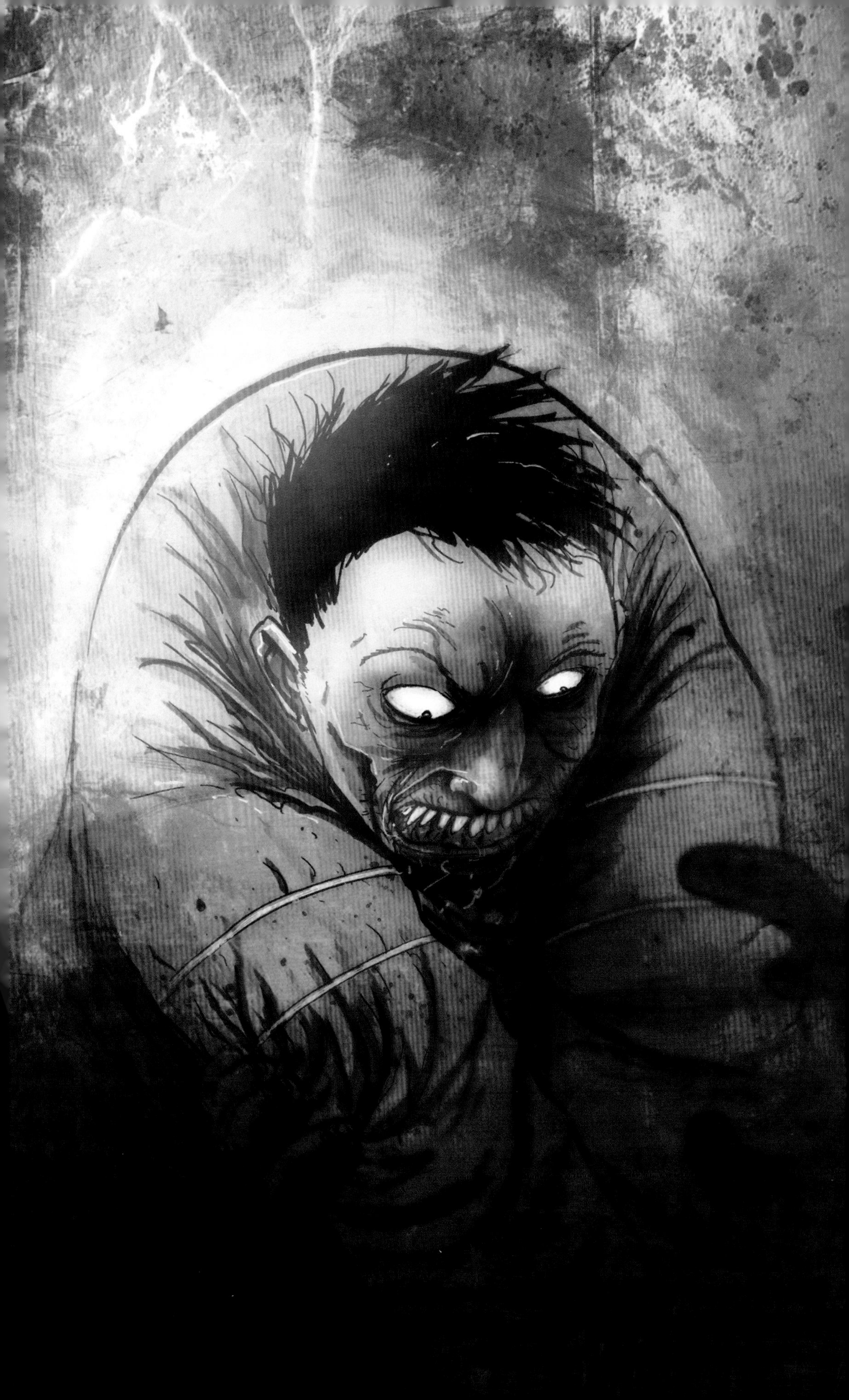

VOLUME 3

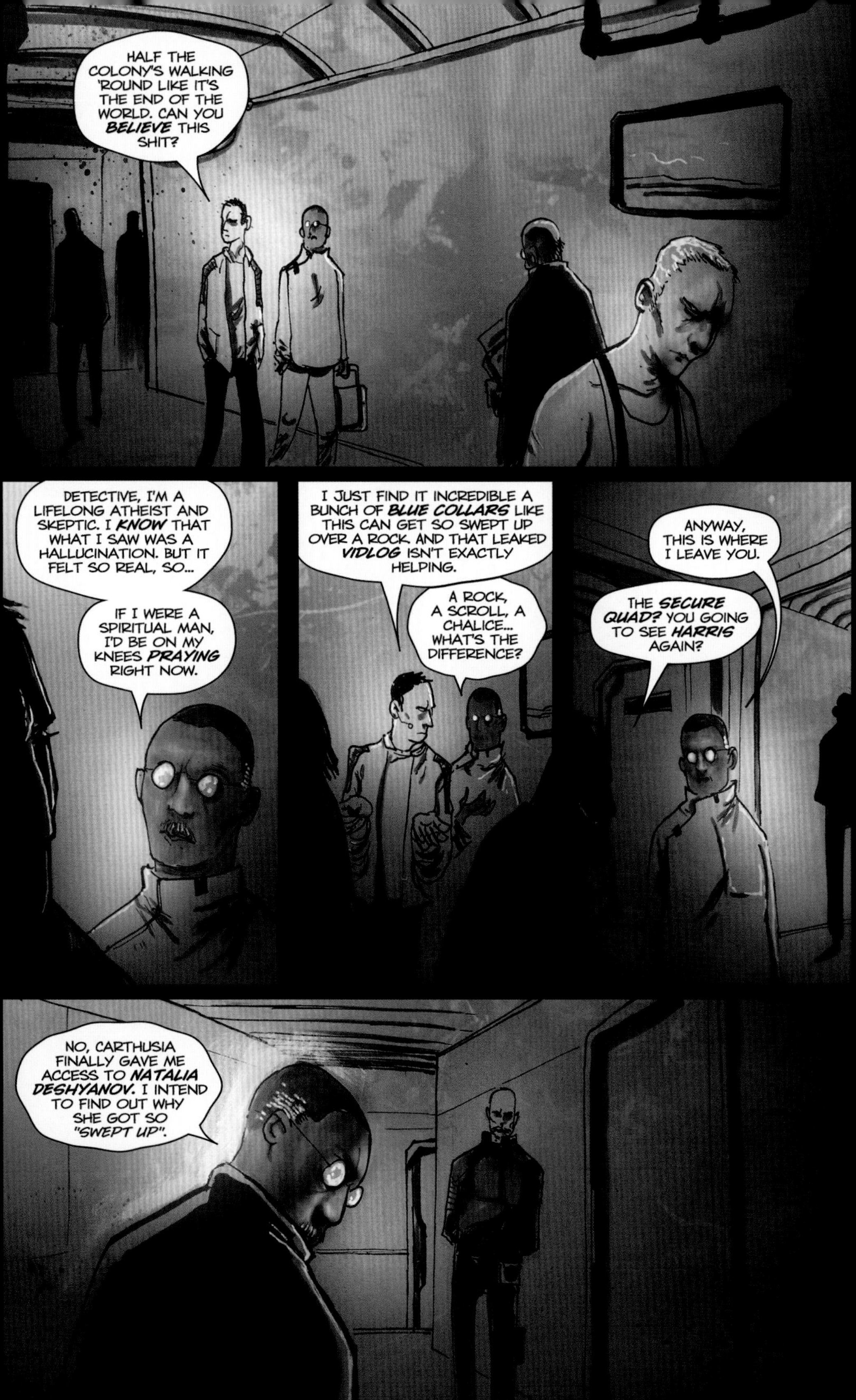
HALF THE COLONY'S WALKING 'ROUND LIKE IT'S THE END OF THE WORLD. CAN YOU *BELIEVE* THIS SHIT?
DETECTIVE, I'M A LIFELONG ATHEIST AND SKEPTIC. I *KNOW* THAT WHAT I SAW WAS A HALLUCINATION. BUT IT FELT SO REAL, SO...
IF I WERE A SPIRITUAL MAN, I'D BE ON MY KNEES *PRAYING* RIGHT NOW.
I JUST FIND IT INCREDIBLE A BUNCH OF *BLUE COLLARS* LIKE THIS CAN GET SO SWEPT UP OVER A ROCK. AND THAT LEAKED *VIDLOG* ISN'T EXACTLY HELPING.
A ROCK, A SCROLL, A CHALICE... WHAT'S THE DIFFERENCE?
ANYWAY, THIS IS WHERE I LEAVE YOU.
THE *SECURE QUAD?* YOU GOING TO SEE *HARRIS* AGAIN?
NO, CARTHUSIA FINALLY GAVE ME ACCESS TO *NATALIA DESHYANOV*. I INTEND TO FIND OUT WHY SHE GOT SO *"SWEPT UP"*.

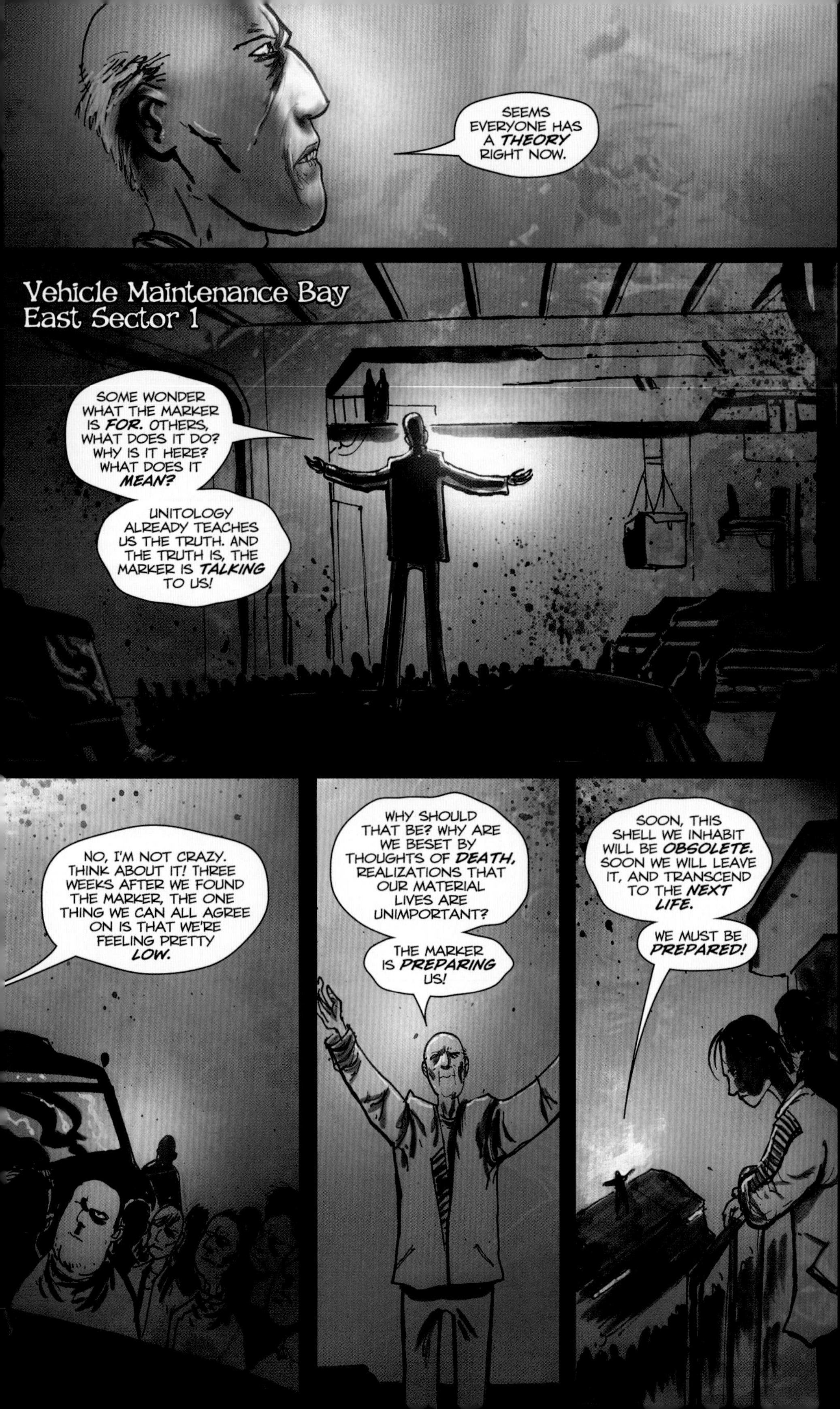
SEEMS EVERYONE HAS A THEORY RIGHT NOW.
Vehicle Maintenance Bay
East Sector 1
SOME WONDER WHAT THE MARKER IS FOR. OTHERS, WHAT DOES IT DO? WHY IS IT HERE? WHAT DOES IT MEAN?
UNITOLOGY ALREADY TEACHES US THE TRUTH. AND THE TRUTH IS, THE MARKER IS TALKING TO US!
NO, I'M NOT CRAZY. THINK ABOUT IT! THREE WEEKS AFTER WE FOUND THE MARKER, THE ONE THING WE CAN ALL AGREE ON IS THAT WE'RE FEELING PRETTY LOW.
WHY SHOULD THAT BE? WHY ARE WE BESET BY THOUGHTS OF DEATH, REALIZATIONS THAT OUR MATERIAL LIVES ARE UNIMPORTANT?
THE MARKER IS PREPARING US!
SOON, THIS SHELL WE INHABIT WILL BE OBSOLETE. SOON WE WILL LEAVE IT, AND TRANSCEND TO THE NEXT LIFE.
WE MUST BE PREPARED!

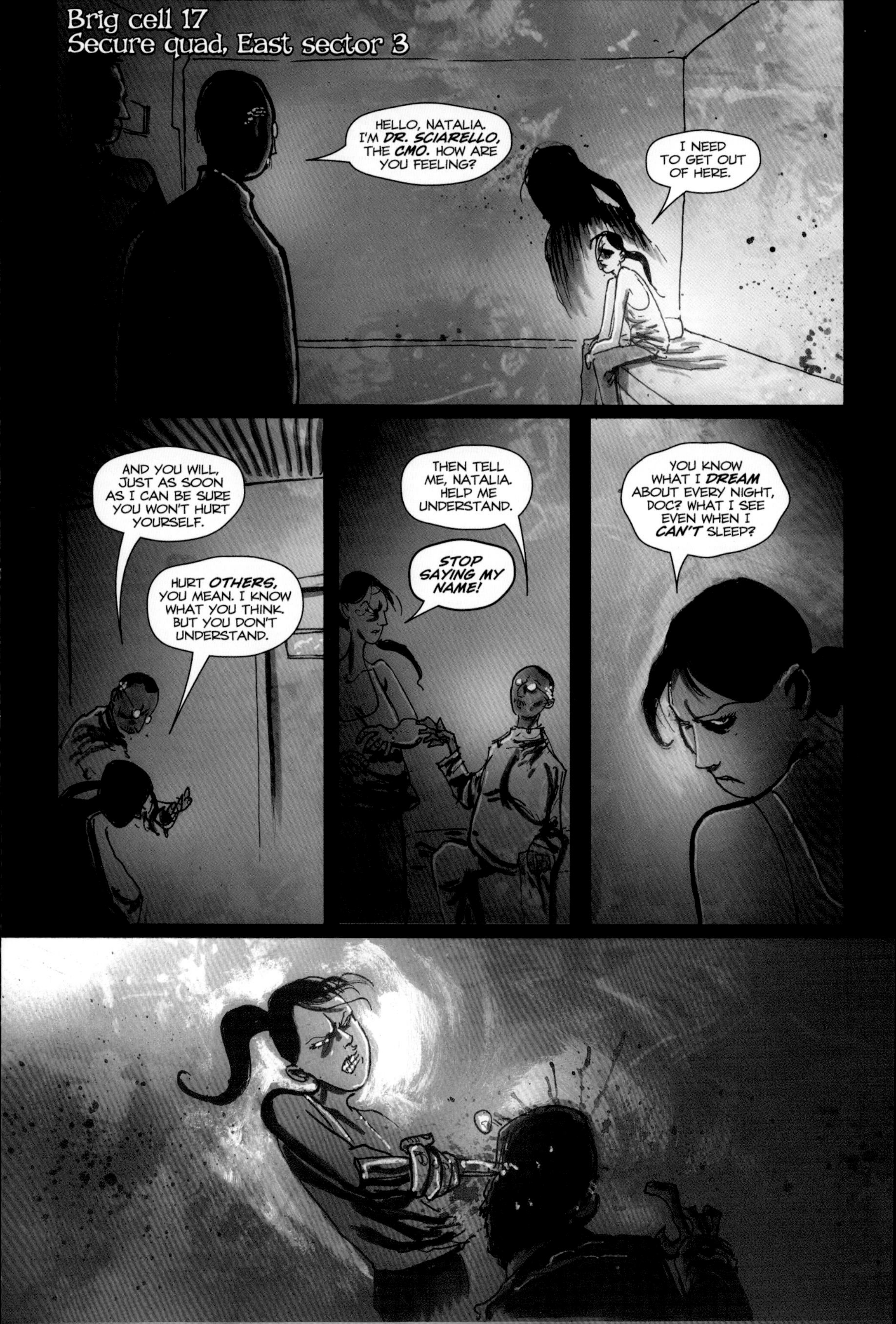
Brig cell 17
Secure quad, East sector 3
HELLO, NATALIA. I'M DR. SCIARELLO, THE CMO. HOW ARE YOU FEELING?
I NEED TO GET OUT OF HERE.
AND YOU WILL, JUST AS SOON AS I CAN BE SURE YOU WON'T HURT YOURSELF.
HURT OTHERS, YOU MEAN. I KNOW WHAT YOU THINK. BUT YOU DON'T UNDERSTAND.
THEN TELL ME, NATALIA. HELP ME UNDERSTAND.
STOP SAYING MY NAME!
YOU KNOW WHAT I DREAM ABOUT EVERY NIGHT, DOC? WHAT I SEE EVEN WHEN I CAN'T SLEEP?

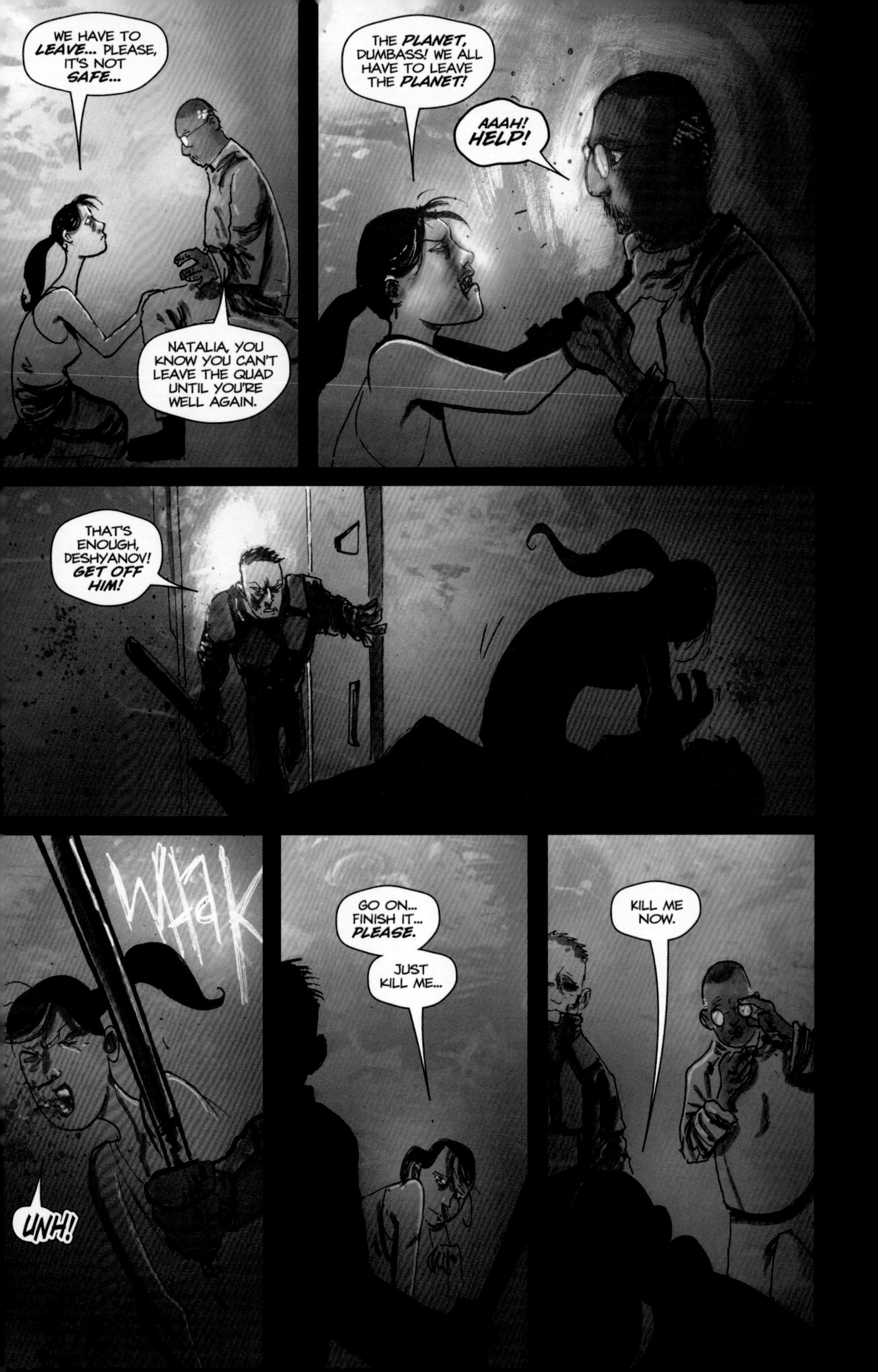
WE HAVE TO LEAVE... PLEASE, IT'S NOT SAFE...
NATALIA, YOU KNOW YOU CAN'T LEAVE THE QUAD UNTIL YOU'RE WELL AGAIN.
THE PLANET, DUMBASS! WE ALL HAVE TO LEAVE THE PLANET!
AAAH! HELP!
THAT'S ENOUGH, DESHYANOV! GET OFF HIM!
WHAK
UNH!
GO ON... FINISH IT... PLEASE.
JUST KILL ME...
KILL ME NOW.

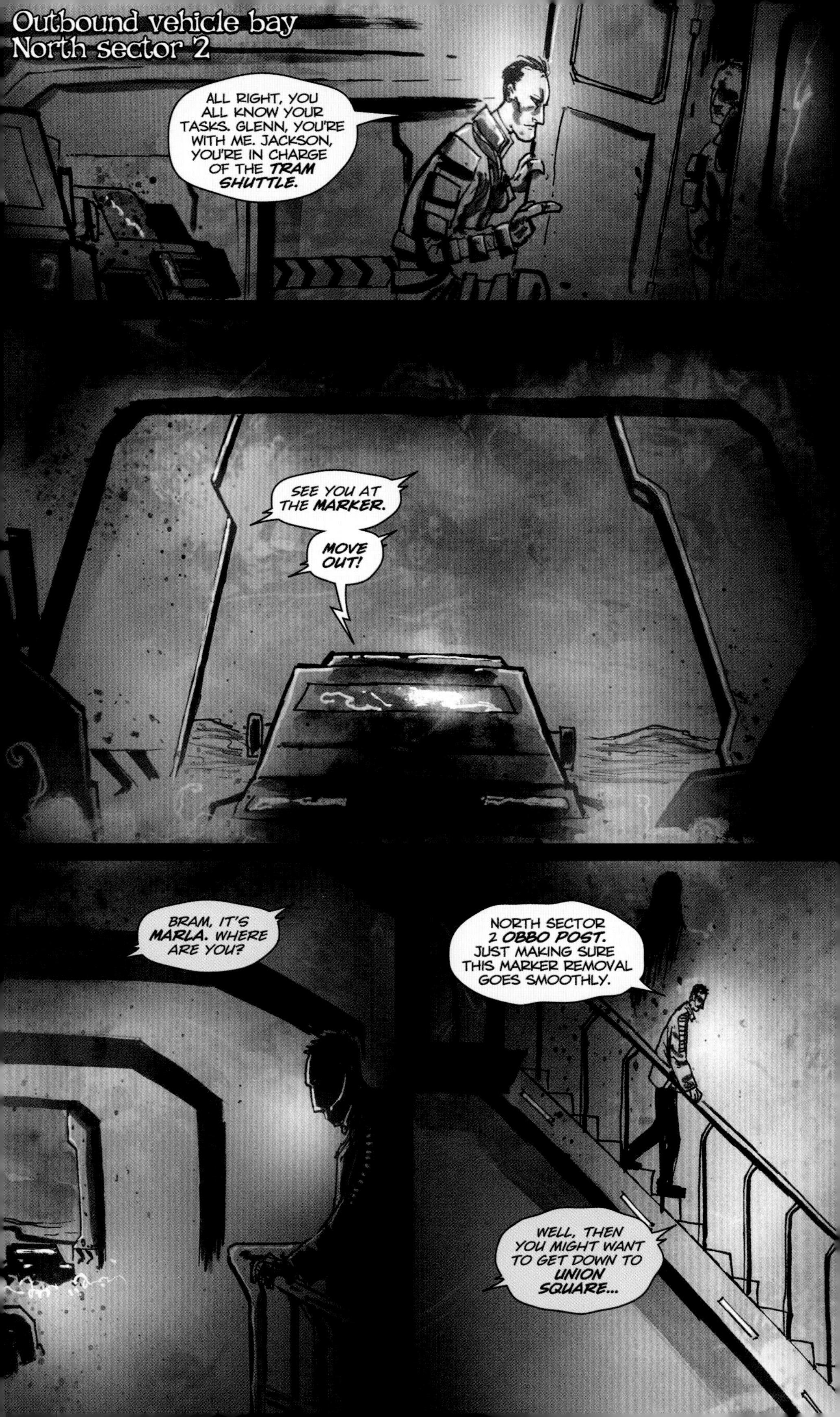
Outbound vehicle bay
North sector 2
ALL RIGHT, YOU ALL KNOW YOUR TASKS. GLENN, YOU'RE WITH ME. JACKSON, YOU'RE IN CHARGE OF THE TRAM SHUTTLE.
SEE YOU AT THE MARKER.
MOVE OUT!
BRAM, IT'S MARLA. WHERE ARE YOU?
NORTH SECTOR 2 OBBO POST. JUST MAKING SURE THIS MARKER REMOVAL GOES SMOOTHLY.
WELL, THEN YOU MIGHT WANT TO GET DOWN TO UNION SQUARE...

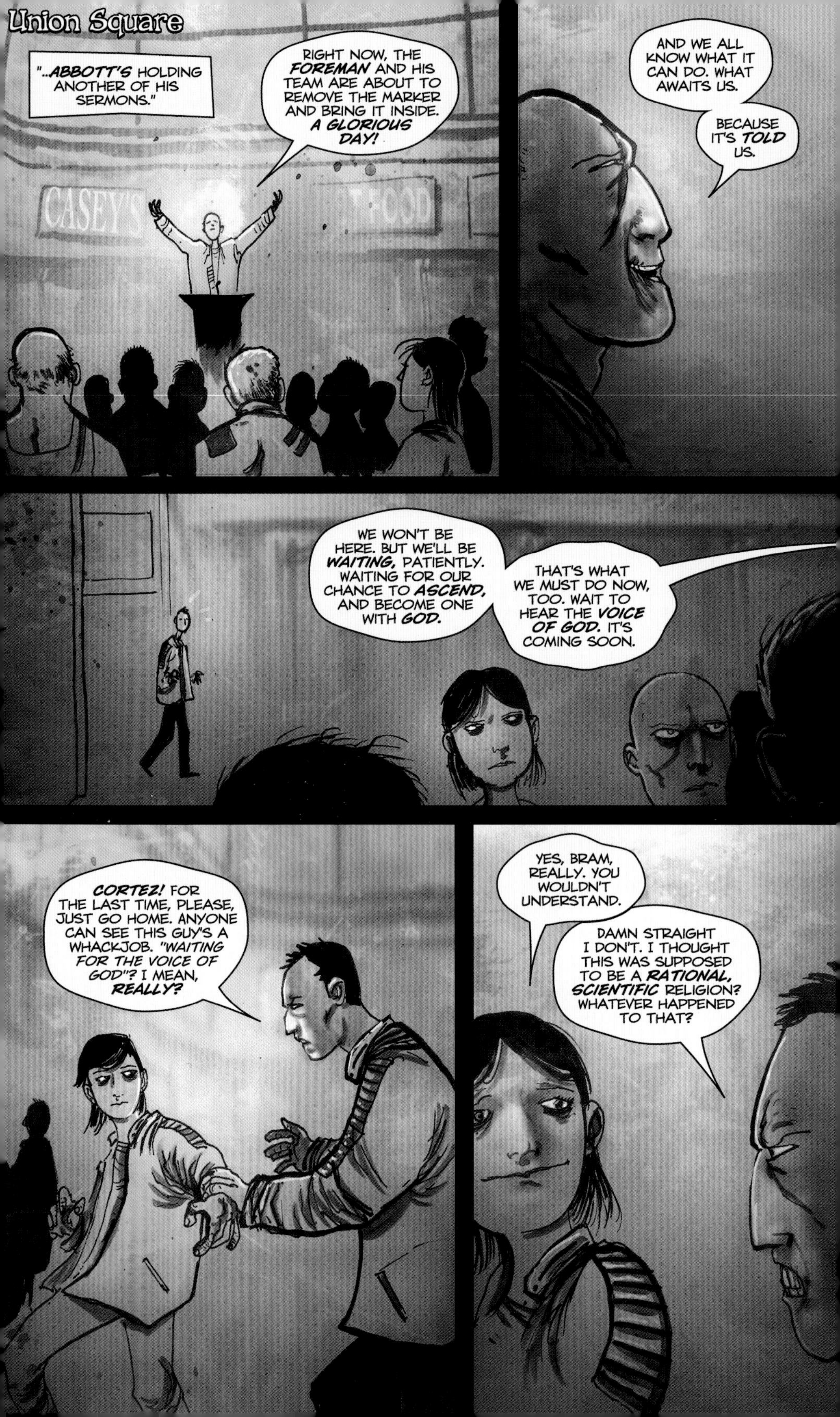
Union Square
"...ABBOTT'S HOLDING ANOTHER OF HIS SERMONS."
RIGHT NOW, THE FOREMAN AND HIS TEAM ARE ABOUT TO REMOVE THE MARKER AND BRING IT INSIDE. A GLORIOUS DAY!
CASEY'S
AND WE ALL KNOW WHAT IT CAN DO. WHAT AWAITS US.
BECAUSE IT'S TOLD US.
WE WON'T BE HERE. BUT WE'LL BE WAITING, PATIENTLY. WAITING FOR OUR CHANCE TO ASCEND, AND BECOME ONE WITH GOD.
THAT'S WHAT WE MUST DO NOW, TOO. WAIT TO HEAR THE VOICE OF GOD. IT'S COMING SOON.
CORTEZ! FOR THE LAST TIME, PLEASE, JUST GO HOME. ANYONE CAN SEE THIS GUY'S A WHACKJOB. "WAITING FOR THE VOICE OF GOD"? I MEAN, REALLY?
YES, BRAM, REALLY. YOU WOULDN'T UNDERSTAND.
DAMN STRAIGHT I DON'T. I THOUGHT THIS WAS SUPPOSED TO BE A RATIONAL, SCIENTIFIC RELIGION? WHATEVER HAPPENED TO THAT?

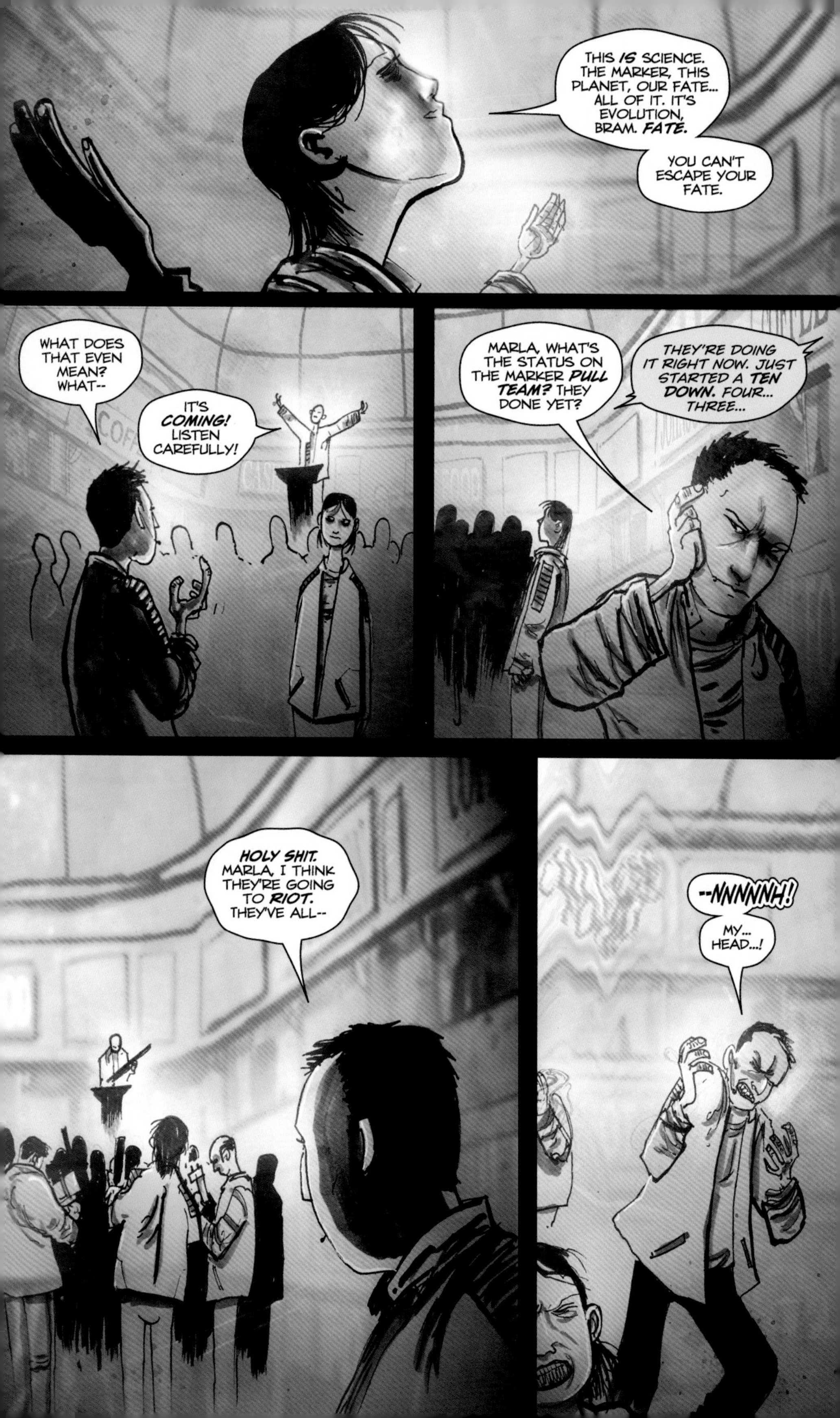
THIS *IS* SCIENCE. THE MARKER, THIS PLANET, OUR FATE... ALL OF IT. IT'S EVOLUTION, BRAM. ***FATE.***
YOU CAN'T ESCAPE YOUR FATE.
WHAT DOES THAT EVEN MEAN? WHAT--
IT'S ***COMING!*** LISTEN CAREFULLY!
MARLA, WHAT'S THE STATUS ON THE MARKER ***PULL TEAM?*** THEY DONE YET?
THEY'RE DOING IT RIGHT NOW. JUST STARTED A ***TEN DOWN.*** *FOUR... THREE...*
HOLY SHIT. MARLA, I THINK THEY'RE GOING TO ***RIOT.*** THEY'VE ALL--
--NNNNNH!
MY... HEAD...!

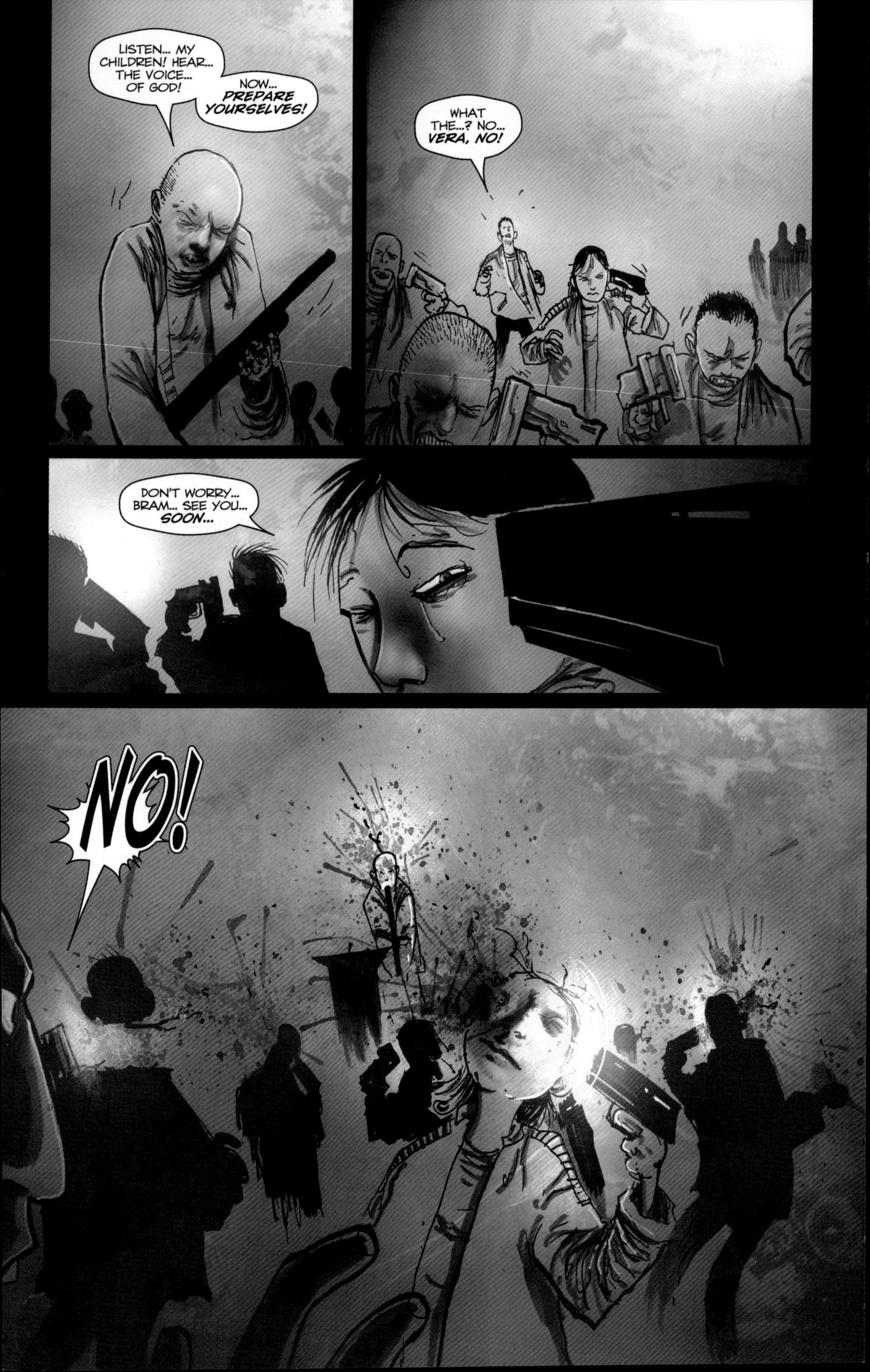
LISTEN... MY CHILDREN! HEAR... THE VOICE... OF GOD!
NOW... PREPARE YOURSELVES!
WHAT THE...? NO... VERA, NO!
DON'T WORRY... BRAM... SEE YOU... SOON...
NO!

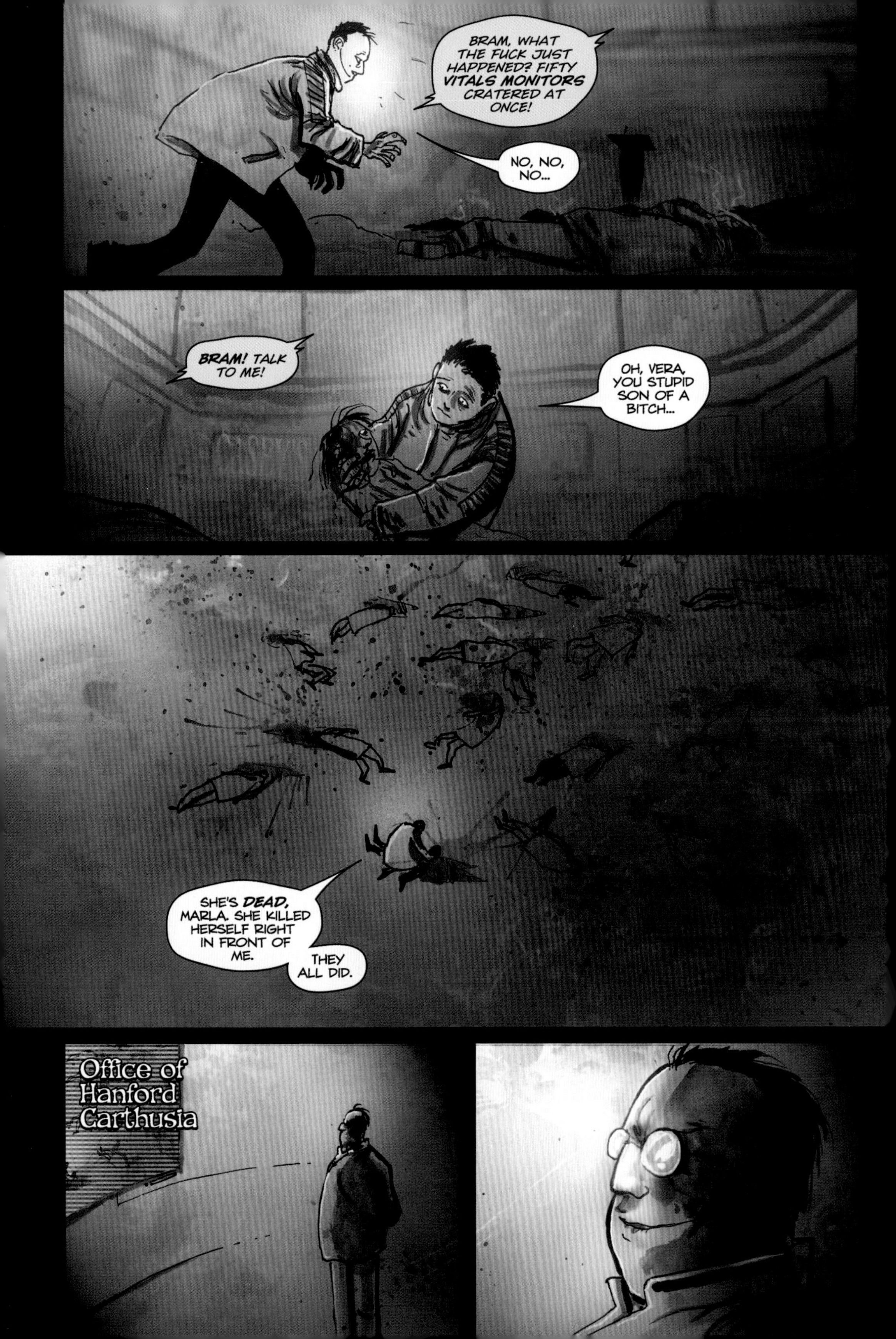
BRAM, WHAT THE FUCK JUST HAPPENED? FIFTY VITALS MONITORS CRATERED AT ONCE!
NO, NO, NO...
BRAM! TALK TO ME!
OH, VERA, YOU STUPID SON OF A BITCH...
SHE'S DEAD, MARLA. SHE KILLED HERSELF RIGHT IN FRONT OF ME.
THEY ALL DID.
Office of Hanford Carthusia

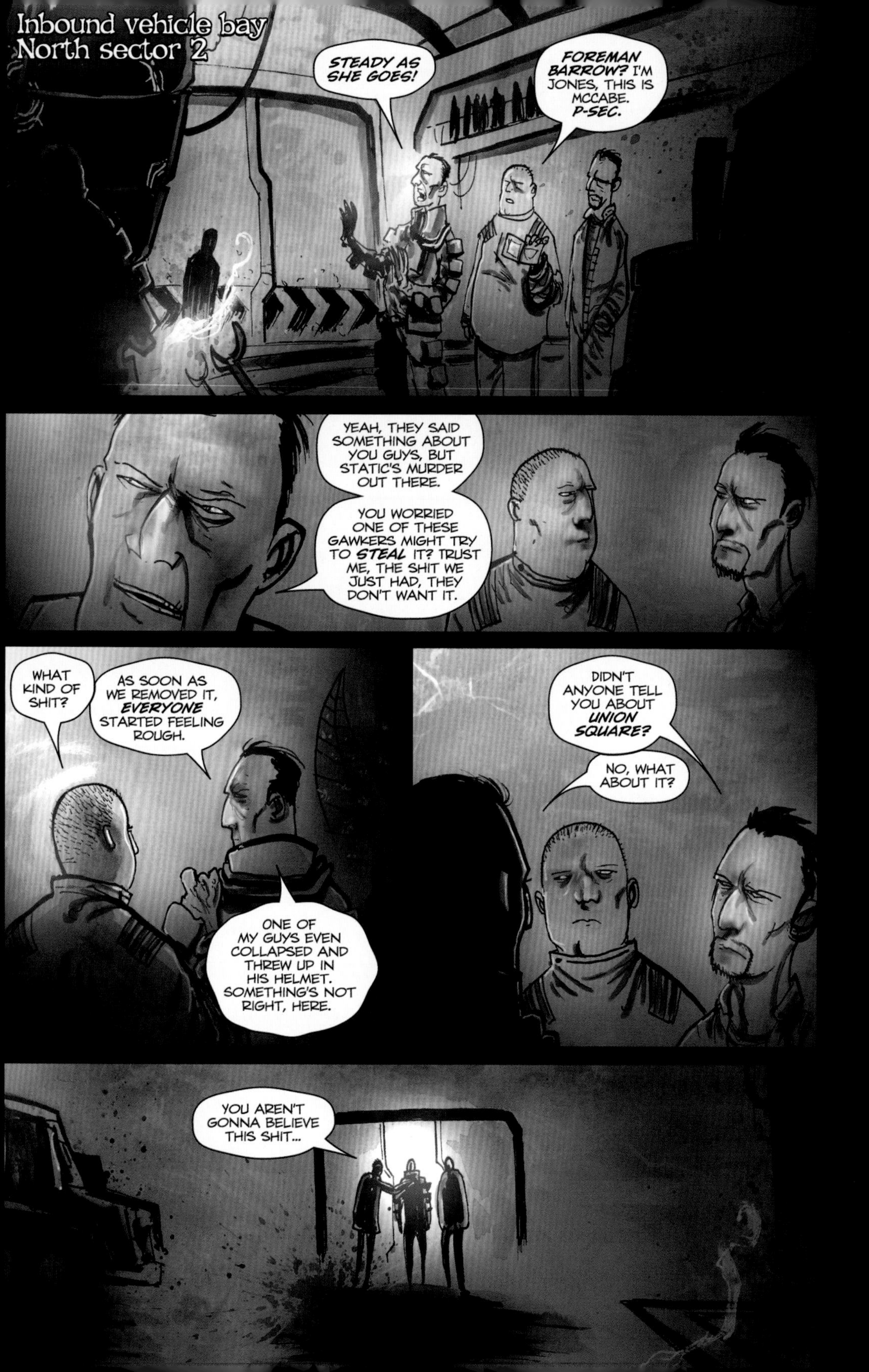
Inbound vehicle bay
North sector 2
STEADY AS SHE GOES!
FOREMAN BARROW? I'M JONES, THIS IS MCCABE. P-SEC.
YEAH, THEY SAID SOMETHING ABOUT YOU GUYS, BUT STATIC'S MURDER OUT THERE.
YOU WORRIED ONE OF THESE GAWKERS MIGHT TRY TO STEAL IT? TRUST ME, THE SHIT WE JUST HAD, THEY DON'T WANT IT.
WHAT KIND OF SHIT?
AS SOON AS WE REMOVED IT, EVERYONE STARTED FEELING ROUGH.
ONE OF MY GUYS EVEN COLLAPSED AND THREW UP IN HIS HELMET. SOMETHING'S NOT RIGHT, HERE.
DIDN'T ANYONE TELL YOU ABOUT UNION SQUARE?
NO, WHAT ABOUT IT?
YOU AREN'T GONNA BELIEVE THIS SHIT...

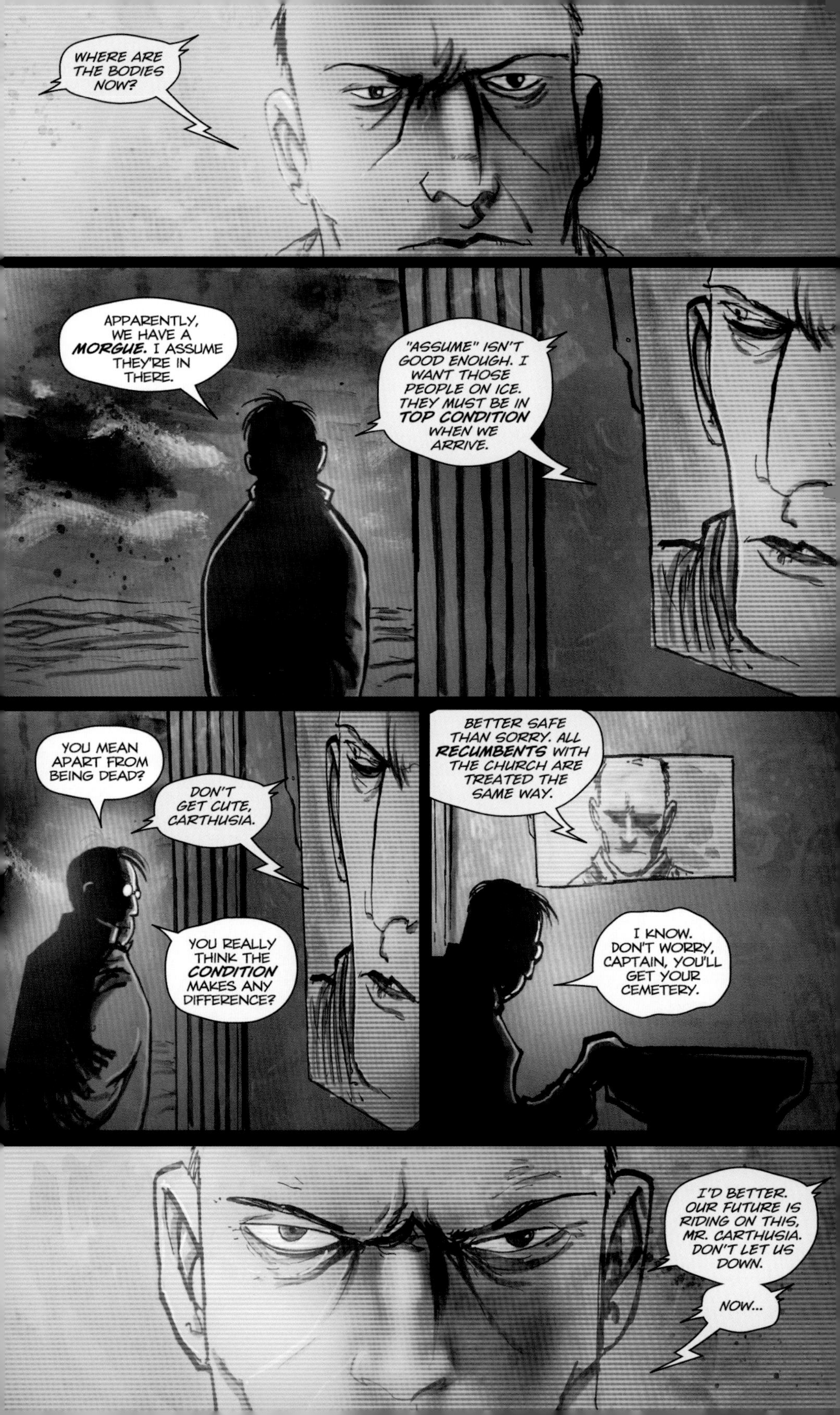

WHERE ARE THE BODIES NOW?
APPARENTLY, WE HAVE A MORGUE. I ASSUME THEY'RE IN THERE.
"ASSUME" ISN'T GOOD ENOUGH. I WANT THOSE PEOPLE ON ICE. THEY MUST BE IN TOP CONDITION WHEN WE ARRIVE.
YOU MEAN APART FROM BEING DEAD?
DON'T GET CUTE, CARTHUSIA.
YOU REALLY THINK THE CONDITION MAKES ANY DIFFERENCE?
BETTER SAFE THAN SORRY. ALL RECUMBENTS WITH THE CHURCH ARE TREATED THE SAME WAY.
I KNOW. DON'T WORRY, CAPTAIN, YOU'LL GET YOUR CEMETERY.
I'D BETTER. OUR FUTURE IS RIDING ON THIS, MR. CARTHUSIA. DON'T LET US DOWN.
NOW...

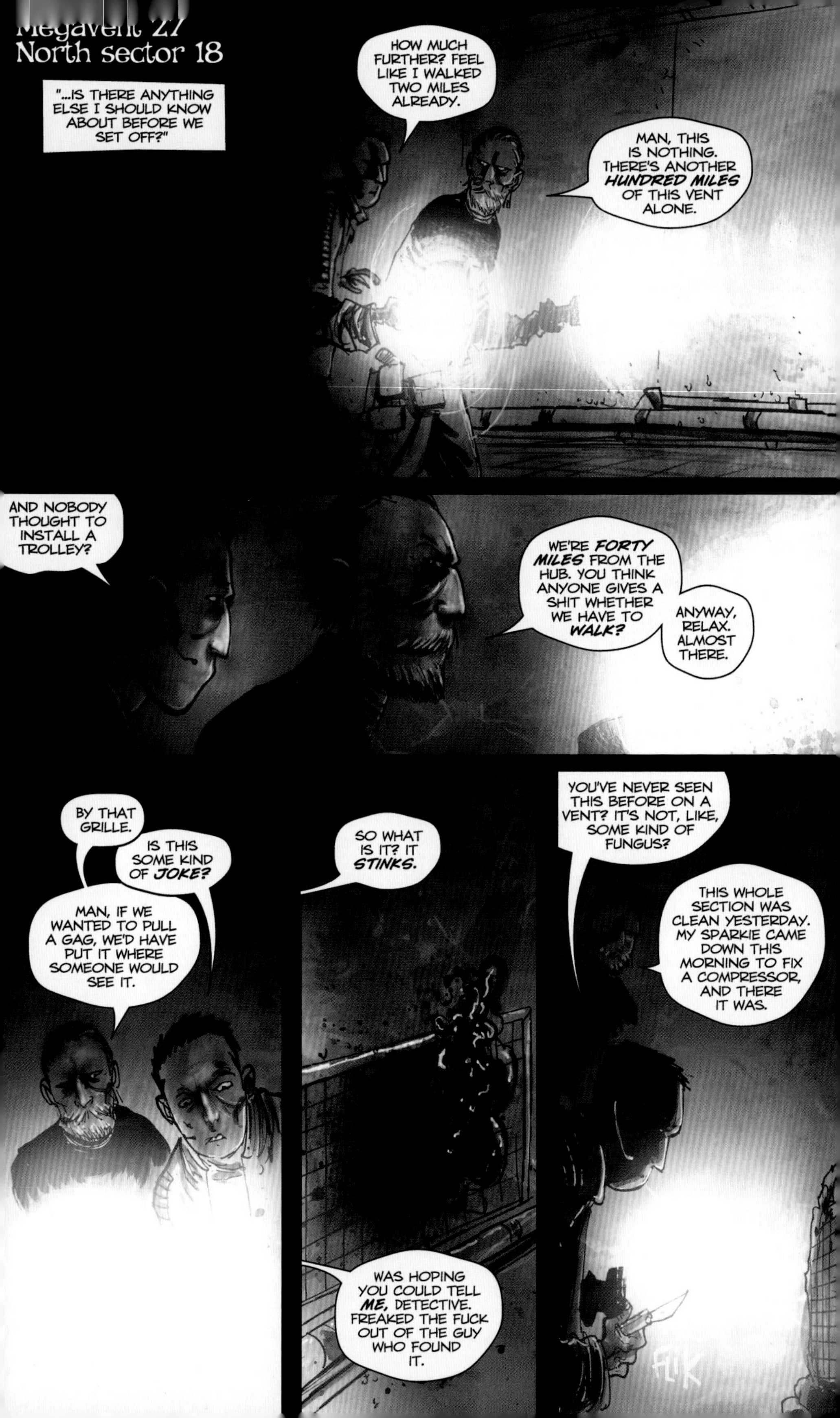
Megavent 27
North sector 18
"...IS THERE ANYTHING ELSE I SHOULD KNOW ABOUT BEFORE WE SET OFF?"
HOW MUCH FURTHER? FEEL LIKE I WALKED TWO MILES ALREADY.
MAN, THIS IS NOTHING. THERE'S ANOTHER HUNDRED MILES OF THIS VENT ALONE.
AND NOBODY THOUGHT TO INSTALL A TROLLEY?
WE'RE FORTY MILES FROM THE HUB. YOU THINK ANYONE GIVES A SHIT WHETHER WE HAVE TO WALK?
ANYWAY, RELAX. ALMOST THERE.
BY THAT GRILLE.
IS THIS SOME KIND OF JOKE?
MAN, IF WE WANTED TO PULL A GAG, WE'D HAVE PUT IT WHERE SOMEONE WOULD SEE IT.
SO WHAT IS IT? IT STINKS.
WAS HOPING YOU COULD TELL ME, DETECTIVE. FREAKED THE FUCK OUT OF THE GUY WHO FOUND IT.
YOU'VE NEVER SEEN THIS BEFORE ON A VENT? IT'S NOT, LIKE, SOME KIND OF FUNGUS?
THIS WHOLE SECTION WAS CLEAN YESTERDAY. MY SPARKIE CAME DOWN THIS MORNING TO FIX A COMPRESSOR, AND THERE IT WAS.
FLIK

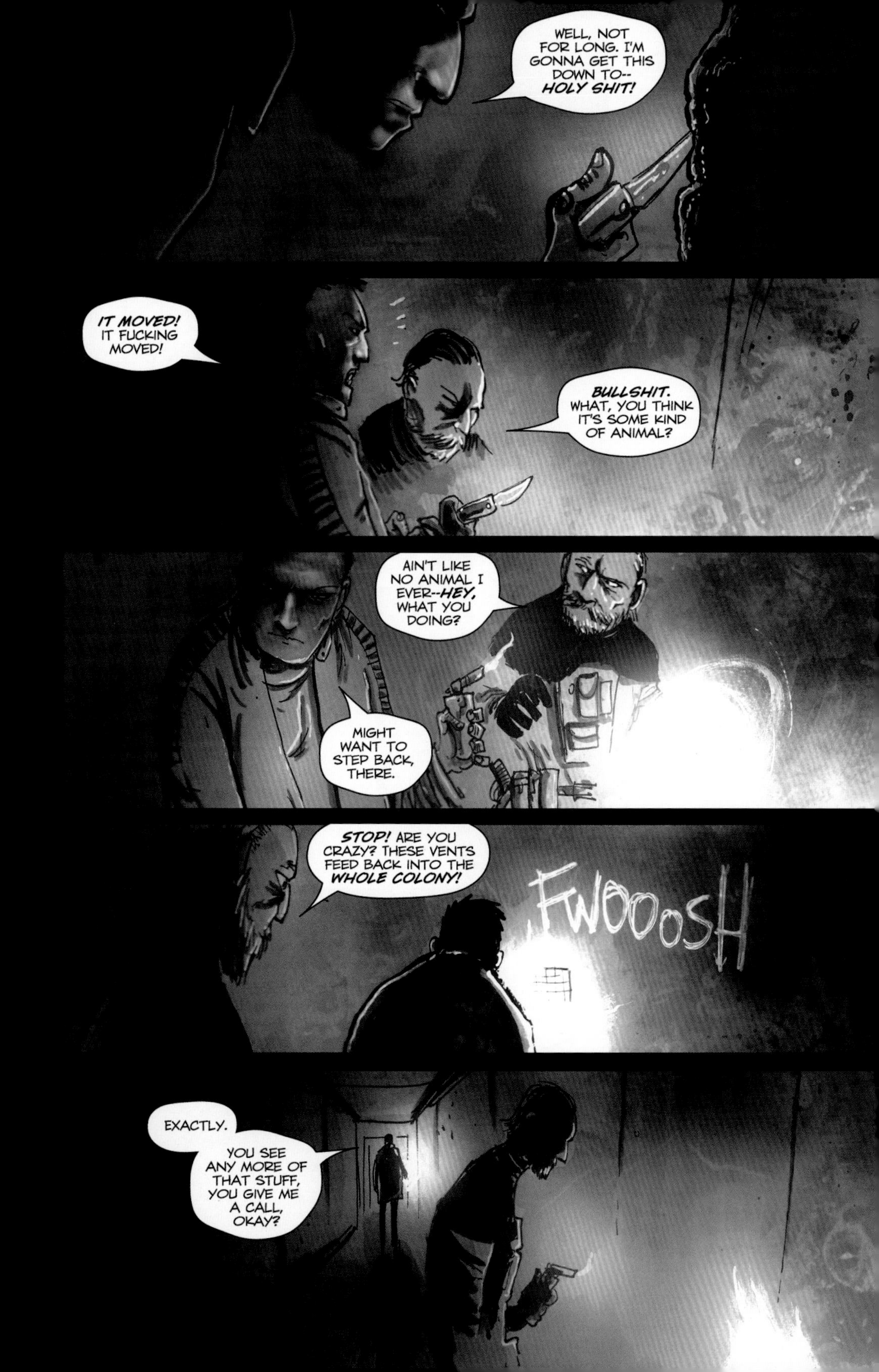
WELL, NOT FOR LONG. I'M GONNA GET THIS DOWN TO-- HOLY SHIT!
IT MOVED! IT FUCKING MOVED!
BULLSHIT. WHAT, YOU THINK IT'S SOME KIND OF ANIMAL?
AIN'T LIKE NO ANIMAL I EVER--HEY, WHAT YOU DOING?
MIGHT WANT TO STEP BACK, THERE.
STOP! ARE YOU CRAZY? THESE VENTS FEED BACK INTO THE WHOLE COLONY!
FWOOOOSH
EXACTLY.
YOU SEE ANY MORE OF THAT STUFF, YOU GIVE ME A CALL, OKAY?

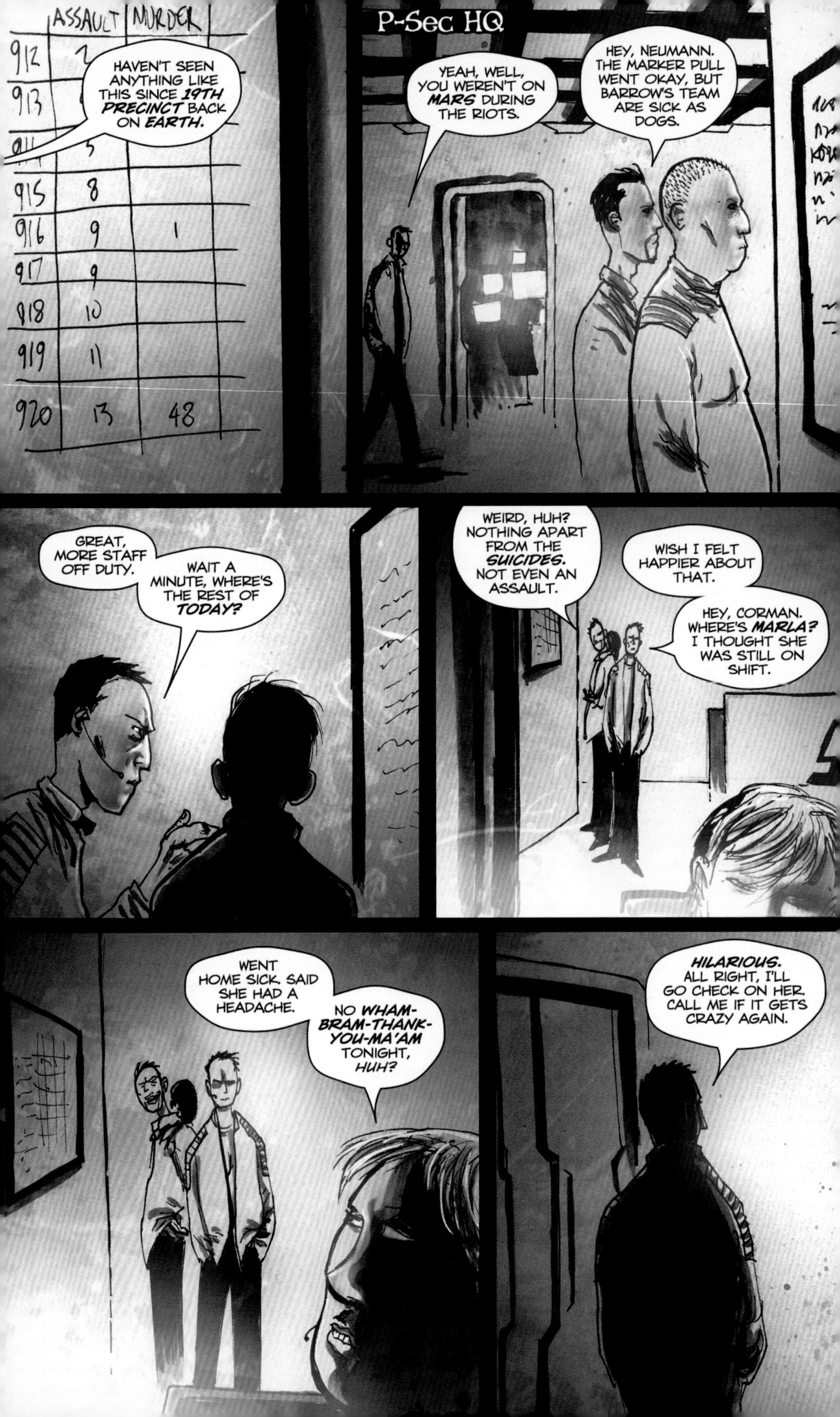
P-Sec HQ
ASSAULT MURDER
912 2
913
915 8
916 9 1
917 9
918 10
919 11
920 13 48
HAVEN'T SEEN ANYTHING LIKE THIS SINCE 19TH PRECINCT BACK ON EARTH.
YEAH, WELL, YOU WEREN'T ON MARS DURING THE RIOTS.
HEY, NEUMANN. THE MARKER PULL WENT OKAY, BUT BARROW'S TEAM ARE SICK AS DOGS.
GREAT, MORE STAFF OFF DUTY.
WAIT A MINUTE, WHERE'S THE REST OF TODAY?
WEIRD, HUH? NOTHING APART FROM THE SUICIDES. NOT EVEN AN ASSAULT.
WISH I FELT HAPPIER ABOUT THAT.
HEY, CORMAN. WHERE'S MARLA? I THOUGHT SHE WAS STILL ON SHIFT.
WENT HOME SICK. SAID SHE HAD A HEADACHE.
NO WHAM-BRAM-THANK-YOU-MA'AM TONIGHT, HUH?
HILARIOUS. ALL RIGHT, I'LL GO CHECK ON HER. CALL ME IF IT GETS CRAZY AGAIN.

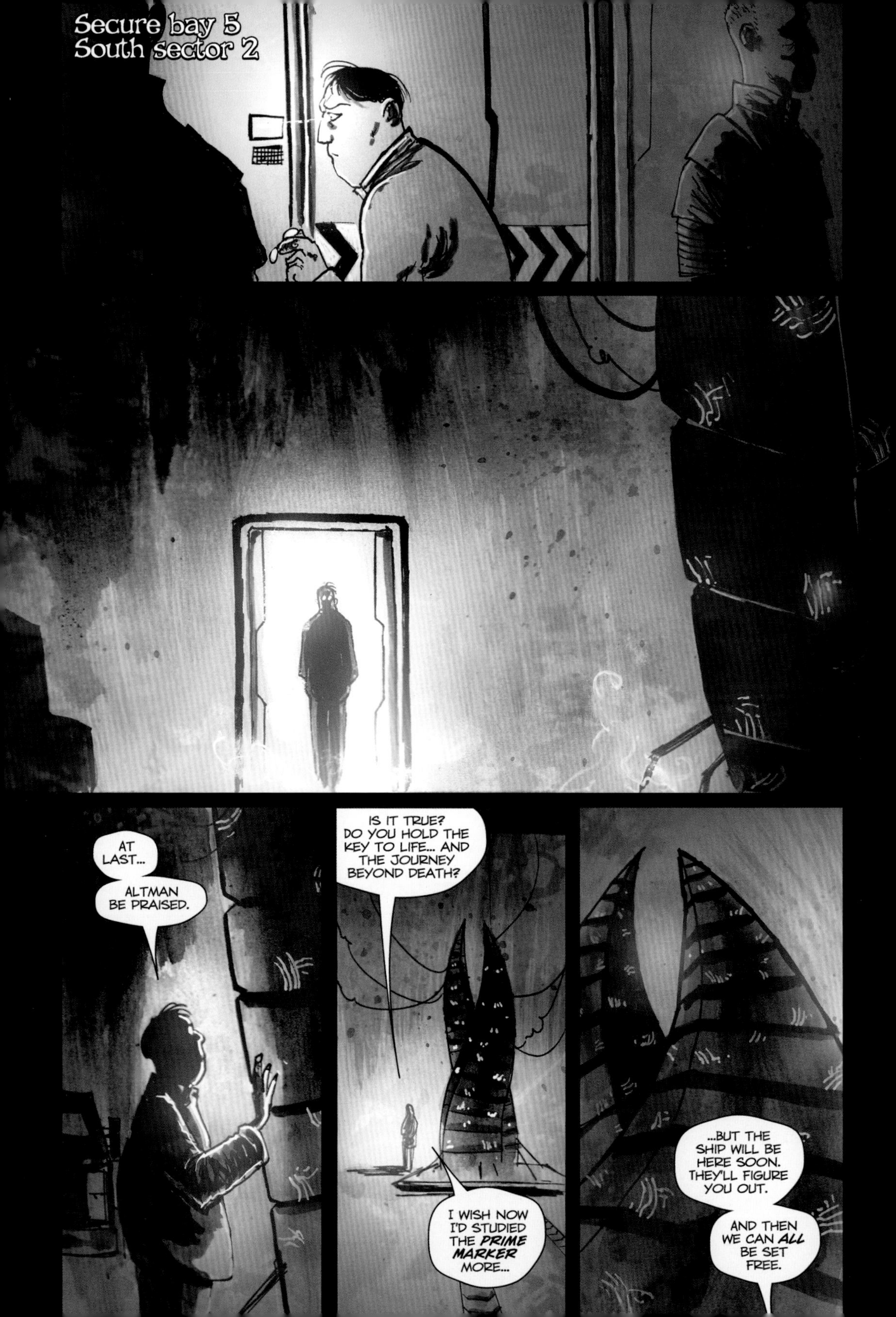
Secure bay 5
South sector 2
AT LAST...
ALTMAN BE PRAISED.
IS IT TRUE? DO YOU HOLD THE KEY TO LIFE... AND THE JOURNEY BEYOND DEATH?
I WISH NOW I'D STUDIED THE *PRIME MARKER* MORE...
...BUT THE SHIP WILL BE HERE SOON. THEY'LL FIGURE YOU OUT.
AND THEN WE CAN *ALL* BE SET FREE.

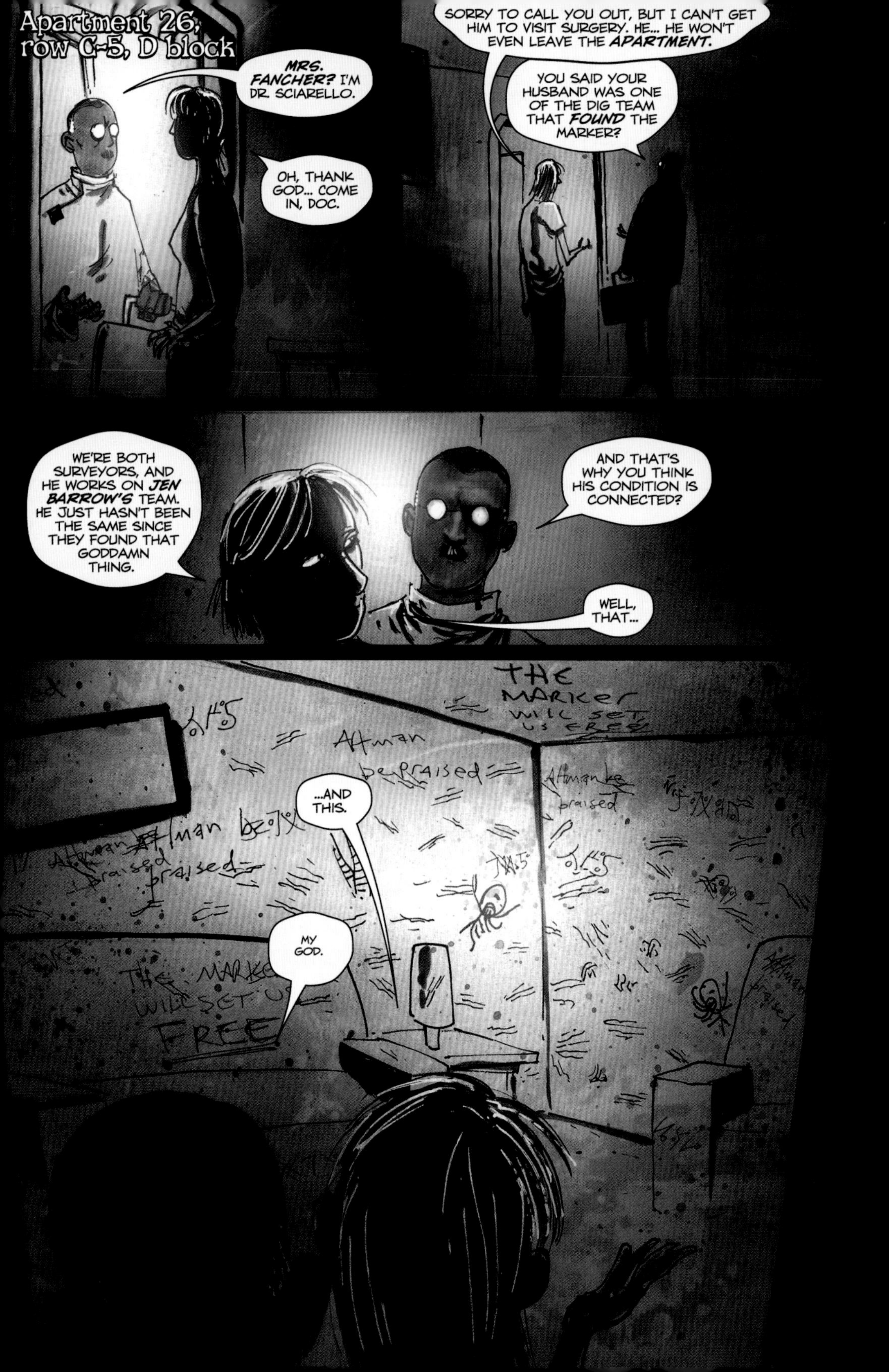

Apartment 26, row C-5, D block
MRS. FANCHER? I'M DR. SCIARELLO.
OH, THANK GOD... COME IN, DOC.
SORRY TO CALL YOU OUT, BUT I CAN'T GET HIM TO VISIT SURGERY. HE... HE WON'T EVEN LEAVE THE APARTMENT.
YOU SAID YOUR HUSBAND WAS ONE OF THE DIG TEAM THAT FOUND THE MARKER?
WE'RE BOTH SURVEYORS, AND HE WORKS ON JEN BARROW'S TEAM. HE JUST HASN'T BEEN THE SAME SINCE THEY FOUND THAT GODDAMN THING.
AND THAT'S WHY YOU THINK HIS CONDITION IS CONNECTED?
WELL, THAT...
THE MARKER WILL SET US FREE
Altman be praised
...AND THIS.
MY GOD.

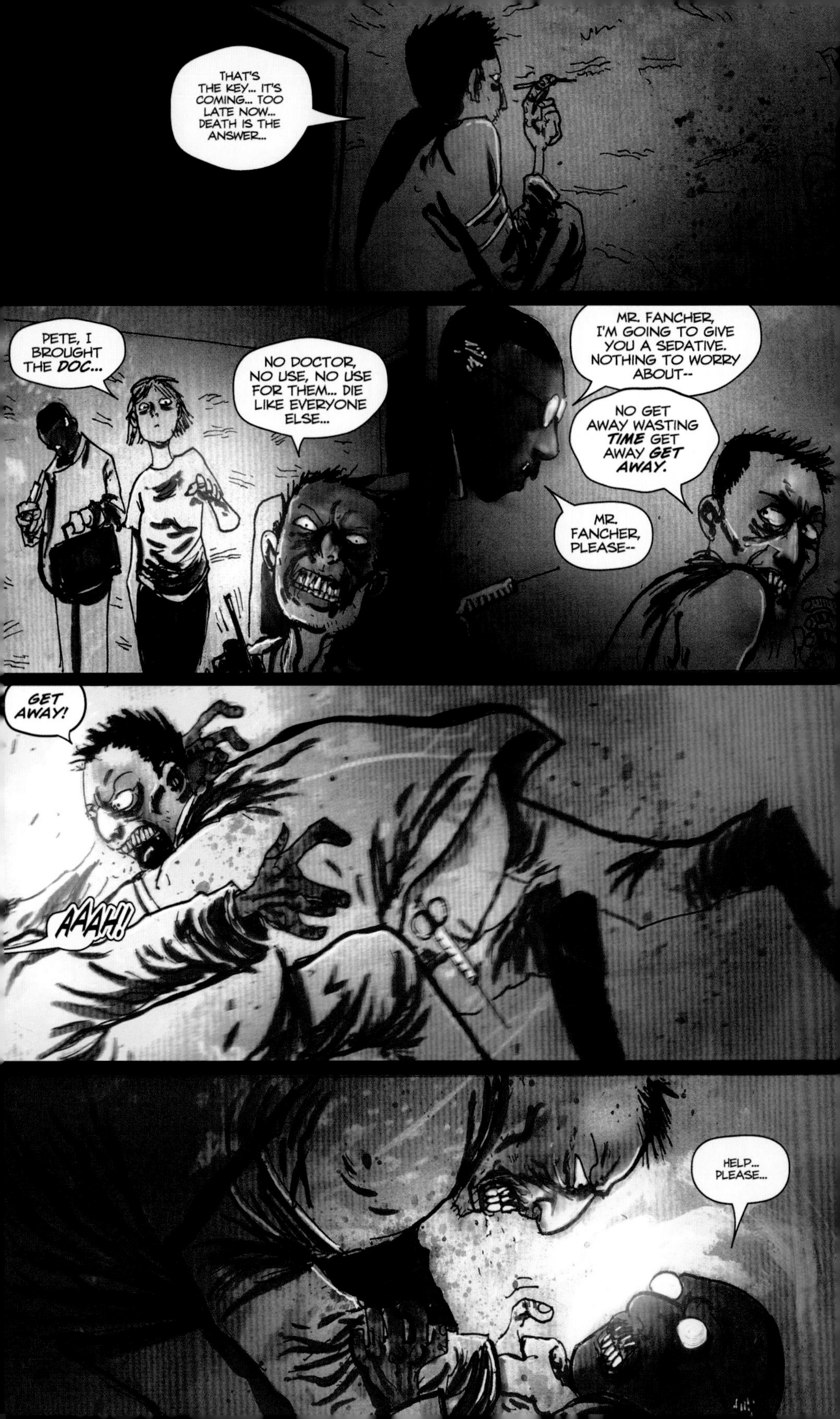
THAT'S THE KEY... IT'S COMING... TOO LATE NOW... DEATH IS THE ANSWER...
PETE, I BROUGHT THE *DOC*...
NO DOCTOR, NO USE, NO USE FOR THEM... DIE LIKE EVERYONE ELSE...
MR. FANCHER, I'M GOING TO GIVE YOU A SEDATIVE. NOTHING TO WORRY ABOUT--
NO GET AWAY WASTING *TIME* GET AWAY *GET AWAY.*
MR. FANCHER, PLEASE--
GET AWAY!
AAAH!
HELP... PLEASE...

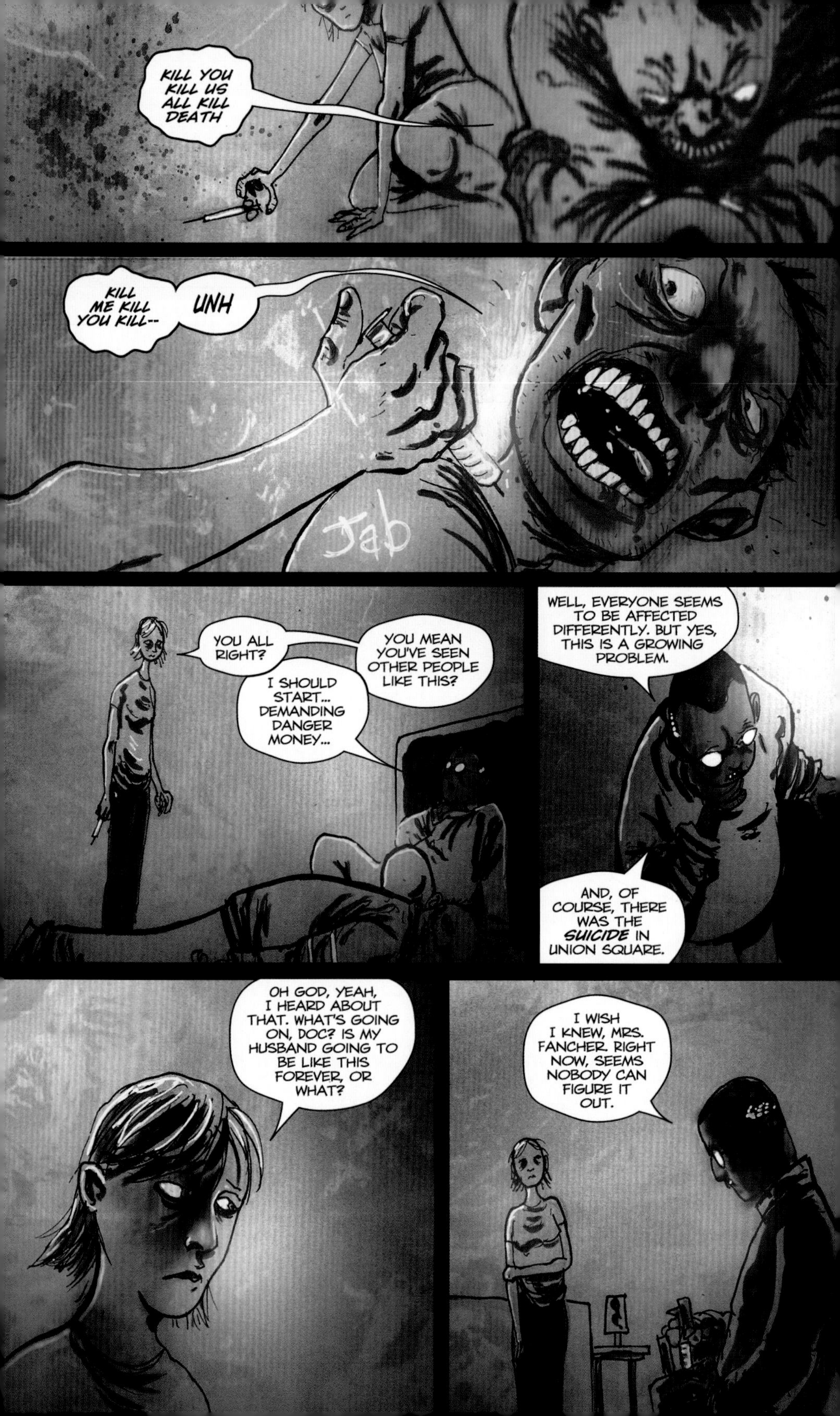
KILL YOU KILL US ALL KILL DEATH
KILL ME KILL YOU KILL--
UNH
JAB
YOU ALL RIGHT?
I SHOULD START... DEMANDING DANGER MONEY...
YOU MEAN YOU'VE SEEN OTHER PEOPLE LIKE THIS?
WELL, EVERYONE SEEMS TO BE AFFECTED DIFFERENTLY. BUT YES, THIS IS A GROWING PROBLEM.
AND, OF COURSE, THERE WAS THE SUICIDE IN UNION SQUARE.
OH GOD, YEAH, I HEARD ABOUT THAT. WHAT'S GOING ON, DOC? IS MY HUSBAND GOING TO BE LIKE THIS FOREVER, OR WHAT?
I WISH I KNEW, MRS. FANCHER. RIGHT NOW, SEEMS NOBODY CAN FIGURE IT OUT.

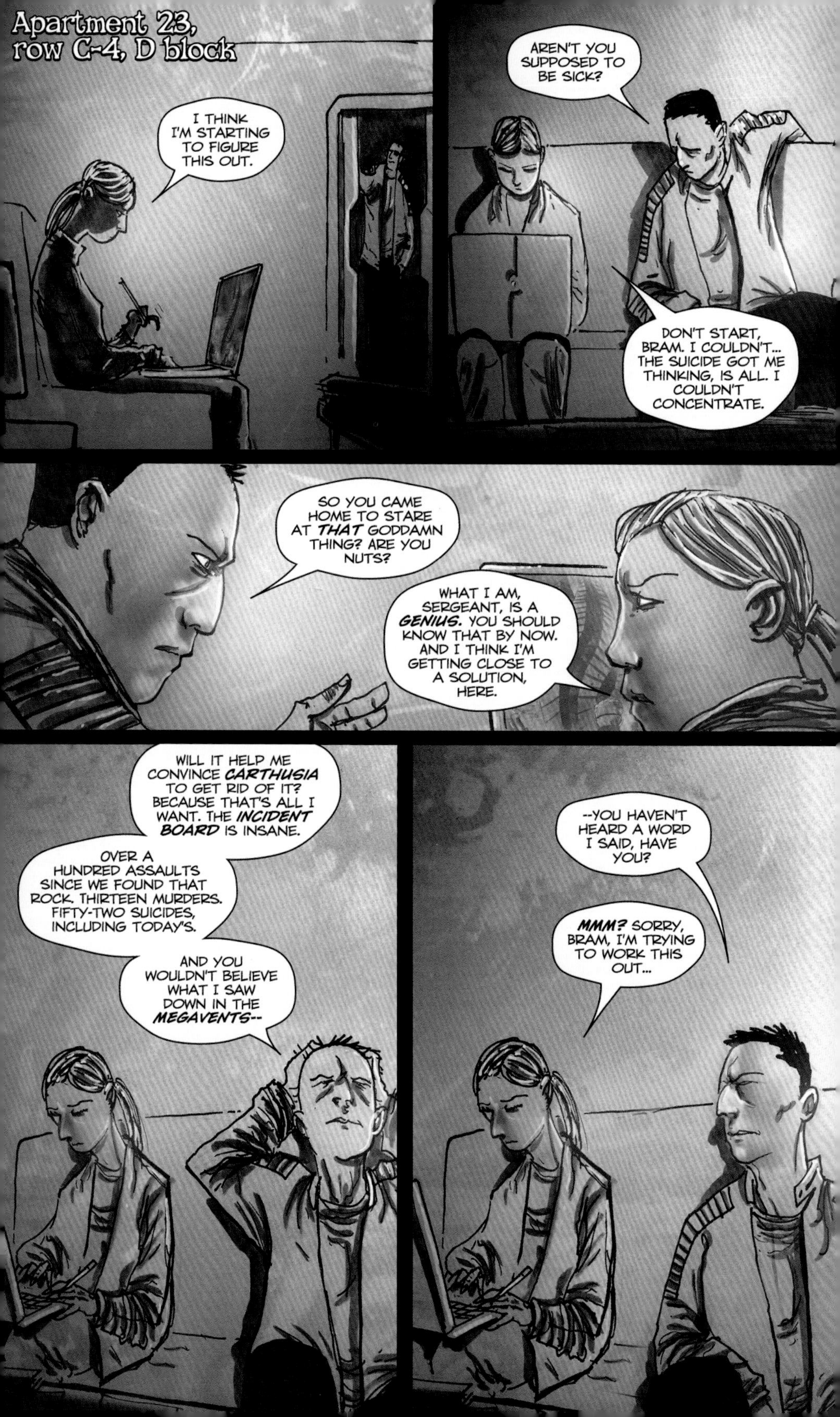
Apartment 23, row C-4, D block
I THINK I'M STARTING TO FIGURE THIS OUT.
AREN'T YOU SUPPOSED TO BE SICK?
DON'T START, BRAM. I COULDN'T... THE SUICIDE GOT ME THINKING, IS ALL. I COULDN'T CONCENTRATE.
SO YOU CAME HOME TO STARE AT THAT GODDAMN THING? ARE YOU NUTS?
WHAT I AM, SERGEANT, IS A GENIUS. YOU SHOULD KNOW THAT BY NOW. AND I THINK I'M GETTING CLOSE TO A SOLUTION, HERE.
WILL IT HELP ME CONVINCE CARTHUSIA TO GET RID OF IT? BECAUSE THAT'S ALL I WANT. THE INCIDENT BOARD IS INSANE.
OVER A HUNDRED ASSAULTS SINCE WE FOUND THAT ROCK. THIRTEEN MURDERS. FIFTY-TWO SUICIDES, INCLUDING TODAY'S.
AND YOU WOULDN'T BELIEVE WHAT I SAW DOWN IN THE MEGAVENTS--
--YOU HAVEN'T HEARD A WORD I SAID, HAVE YOU?
MMM? SORRY, BRAM, I'M TRYING TO WORK THIS OUT...

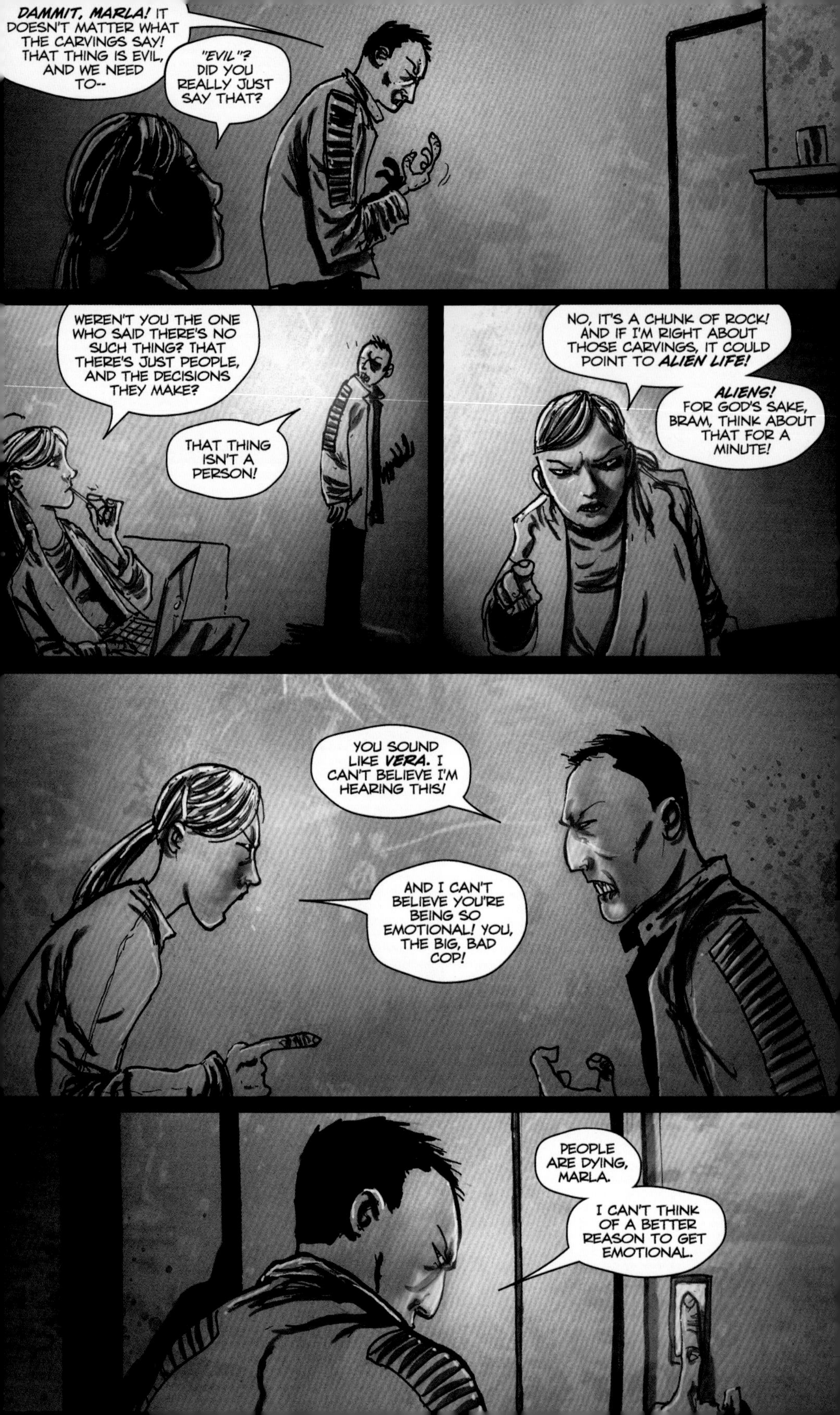
DAMMIT, MARLA! IT DOESN'T MATTER WHAT THE CARVINGS SAY! THAT THING IS EVIL, AND WE NEED TO--
"EVIL"? DID YOU REALLY JUST SAY THAT?
WEREN'T YOU THE ONE WHO SAID THERE'S NO SUCH THING? THAT THERE'S JUST PEOPLE, AND THE DECISIONS THEY MAKE?
THAT THING ISN'T A PERSON!
NO, IT'S A CHUNK OF ROCK! AND IF I'M RIGHT ABOUT THOSE CARVINGS, IT COULD POINT TO ALIEN LIFE!
ALIENS! FOR GOD'S SAKE, BRAM, THINK ABOUT THAT FOR A MINUTE!
YOU SOUND LIKE VERA. I CAN'T BELIEVE I'M HEARING THIS!
AND I CAN'T BELIEVE YOU'RE BEING SO EMOTIONAL! YOU, THE BIG, BAD COP!
PEOPLE ARE DYING, MARLA.
I CAN'T THINK OF A BETTER REASON TO GET EMOTIONAL.

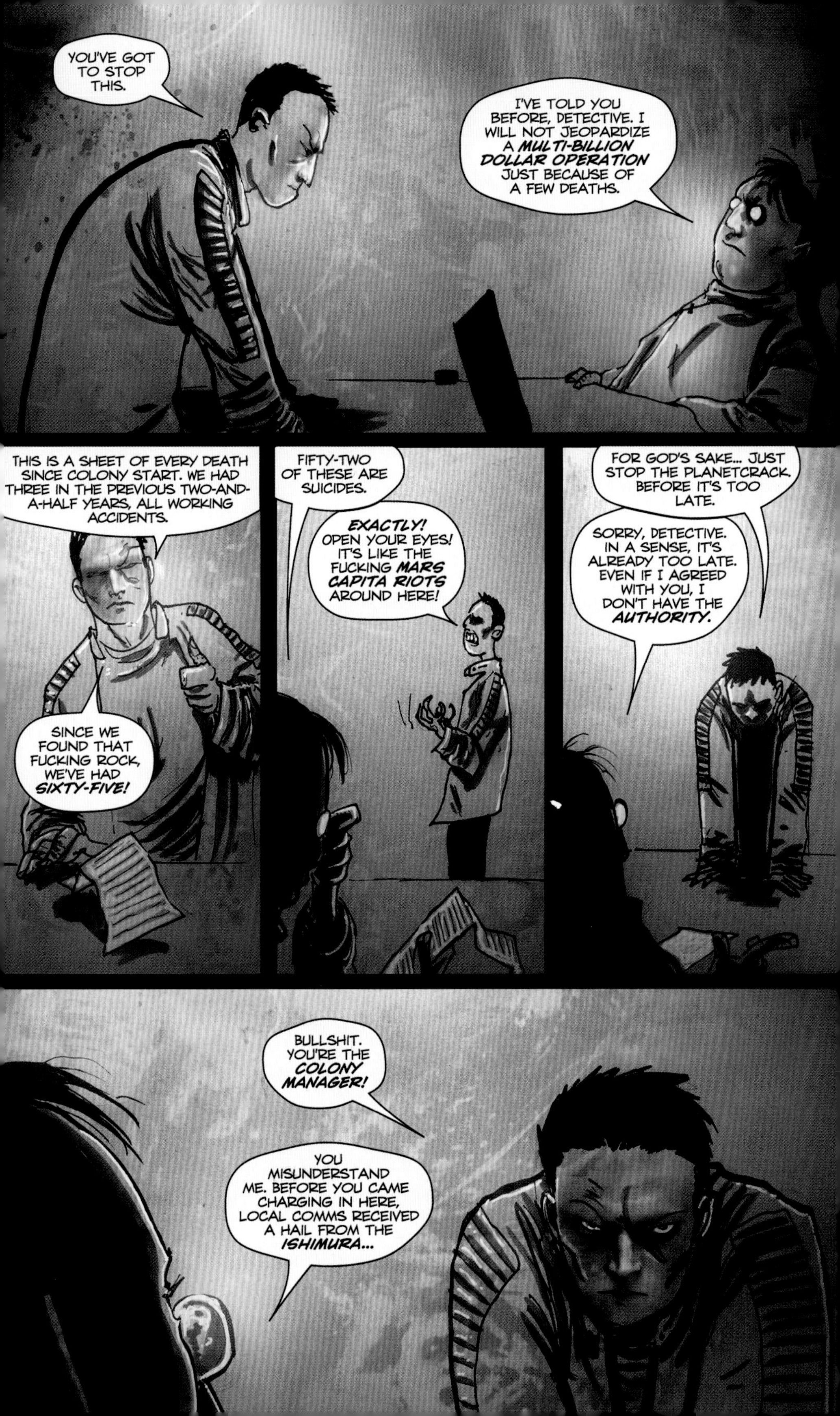
YOU'VE GOT TO STOP THIS.
I'VE TOLD YOU BEFORE, DETECTIVE. I WILL NOT JEOPARDIZE A MULTI-BILLION DOLLAR OPERATION JUST BECAUSE OF A FEW DEATHS.
THIS IS A SHEET OF EVERY DEATH SINCE COLONY START. WE HAD THREE IN THE PREVIOUS TWO-AND-A-HALF YEARS, ALL WORKING ACCIDENTS.
SINCE WE FOUND THAT FUCKING ROCK, WE'VE HAD SIXTY-FIVE!
FIFTY-TWO OF THESE ARE SUICIDES.
EXACTLY! OPEN YOUR EYES! IT'S LIKE THE FUCKING MARS CAPITA RIOTS AROUND HERE!
FOR GOD'S SAKE... JUST STOP THE PLANETCRACK. BEFORE IT'S TOO LATE.
SORRY, DETECTIVE. IN A SENSE, IT'S ALREADY TOO LATE. EVEN IF I AGREED WITH YOU, I DON'T HAVE THE AUTHORITY.
BULLSHIT. YOU'RE THE COLONY MANAGER!
YOU MISUNDERSTAND ME. BEFORE YOU CAME CHARGING IN HERE, LOCAL COMMS RECEIVED A HAIL FROM THE ISHIMURA...

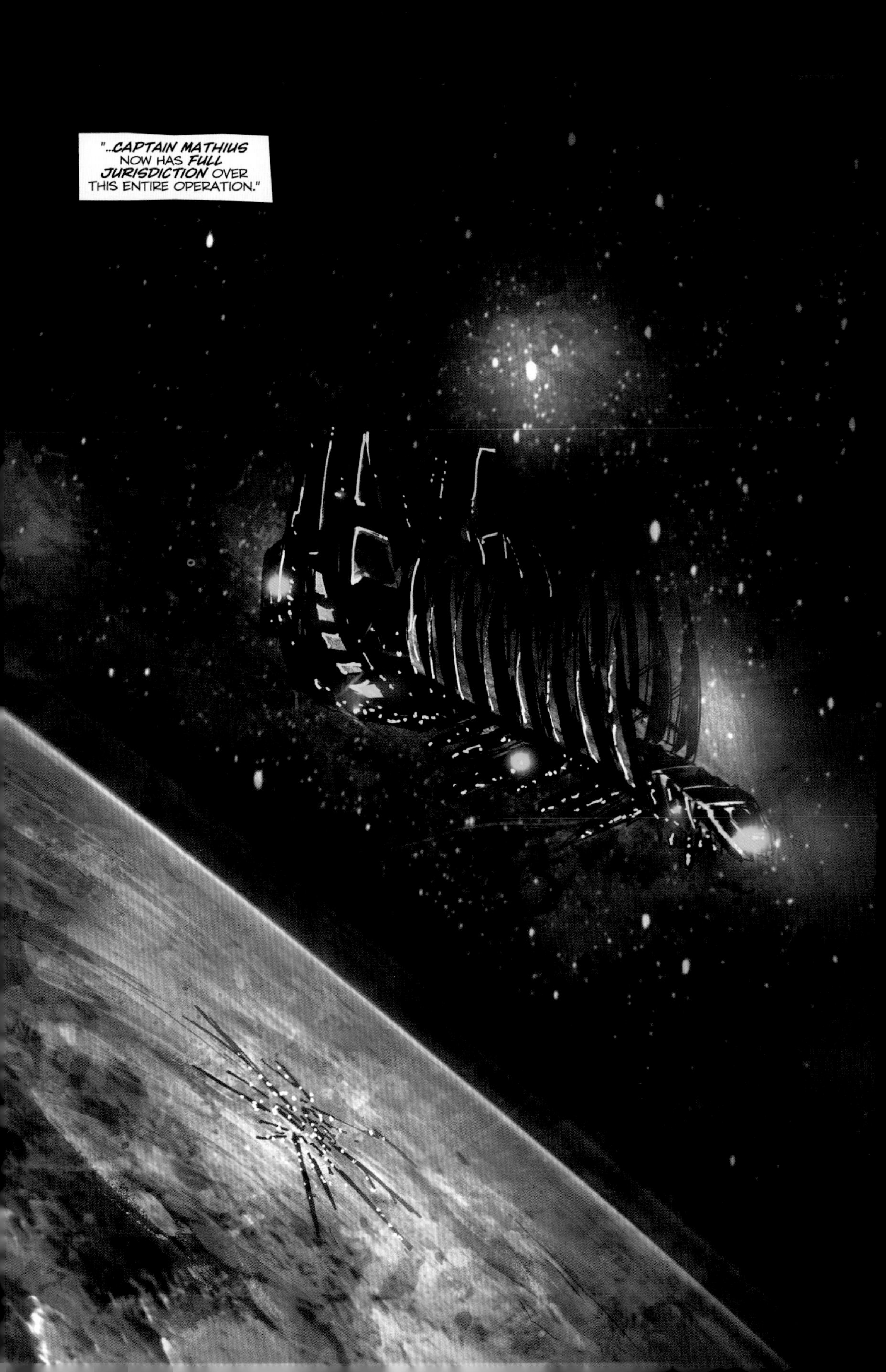
"...CAPTAIN MATHIUS NOW HAS FULL JURISDICTION OVER THIS ENTIRE OPERATION."

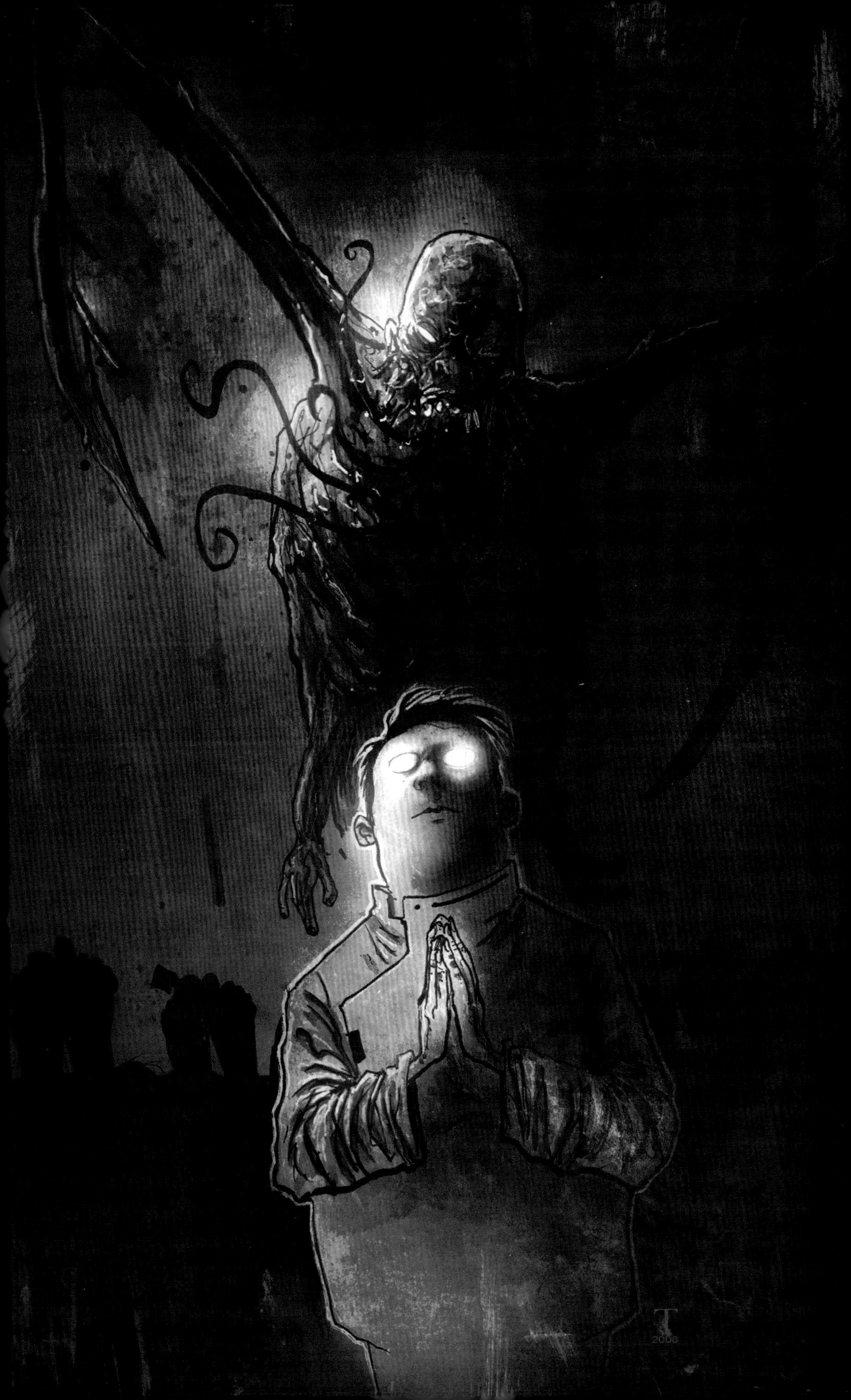

VOLUME 4

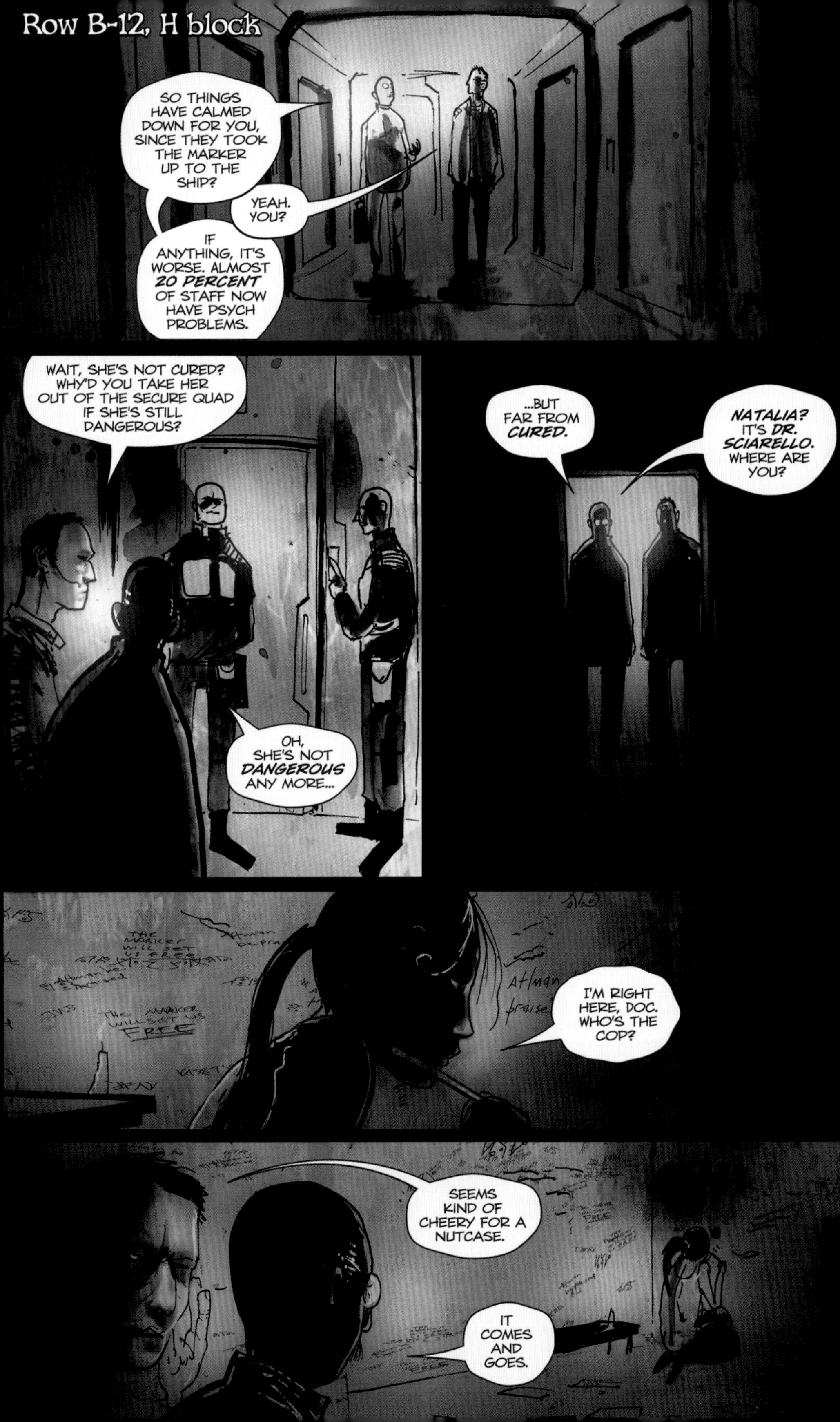
Row B-12, H block
SO THINGS HAVE CALMED DOWN FOR YOU, SINCE THEY TOOK THE MARKER UP TO THE SHIP?
YEAH. YOU?
IF ANYTHING, IT'S WORSE. ALMOST 20 PERCENT OF STAFF NOW HAVE PSYCH PROBLEMS.
WAIT, SHE'S NOT CURED? WHY'D YOU TAKE HER OUT OF THE SECURE QUAD IF SHE'S STILL DANGEROUS?
OH, SHE'S NOT DANGEROUS ANY MORE...
...BUT FAR FROM CURED.
NATALIA? IT'S DR. SCIARELLO. WHERE ARE YOU?
I'M RIGHT HERE, DOC. WHO'S THE COP?
SEEMS KIND OF CHEERY FOR A NUTCASE.
IT COMES AND GOES.

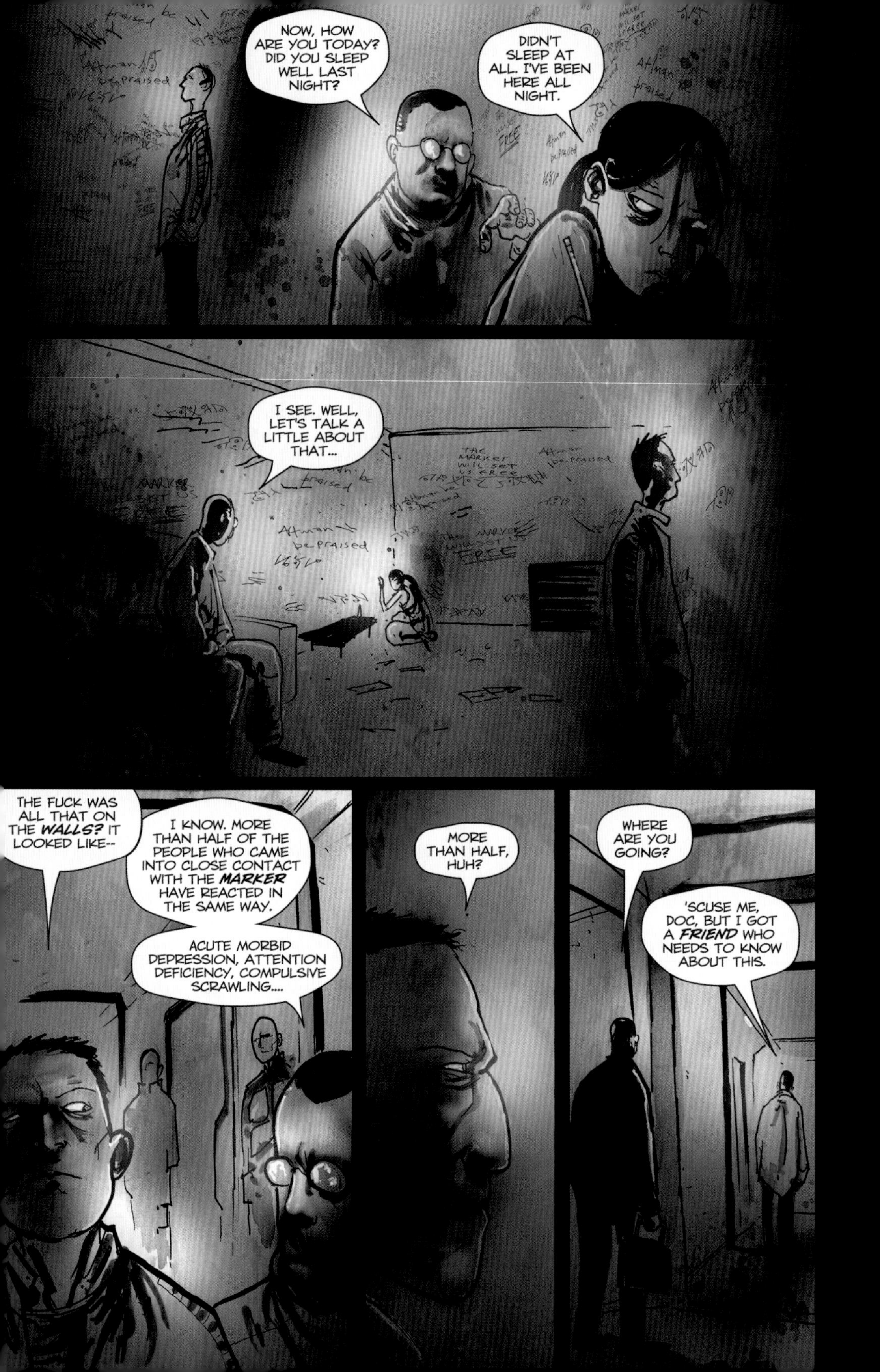
NOW, HOW ARE YOU TODAY? DID YOU SLEEP WELL LAST NIGHT?
DIDN'T SLEEP AT ALL. I'VE BEEN HERE ALL NIGHT.
I SEE. WELL, LET'S TALK A LITTLE ABOUT THAT...
THE FUCK WAS ALL THAT ON THE *WALLS?* IT LOOKED LIKE--
I KNOW. MORE THAN HALF OF THE PEOPLE WHO CAME INTO CLOSE CONTACT WITH THE *MARKER* HAVE REACTED IN THE SAME WAY.
ACUTE MORBID DEPRESSION, ATTENTION DEFICIENCY, COMPULSIVE SCRAWLING....
MORE THAN HALF, HUH?
WHERE ARE YOU GOING?
'SCUSE ME, DOC, BUT I GOT A *FRIEND* WHO NEEDS TO KNOW ABOUT THIS.

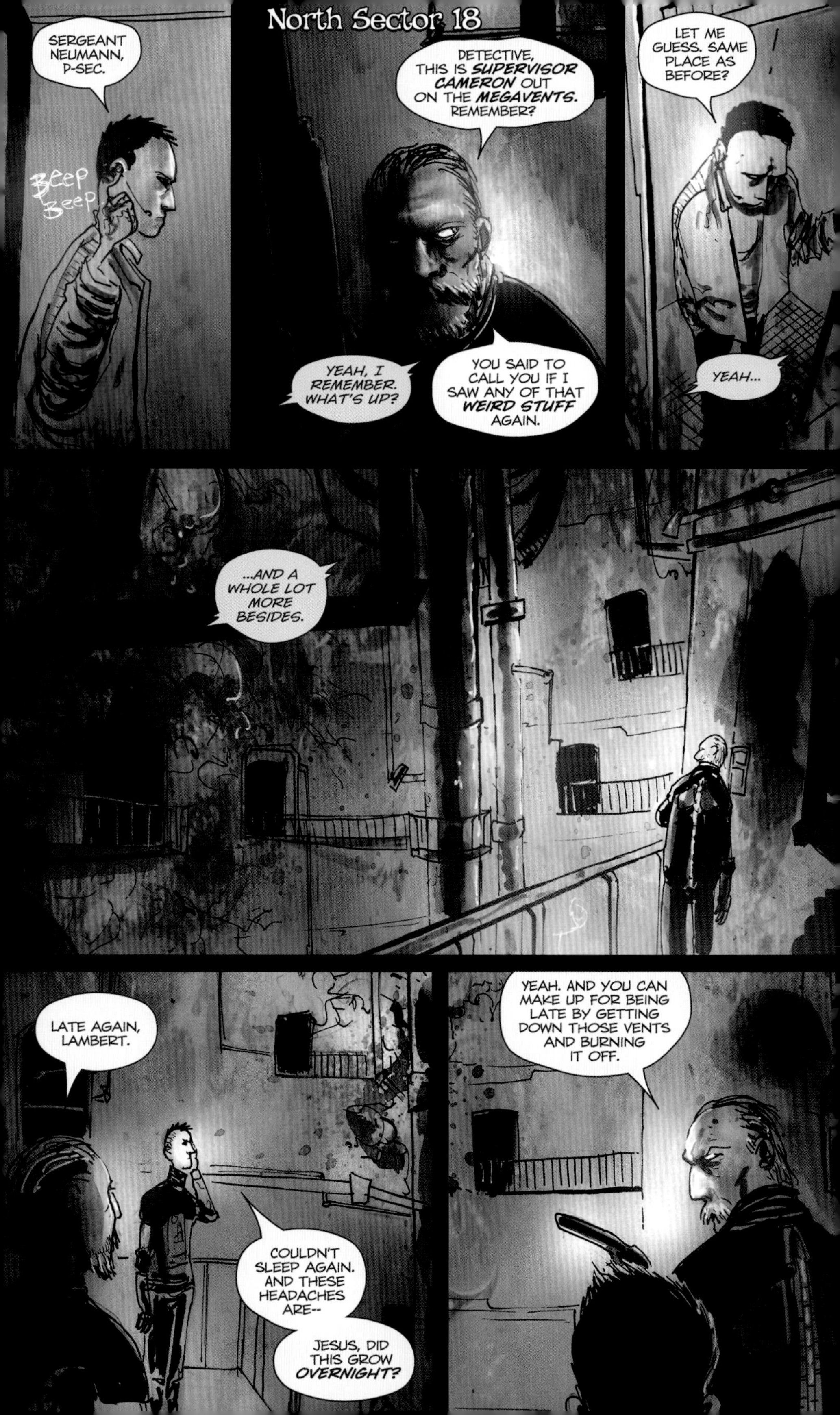
North Sector 18
SERGEANT NEUMANN, P-SEC.
BEEP BEEP
DETECTIVE, THIS IS SUPERVISOR CAMERON OUT ON THE MEGAVENTS. REMEMBER?
YEAH, I REMEMBER. WHAT'S UP?
YOU SAID TO CALL YOU IF I SAW ANY OF THAT WEIRD STUFF AGAIN.
LET ME GUESS. SAME PLACE AS BEFORE?
YEAH...
...AND A WHOLE LOT MORE BESIDES.
LATE AGAIN, LAMBERT.
COULDN'T SLEEP AGAIN. AND THESE HEADACHES ARE--
JESUS, DID THIS GROW OVERNIGHT?
YEAH. AND YOU CAN MAKE UP FOR BEING LATE BY GETTING DOWN THOSE VENTS AND BURNING IT OFF.

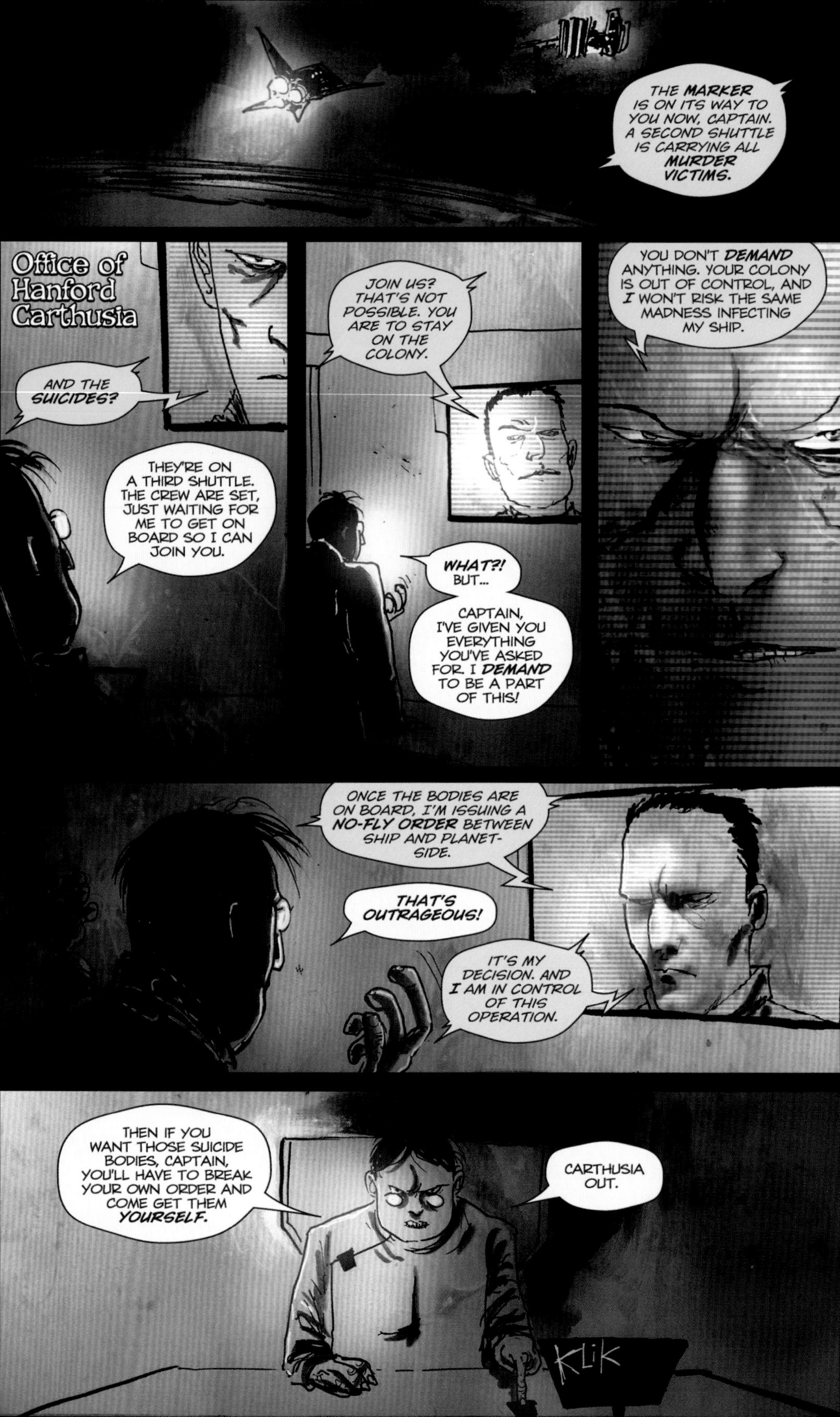
THE MARKER IS ON ITS WAY TO YOU NOW, CAPTAIN. A SECOND SHUTTLE IS CARRYING ALL MURDER VICTIMS.
Office of Hanford Carthusia
AND THE SUICIDES?
THEY'RE ON A THIRD SHUTTLE. THE CREW ARE SET, JUST WAITING FOR ME TO GET ON BOARD SO I CAN JOIN YOU.
JOIN US? THAT'S NOT POSSIBLE. YOU ARE TO STAY ON THE COLONY.
WHAT?! BUT...
CAPTAIN, I'VE GIVEN YOU EVERYTHING YOU'VE ASKED FOR. I DEMAND TO BE A PART OF THIS!
YOU DON'T DEMAND ANYTHING. YOUR COLONY IS OUT OF CONTROL, AND I WON'T RISK THE SAME MADNESS INFECTING MY SHIP.
ONCE THE BODIES ARE ON BOARD, I'M ISSUING A NO-FLY ORDER BETWEEN SHIP AND PLANET-SIDE.
THAT'S OUTRAGEOUS!
IT'S MY DECISION. AND I AM IN CONTROL OF THIS OPERATION.
THEN IF YOU WANT THOSE SUICIDE BODIES, CAPTAIN, YOU'LL HAVE TO BREAK YOUR OWN ORDER AND COME GET THEM YOURSELF.
CARTHUSIA OUT.
KLIK

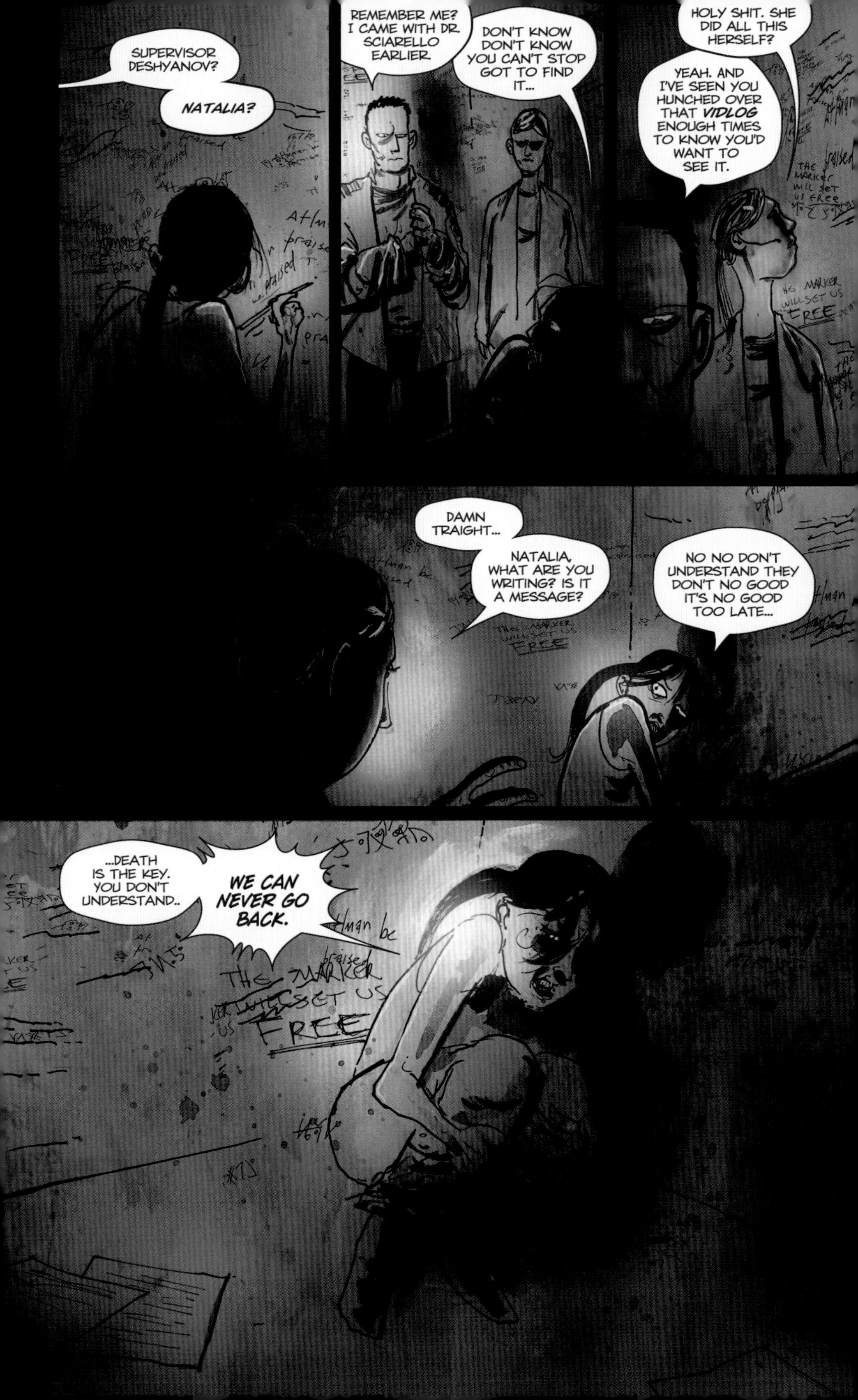
SUPERVISOR DESHYANOV?
NATALIA?
REMEMBER ME? I CAME WITH DR. SCIARELLO EARLIER.
DON'T KNOW DON'T KNOW YOU CAN'T STOP GOT TO FIND IT...
HOLY SHIT. SHE DID ALL THIS HERSELF?
YEAH. AND I'VE SEEN YOU HUNCHED OVER THAT VIDLOG ENOUGH TIMES TO KNOW YOU'D WANT TO SEE IT.
DAMN TRAIGHT...
NATALIA, WHAT ARE YOU WRITING? IS IT A MESSAGE?
NO NO DON'T UNDERSTAND THEY DON'T NO GOOD IT'S NO GOOD TOO LATE...
...DEATH IS THE KEY. YOU DON'T UNDERSTAND..
WE CAN NEVER GO BACK.
THE MARKER WILL SET US FREE

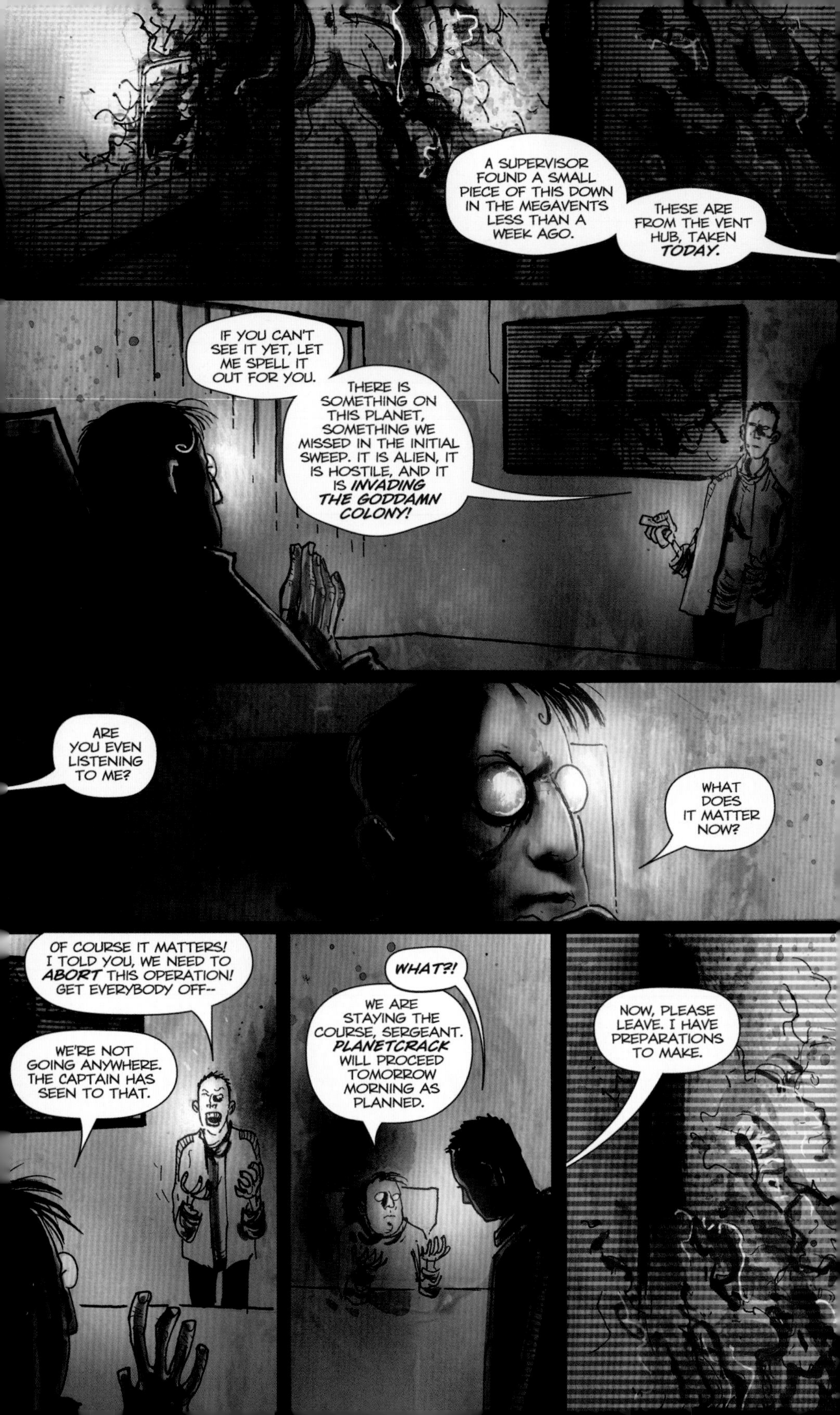
A SUPERVISOR FOUND A SMALL PIECE OF THIS DOWN IN THE MEGAVENTS LESS THAN A WEEK AGO.
THESE ARE FROM THE VENT HUB, TAKEN *TODAY.*
IF YOU CAN'T SEE IT YET, LET ME SPELL IT OUT FOR YOU.
THERE IS SOMETHING ON THIS PLANET, SOMETHING WE MISSED IN THE INITIAL SWEEP. IT IS ALIEN, IT IS HOSTILE, AND IT IS *INVADING THE GODDAMN COLONY!*
ARE YOU EVEN LISTENING TO ME?
WHAT DOES IT MATTER NOW?
OF COURSE IT MATTERS! I TOLD YOU, WE NEED TO *ABORT* THIS OPERATION! GET EVERYBODY OFF--
WE'RE NOT GOING ANYWHERE. THE CAPTAIN HAS SEEN TO THAT.
WE ARE STAYING THE COURSE, SERGEANT. *PLANETCRACK* WILL PROCEED TOMORROW MORNING AS PLANNED.
WHAT?!
NOW, PLEASE LEAVE. I HAVE PREPARATIONS TO MAKE.

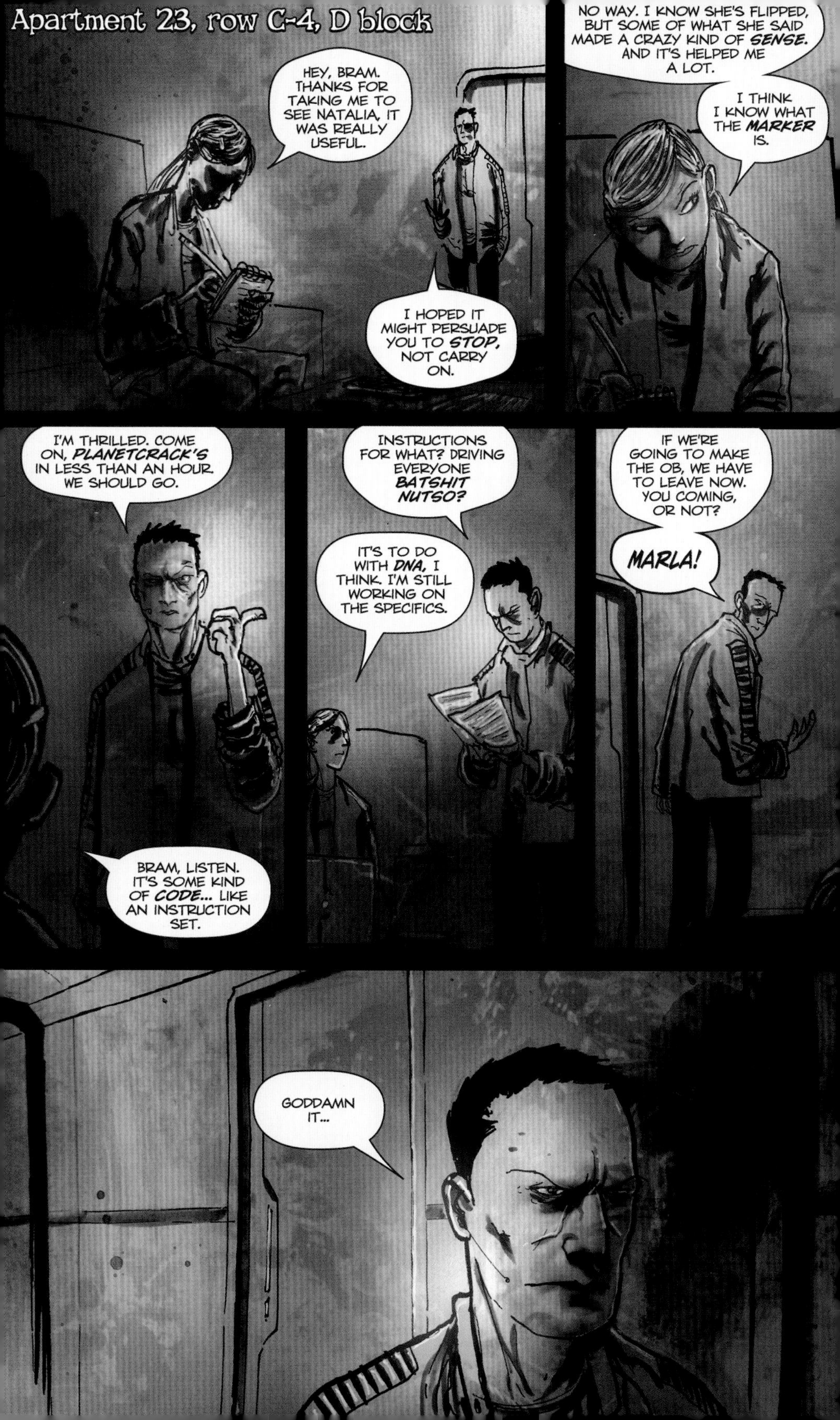
Apartment 23, row C-4, D block
HEY, BRAM. THANKS FOR TAKING ME TO SEE NATALIA, IT WAS REALLY USEFUL.
I HOPED IT MIGHT PERSUADE YOU TO STOP, NOT CARRY ON.
NO WAY. I KNOW SHE'S FLIPPED, BUT SOME OF WHAT SHE SAID MADE A CRAZY KIND OF SENSE. AND IT'S HELPED ME A LOT.
I THINK I KNOW WHAT THE MARKER IS.
I'M THRILLED. COME ON, PLANETCRACK'S IN LESS THAN AN HOUR WE SHOULD GO.
BRAM, LISTEN. IT'S SOME KIND OF CODE... LIKE AN INSTRUCTION SET.
INSTRUCTIONS FOR WHAT? DRIVING EVERYONE BATSHIT NUTSO?
IT'S TO DO WITH DNA, I THINK. I'M STILL WORKING ON THE SPECIFICS.
IF WE'RE GOING TO MAKE THE OB, WE HAVE TO LEAVE NOW. YOU COMING, OR NOT?
MARLA!
GODDAMN IT...

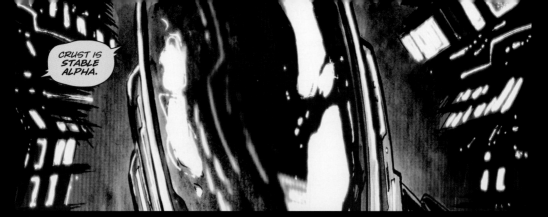

CRUST IS STABLE ALPHA.

GRAVITY TETHERS 13 THROUGH 16, STATUS GREEN.

GEOSTAT AV IS IN PLACE. CONFIRM FINAL.

ROGER THAT, GROUND. STAND BY.

ALL TETHER LOCKS CONFIRMED. ALL UNITS CORRECT AND GREEN.

THIS IS GLIDER TWO, ALL SYSTEMS LOOK GOOD.

ROGER THAT, GLIDER TWO.

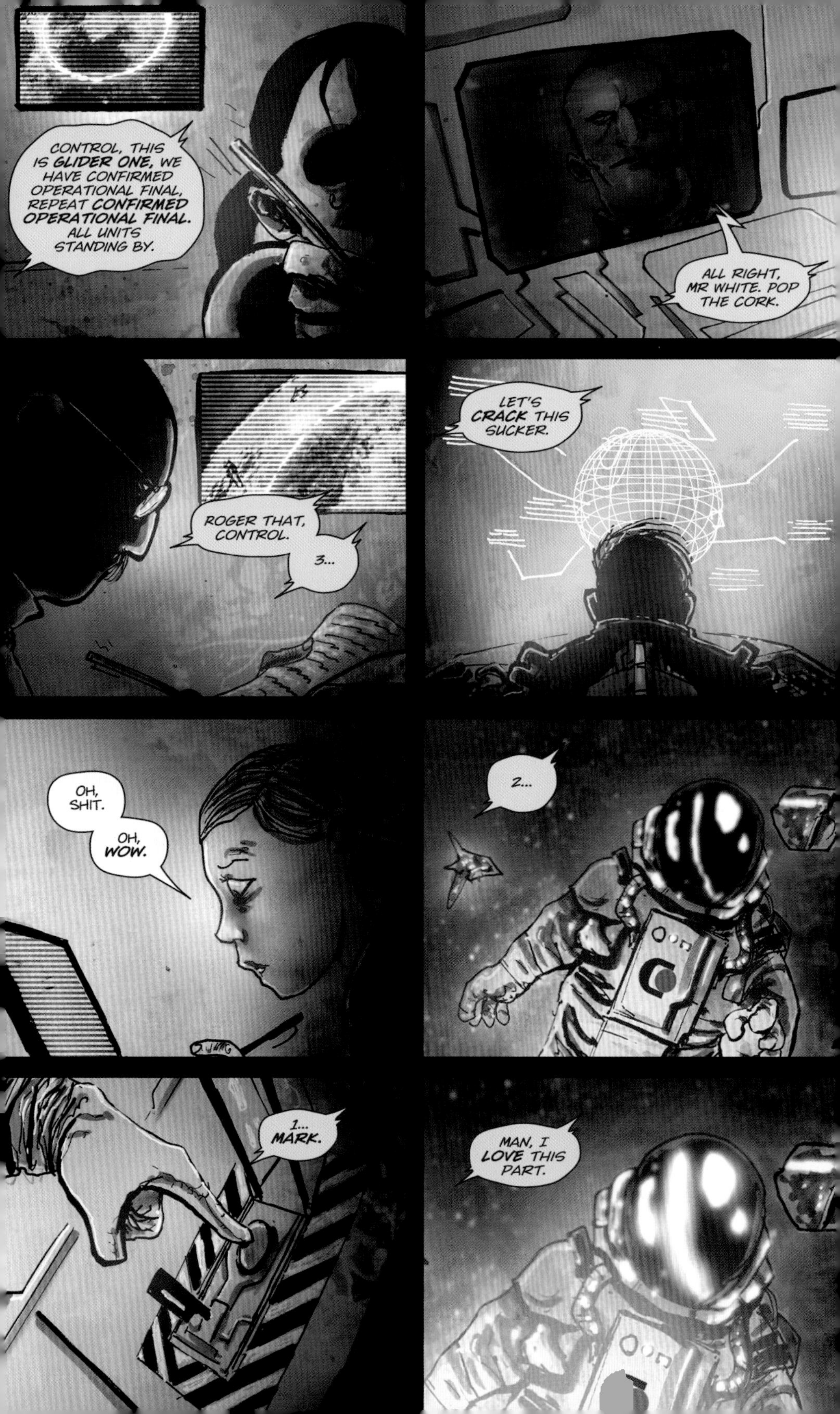
CONTROL, THIS IS GLIDER ONE, WE HAVE CONFIRMED OPERATIONAL FINAL, REPEAT CONFIRMED OPERATIONAL FINAL. ALL UNITS STANDING BY.
ALL RIGHT, MR WHITE. POP THE CORK.
ROGER THAT, CONTROL.
3...
LET'S CRACK THIS SUCKER.
OH, SHIT.
OH, WOW.
2...
1... MARK.
MAN, I LOVE THIS PART.

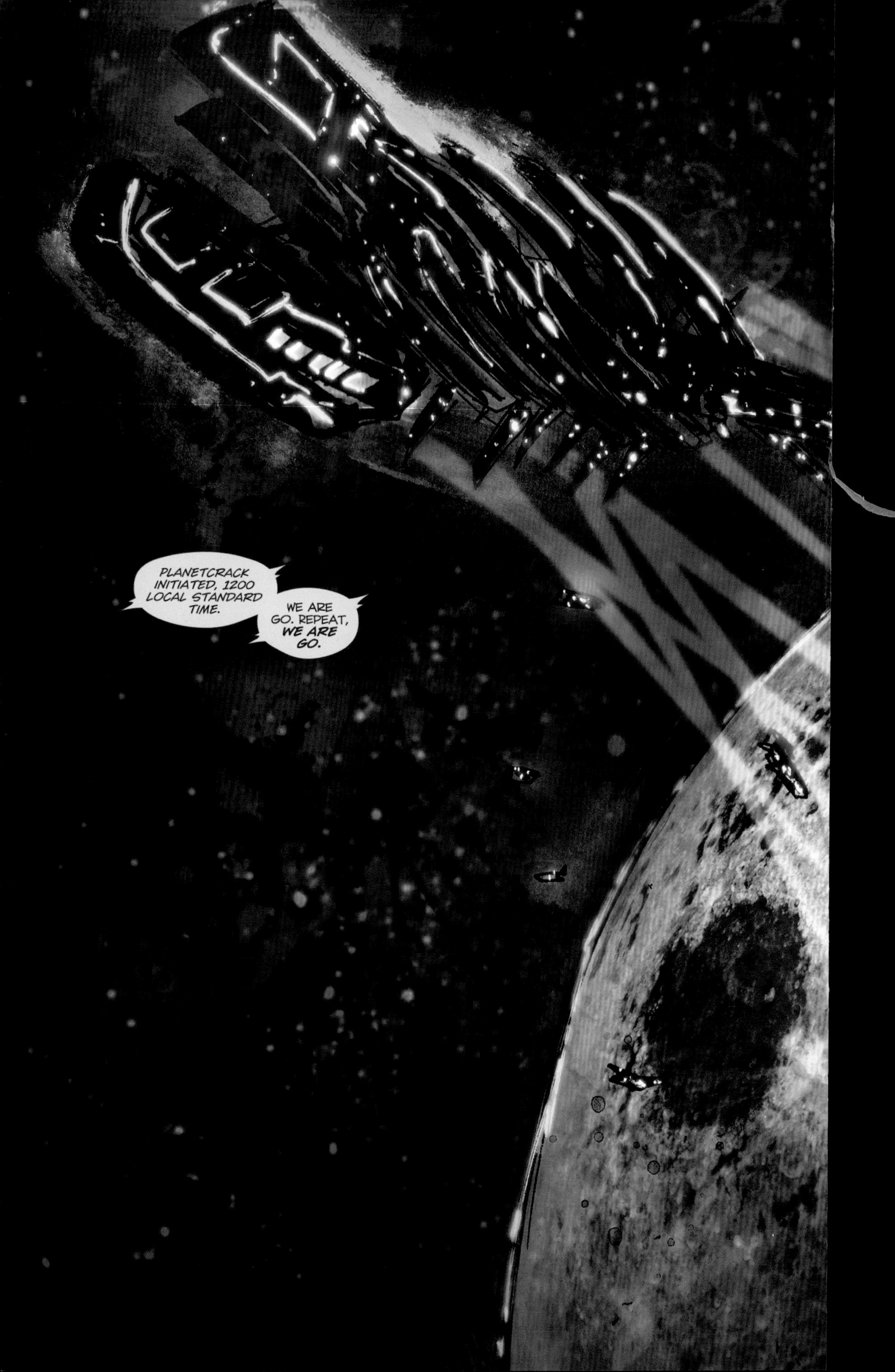
PLANETCRACK INITIATED, 1200 LOCAL STANDARD TIME.
WE ARE GO. REPEAT, WE ARE GO.

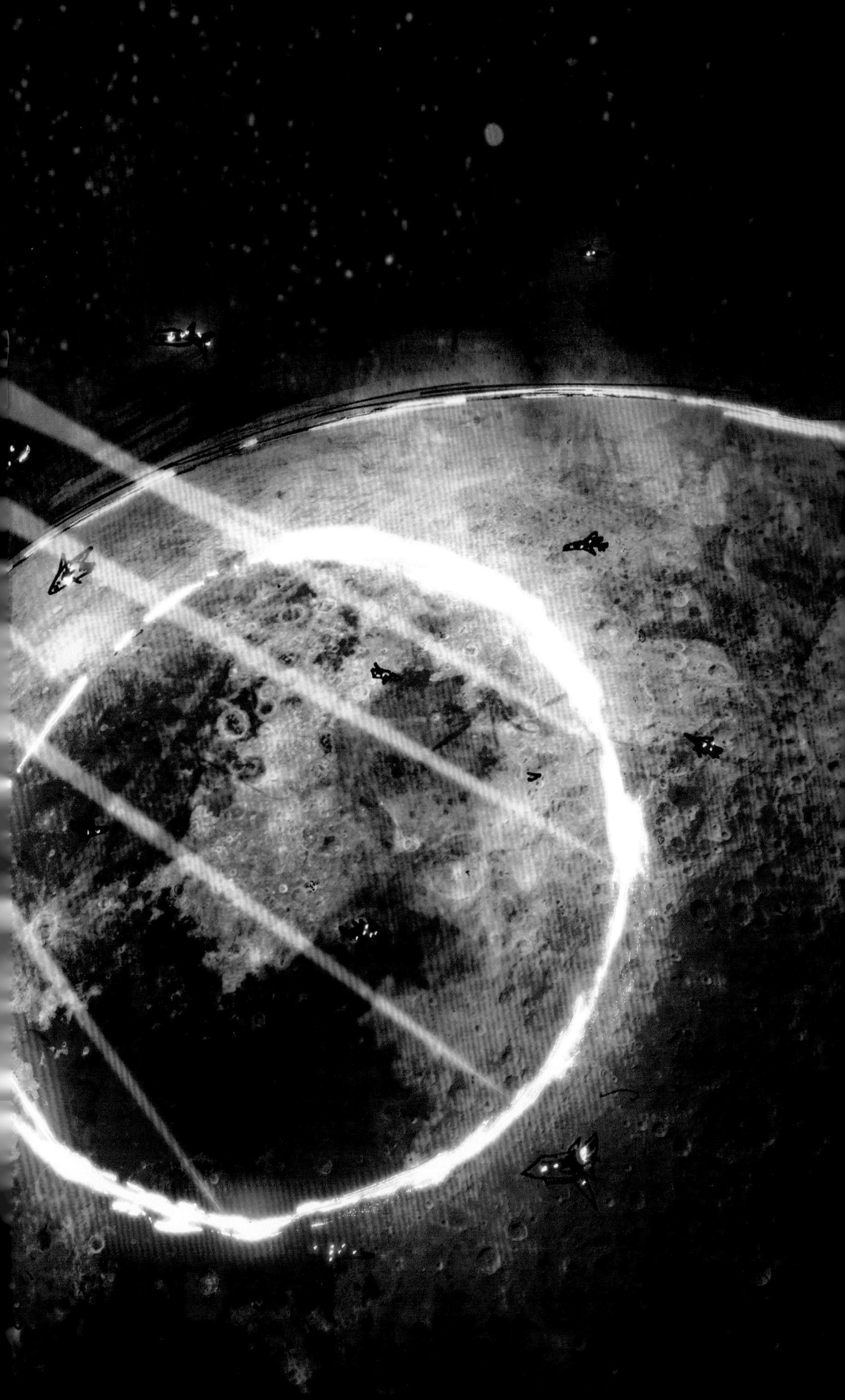

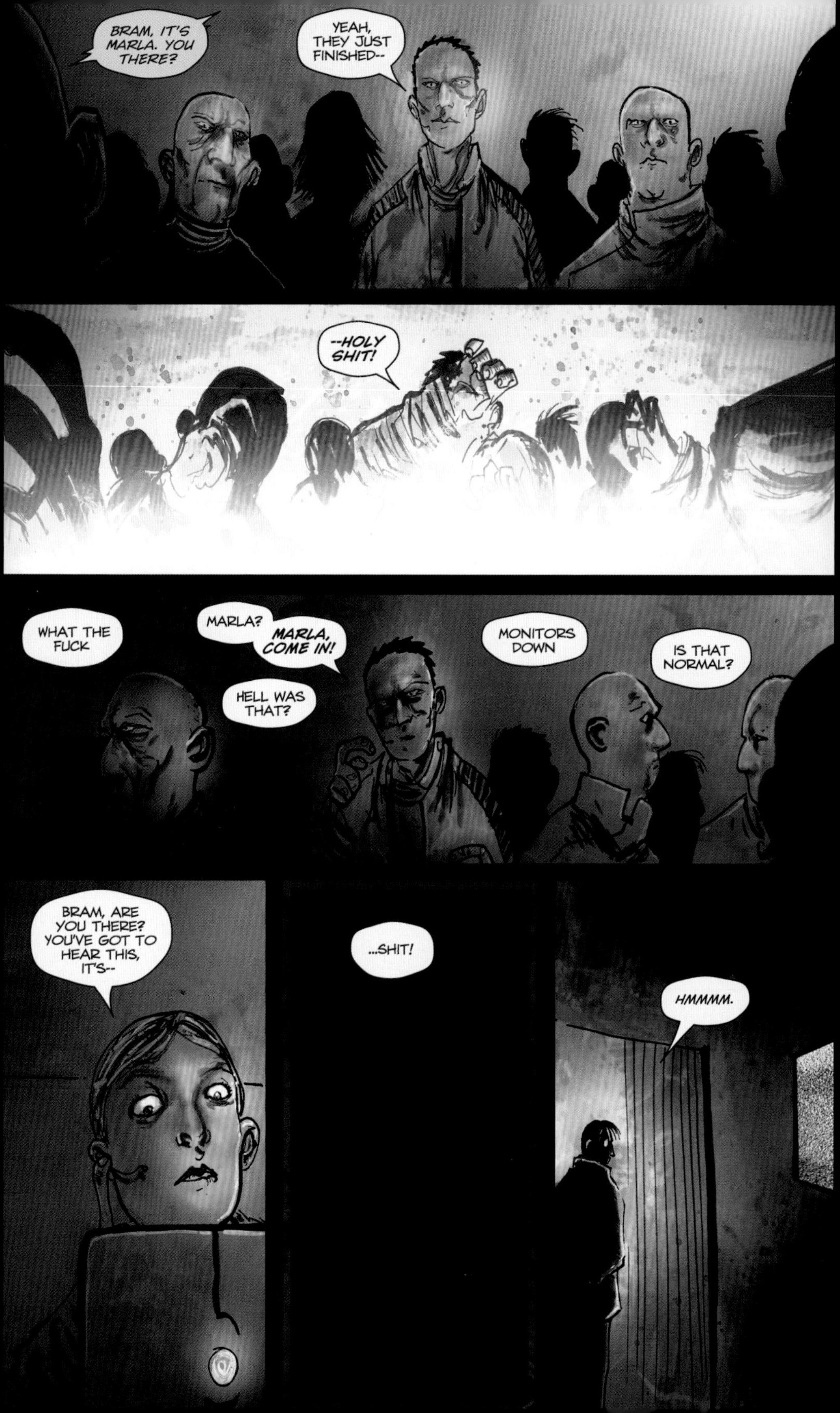
BRAM, IT'S MARLA. YOU THERE?
YEAH, THEY JUST FINISHED--
--HOLY SHIT!
WHAT THE FUCK
MARLA? MARLA, COME IN!
HELL WAS THAT?
MONITORS DOWN
IS THAT NORMAL?
BRAM, ARE YOU THERE? YOU'VE GOT TO HEAR THIS, IT'S--
...SHIT!
HMMMM.

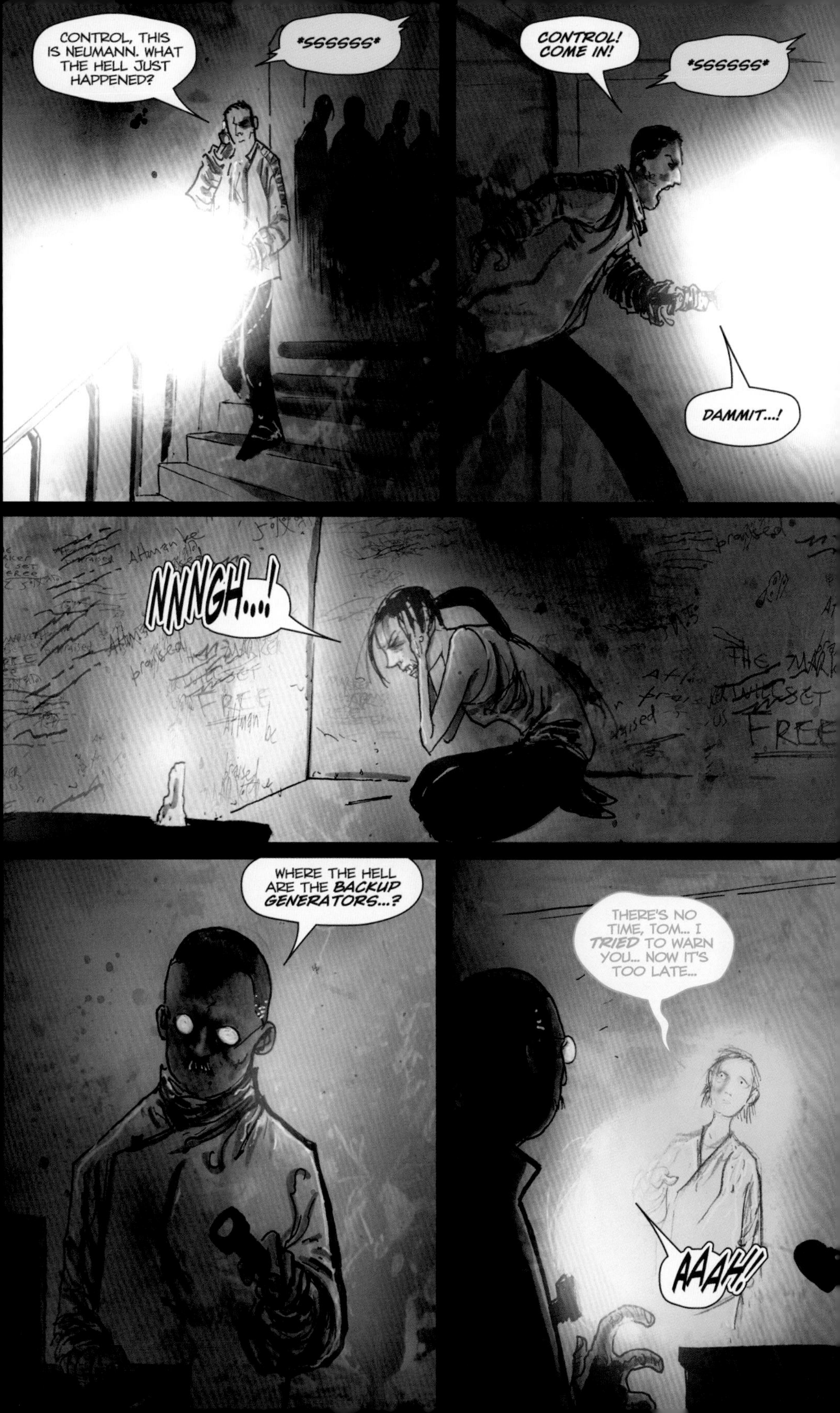
CONTROL, THIS IS NEUMANN. WHAT THE HELL JUST HAPPENED?
SSSSSS
CONTROL! COME IN!
SSSSSS
DAMMIT...!
NNNGH...!
WHERE THE HELL ARE THE BACKUP GENERATORS...?
THERE'S NO TIME, TOM... I TRIED TO WARN YOU... NOW IT'S TOO LATE...
AAAH!

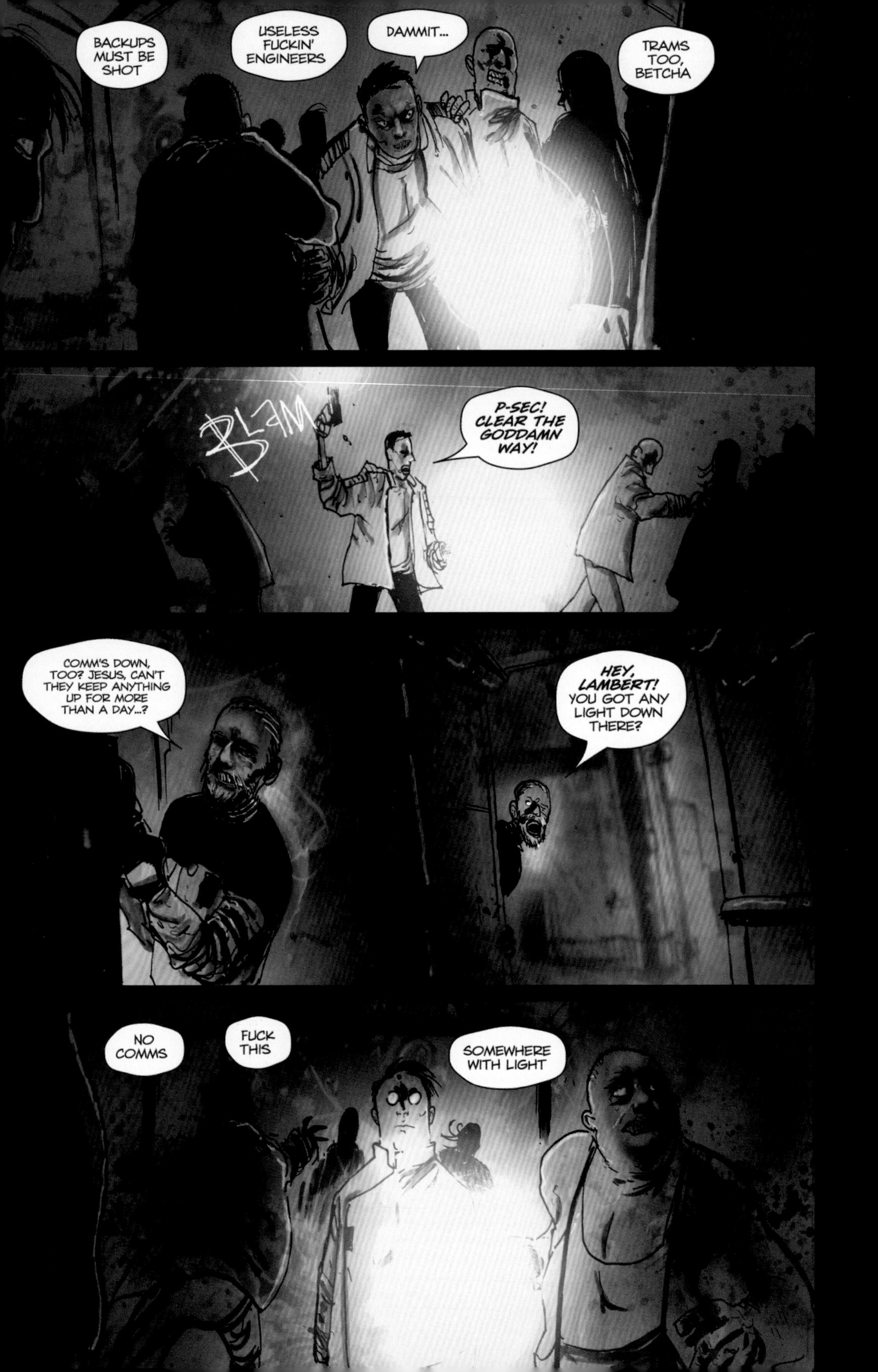
BACKUPS MUST BE SHOT
USELESS FUCKIN' ENGINEERS
DAMMIT...
TRAMS TOO, BETCHA
BLAM
P-SEC! CLEAR THE GODDAMN WAY!
COMM'S DOWN, TOO? JESUS, CAN'T THEY KEEP ANYTHING UP FOR MORE THAN A DAY...?
HEY, LAMBERT! YOU GOT ANY LIGHT DOWN THERE?
NO COMMS
FUCK THIS
SOMEWHERE WITH LIGHT

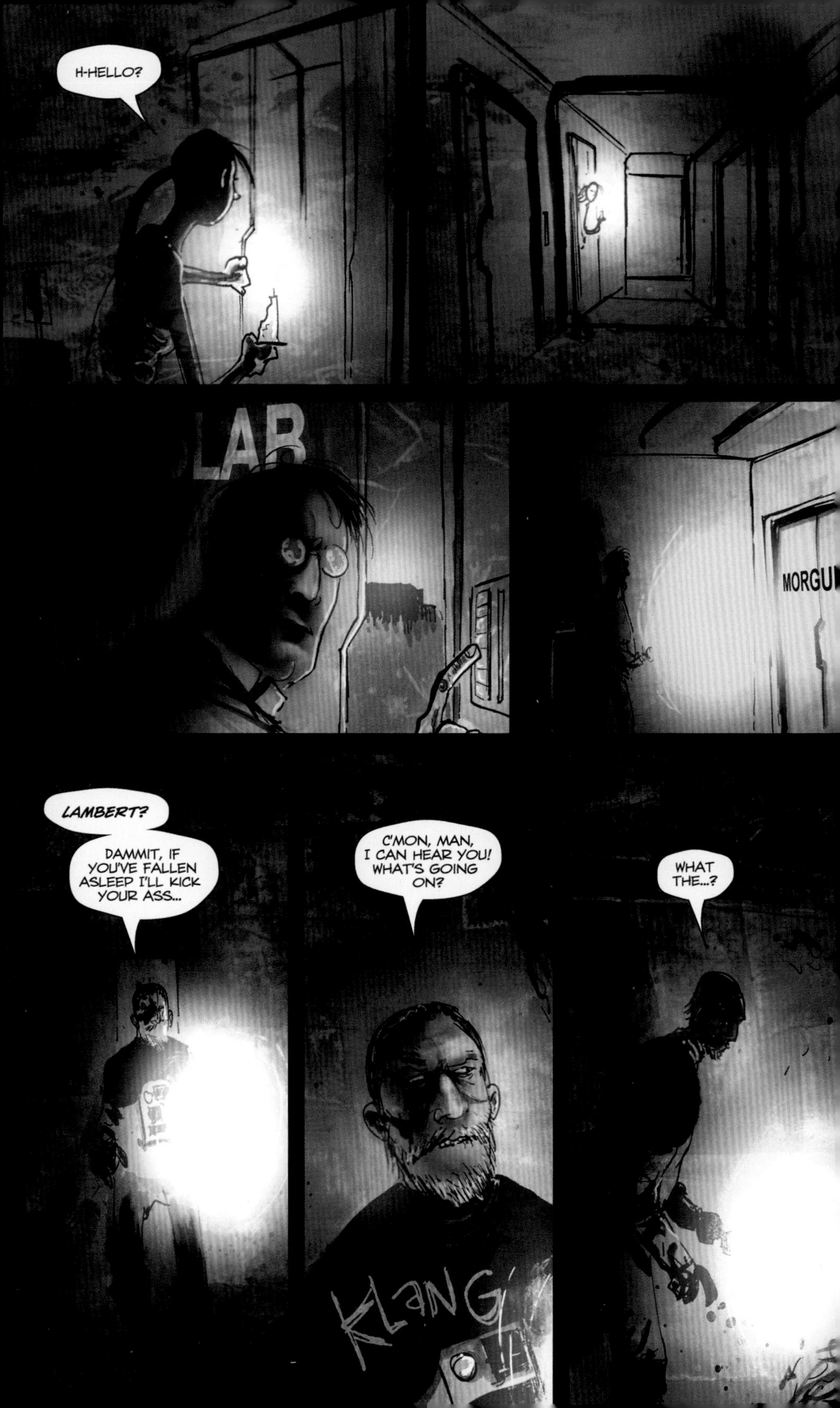
H-HELLO?
LAB
MORGU
LAMBERT?
DAMMIT, IF YOU'VE FALLEN ASLEEP I'LL KICK YOUR ASS...
C'MON, MAN, I CAN HEAR YOU! WHAT'S GOING ON?
WHAT THE...?
KLANG

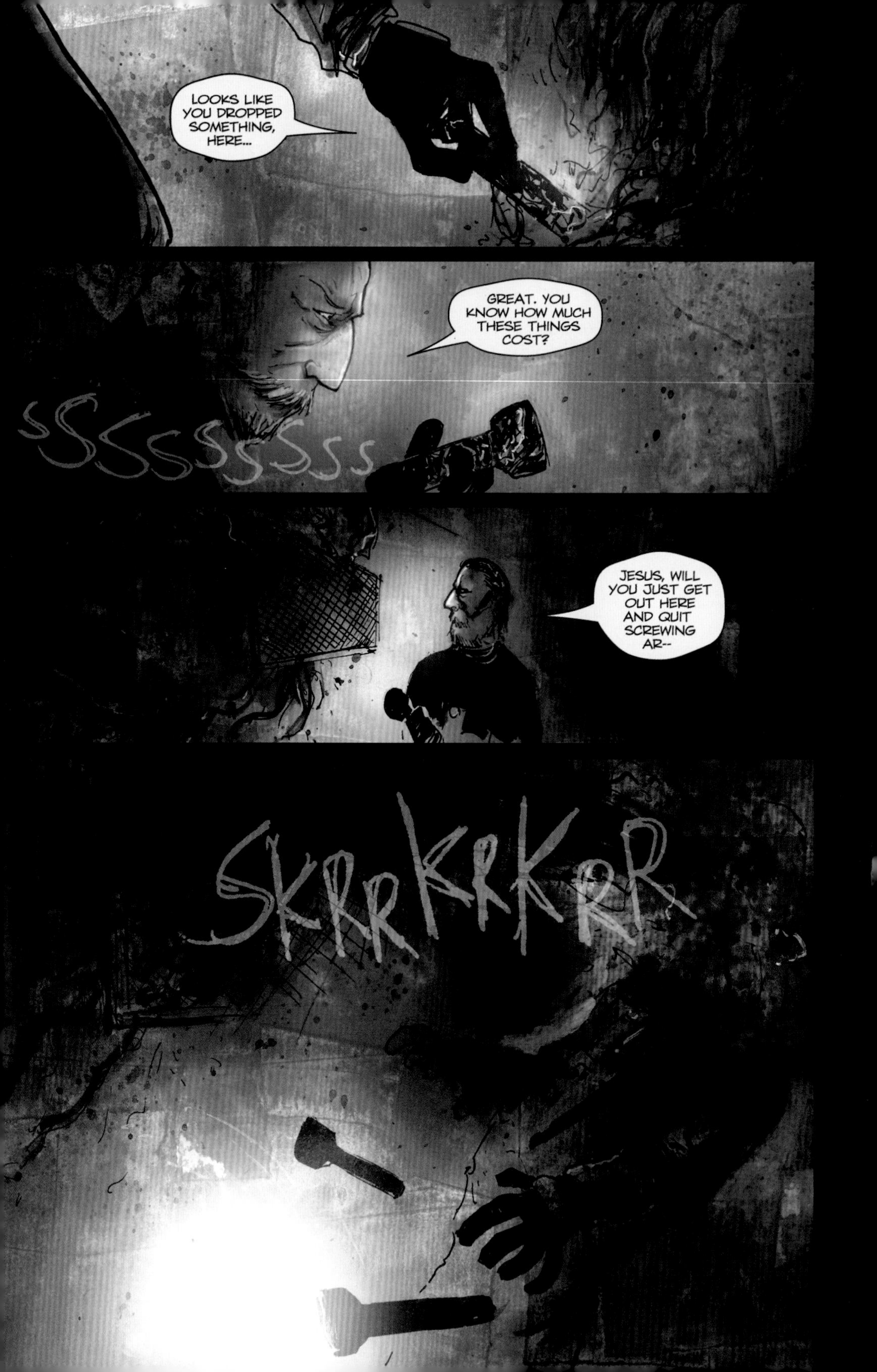
LOOKS LIKE YOU DROPPED SOMETHING, HERE...
GREAT. YOU KNOW HOW MUCH THESE THINGS COST?
SSSSSSSSS
JESUS, WILL YOU JUST GET OUT HERE AND QUIT SCREWING AR--
SKRRKRKRR

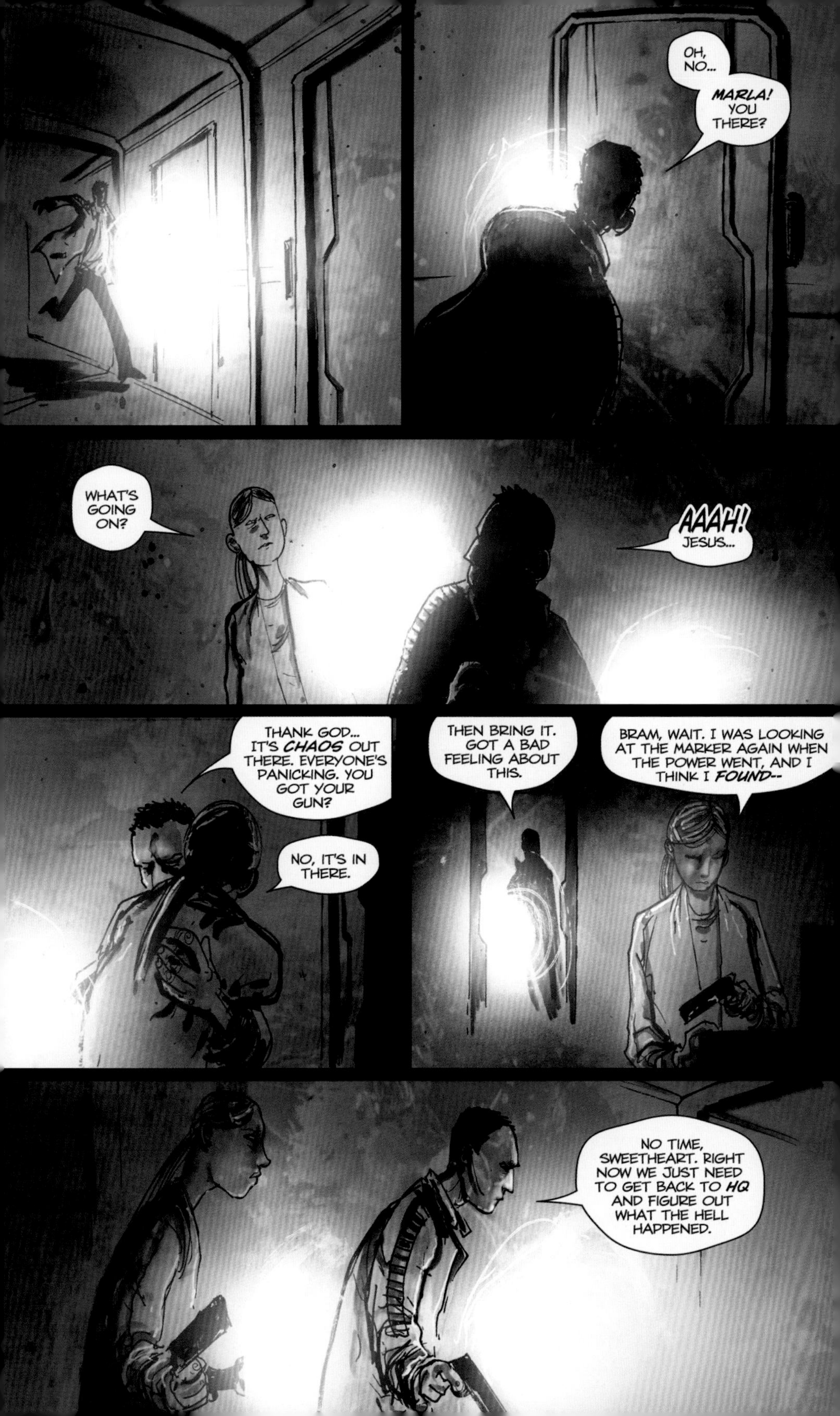
OH, NO... MARLA! YOU THERE?
WHAT'S GOING ON?
AAAH! JESUS...
THANK GOD... IT'S CHAOS OUT THERE. EVERYONE'S PANICKING. YOU GOT YOUR GUN?
NO, IT'S IN THERE.
THEN BRING IT. GOT A BAD FEELING ABOUT THIS.
BRAM, WAIT. I WAS LOOKING AT THE MARKER AGAIN WHEN THE POWER WENT, AND I THINK I FOUND--
NO TIME, SWEETHEART. RIGHT NOW WE JUST NEED TO GET BACK TO HQ AND FIGURE OUT WHAT THE HELL HAPPENED.

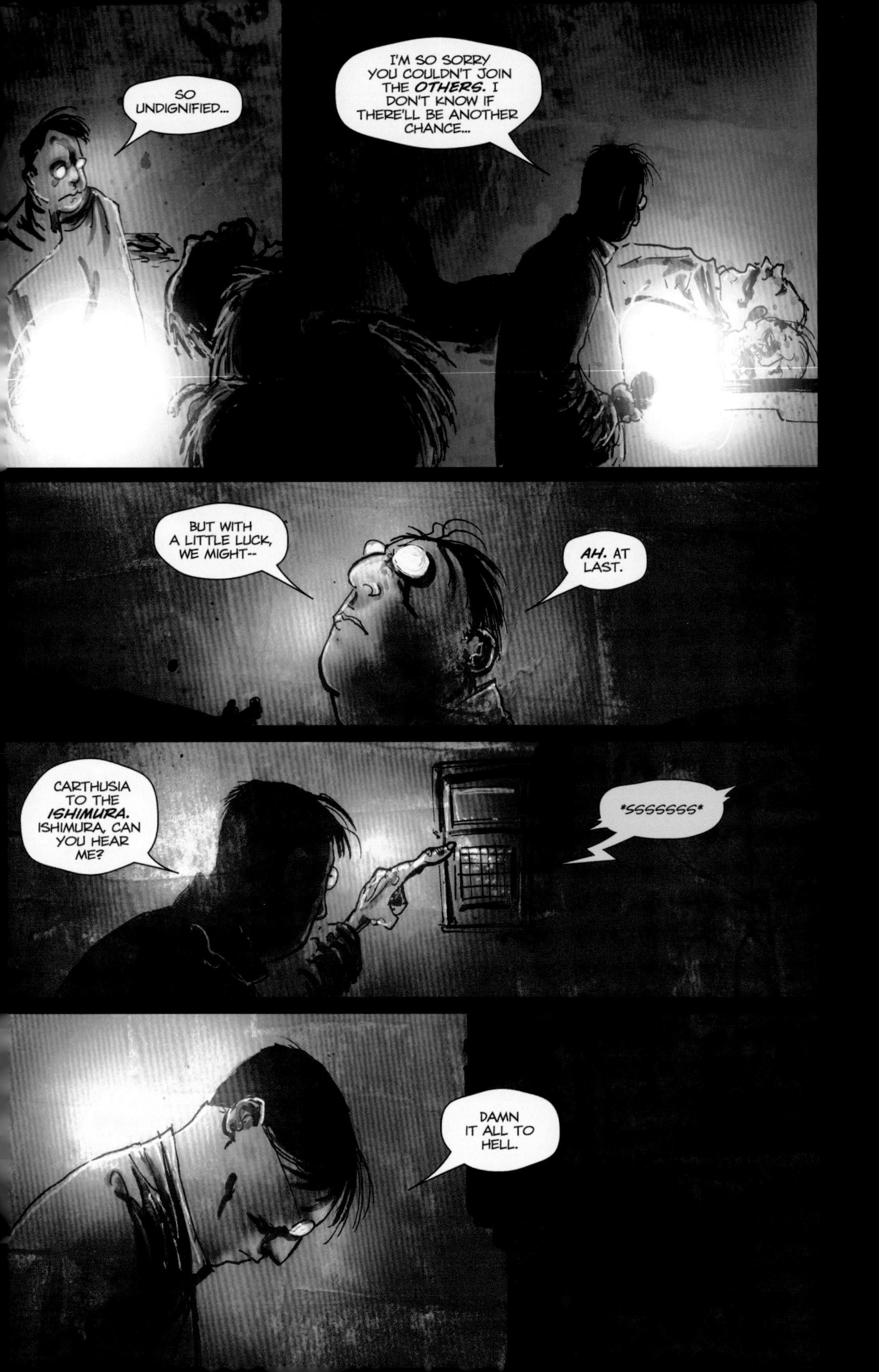
SO UNDIGNIFIED...
I'M SO SORRY YOU COULDN'T JOIN THE *OTHERS.* I DON'T KNOW IF THERE'LL BE ANOTHER CHANCE...
BUT WITH A LITTLE LUCK, WE MIGHT--
AH. AT LAST.
CARTHUSIA TO THE *ISHIMURA.* ISHIMURA, CAN YOU HEAR ME?
SSSSSSS
DAMN IT ALL TO HELL.

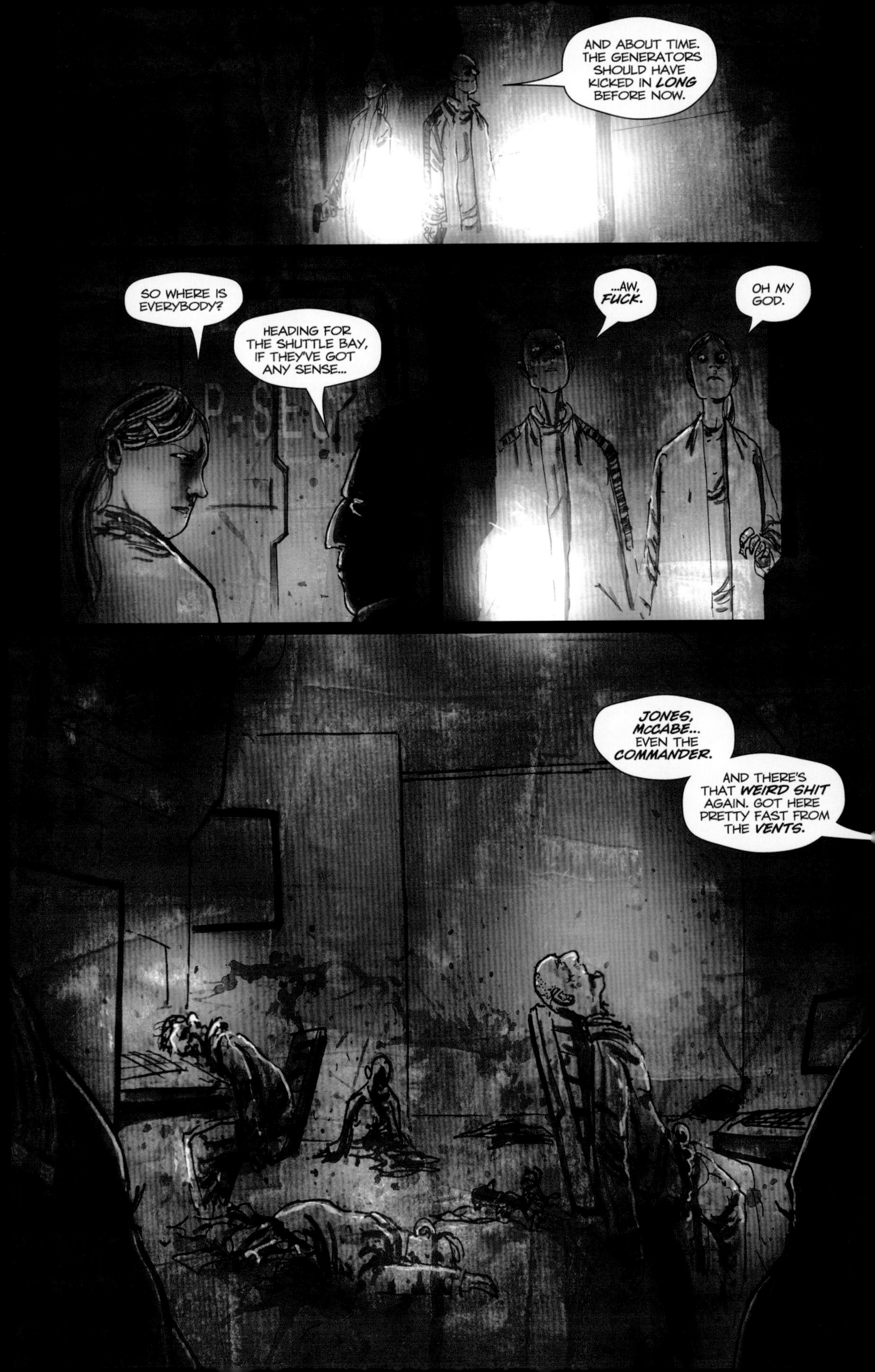
AND ABOUT TIME. THE GENERATORS SHOULD HAVE KICKED IN LONG BEFORE NOW.
SO WHERE IS EVERYBODY?
HEADING FOR THE SHUTTLE BAY, IF THEY'VE GOT ANY SENSE...
...AW, FUCK.
OH MY GOD.
JONES, McCABE... EVEN THE COMMANDER.
AND THERE'S THAT WEIRD SHIT AGAIN. GOT HERE PRETTY FAST FROM THE VENTS.

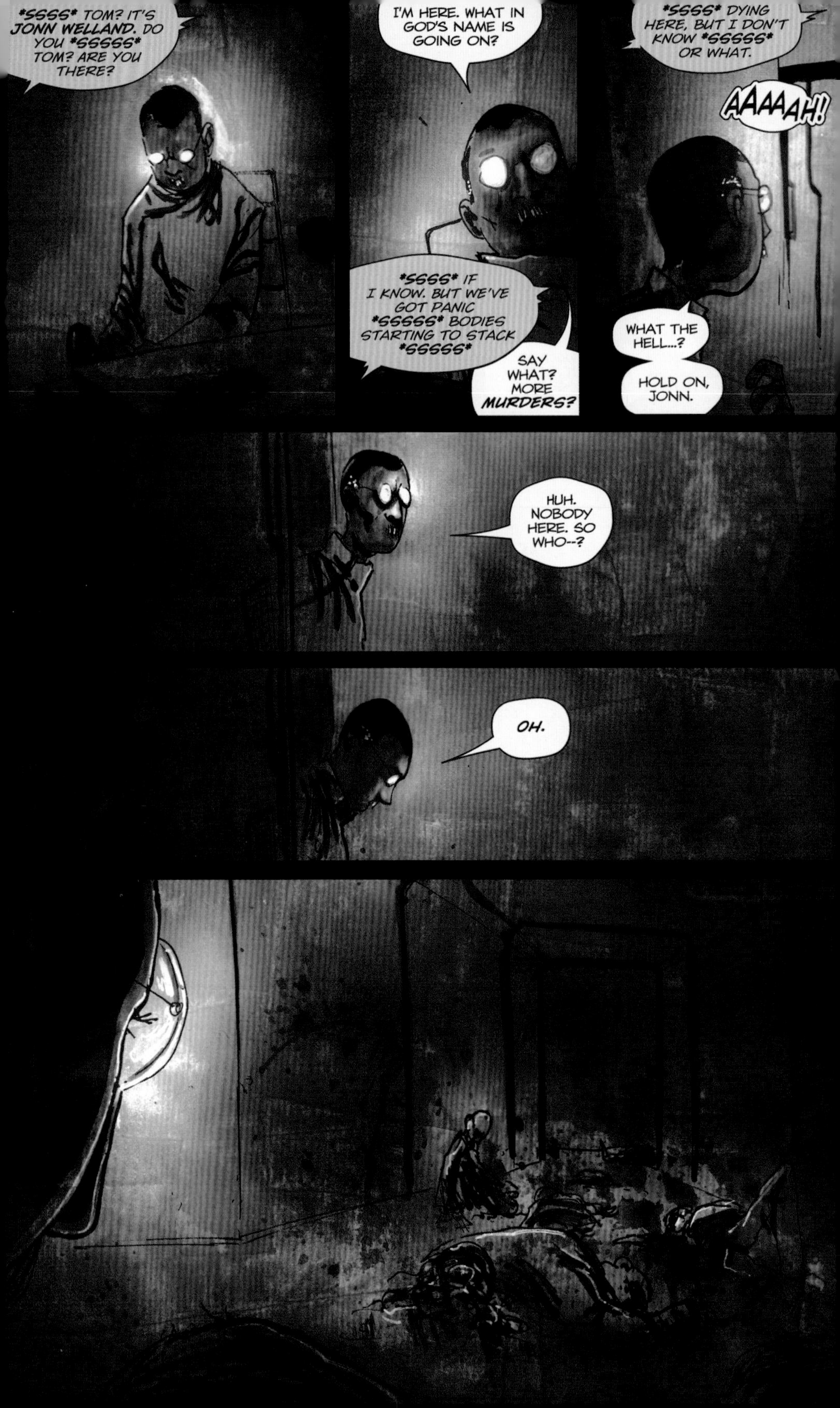
SSSS TOM? IT'S JONN WELLAND. DO YOU *SSSSS* TOM? ARE YOU THERE?
I'M HERE. WHAT IN GOD'S NAME IS GOING ON?
SSSS IF I KNOW. BUT WE'VE GOT PANIC *SSSSS* BODIES STARTING TO STACK *SSSSS*
SAY WHAT? MORE MURDERS?
SSSS DYING HERE, BUT I DON'T KNOW *SSSSS* OR WHAT.
AAAAAH!
WHAT THE HELL...?
HOLD ON, JONN.
HUH. NOBODY HERE. SO WHO--?
OH.

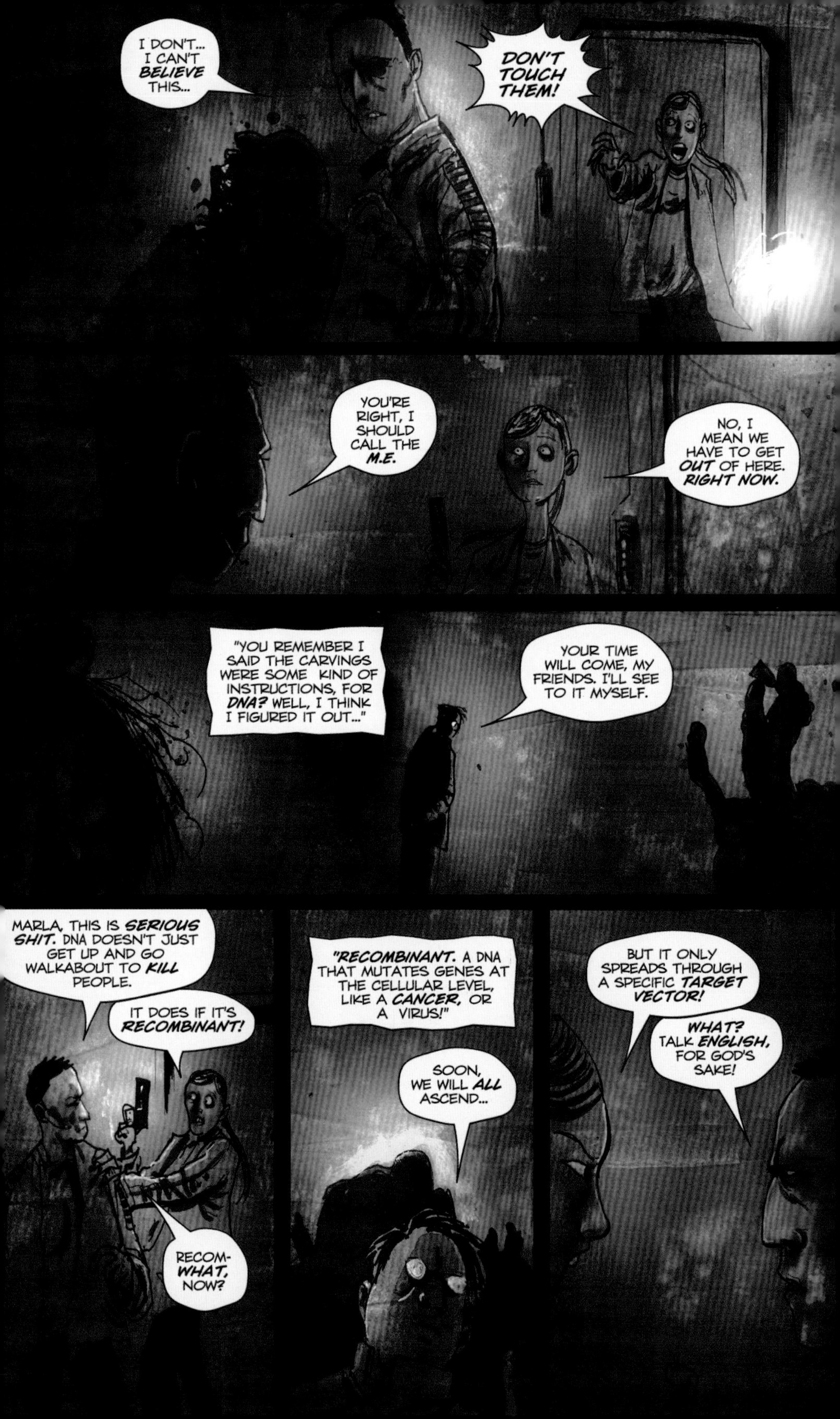
I DON'T... I CAN'T *BELIEVE* THIS...
DON'T TOUCH THEM!
YOU'RE RIGHT, I SHOULD CALL THE *M.E.*
NO, I MEAN WE HAVE TO GET *OUT* OF HERE. *RIGHT NOW.*
"YOU REMEMBER I SAID THE CARVINGS WERE SOME KIND OF INSTRUCTIONS, FOR *DNA?* WELL, I THINK I FIGURED IT OUT..."
YOUR TIME WILL COME, MY FRIENDS. I'LL SEE TO IT MYSELF.
MARLA, THIS IS *SERIOUS SHIT.* DNA DOESN'T JUST GET UP AND GO WALKABOUT TO *KILL* PEOPLE.
IT DOES IF IT'S *RECOMBINANT!*
RECOM-*WHAT,* NOW?
"RECOMBINANT. A DNA THAT MUTATES GENES AT THE CELLULAR LEVEL, LIKE A *CANCER,* OR A VIRUS!"
SOON, WE WILL *ALL* ASCEND...
BUT IT ONLY SPREADS THROUGH A SPECIFIC *TARGET VECTOR!*
WHAT? TALK *ENGLISH,* FOR GOD'S SAKE!

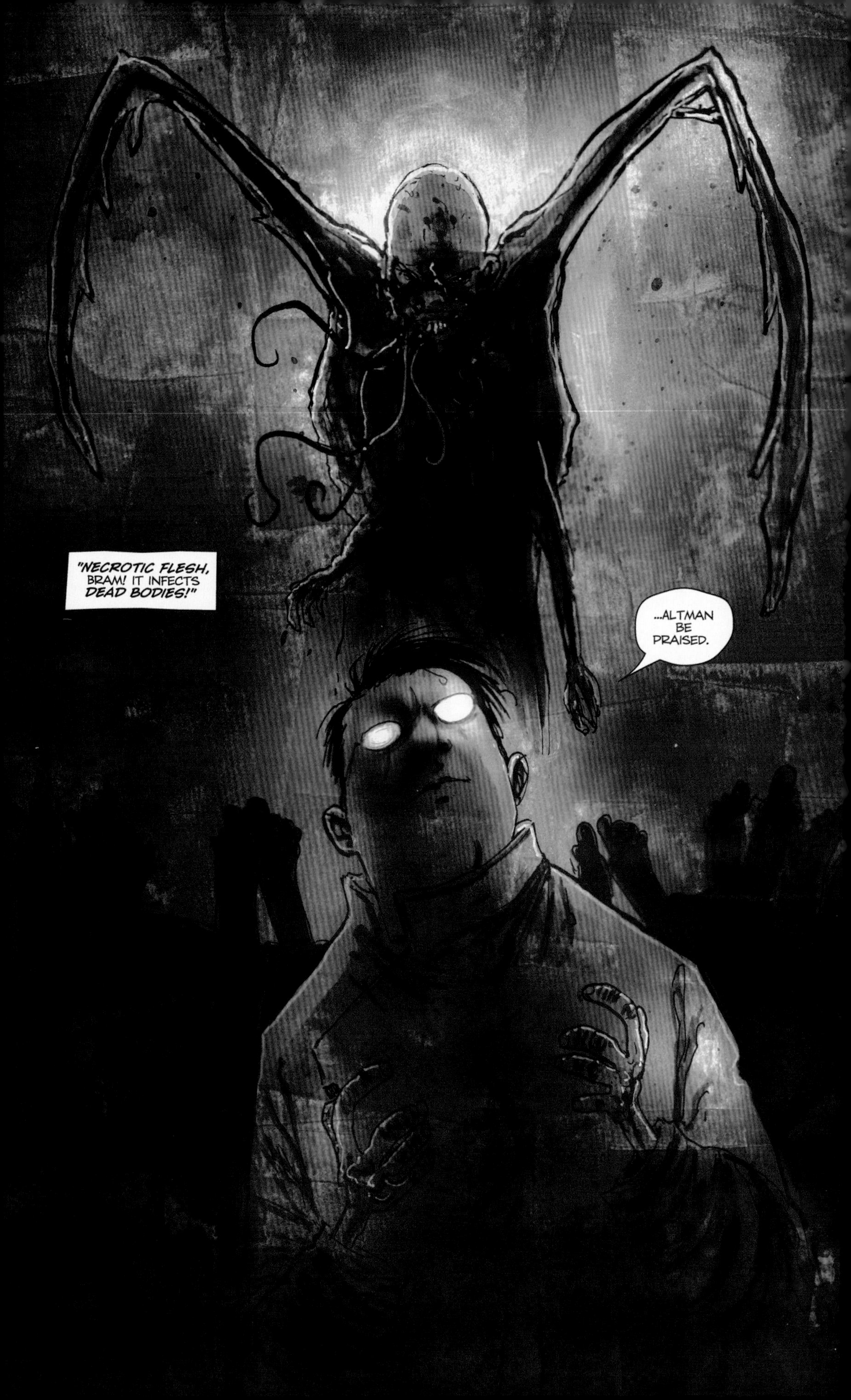
"NECROTIC FLESH, BRAM! IT INFECTS DEAD BODIES!"
...ALTMAN BE PRAISED.

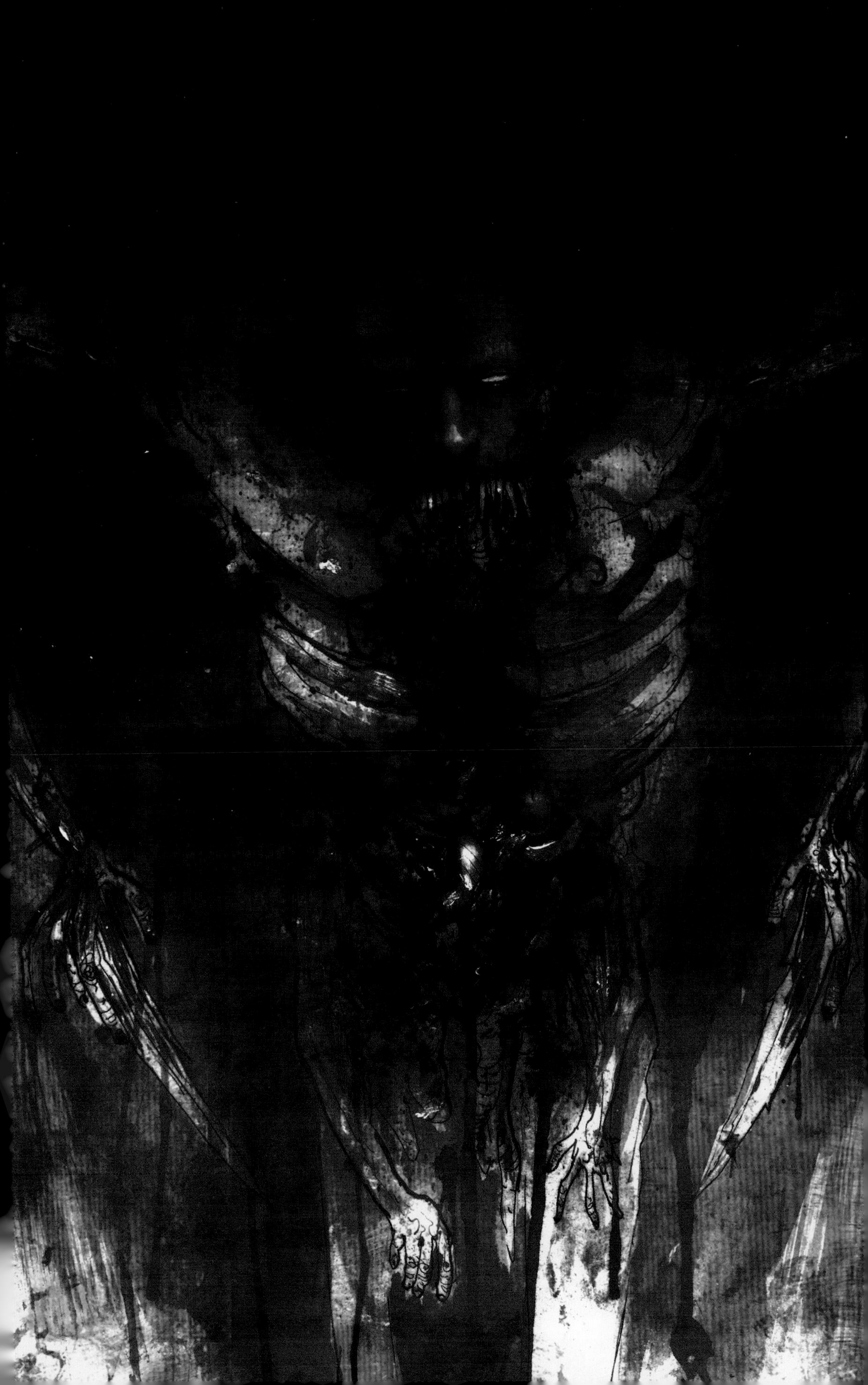

VULUME 5

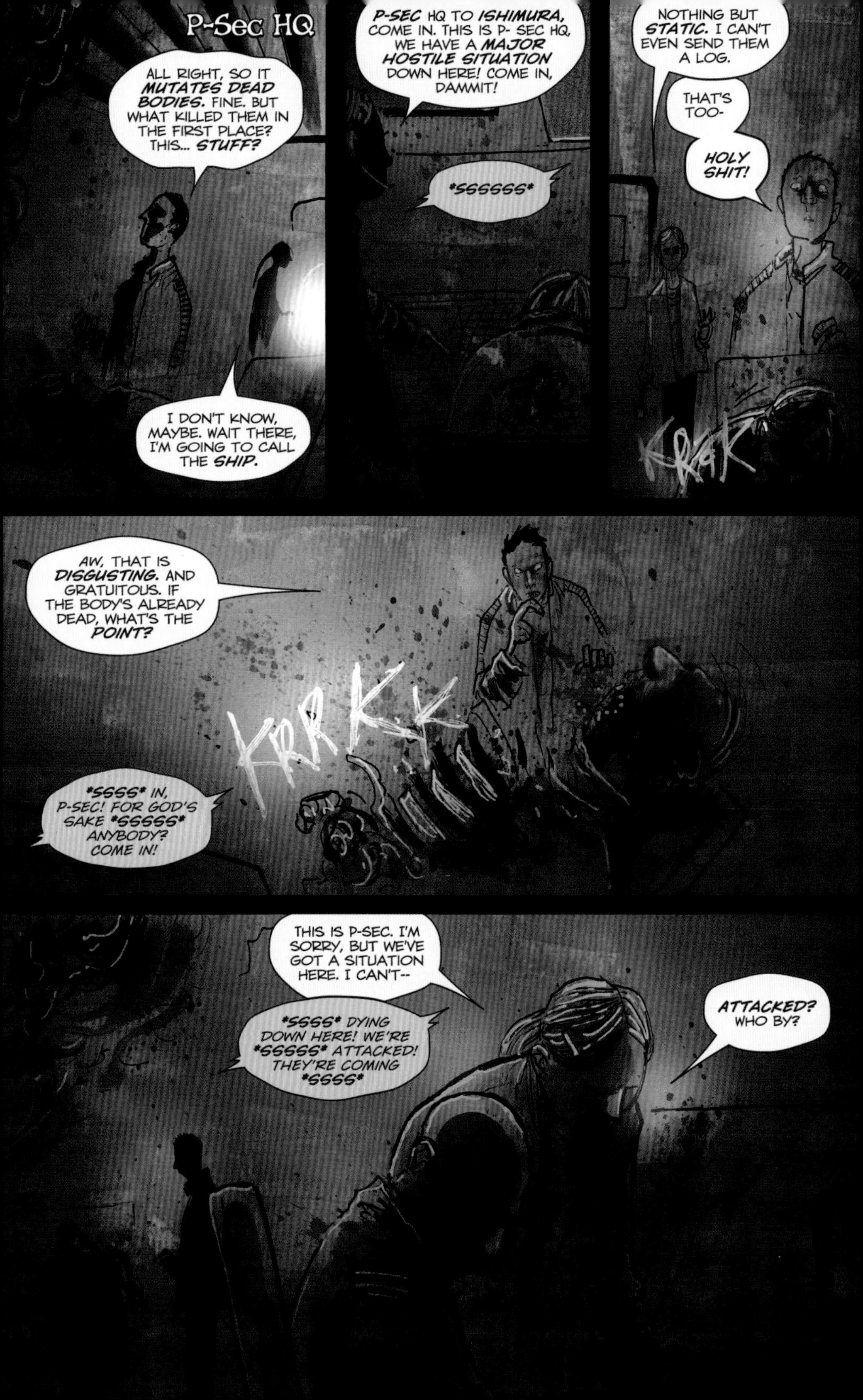
P-Sec HQ
ALL RIGHT, SO IT MUTATES DEAD BODIES. FINE. BUT WHAT KILLED THEM IN THE FIRST PLACE? THIS... STUFF?
I DON'T KNOW, MAYBE. WAIT THERE, I'M GOING TO CALL THE SHIP.
P-SEC HQ TO ISHIMURA, COME IN. THIS IS P- SEC HQ, WE HAVE A MAJOR HOSTILE SITUATION DOWN HERE! COME IN, DAMMIT!
SSSSSS
NOTHING BUT STATIC. I CAN'T EVEN SEND THEM A LOG.
THAT'S TOO-
HOLY SHIT!
KRAK
AW, THAT IS DISGUSTING. AND GRATUITOUS. IF THE BODY'S ALREADY DEAD, WHAT'S THE POINT?
KRRKK
SSSS IN, P-SEC! FOR GOD'S SAKE *SSSSS* ANYBODY? COME IN!
THIS IS P-SEC. I'M SORRY, BUT WE'VE GOT A SITUATION HERE. I CAN'T--
SSSS DYING DOWN HERE! WE'RE *SSSSS* ATTACKED! THEY'RE COMING *SSSS*
ATTACKED? WHO BY?

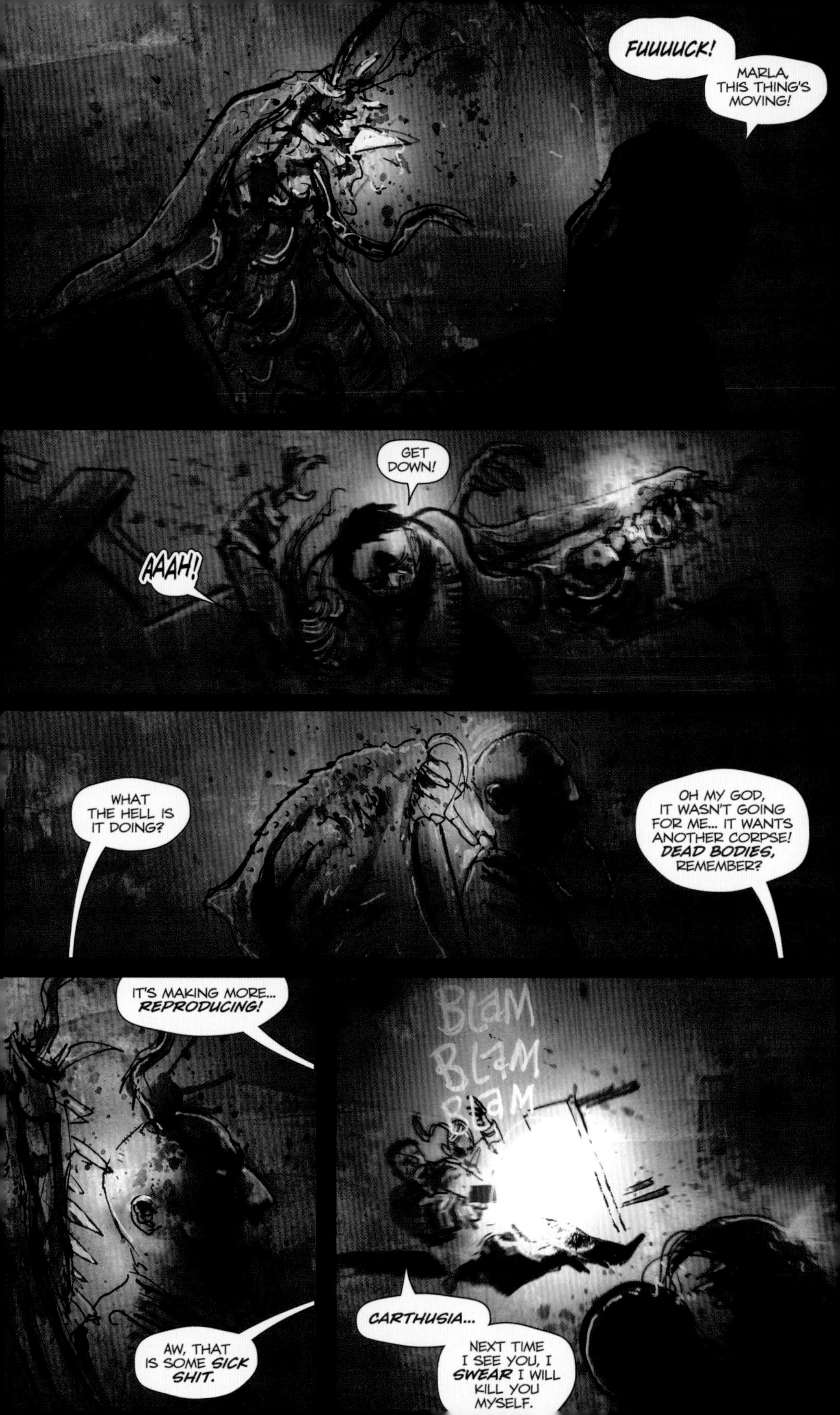
FUUUUCK!
MARLA, THIS THING'S MOVING!
GET DOWN!
AAAH!
WHAT THE HELL IS IT DOING?
OH MY GOD, IT WASN'T GOING FOR ME... IT WANTS ANOTHER CORPSE! DEAD BODIES, REMEMBER?
IT'S MAKING MORE... REPRODUCING!
AW, THAT IS SOME SICK SHIT.
BLAM BLAM BLAM
CARTHUSIA...
NEXT TIME I SEE YOU, I SWEAR I WILL KILL YOU MYSELF.

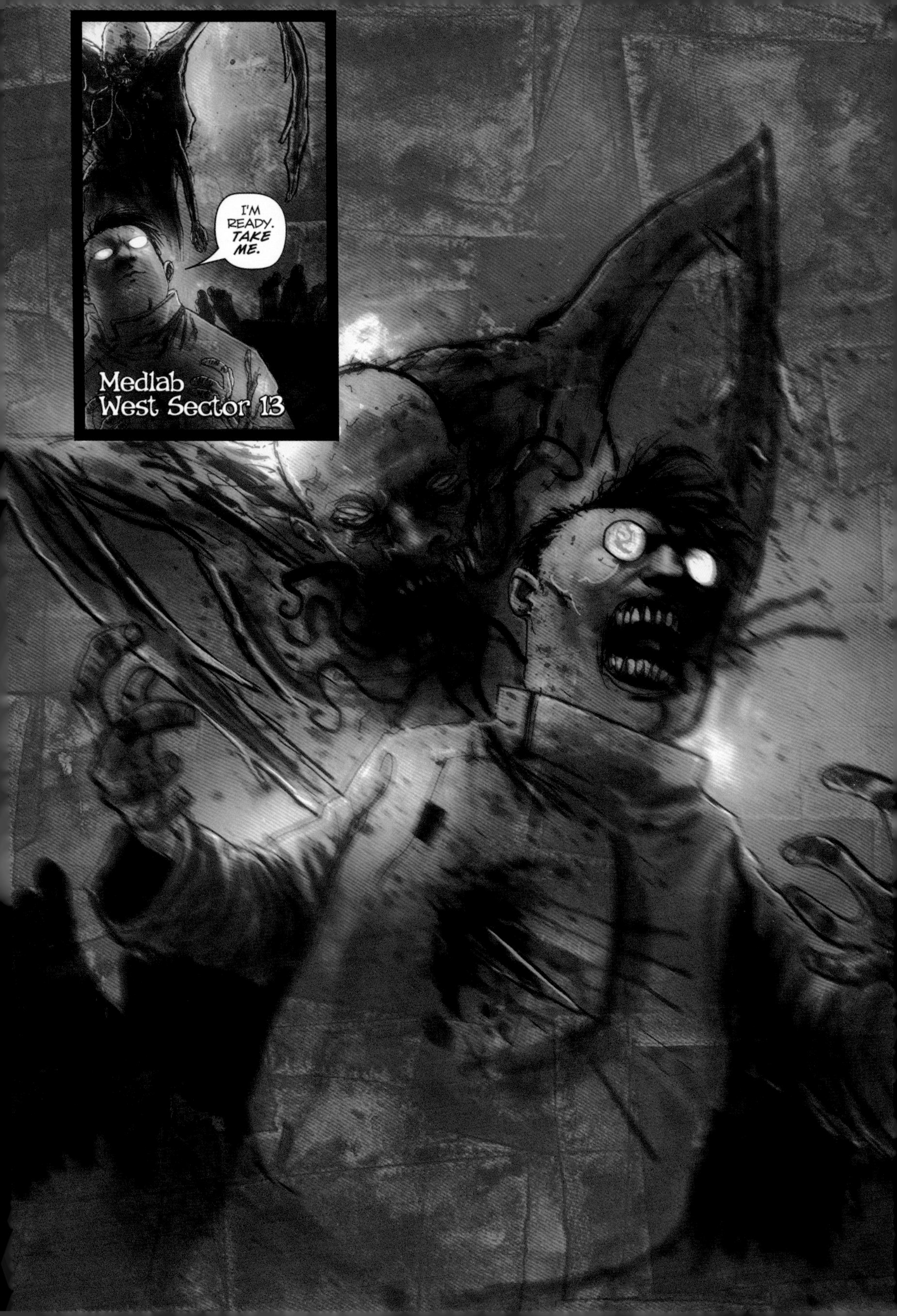
I'M READY. TAKE ME.
Medlab West Sector 13

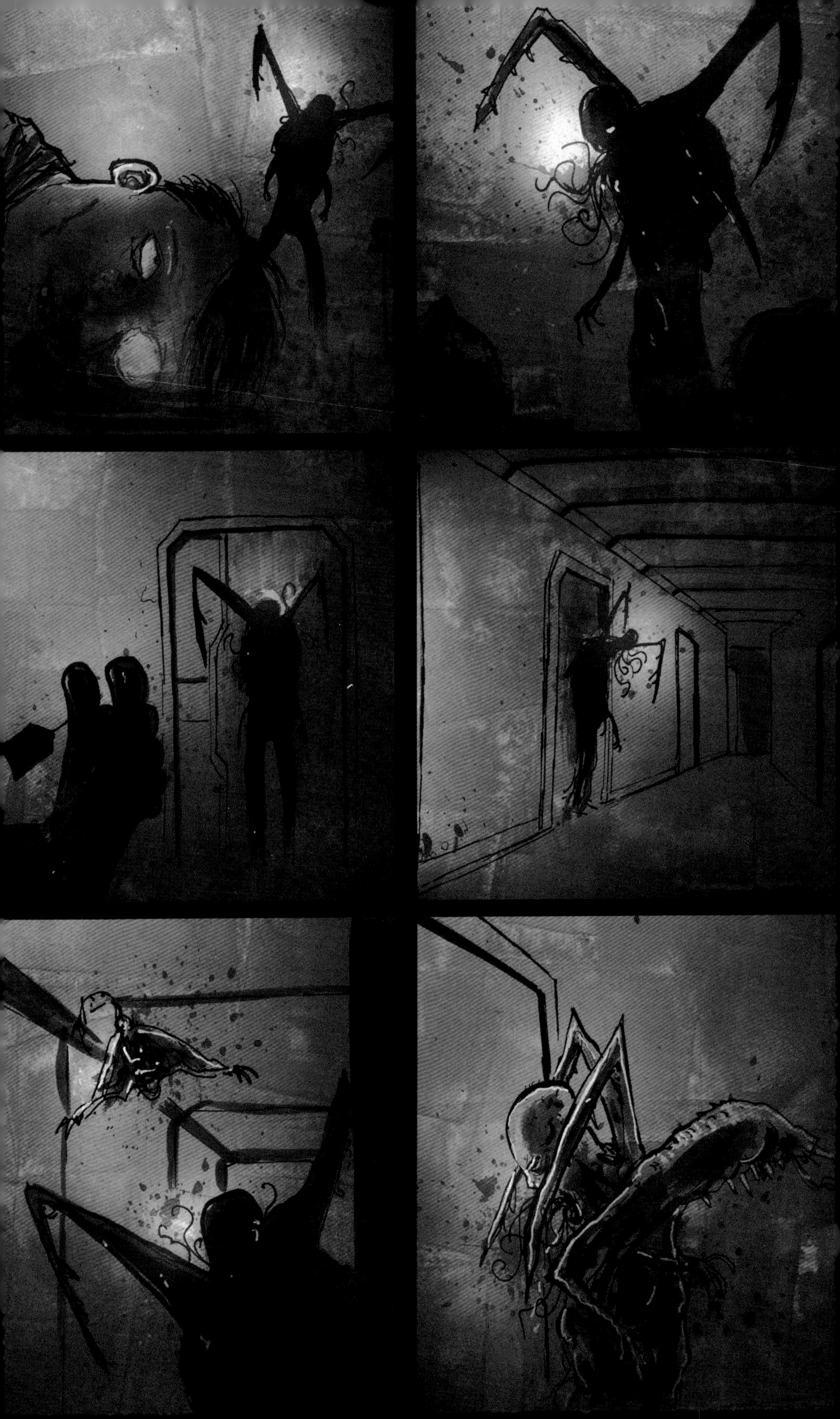

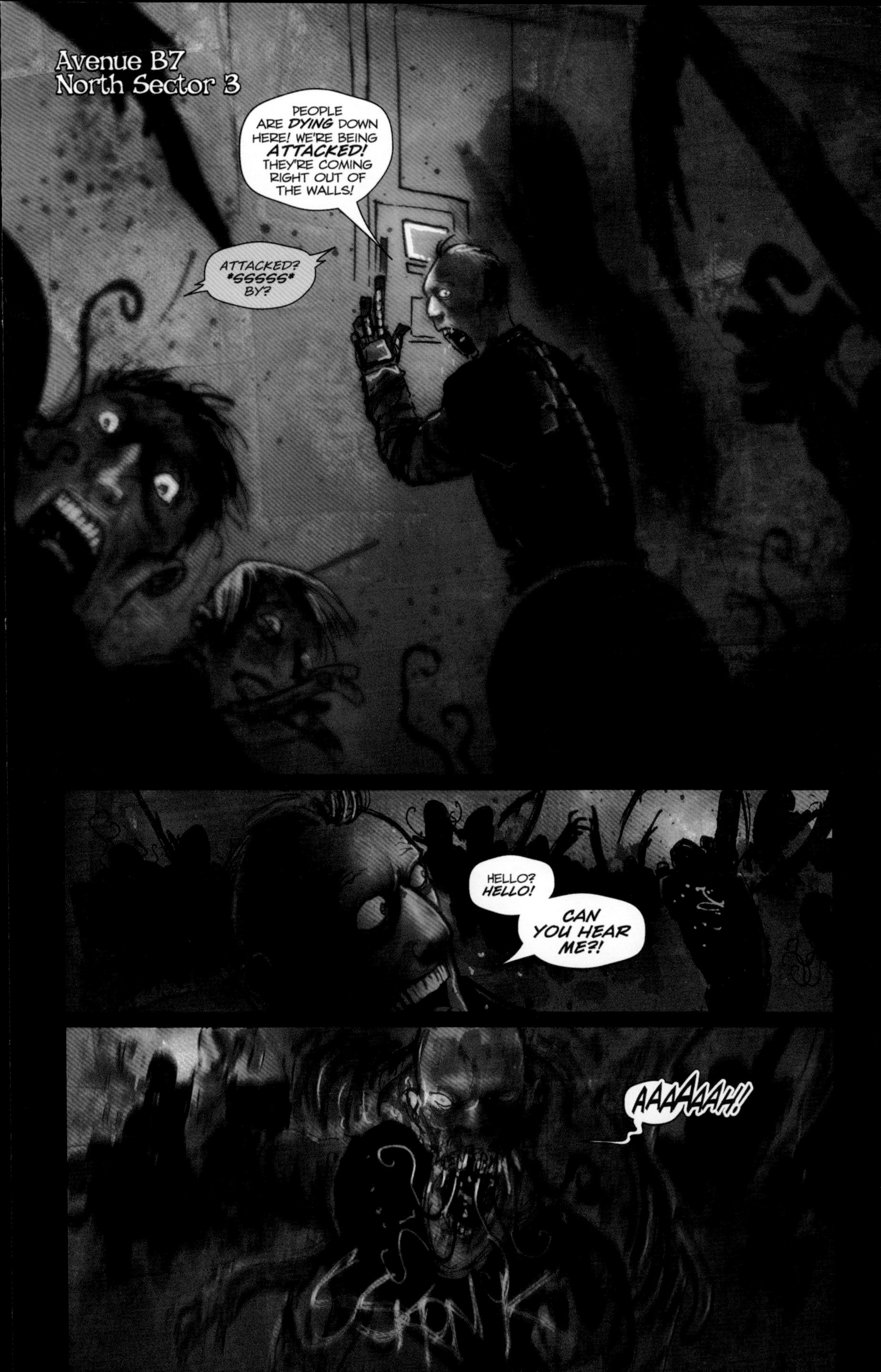
Avenue B7
North Sector 3
PEOPLE ARE DYING DOWN HERE! WE'RE BEING ATTACKED! THEY'RE COMING RIGHT OUT OF THE WALLS!
ATTACKED? *SSSSS* BY?
HELLO? HELLO!
CAN YOU HEAR ME?!
AAAAAAH!!

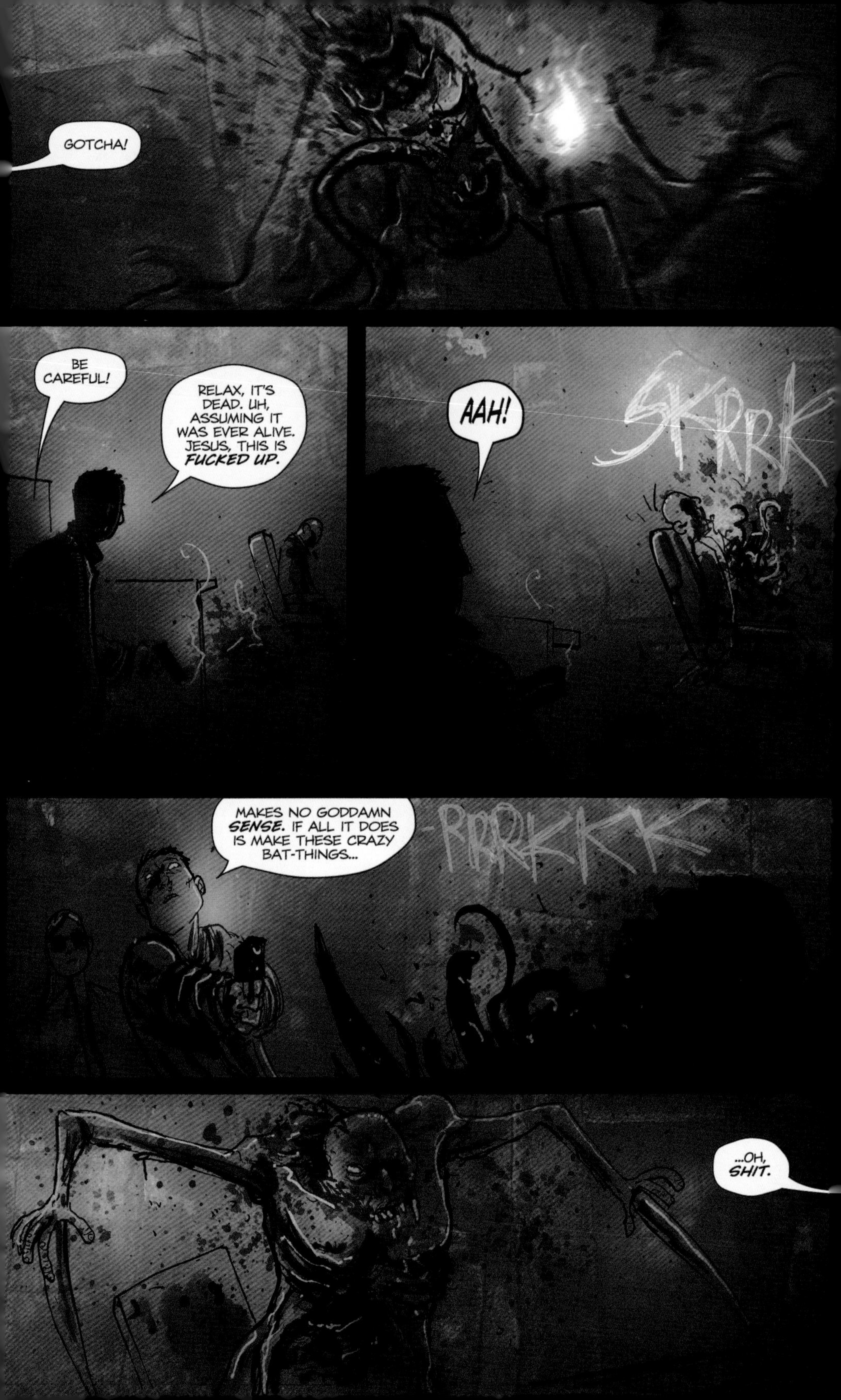
GOTCHA!
BE CAREFUL!
RELAX, IT'S DEAD. UH, ASSUMING IT WAS EVER ALIVE. JESUS, THIS IS **FUCKED UP**.
AAH!
SKRRK
MAKES NO GODDAMN **SENSE**. IF ALL IT DOES IS MAKE THESE CRAZY BAT-THINGS...
-RRRKKK
...OH, **SHIT**.

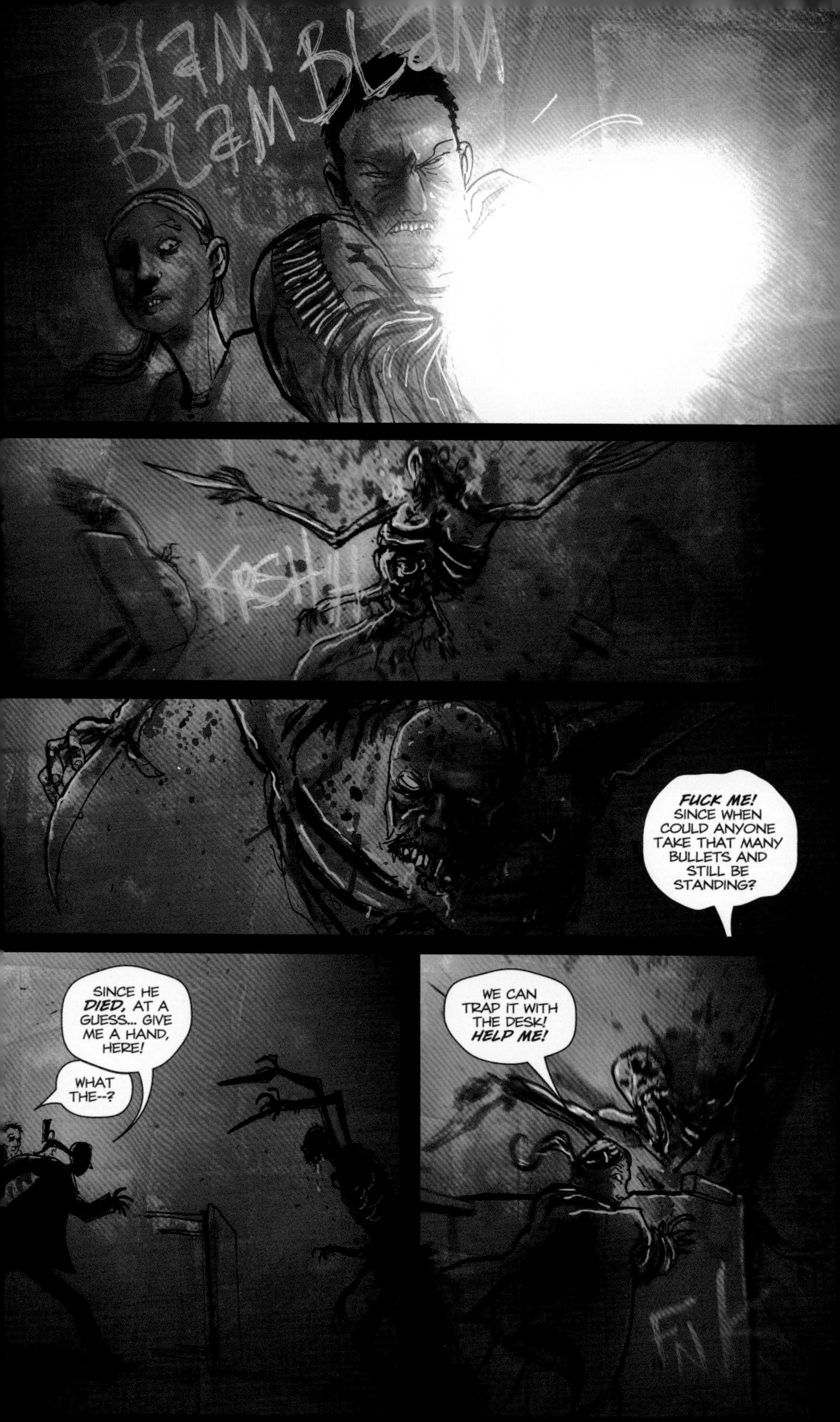
BLAM BLAM
BLAM BLAM
KRSHH
FUCK ME! SINCE WHEN COULD ANYONE TAKE THAT MANY BULLETS AND STILL BE STANDING?
SINCE HE DIED, AT A GUESS... GIVE ME A HAND, HERE!
WHAT THE--?
WE CAN TRAP IT WITH THE DESK! HELP ME!

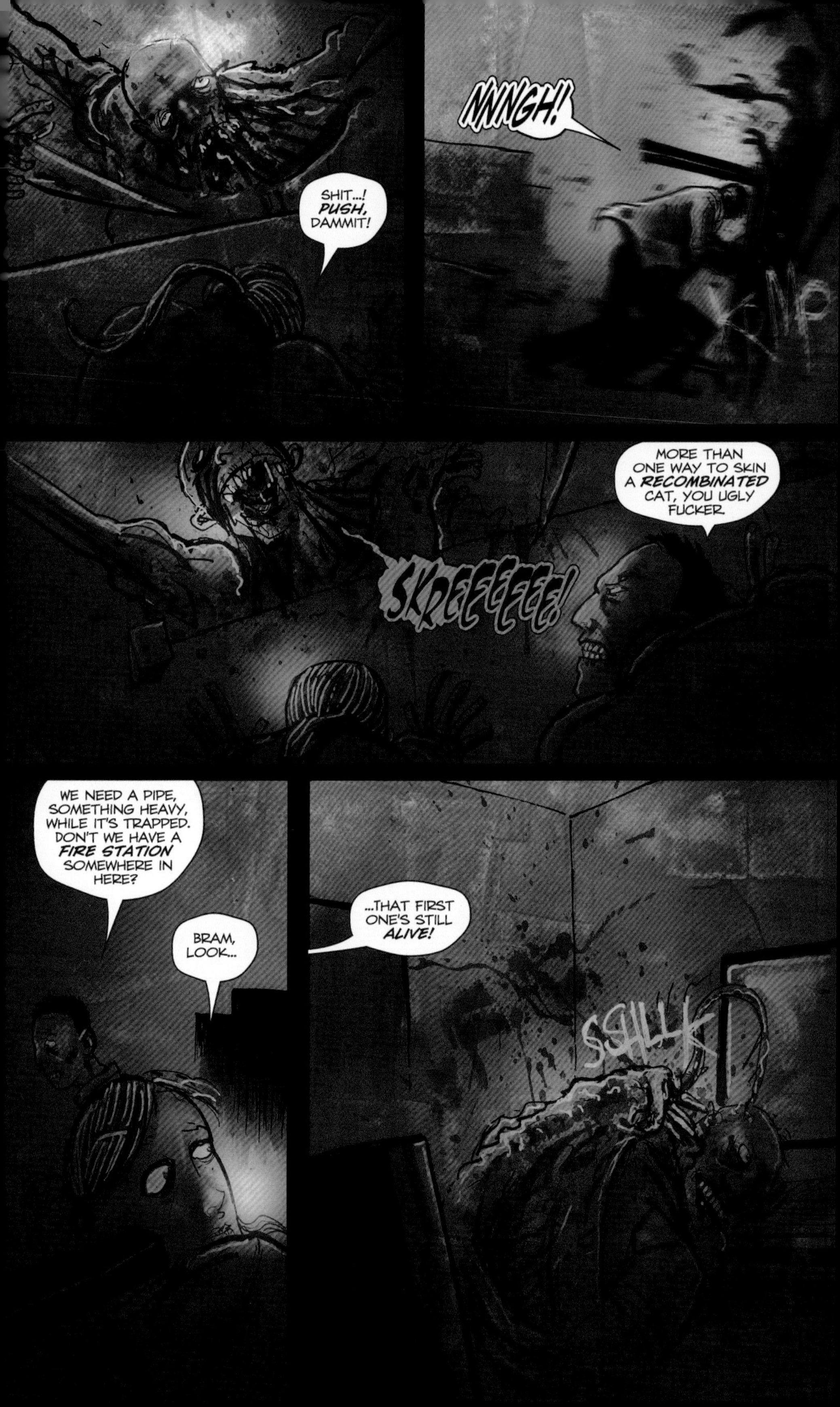
SHIT...! PUSH, DAMMIT!
NNNGH!
MORE THAN ONE WAY TO SKIN A RECOMBINATED CAT, YOU UGLY FUCKER.
SKREEEEEE!
WE NEED A PIPE, SOMETHING HEAVY, WHILE IT'S TRAPPED. DON'T WE HAVE A FIRE STATION SOMEWHERE IN HERE?
BRAM, LOOK...
...THAT FIRST ONE'S STILL ALIVE!
SSHLLK

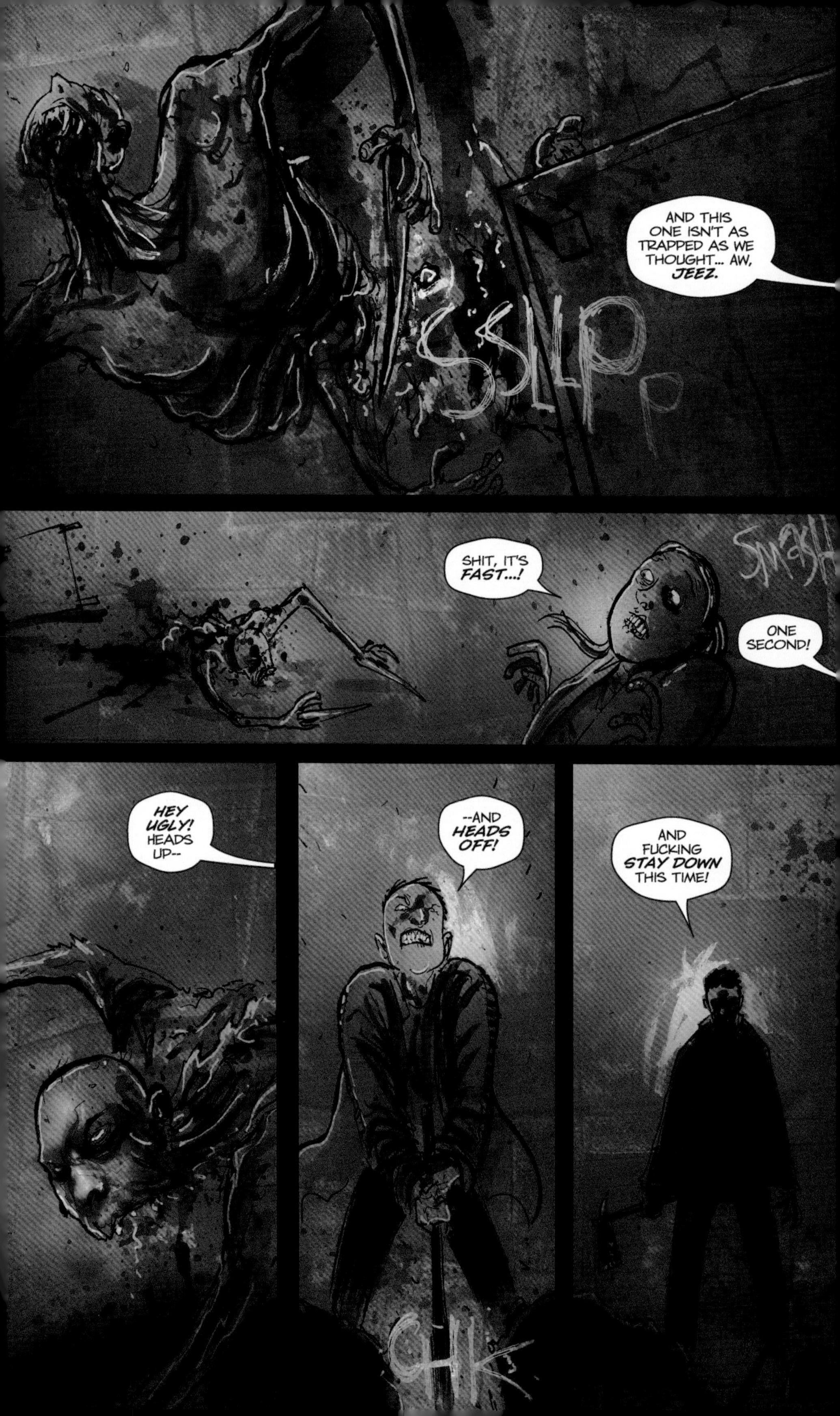
AND THIS ONE ISN'T AS TRAPPED AS WE THOUGHT... AW, JEEZ.
SSLLPP
SHIT, IT'S FAST...!
SMASH
ONE SECOND!
HEY UGLY! HEADS UP--
--AND HEADS OFF!
CHK
AND FUCKING STAY DOWN THIS TIME!

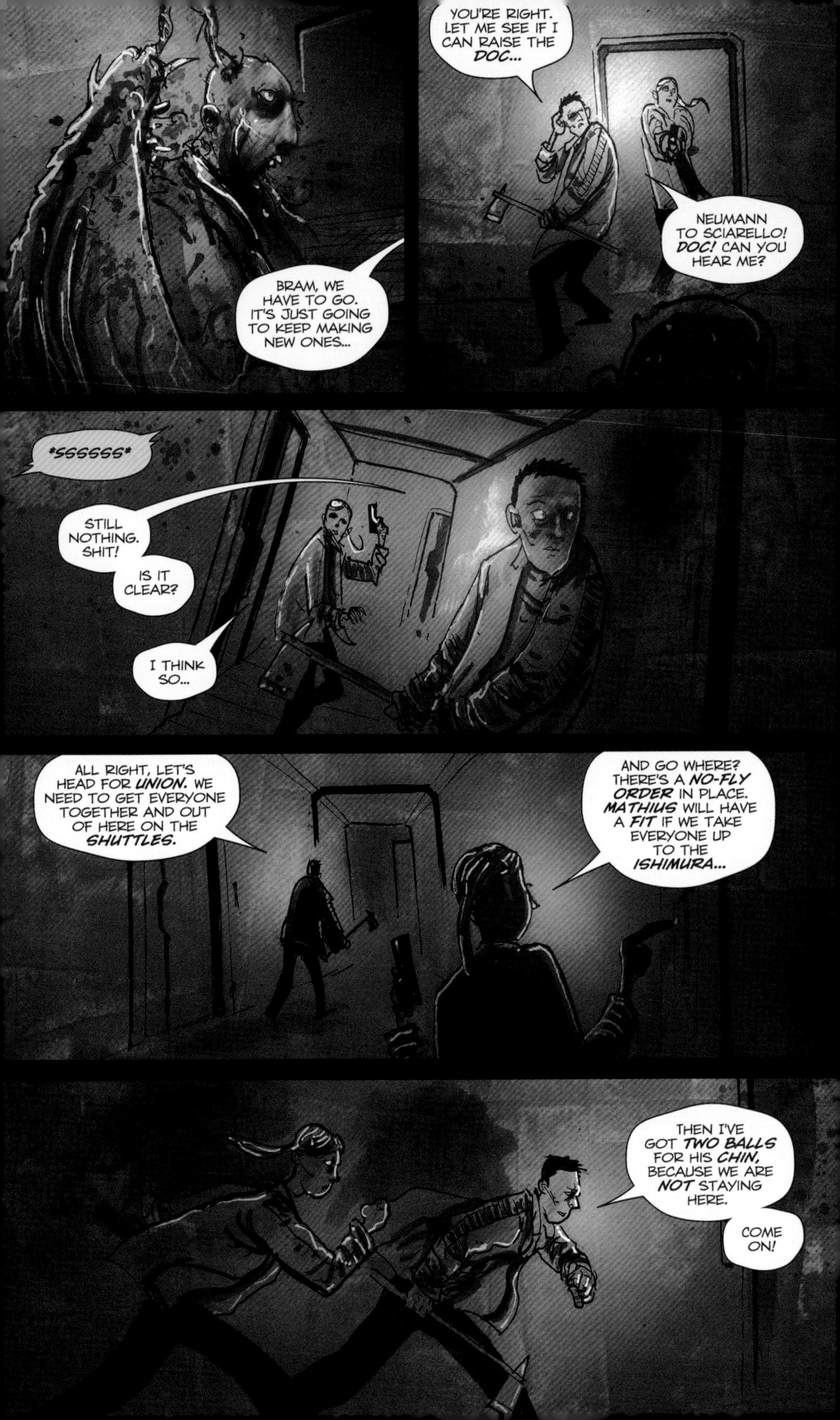
BRAM, WE HAVE TO GO. IT'S JUST GOING TO KEEP MAKING NEW ONES...
YOU'RE RIGHT. LET ME SEE IF I CAN RAISE THE DOC...
NEUMANN TO SCIARELLO! DOC! CAN YOU HEAR ME?
SSSSSS
STILL NOTHING. SHIT!
IS IT CLEAR?
I THINK SO...
ALL RIGHT, LET'S HEAD FOR UNION. WE NEED TO GET EVERYONE TOGETHER AND OUT OF HERE ON THE SHUTTLES.
AND GO WHERE? THERE'S A NO-FLY ORDER IN PLACE. MATHIUS WILL HAVE A FIT IF WE TAKE EVERYONE UP TO THE ISHIMURA...
THEN I'VE GOT TWO BALLS FOR HIS CHIN, BECAUSE WE ARE NOT STAYING HERE.
COME ON!

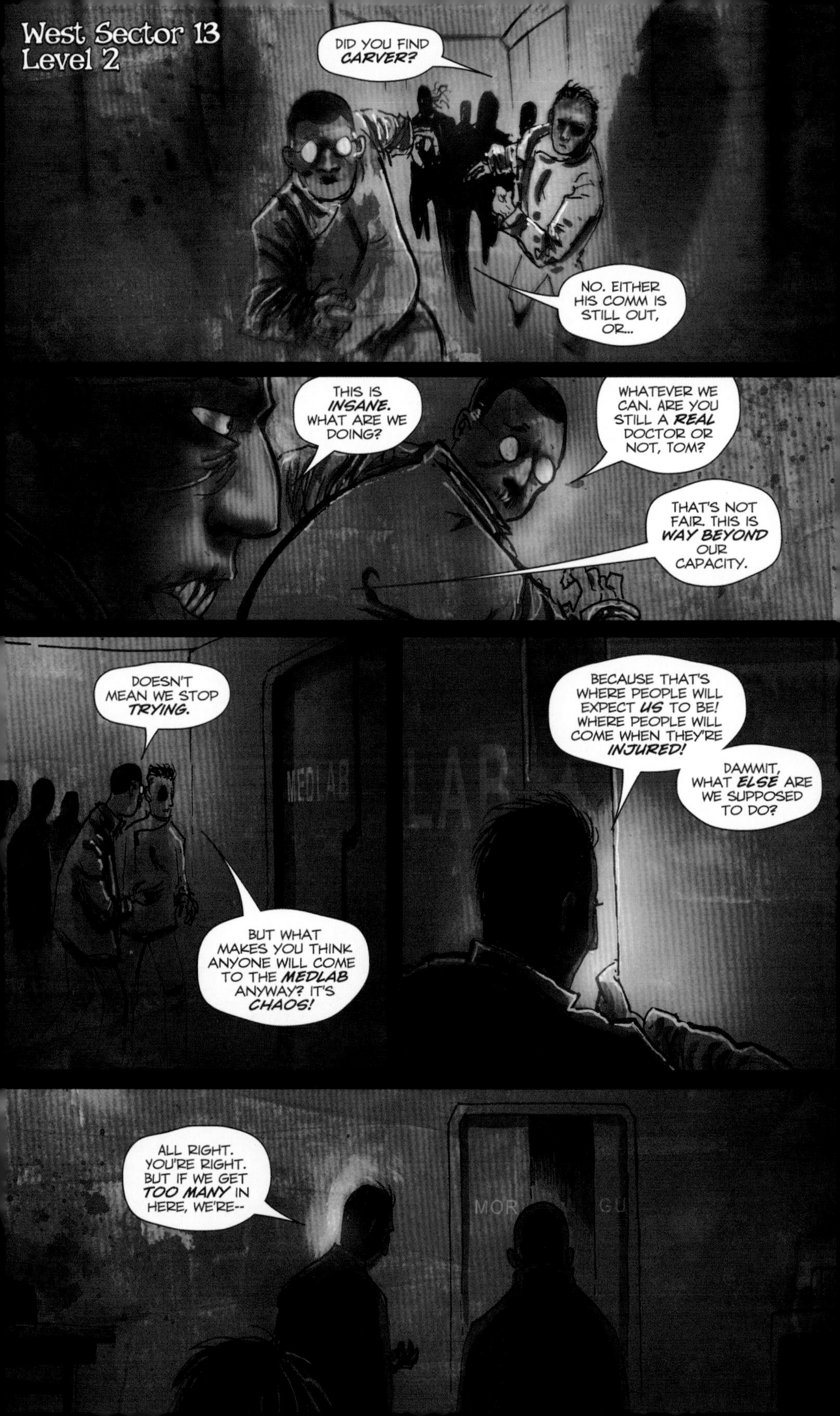
West Sector 13
Level 2
DID YOU FIND CARVER?
NO. EITHER HIS COMM IS STILL OUT, OR...
THIS IS INSANE. WHAT ARE WE DOING?
WHATEVER WE CAN. ARE YOU STILL A REAL DOCTOR OR NOT, TOM?
THAT'S NOT FAIR. THIS IS WAY BEYOND OUR CAPACITY.
DOESN'T MEAN WE STOP TRYING.
MEDLAB
BUT WHAT MAKES YOU THINK ANYONE WILL COME TO THE MEDLAB ANYWAY? IT'S CHAOS!
BECAUSE THAT'S WHERE PEOPLE WILL EXPECT US TO BE! WHERE PEOPLE WILL COME WHEN THEY'RE INJURED!
DAMMIT, WHAT ELSE ARE WE SUPPOSED TO DO?
ALL RIGHT. YOU'RE RIGHT. BUT IF WE GET TOO MANY IN HERE, WE'RE--

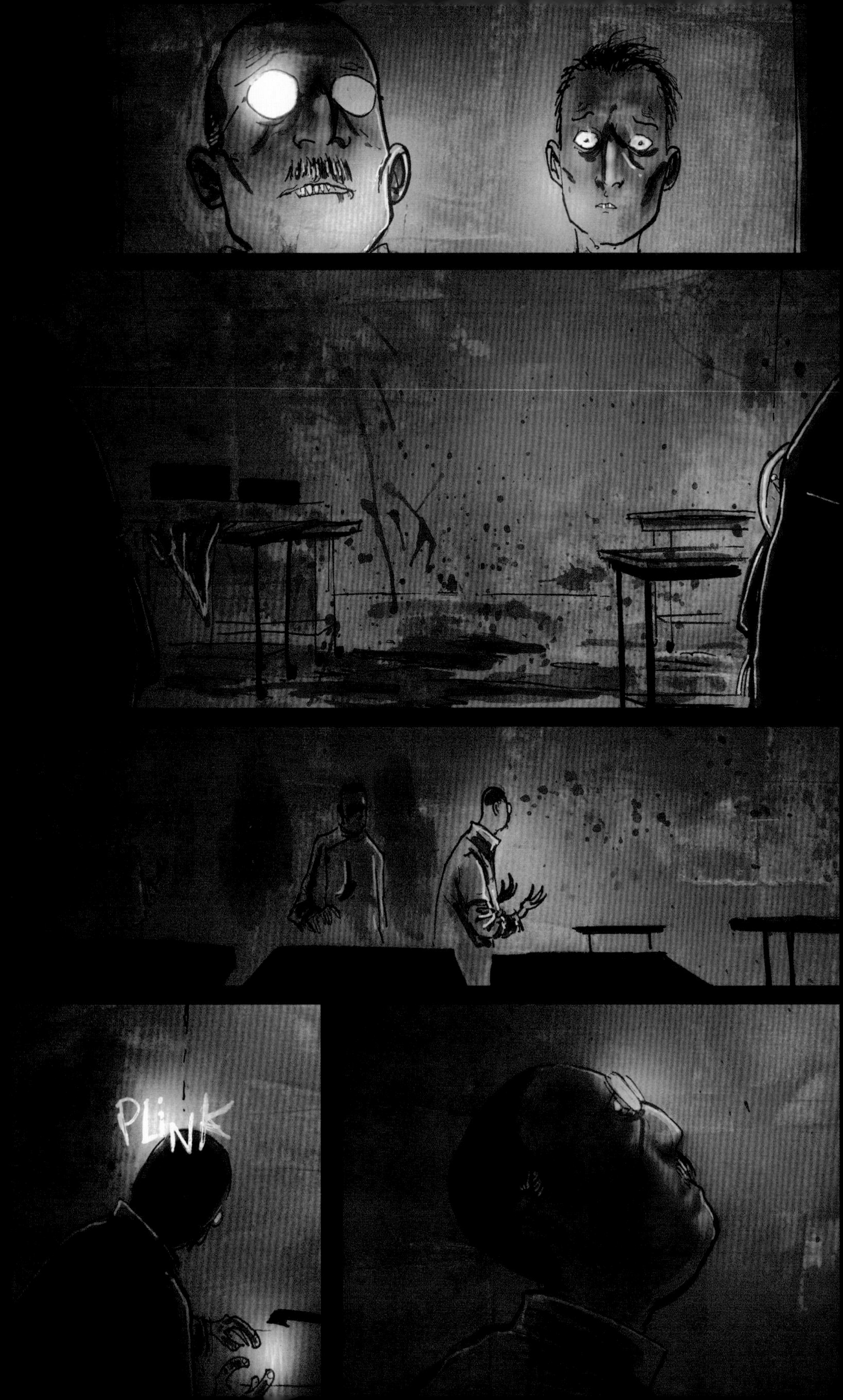
PLINK

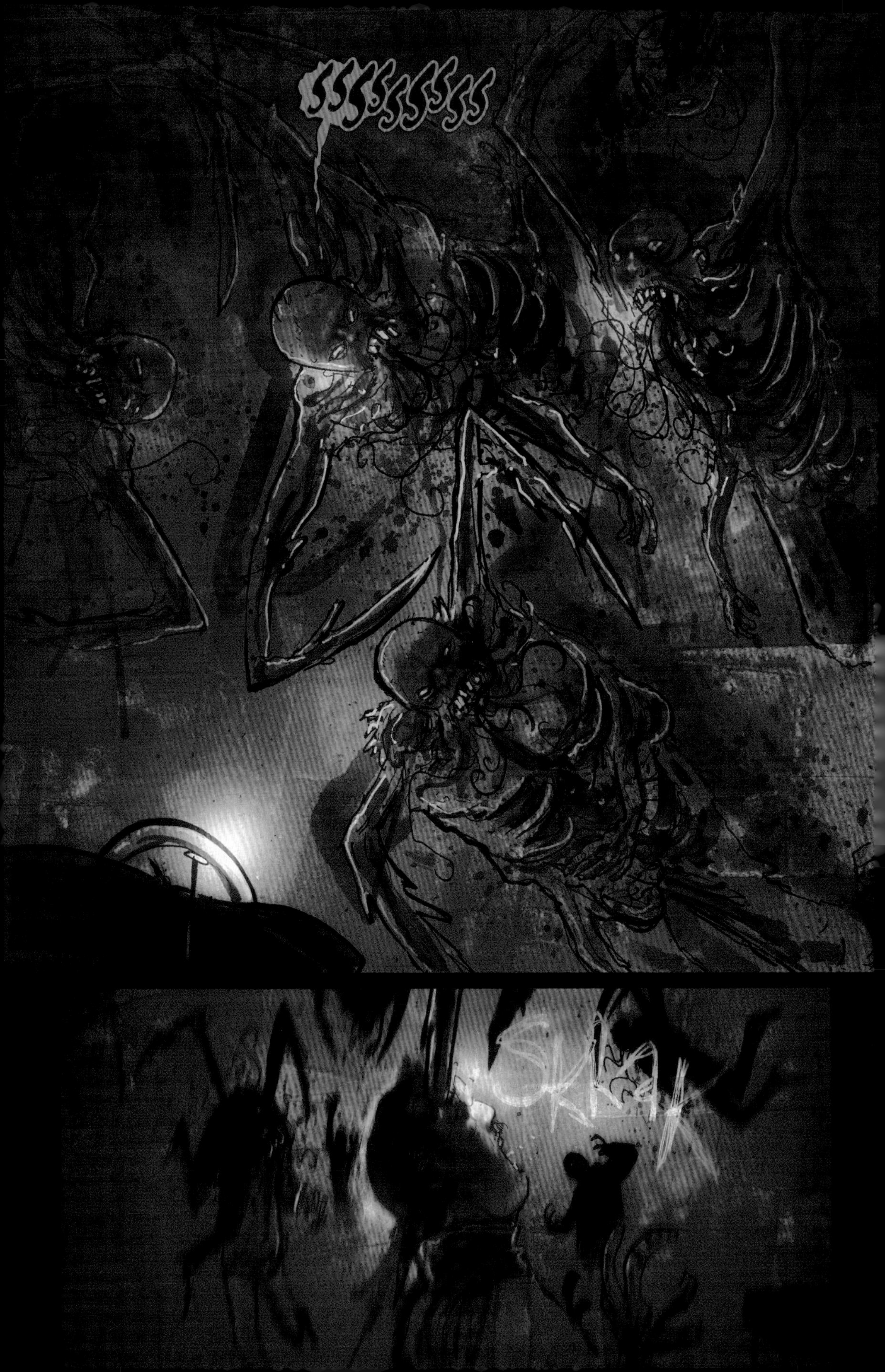
SSSSSSSSS
SKLAK

Union Square

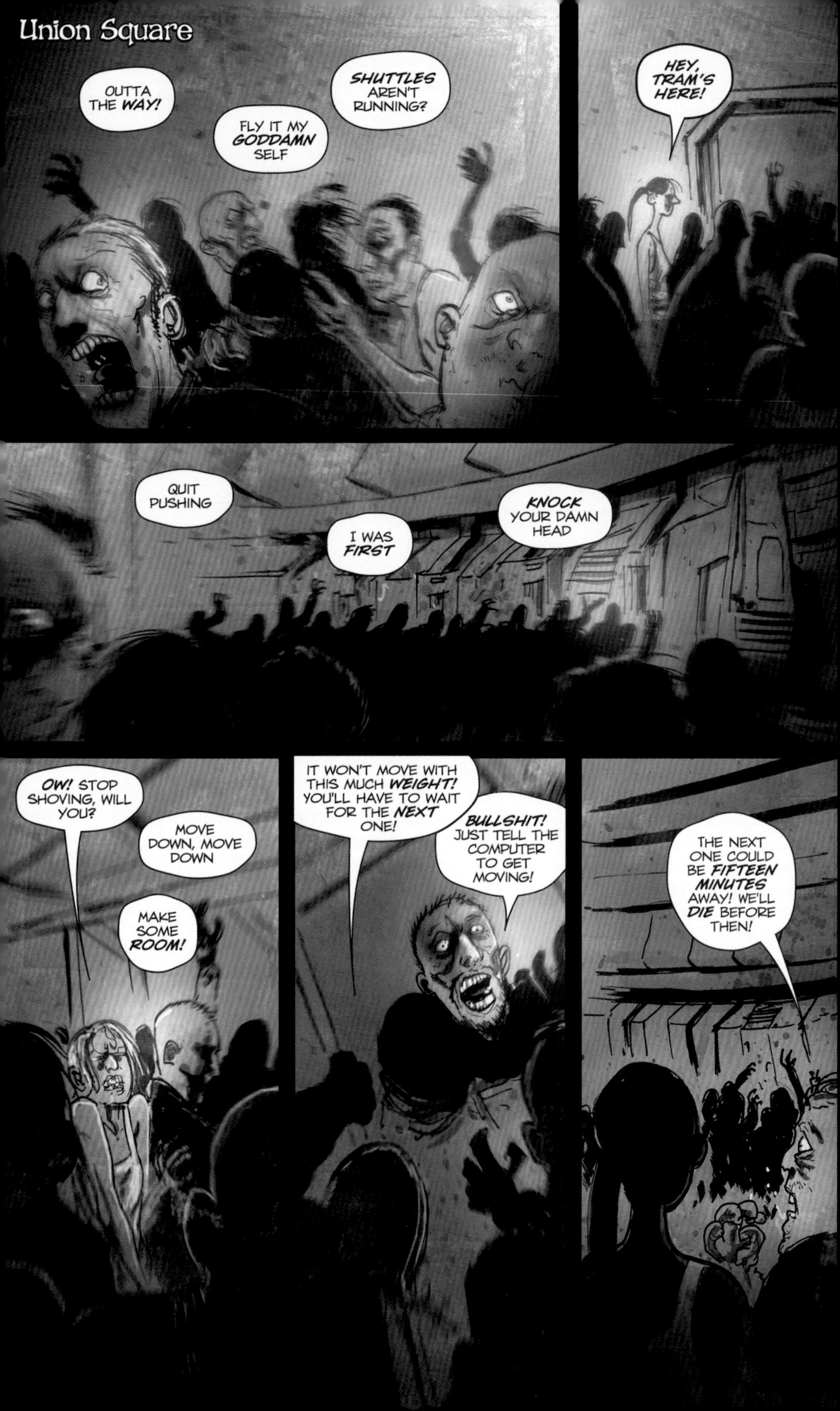
OUTTA THE WAY!
FLY IT MY GODDAMN SELF
SHUTTLES AREN'T RUNNING?
HEY, TRAM'S HERE!
QUIT PUSHING
I WAS FIRST
KNOCK YOUR DAMN HEAD
OW! STOP SHOVING, WILL YOU?
MOVE DOWN, MOVE DOWN
MAKE SOME ROOM!
IT WON'T MOVE WITH THIS MUCH WEIGHT! YOU'LL HAVE TO WAIT FOR THE NEXT ONE!
BULLSHIT! JUST TELL THE COMPUTER TO GET MOVING!
THE NEXT ONE COULD BE FIFTEEN MINUTES AWAY! WE'LL DIE BEFORE THEN!

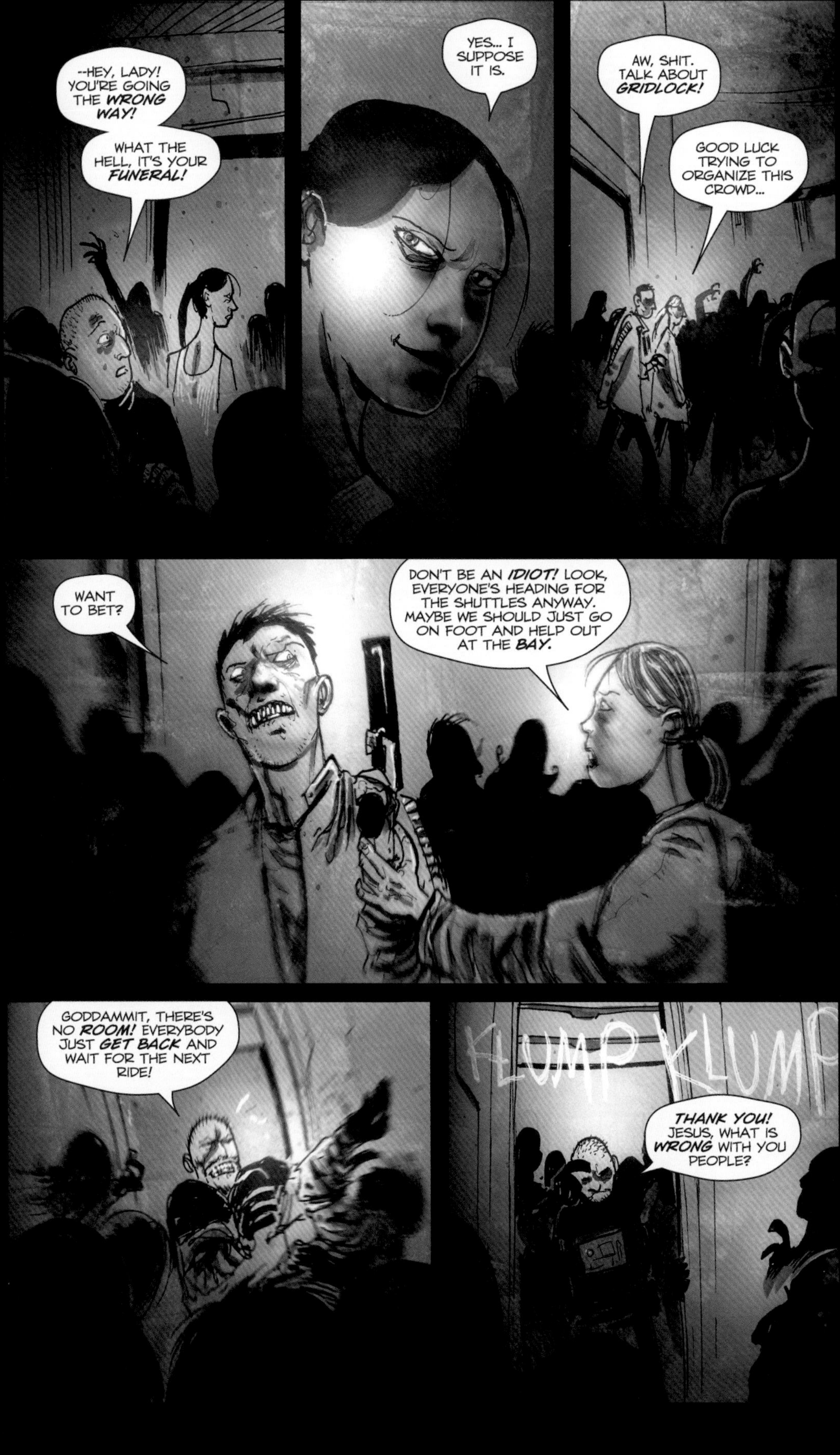
--HEY, LADY! YOU'RE GOING THE WRONG WAY!
WHAT THE HELL, IT'S YOUR FUNERAL!
YES... I SUPPOSE IT IS.
AW, SHIT. TALK ABOUT GRIDLOCK!
GOOD LUCK TRYING TO ORGANIZE THIS CROWD...
WANT TO BET?
DON'T BE AN IDIOT! LOOK, EVERYONE'S HEADING FOR THE SHUTTLES ANYWAY. MAYBE WE SHOULD JUST GO ON FOOT AND HELP OUT AT THE BAY.
GODDAMMIT, THERE'S NO ROOM! EVERYBODY JUST GET BACK AND WAIT FOR THE NEXT RIDE!
KLUMP KLUMP
THANK YOU! JESUS, WHAT IS WRONG WITH YOU PEOPLE?

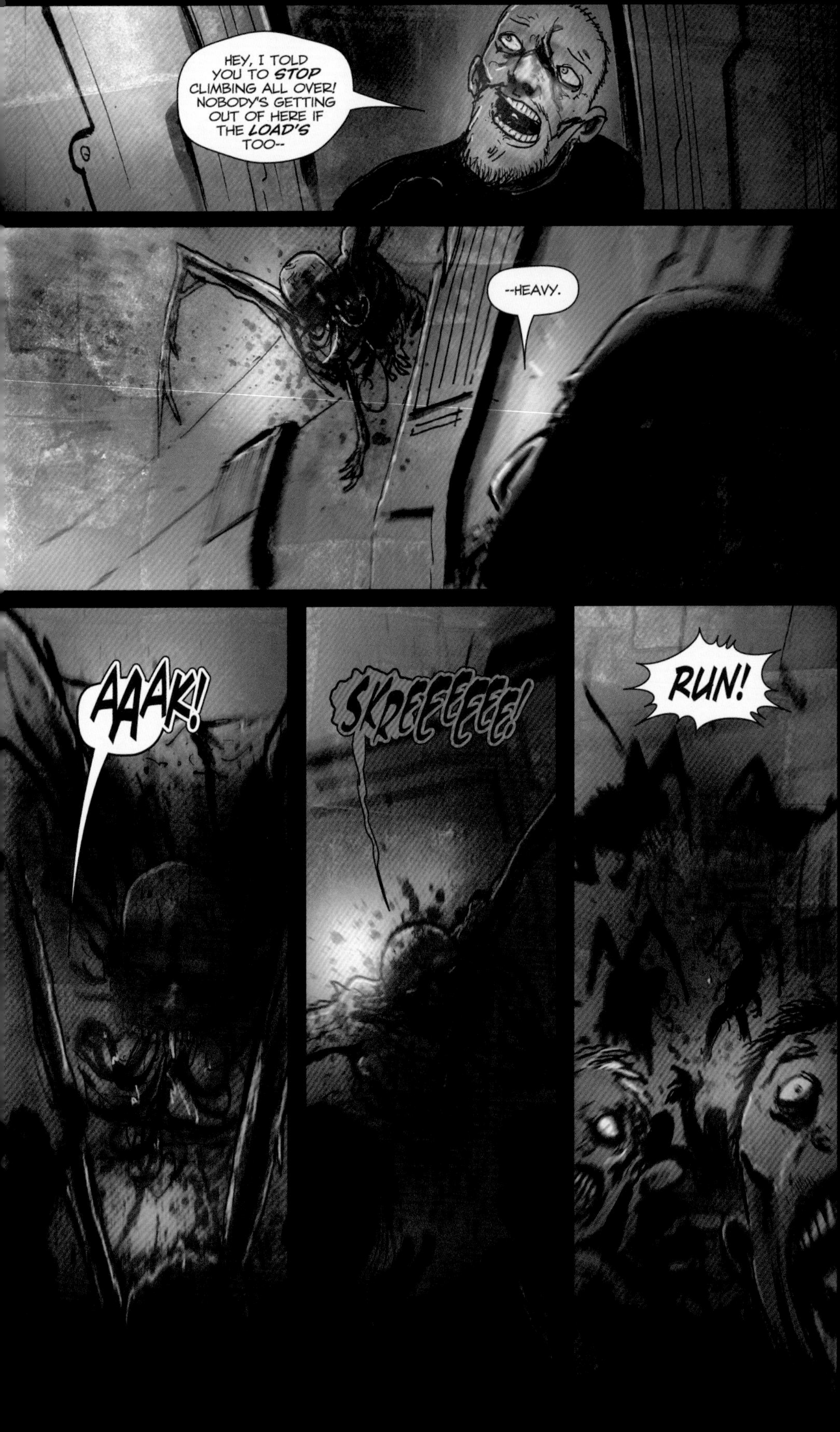
HEY, I TOLD YOU TO STOP CLIMBING ALL OVER! NOBODY'S GETTING OUT OF HERE IF THE LOAD'S TOO--
--HEAVY.
AAAK!
SKREEEEEEE!
RUN!

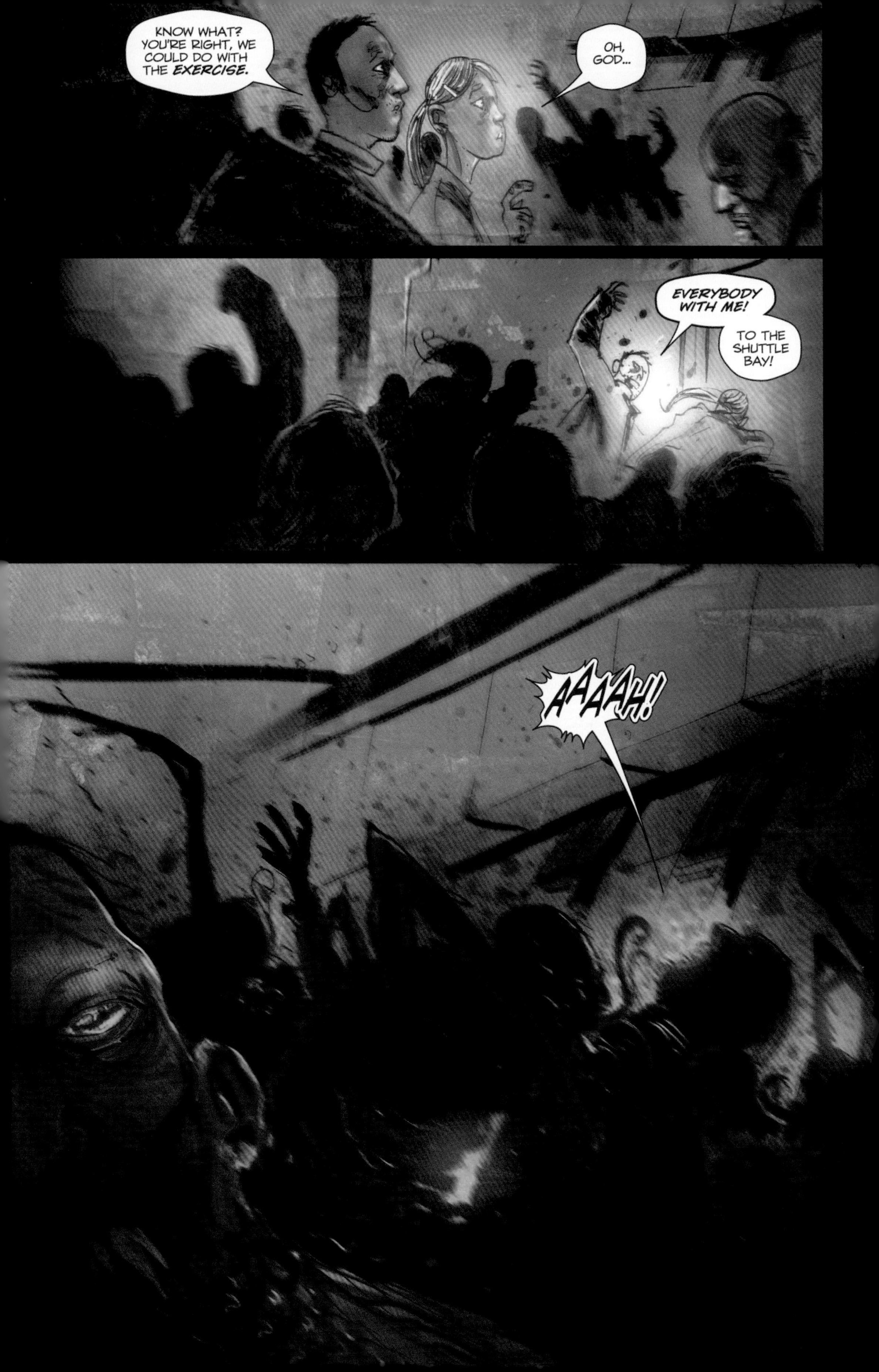
KNOW WHAT? YOU'RE RIGHT, WE COULD DO WITH THE EXERCISE.
OH, GOD...
EVERYBODY WITH ME!
TO THE SHUTTLE BAY!
AAAAH!

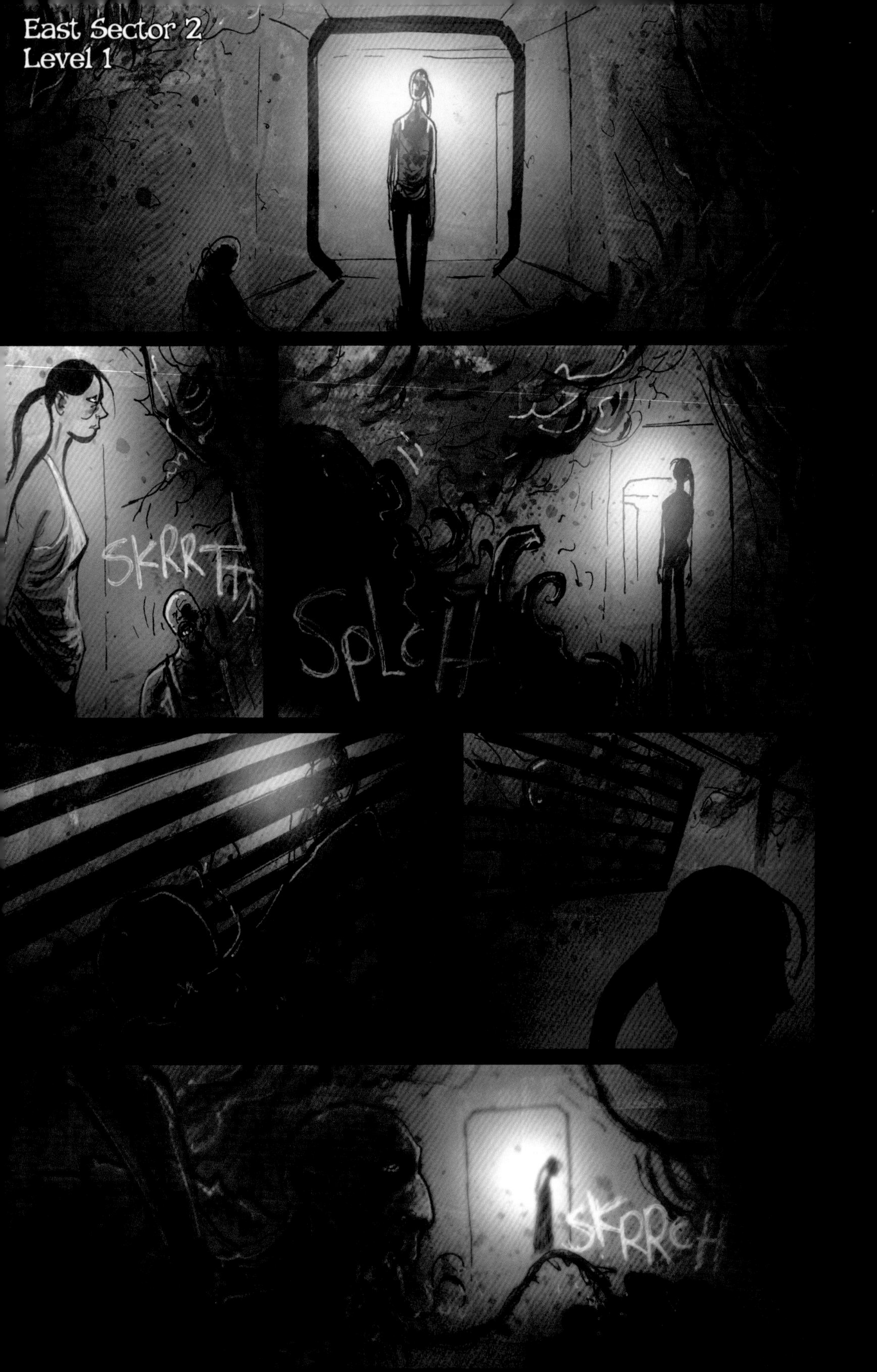
East Sector 2
Level 1
SKRRTT
SPLCH
SKRRCH

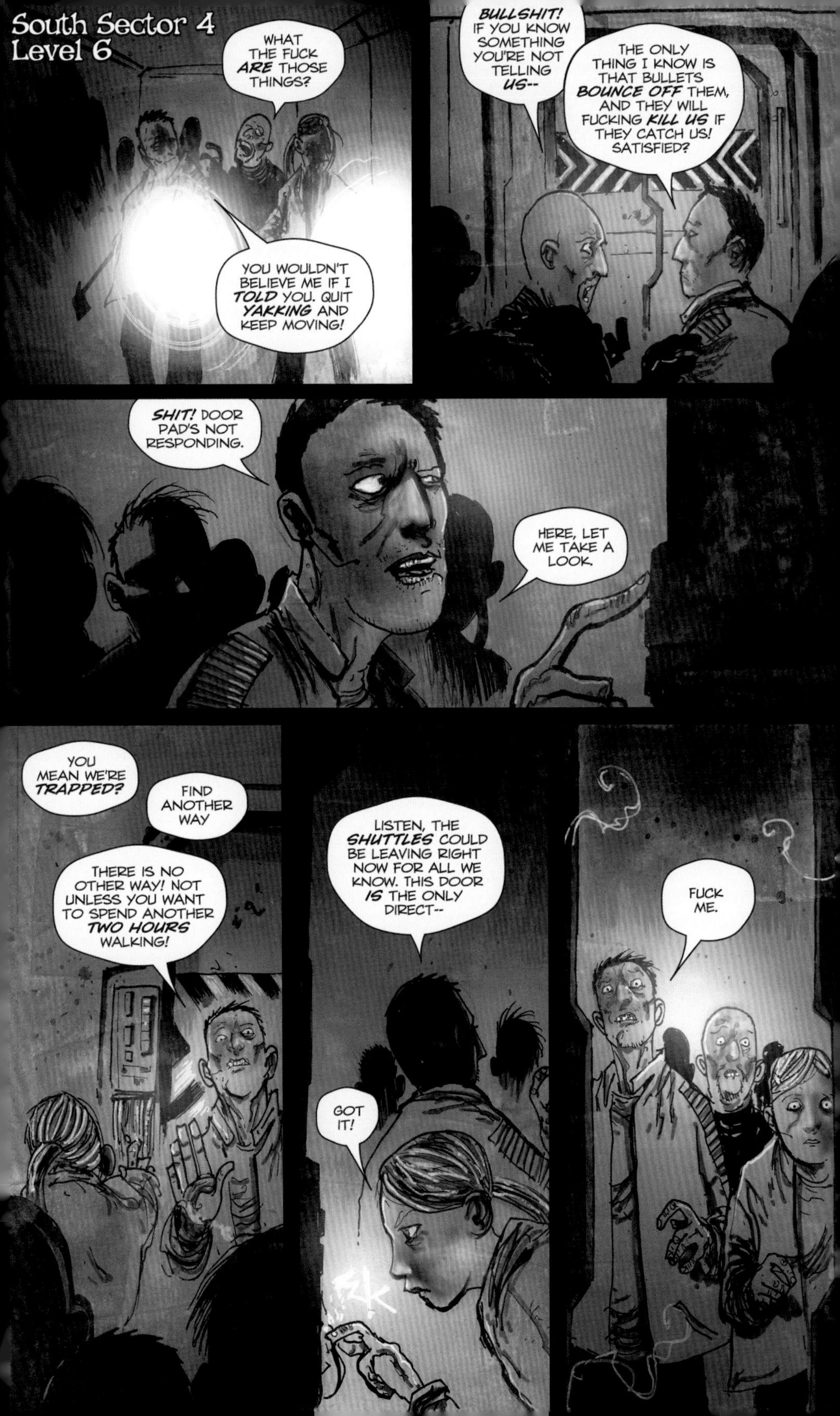
South Sector 4
Level 6
WHAT THE FUCK ARE THOSE THINGS?
YOU WOULDN'T BELIEVE ME IF I TOLD YOU. QUIT YAKKING AND KEEP MOVING!
BULLSHIT! IF YOU KNOW SOMETHING YOU'RE NOT TELLING US--
THE ONLY THING I KNOW IS THAT BULLETS BOUNCE OFF THEM, AND THEY WILL FUCKING KILL US IF THEY CATCH US! SATISFIED?
SHIT! DOOR PAD'S NOT RESPONDING.
HERE, LET ME TAKE A LOOK.
YOU MEAN WE'RE TRAPPED?
FIND ANOTHER WAY
THERE IS NO OTHER WAY! NOT UNLESS YOU WANT TO SPEND ANOTHER TWO HOURS WALKING!
LISTEN, THE SHUTTLES COULD BE LEAVING RIGHT NOW FOR ALL WE KNOW. THIS DOOR IS THE ONLY DIRECT--
GOT IT!
FZK
FUCK ME.

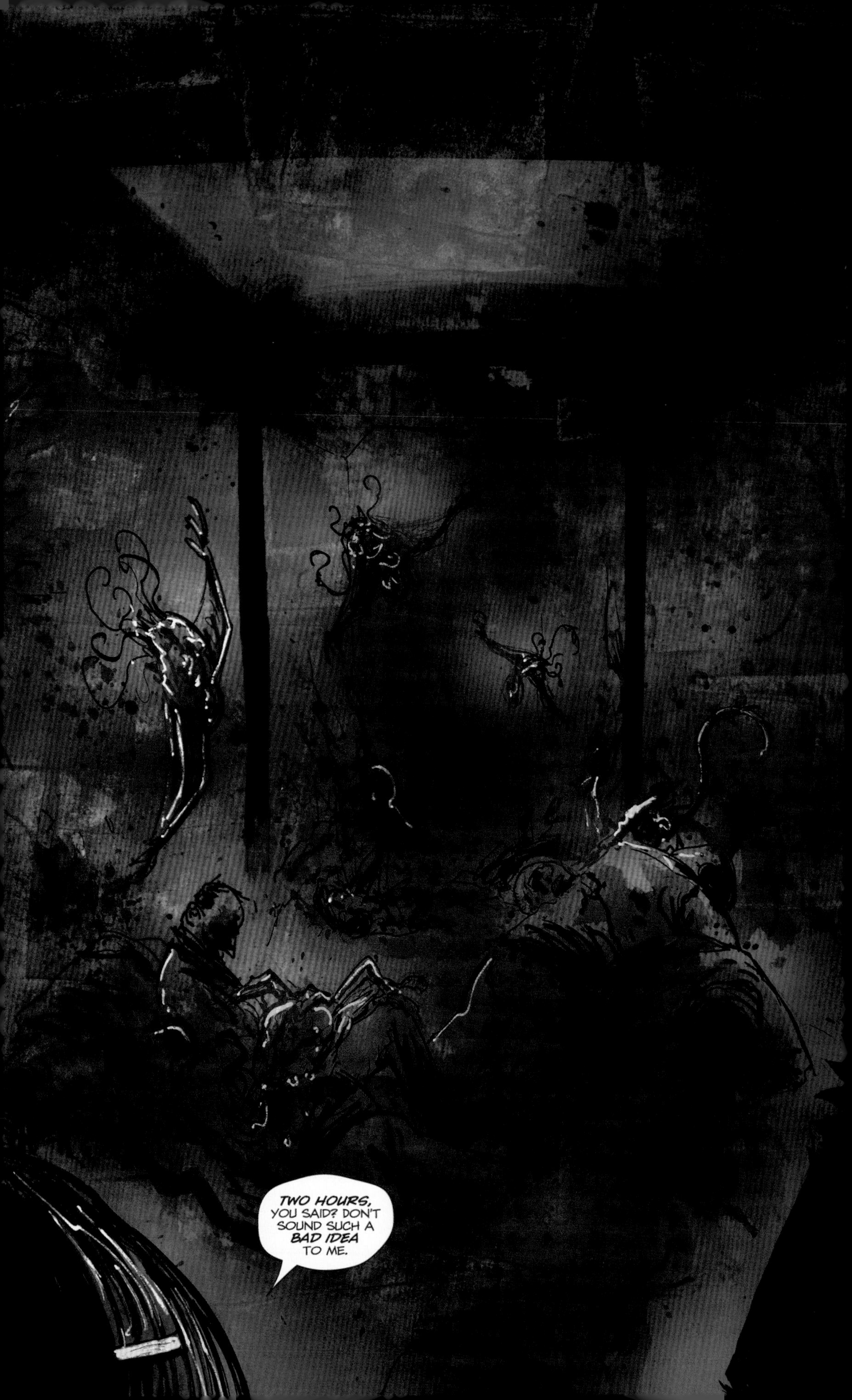
TWO HOURS, YOU SAID? DON'T SOUND SUCH A BAD IDEA TO ME.

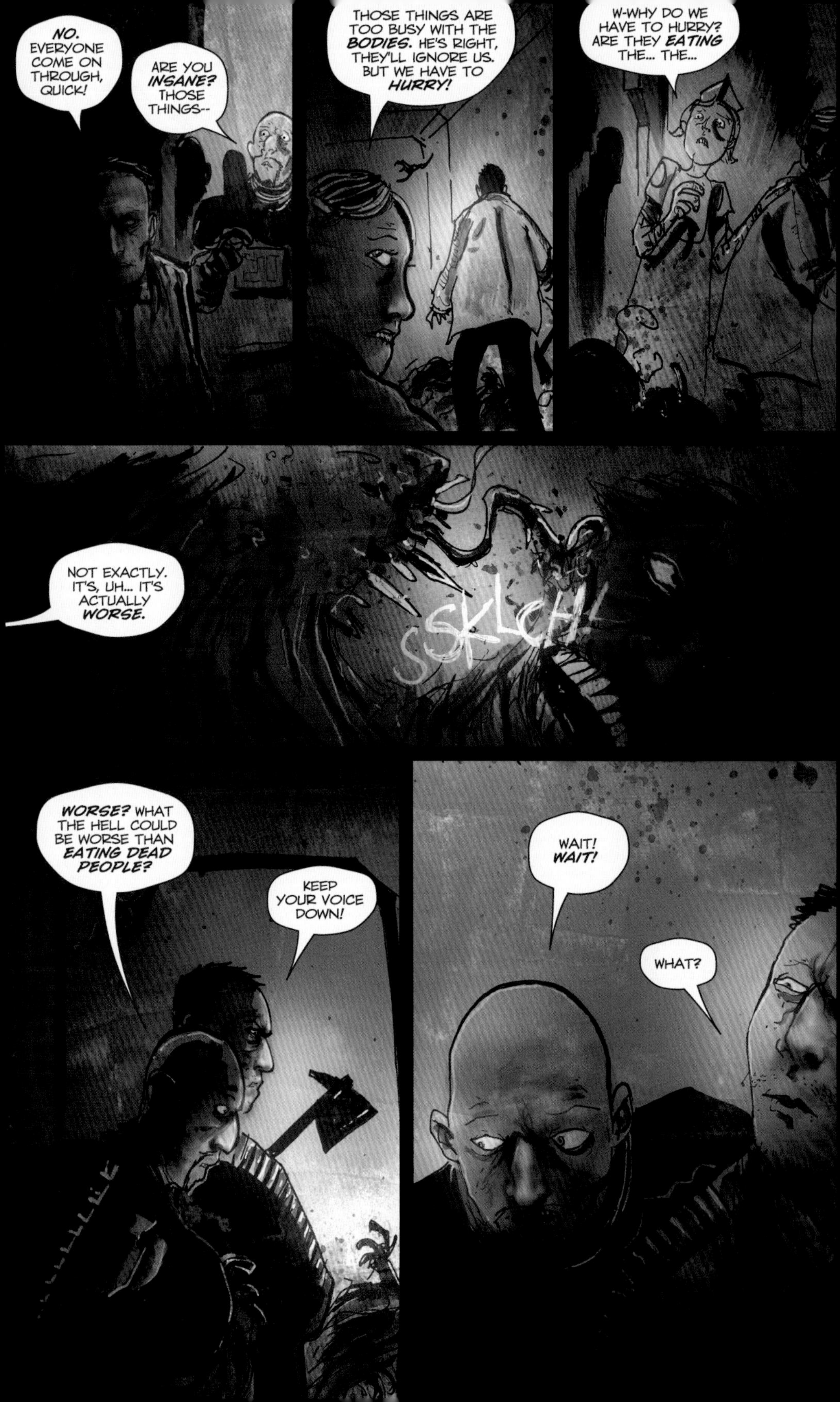
NO. EVERYONE COME ON THROUGH, QUICK!
ARE YOU INSANE? THOSE THINGS--
THOSE THINGS ARE TOO BUSY WITH THE BODIES. HE'S RIGHT, THEY'LL IGNORE US. BUT WE HAVE TO HURRY!
W-WHY DO WE HAVE TO HURRY? ARE THEY EATING THE... THE...
NOT EXACTLY. IT'S, UH... IT'S ACTUALLY WORSE.
SSKLCH!
WORSE? WHAT THE HELL COULD BE WORSE THAN EATING DEAD PEOPLE?
KEEP YOUR VOICE DOWN!
WAIT! WAIT!
WHAT?

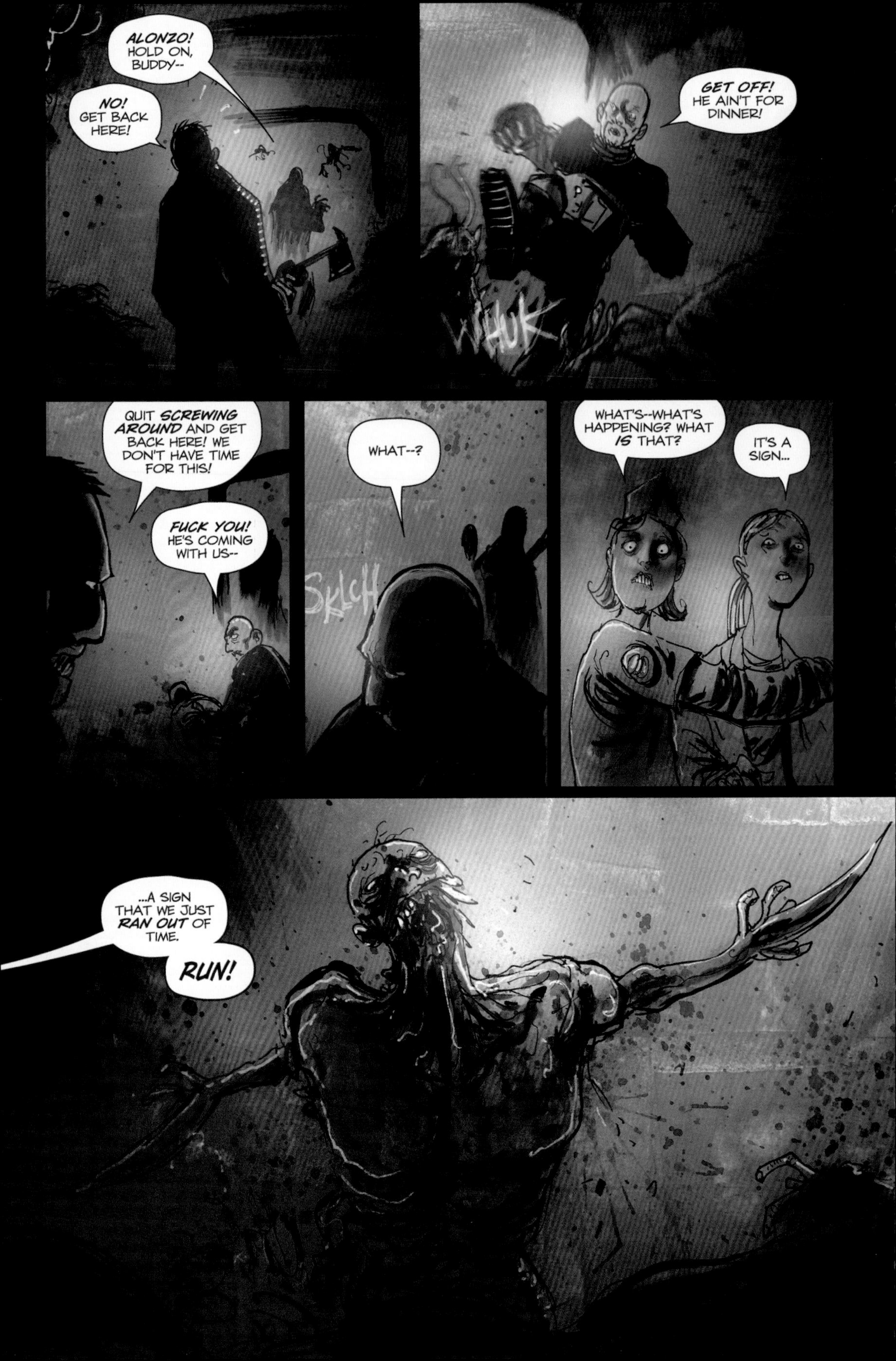
ALONZO! HOLD ON, BUDDY--
NO! GET BACK HERE!
GET OFF! HE AIN'T FOR DINNER!
WHUK
QUIT SCREWING AROUND AND GET BACK HERE! WE DON'T HAVE TIME FOR THIS!
FUCK YOU! HE'S COMING WITH US--
WHAT--?
SKLCH
WHAT'S--WHAT'S HAPPENING? WHAT IS THAT?
IT'S A SIGN...
...A SIGN THAT WE JUST RAN OUT OF TIME.
RUN!

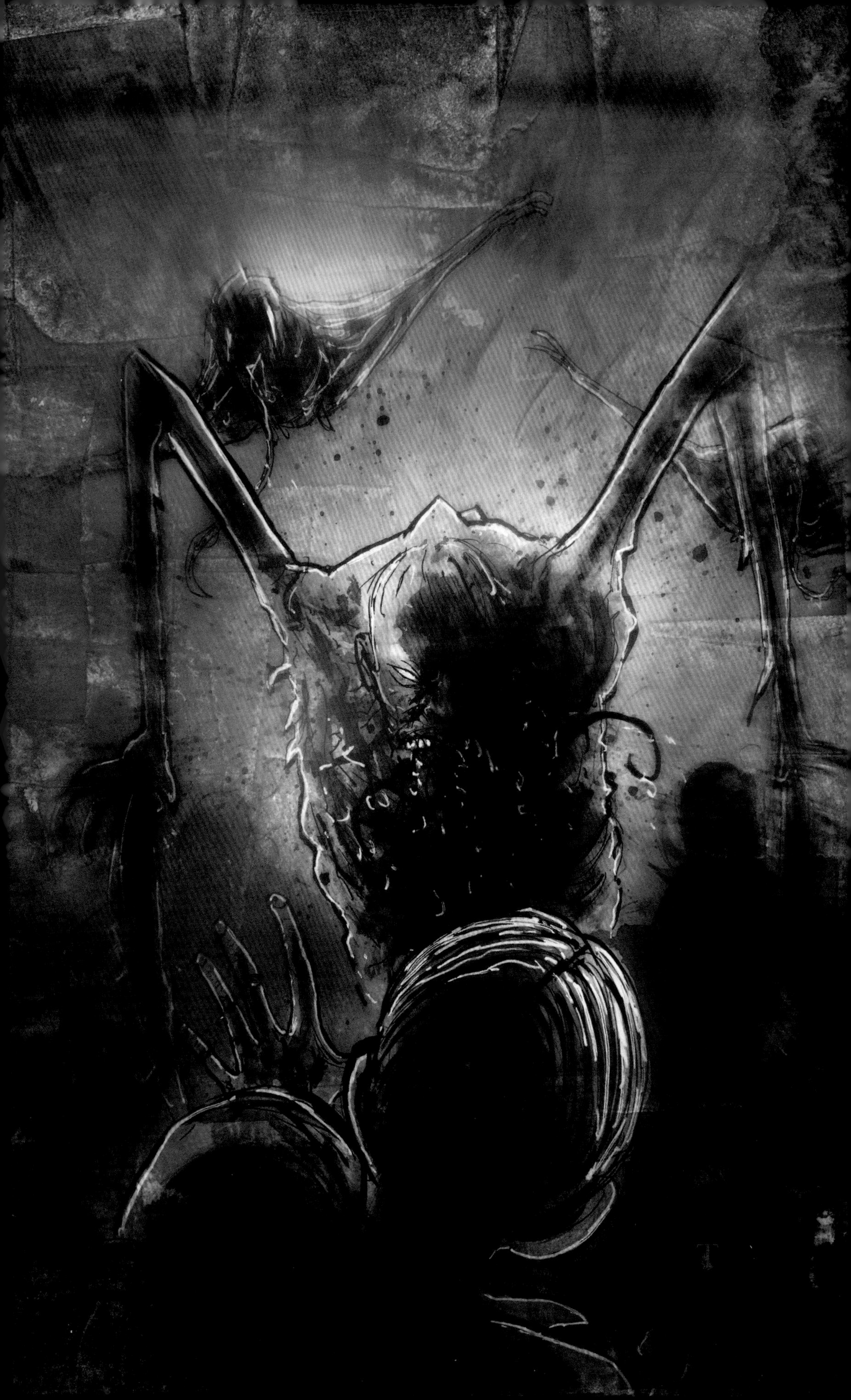

VOLUME 6

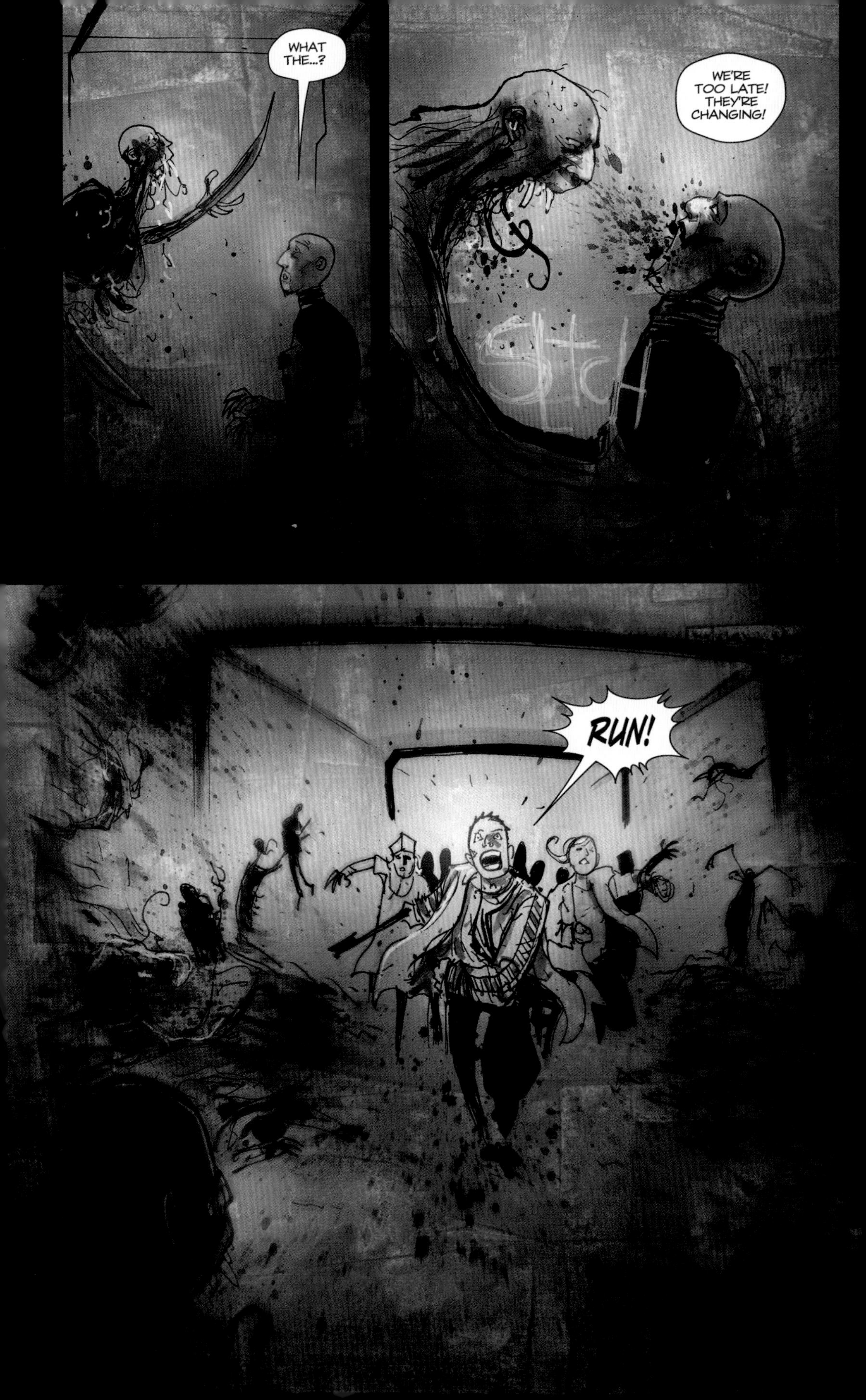
WHAT THE...?
WE'RE TOO LATE! THEY'RE CHANGING!
RUN!

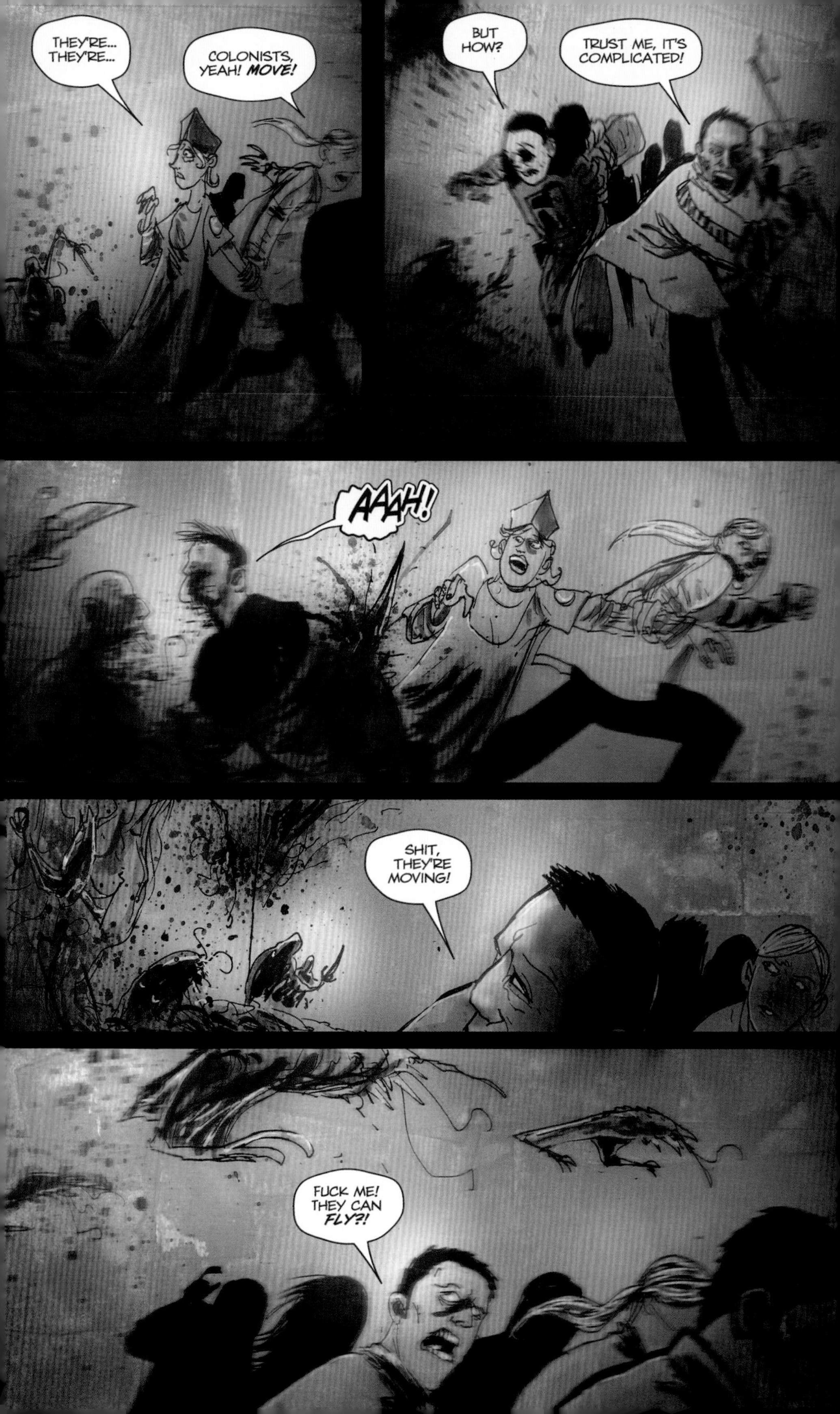
THEY'RE... THEY'RE...
COLONISTS, YEAH! MOVE!
BUT HOW?
TRUST ME, IT'S COMPLICATED!
AAAH!
SHIT, THEY'RE MOVING!
FUCK ME! THEY CAN FLY?!

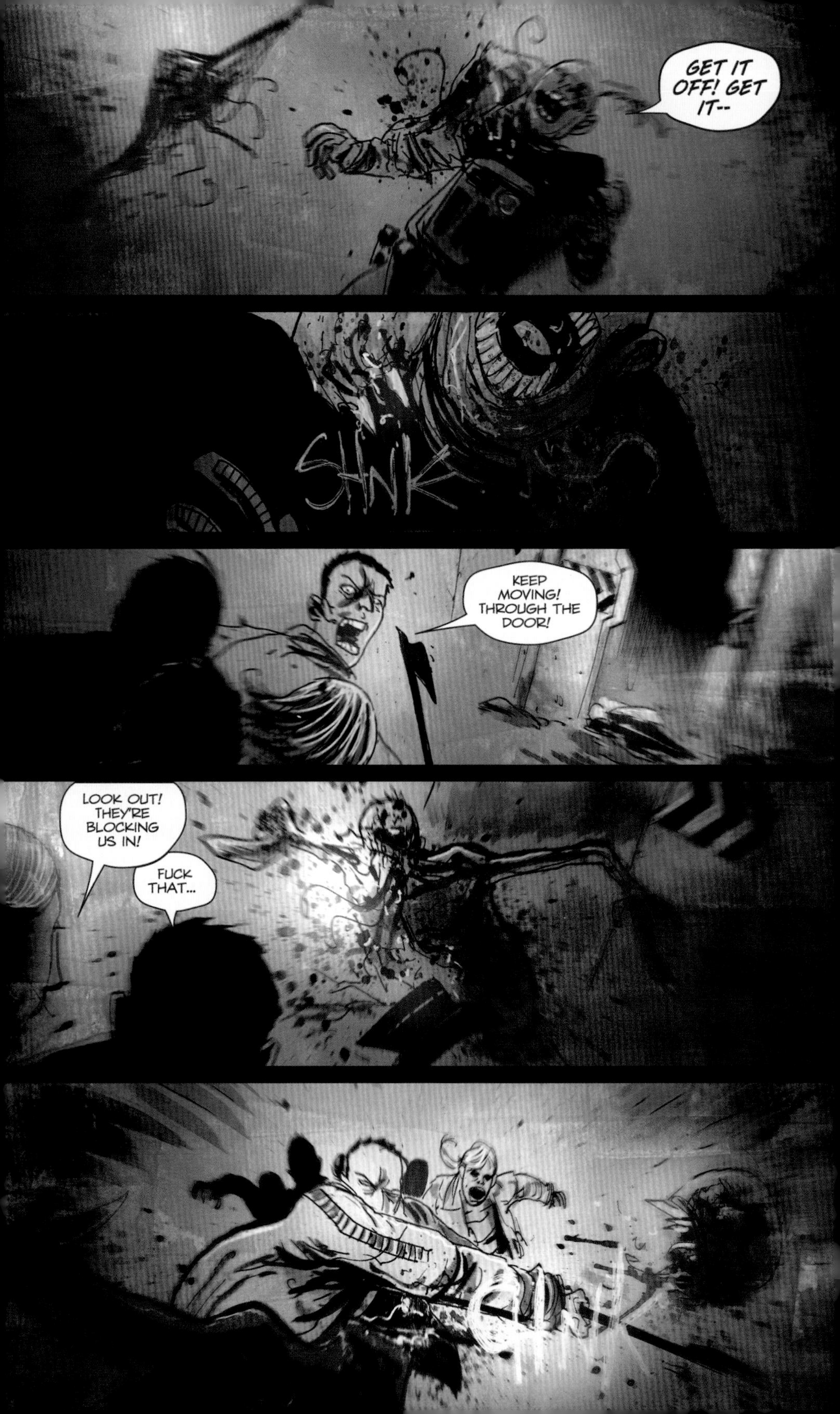

GET IT OFF! GET IT--
SHNK
KEEP MOVING! THROUGH THE DOOR!
LOOK OUT! THEY'RE BLOCKING US IN!
FUCK THAT...

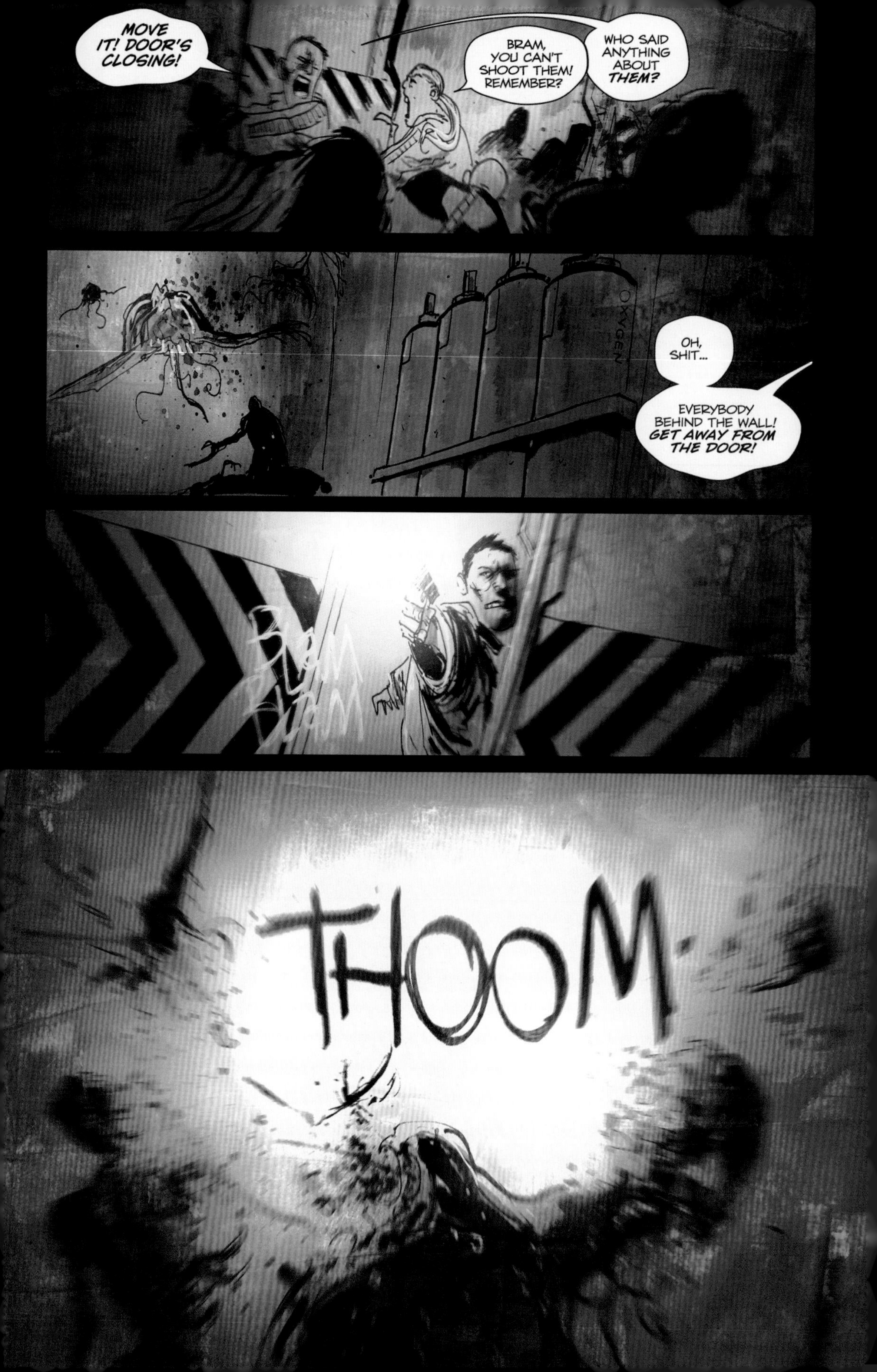
MOVE IT! DOOR'S CLOSING!
BRAM, YOU CAN'T SHOOT THEM! REMEMBER?
WHO SAID ANYTHING ABOUT *THEM?*
OXYGEN
OH, SHIT...
EVERYBODY BEHIND THE WALL! *GET AWAY FROM THE DOOR!*
Blam Blam Blam
THOOM

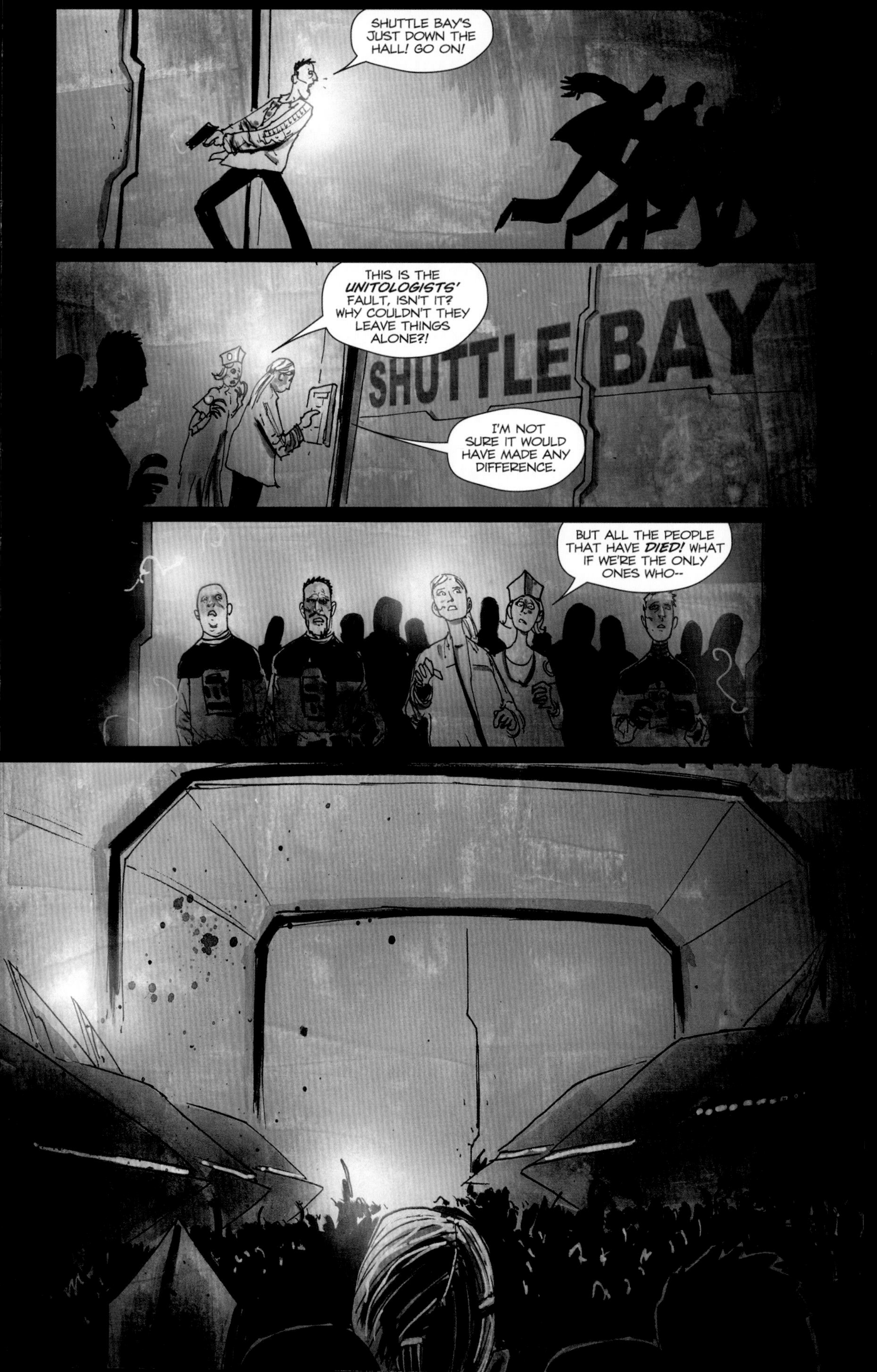
SHUTTLE BAY'S JUST DOWN THE HALL! GO ON!
THIS IS THE *UNITOLOGISTS'* FAULT, ISN'T IT? WHY COULDN'T THEY LEAVE THINGS ALONE?!
SHUTTLE BAY
I'M NOT SURE IT WOULD HAVE MADE ANY DIFFERENCE.
BUT ALL THE PEOPLE THAT HAVE *DIED!* WHAT IF WE'RE THE ONLY ONES WHO--

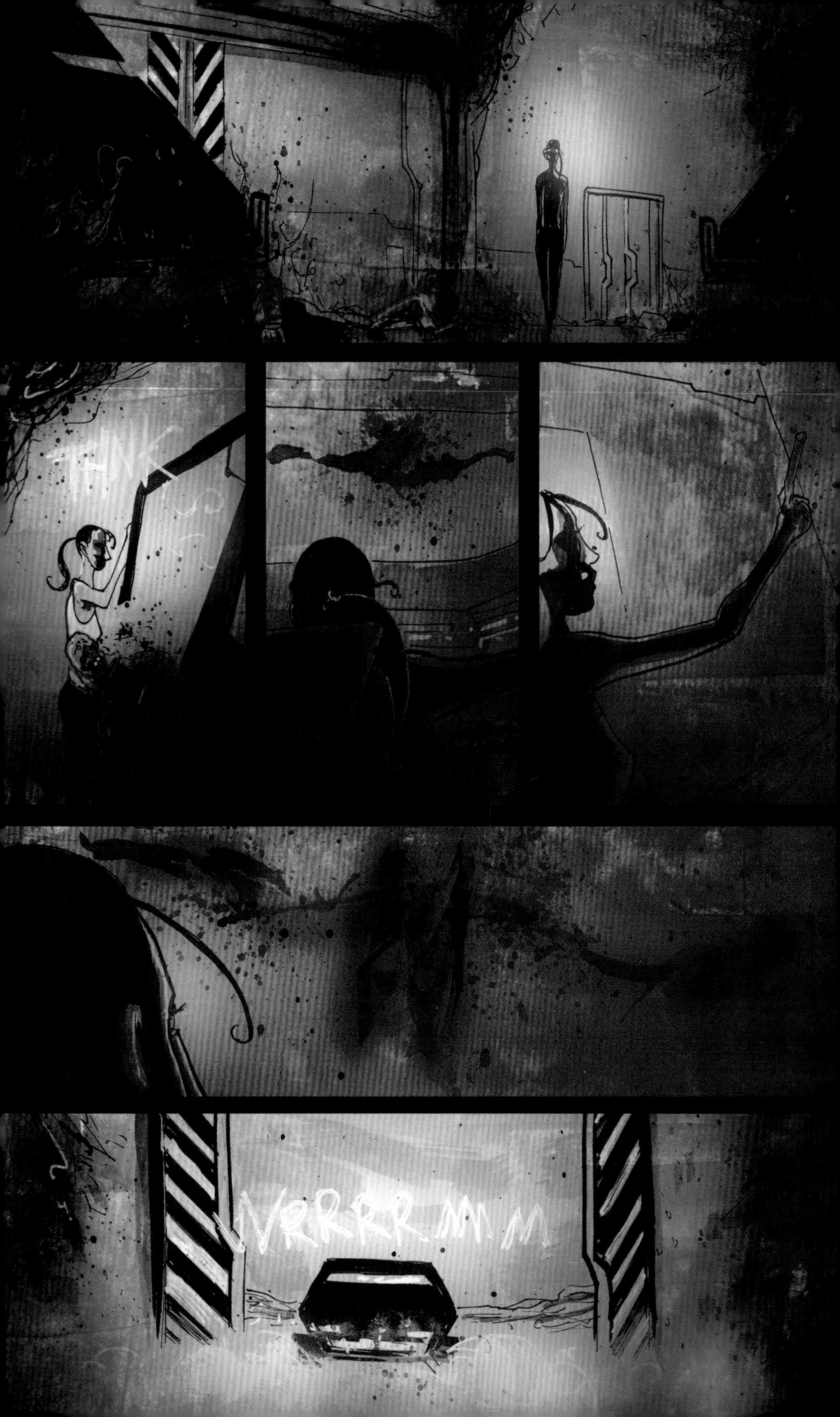
THNK
VRRRRMMM

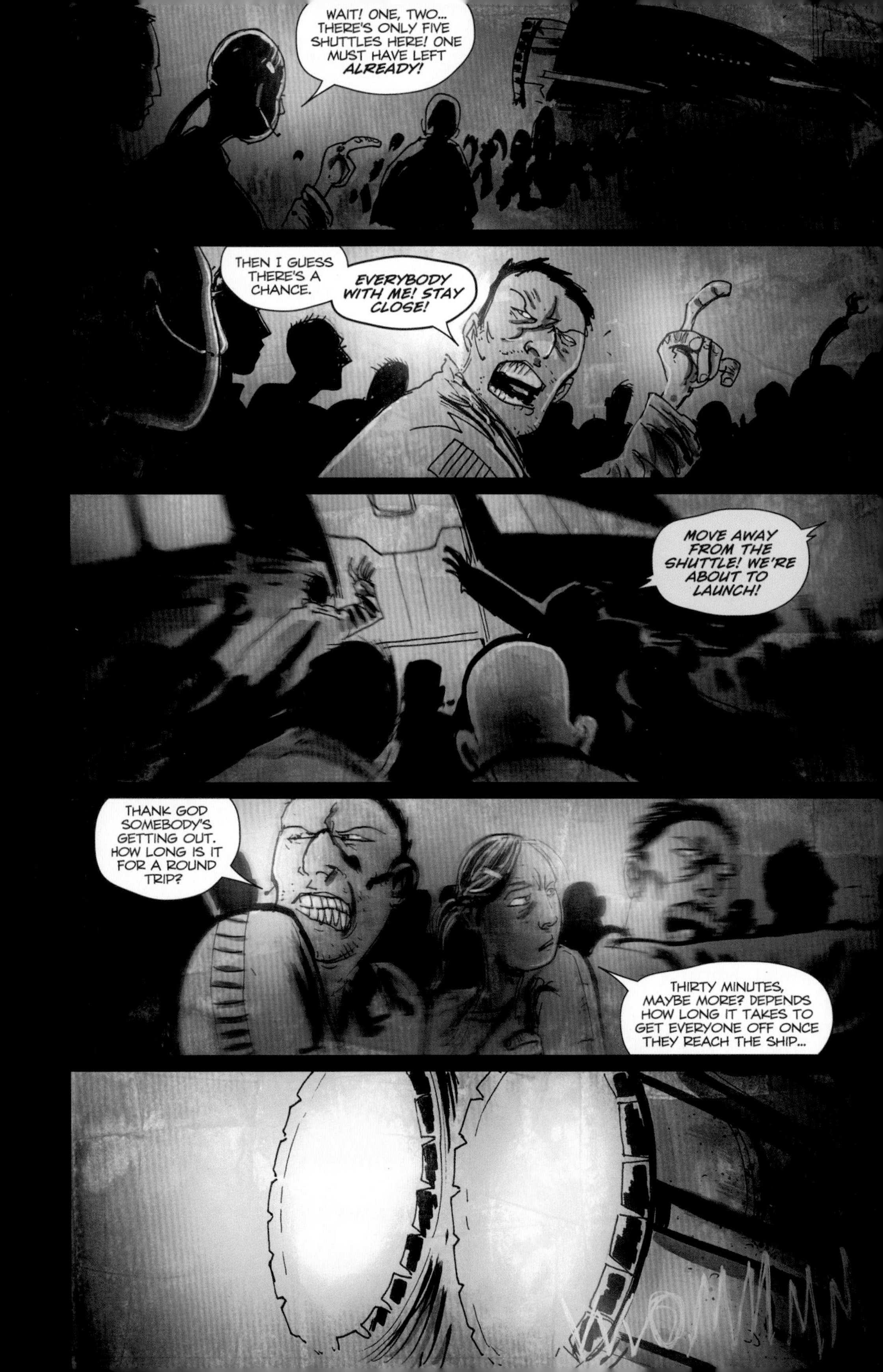
WAIT! ONE, TWO... THERE'S ONLY FIVE SHUTTLES HERE! ONE MUST HAVE LEFT *ALREADY!*
THEN I GUESS THERE'S A CHANCE.
EVERYBODY WITH ME! STAY CLOSE!
MOVE AWAY FROM THE SHUTTLE! WE'RE ABOUT TO LAUNCH!
THANK GOD SOMEBODY'S GETTING OUT. HOW LONG IS IT FOR A ROUND TRIP?
THIRTY MINUTES, MAYBE MORE? DEPENDS HOW LONG IT TAKES TO GET EVERYONE OFF ONCE THEY REACH THE SHIP...
VWOMMMN

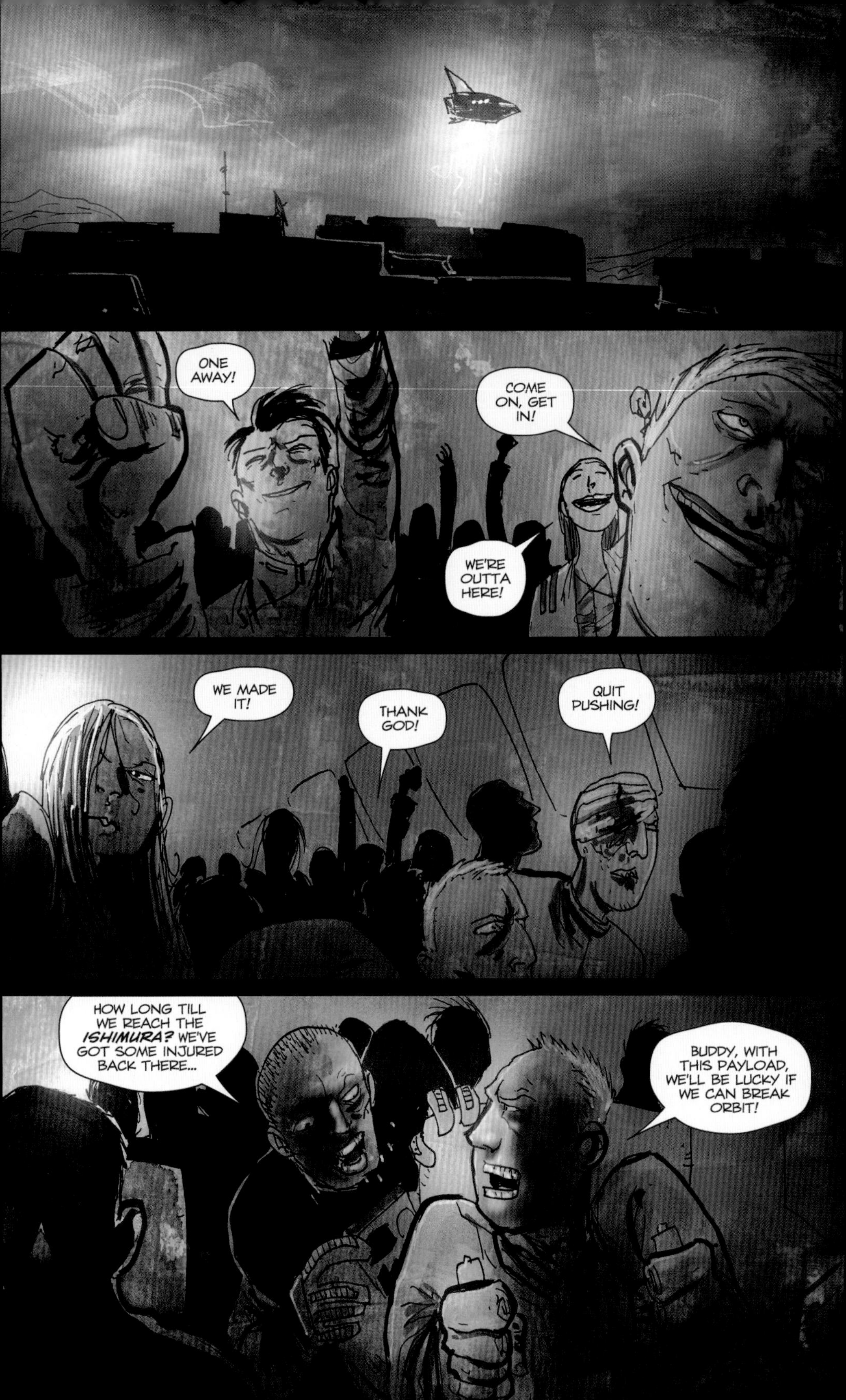
ONE AWAY!
COME ON, GET IN!
WE'RE OUTTA HERE!
WE MADE IT!
THANK GOD!
QUIT PUSHING!
HOW LONG TILL WE REACH THE *ISHIMURA?* WE'VE GOT SOME INJURED BACK THERE...
BUDDY, WITH THIS PAYLOAD, WE'LL BE LUCKY IF WE CAN BREAK ORBIT!

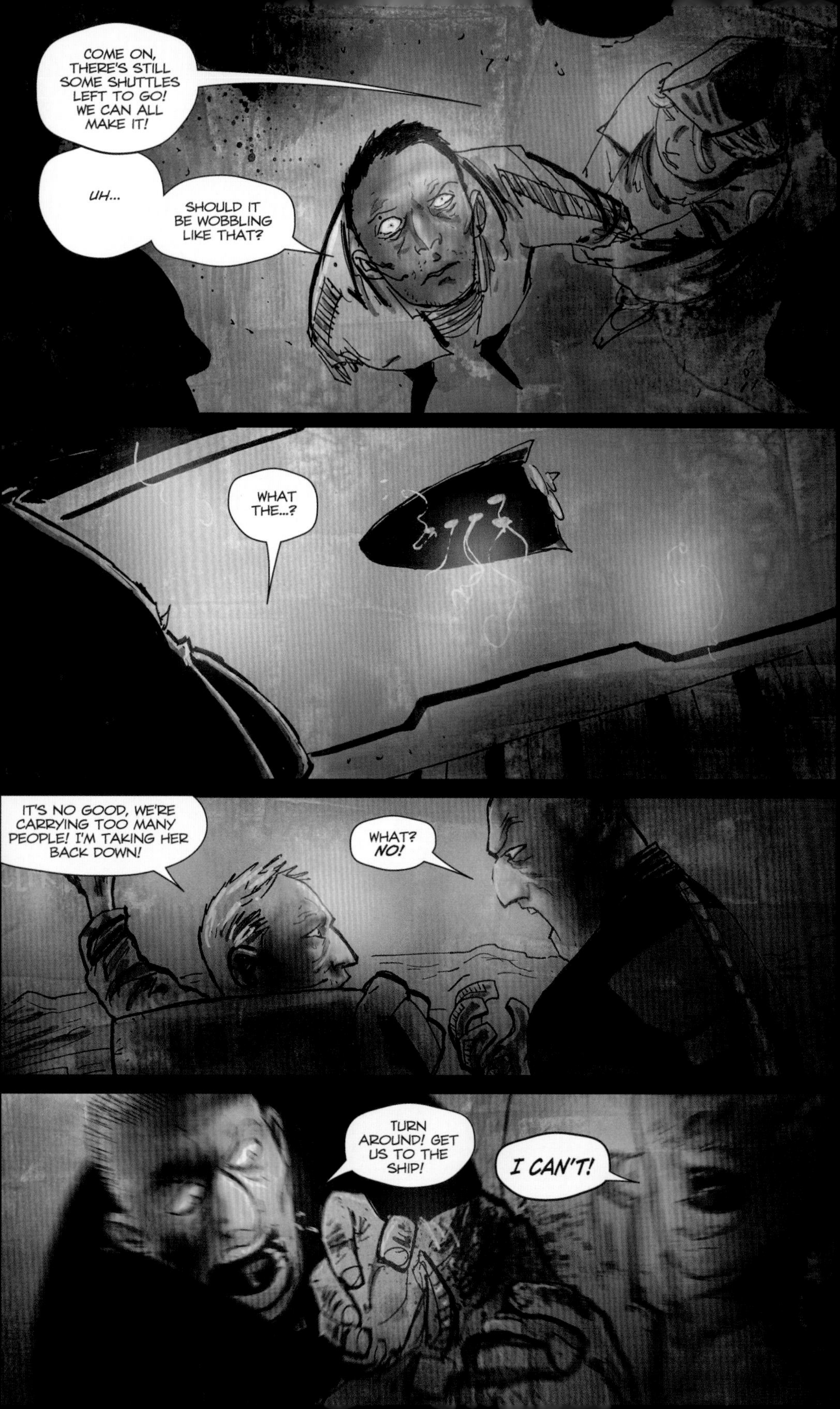
COME ON, THERE'S STILL SOME SHUTTLES LEFT TO GO! WE CAN ALL MAKE IT!
UH...
SHOULD IT BE WOBBLING LIKE THAT?
WHAT THE...?
IT'S NO GOOD, WE'RE CARRYING TOO MANY PEOPLE! I'M TAKING HER BACK DOWN!
WHAT? NO!
TURN AROUND! GET US TO THE SHIP!
I CAN'T!

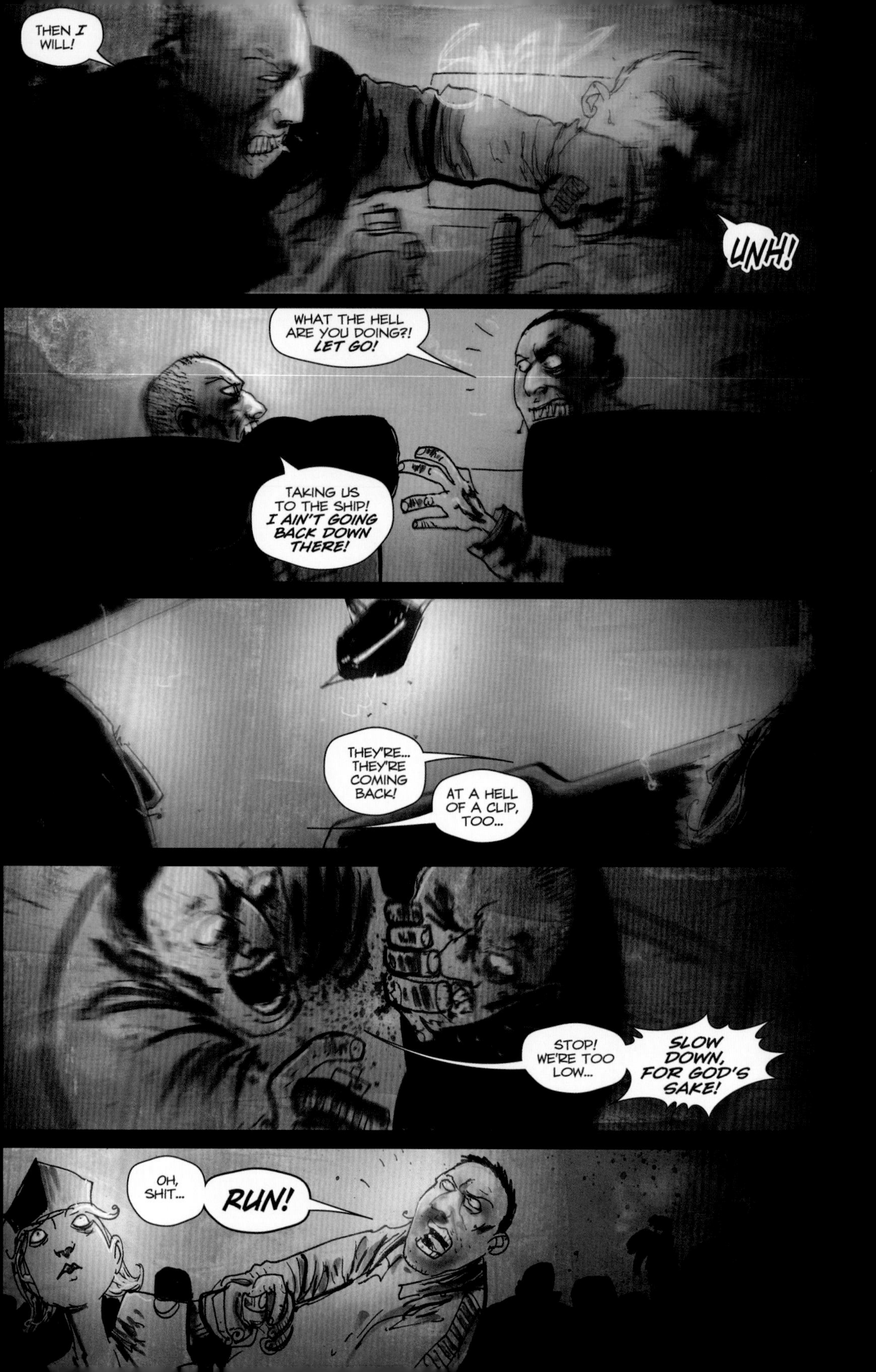
THEN I WILL!
UNH!
WHAT THE HELL ARE YOU DOING?! LET GO!
TAKING US TO THE SHIP! I AIN'T GOING BACK DOWN THERE!
THEY'RE... THEY'RE COMING BACK!
AT A HELL OF A CLIP, TOO...
STOP! WE'RE TOO LOW...
SLOW DOWN, FOR GOD'S SAKE!
OH, SHIT...
RUN!

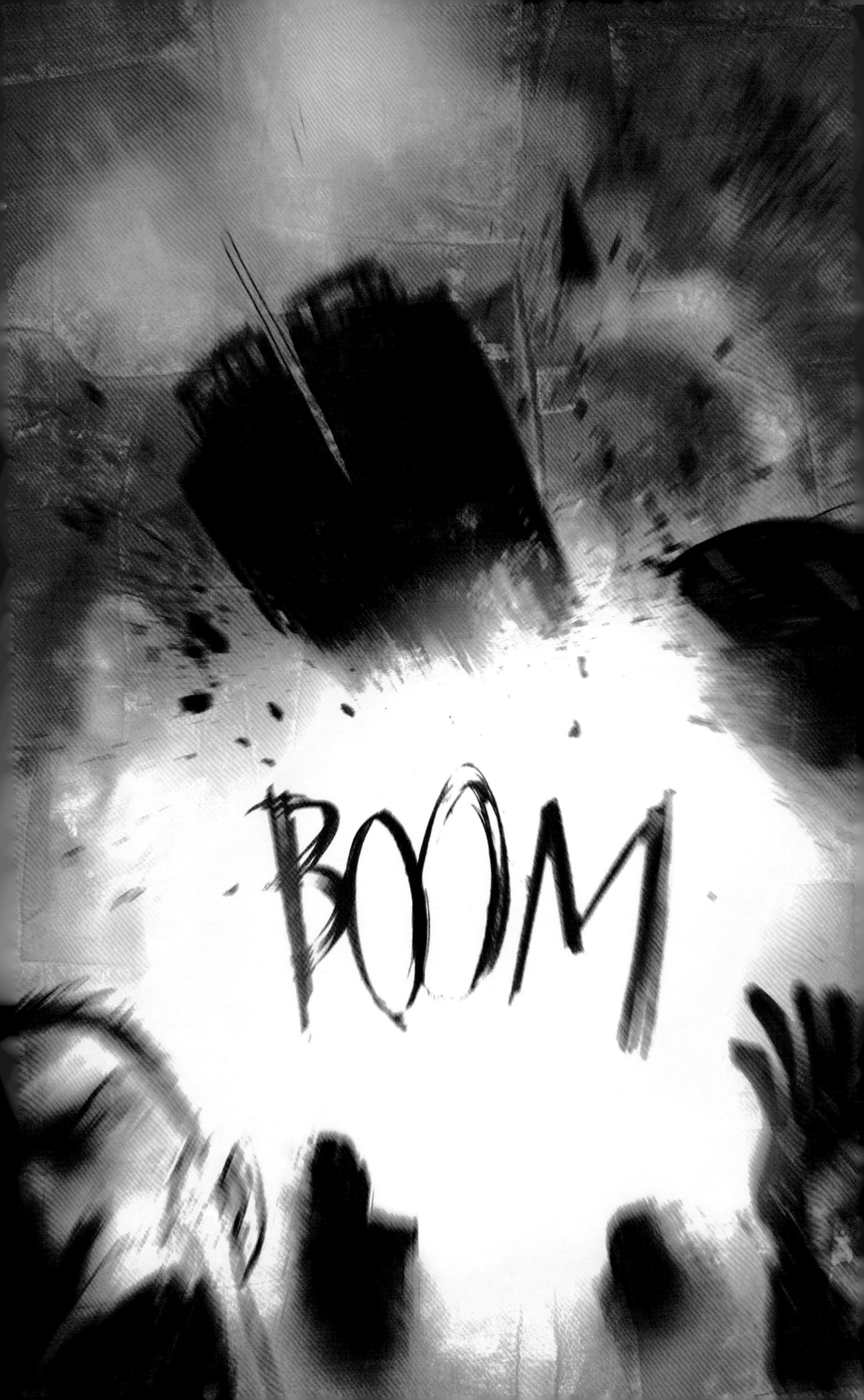
BOOM

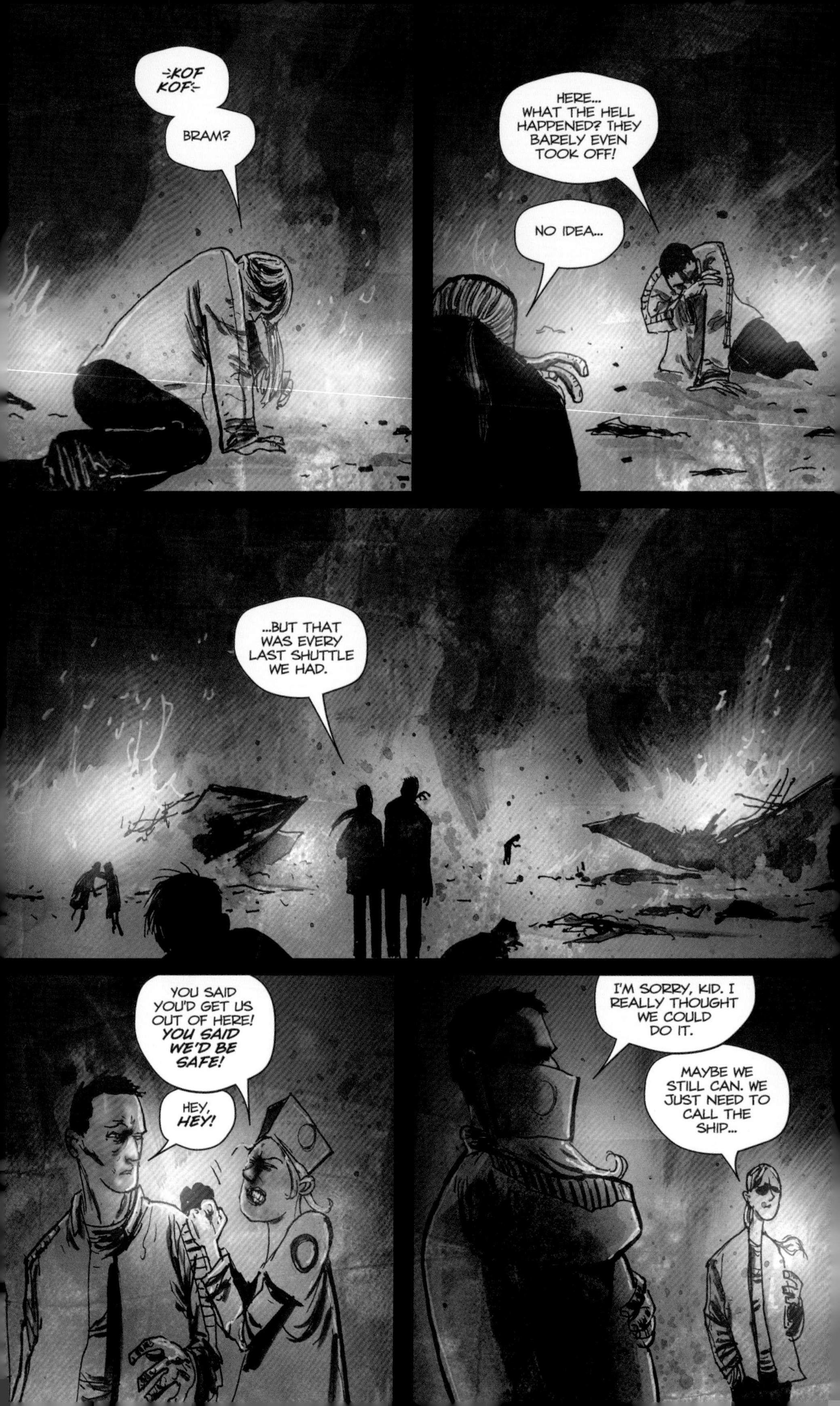
-KOF KOF-
BRAM?
HERE... WHAT THE HELL HAPPENED? THEY BARELY EVEN TOOK OFF!
NO IDEA...
...BUT THAT WAS EVERY LAST SHUTTLE WE HAD.
YOU SAID YOU'D GET US OUT OF HERE! YOU SAID WE'D BE SAFE!
HEY, HEY!
I'M SORRY, KID. I REALLY THOUGHT WE COULD DO IT.
MAYBE WE STILL CAN. WE JUST NEED TO CALL THE SHIP...

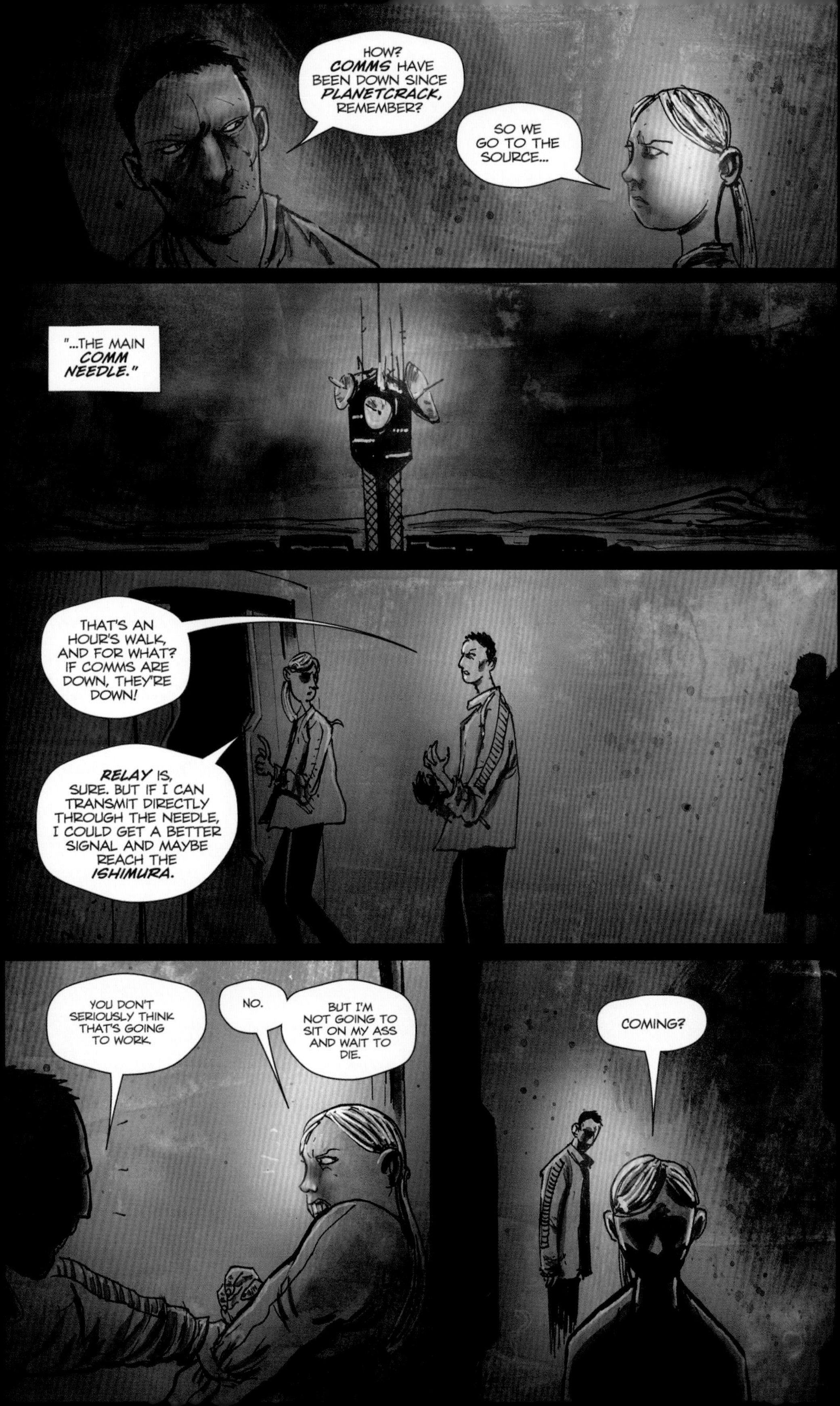
HOW? COMMS HAVE BEEN DOWN SINCE PLANETCRACK, REMEMBER?
SO WE GO TO THE SOURCE...
"...THE MAIN COMM NEEDLE."
THAT'S AN HOUR'S WALK, AND FOR WHAT? IF COMMS ARE DOWN, THEY'RE DOWN!
RELAY IS, SURE. BUT IF I CAN TRANSMIT DIRECTLY THROUGH THE NEEDLE, I COULD GET A BETTER SIGNAL AND MAYBE REACH THE ISHIMURA.
YOU DON'T SERIOUSLY THINK THAT'S GOING TO WORK.
NO.
BUT I'M NOT GOING TO SIT ON MY ASS AND WAIT TO DIE.
COMING?

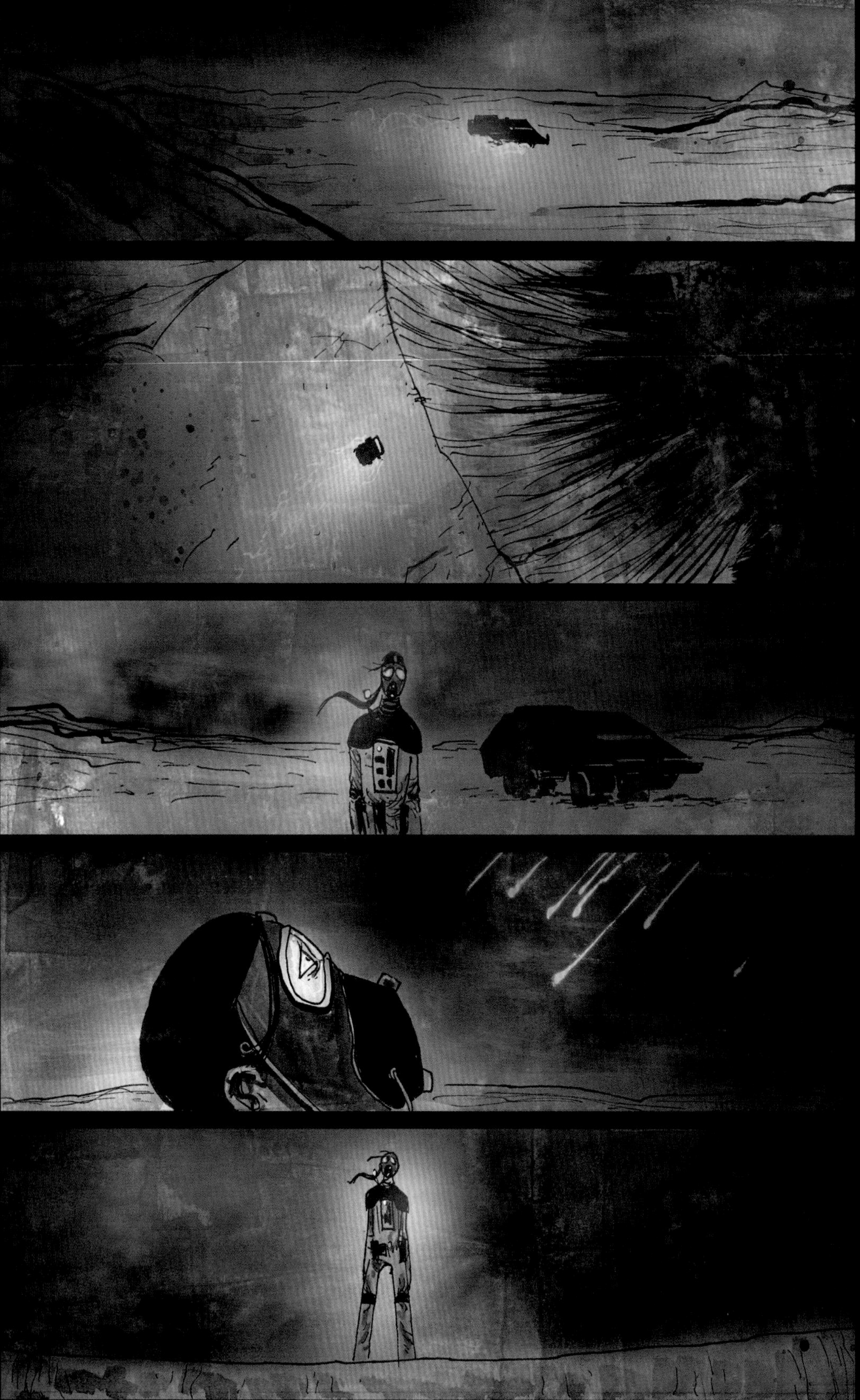

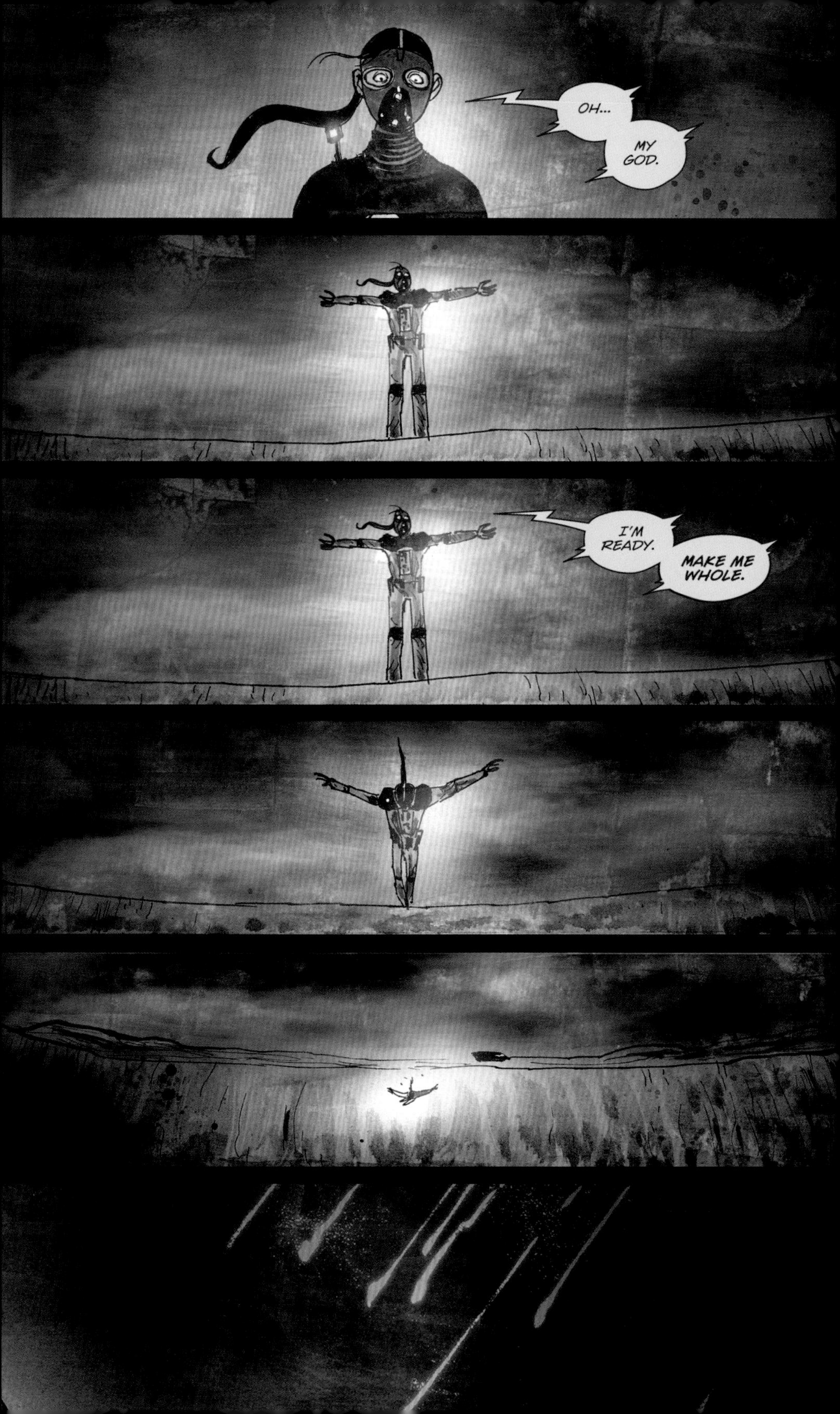
OH...
MY GOD.
I'M READY.
MAKE ME WHOLE.

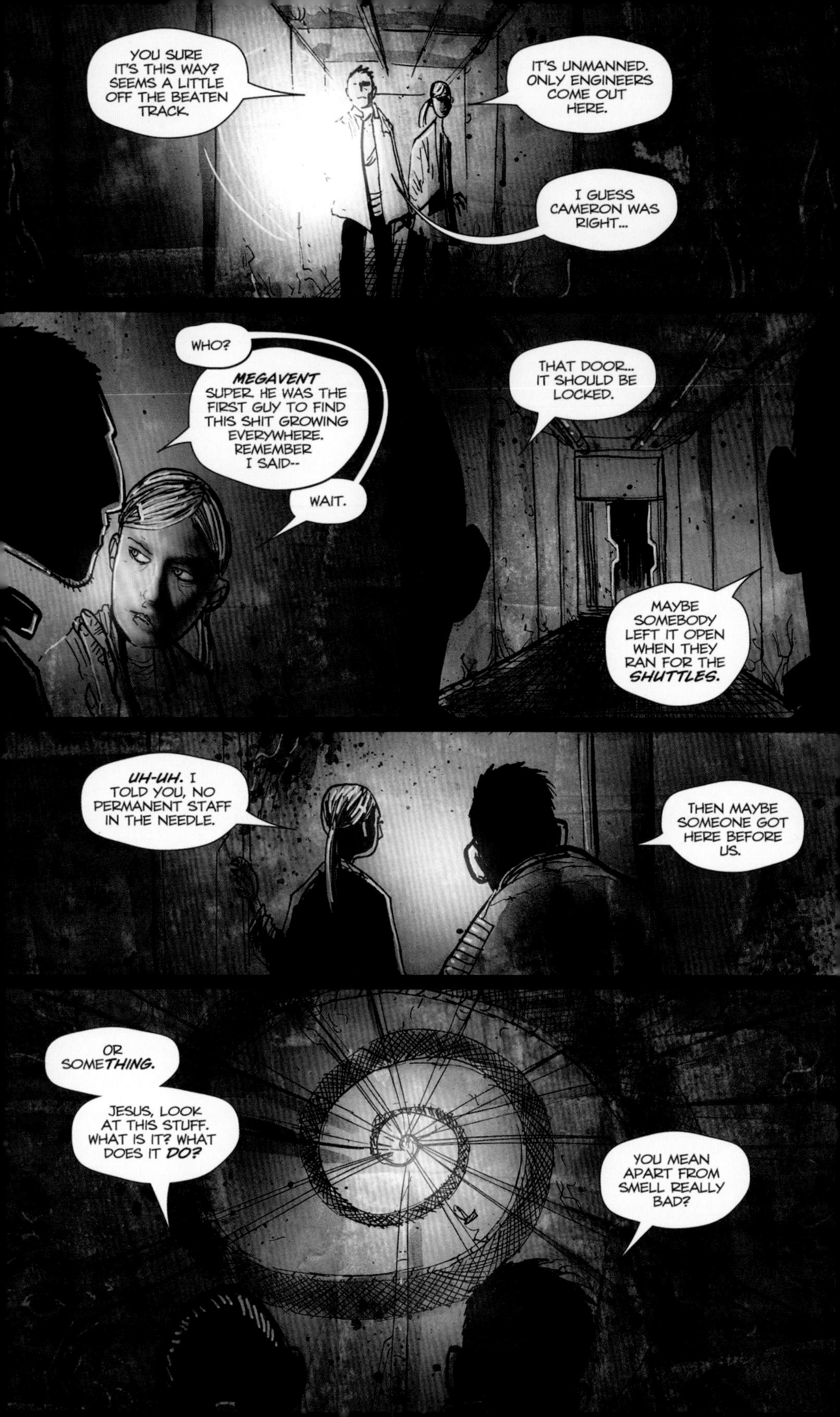
YOU SURE IT'S THIS WAY? SEEMS A LITTLE OFF THE BEATEN TRACK.
IT'S UNMANNED. ONLY ENGINEERS COME OUT HERE.
I GUESS CAMERON WAS RIGHT...
WHO?
MEGAVENT SUPER. HE WAS THE FIRST GUY TO FIND THIS SHIT GROWING EVERYWHERE. REMEMBER I SAID--
WAIT.
THAT DOOR... IT SHOULD BE LOCKED.
MAYBE SOMEBODY LEFT IT OPEN WHEN THEY RAN FOR THE SHUTTLES.
UH-UH. I TOLD YOU, NO PERMANENT STAFF IN THE NEEDLE.
THEN MAYBE SOMEONE GOT HERE BEFORE US.
OR SOMETHING.
JESUS, LOOK AT THIS STUFF. WHAT IS IT? WHAT DOES IT DO?
YOU MEAN APART FROM SMELL REALLY BAD?

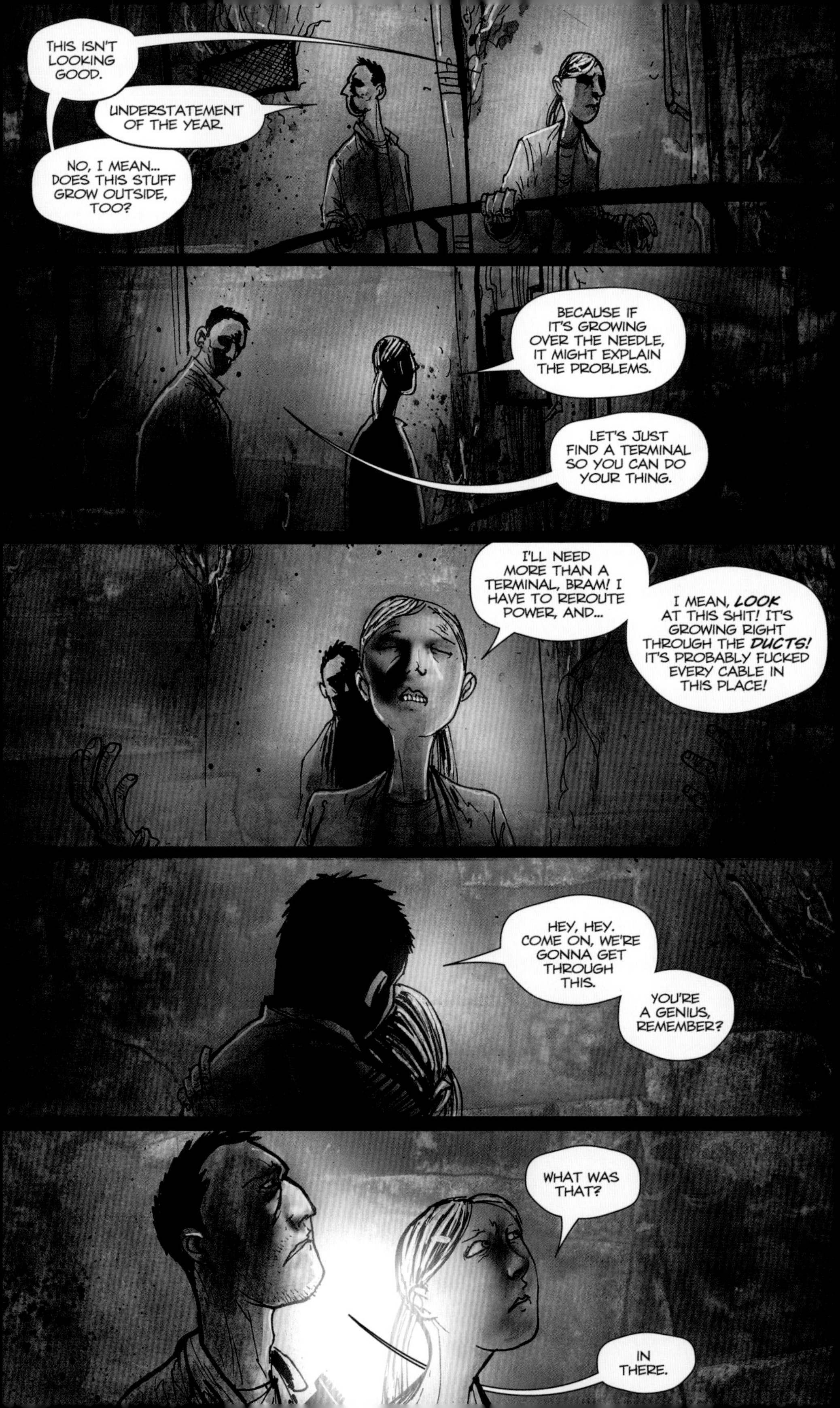
THIS ISN'T LOOKING GOOD.
UNDERSTATEMENT OF THE YEAR.
NO, I MEAN... DOES THIS STUFF GROW OUTSIDE, TOO?
BECAUSE IF IT'S GROWING OVER THE NEEDLE, IT MIGHT EXPLAIN THE PROBLEMS.
LET'S JUST FIND A TERMINAL SO YOU CAN DO YOUR THING.
I'LL NEED MORE THAN A TERMINAL, BRAM! I HAVE TO REROUTE POWER, AND...
I MEAN, LOOK AT THIS SHIT! IT'S GROWING RIGHT THROUGH THE DUCTS! IT'S PROBABLY FUCKED EVERY CABLE IN THIS PLACE!
HEY, HEY. COME ON, WE'RE GONNA GET THROUGH THIS.
YOU'RE A GENIUS, REMEMBER?
WHAT WAS THAT?
IN THERE.

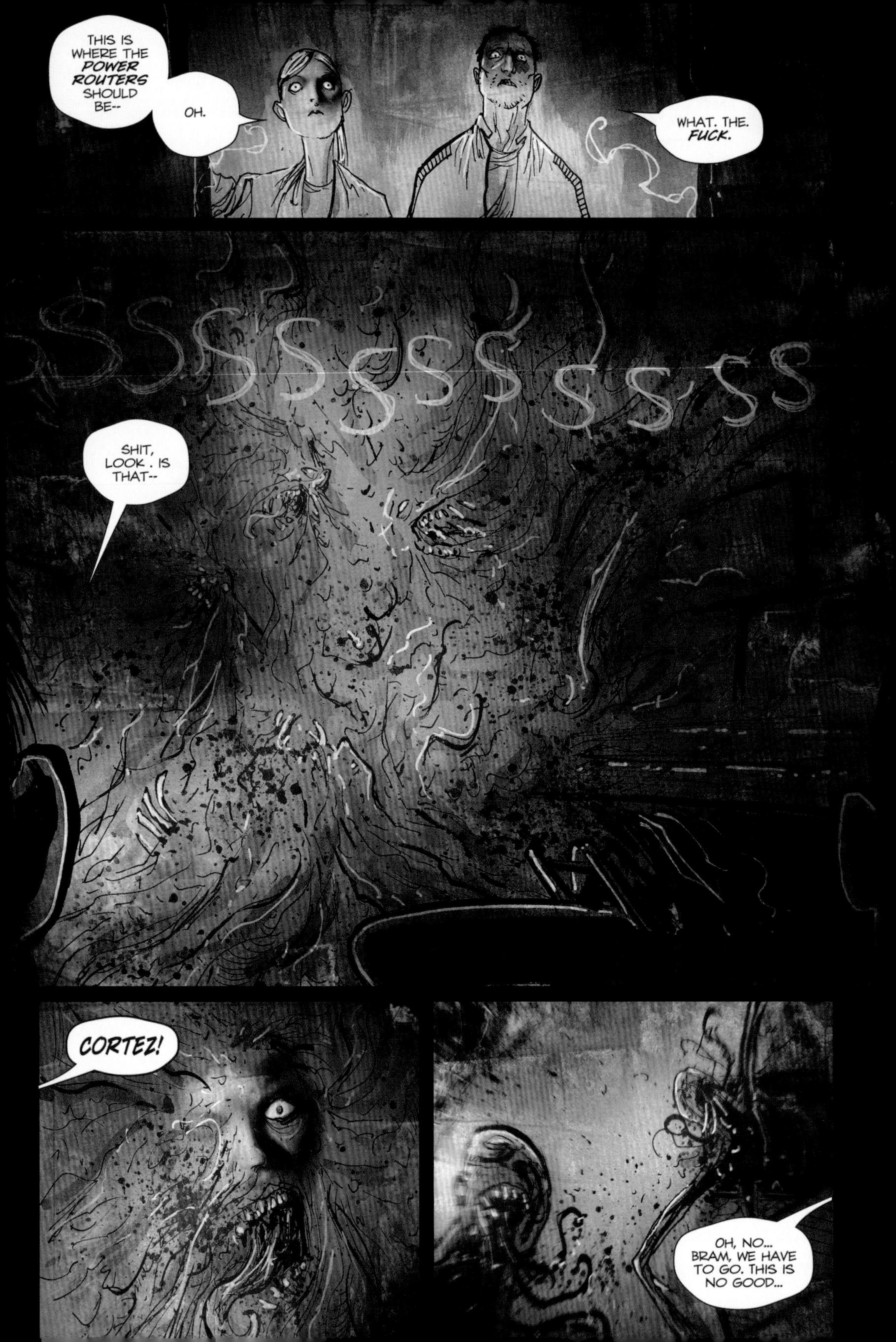
THIS IS WHERE THE POWER ROUTERS SHOULD BE--
OH.
WHAT. THE. FUCK.
SSSSSSSSSSSSSS
SHIT, LOOK . IS THAT--
CORTEZ!
OH, NO... BRAM, WE HAVE TO GO. THIS IS NO GOOD...

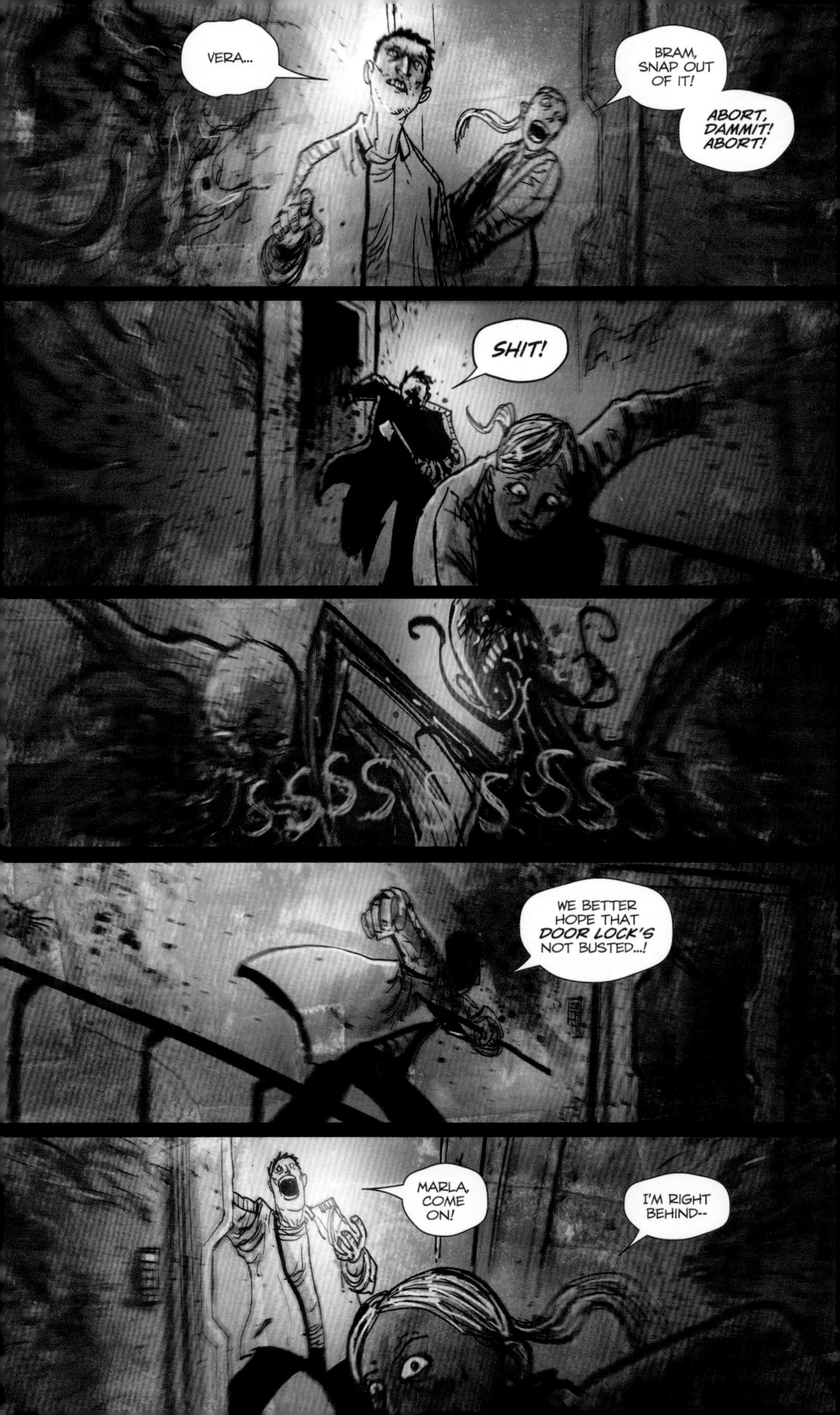
VERA...
BRAM, SNAP OUT OF IT!
ABORT, DAMMIT! ABORT!
SHIT!
SSSSSSSSS
WE BETTER HOPE THAT DOOR LOCK'S NOT BUSTED...!
MARLA, COME ON!
I'M RIGHT BEHIND--

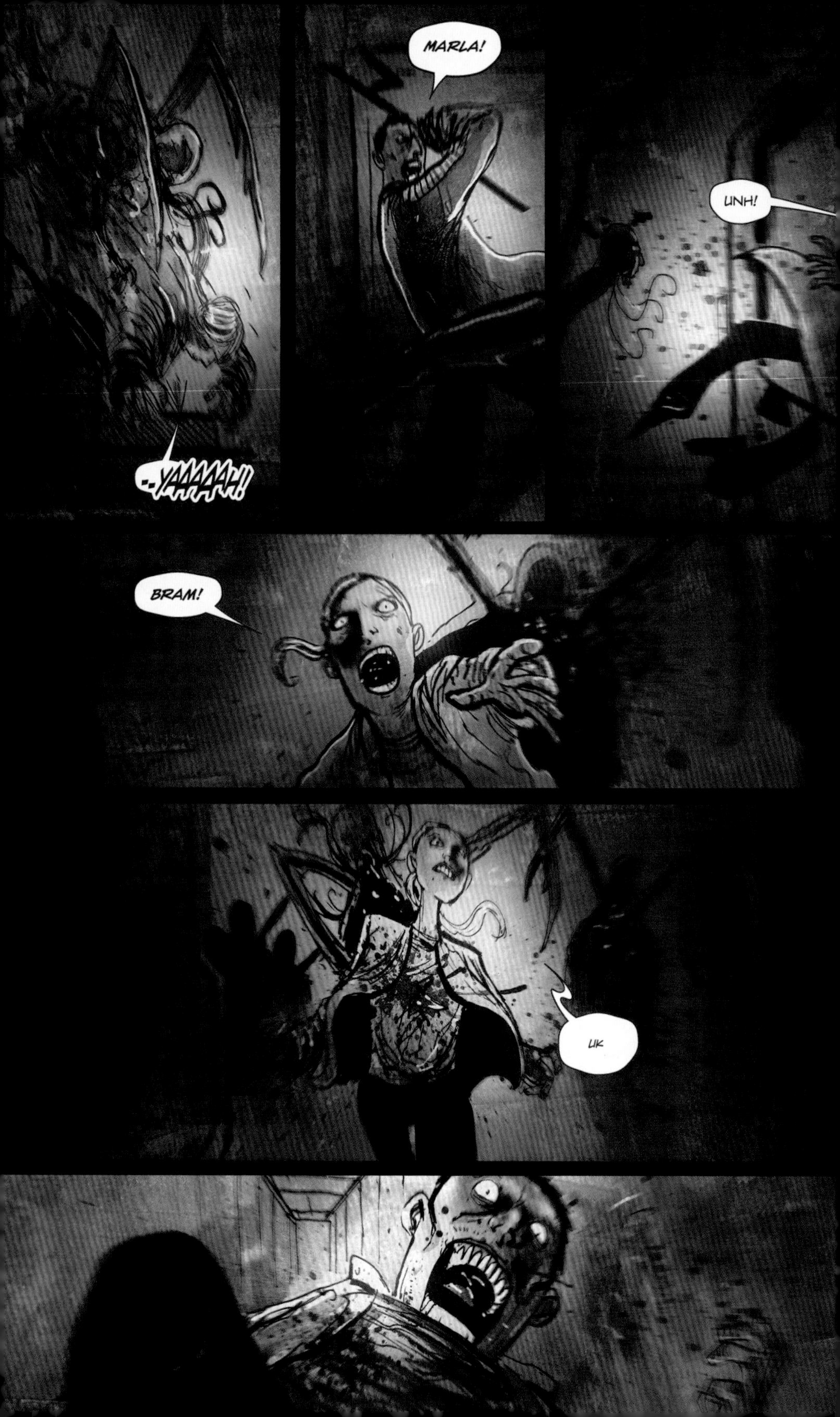

--YAAAAAH!
MARLA!
UNH!
BRAM!
UK

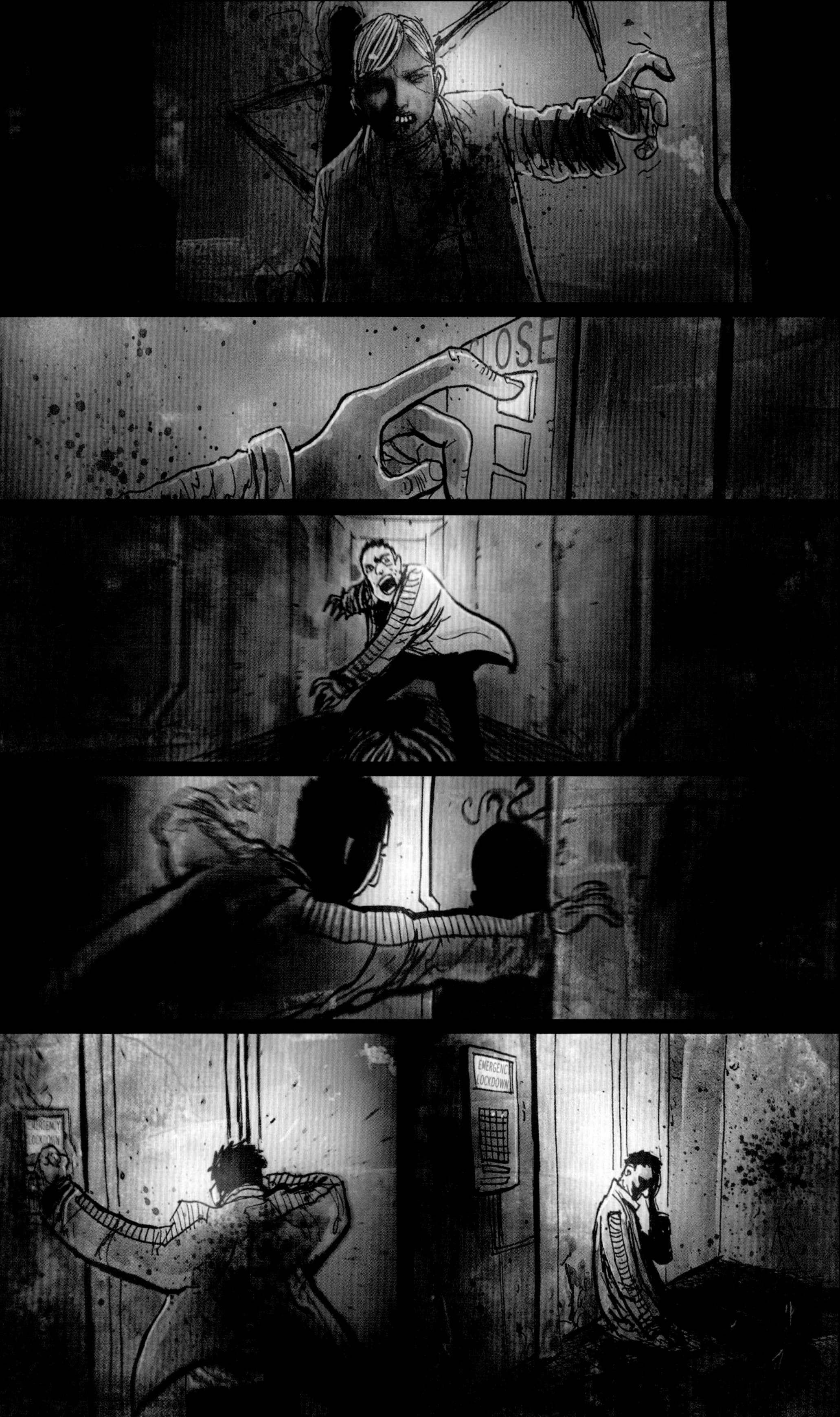
LOSE
EMERGENCY LOCKDOWN
EMERGENC LOCKDOWN

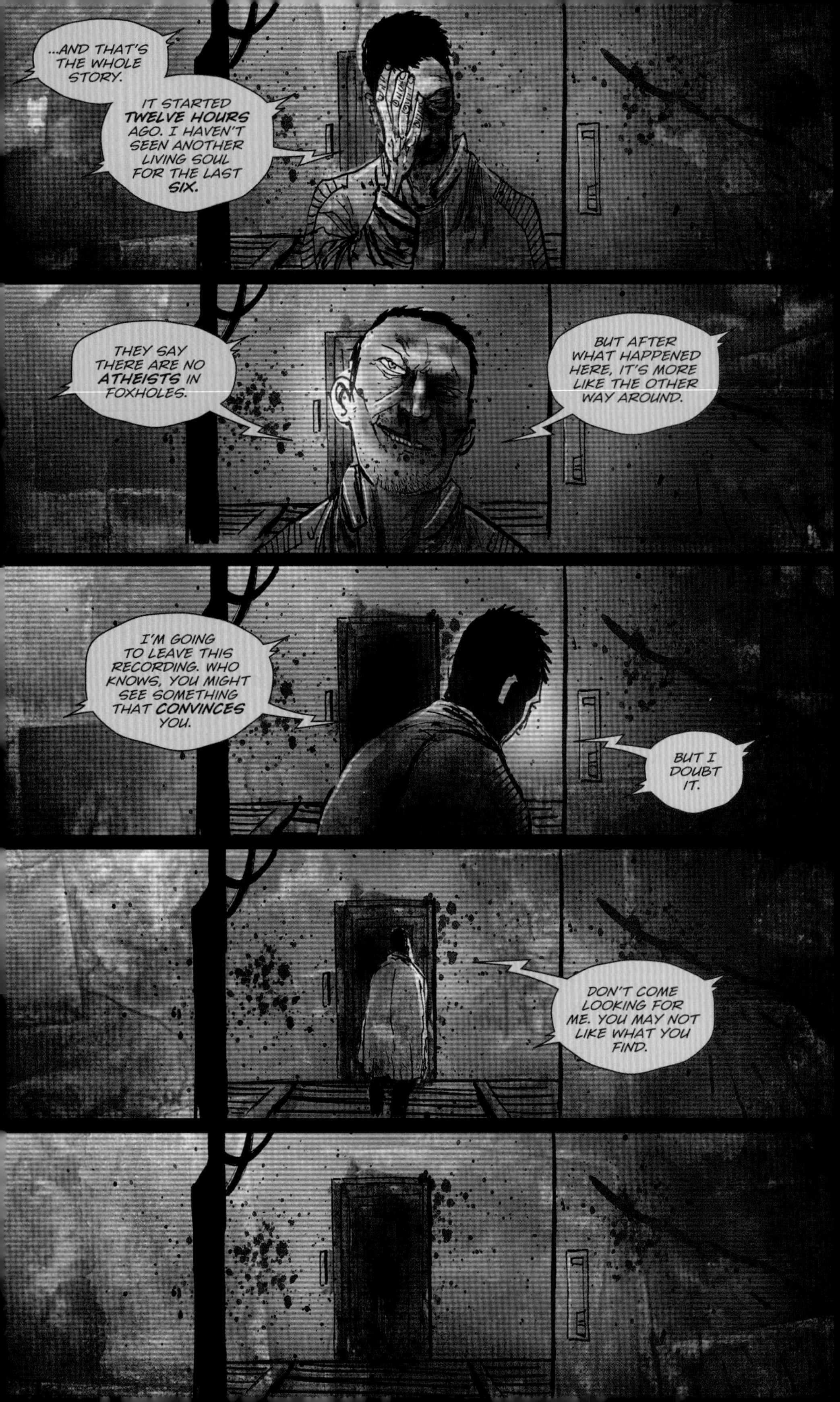
...AND THAT'S THE WHOLE STORY.
IT STARTED **TWELVE HOURS** AGO. I HAVEN'T SEEN ANOTHER LIVING SOUL FOR THE LAST **SIX.**
THEY SAY THERE ARE NO **ATHEISTS** IN FOXHOLES.
BUT AFTER WHAT HAPPENED HERE, IT'S MORE LIKE THE OTHER WAY AROUND.
I'M GOING TO LEAVE THIS RECORDING. WHO KNOWS, YOU MIGHT SEE SOMETHING THAT **CONVINCES** YOU.
BUT I DOUBT IT.
DON'T COME LOOKING FOR ME. YOU MAY NOT LIKE WHAT YOU FIND.

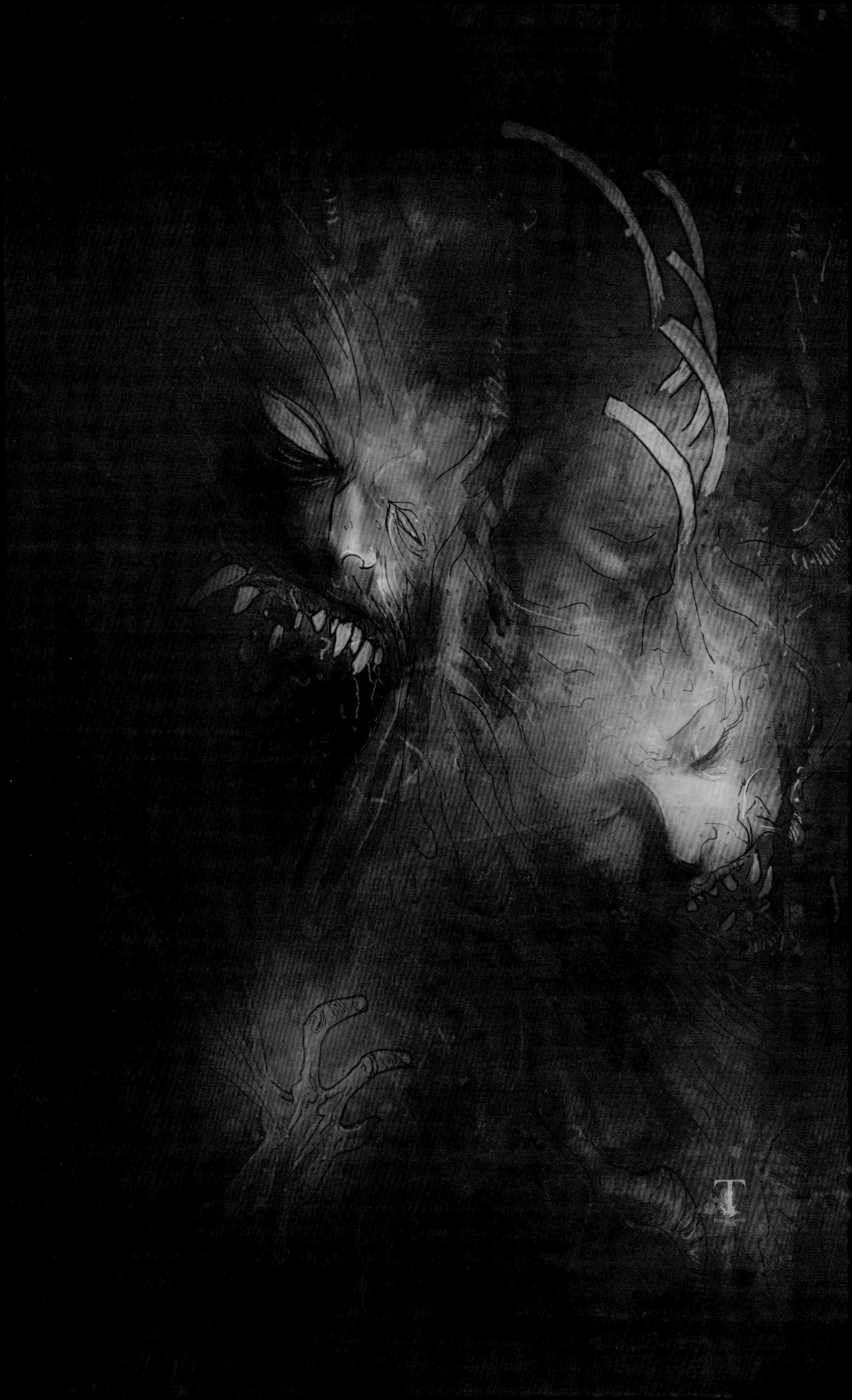

DEAD SPACE
EXTRACTION

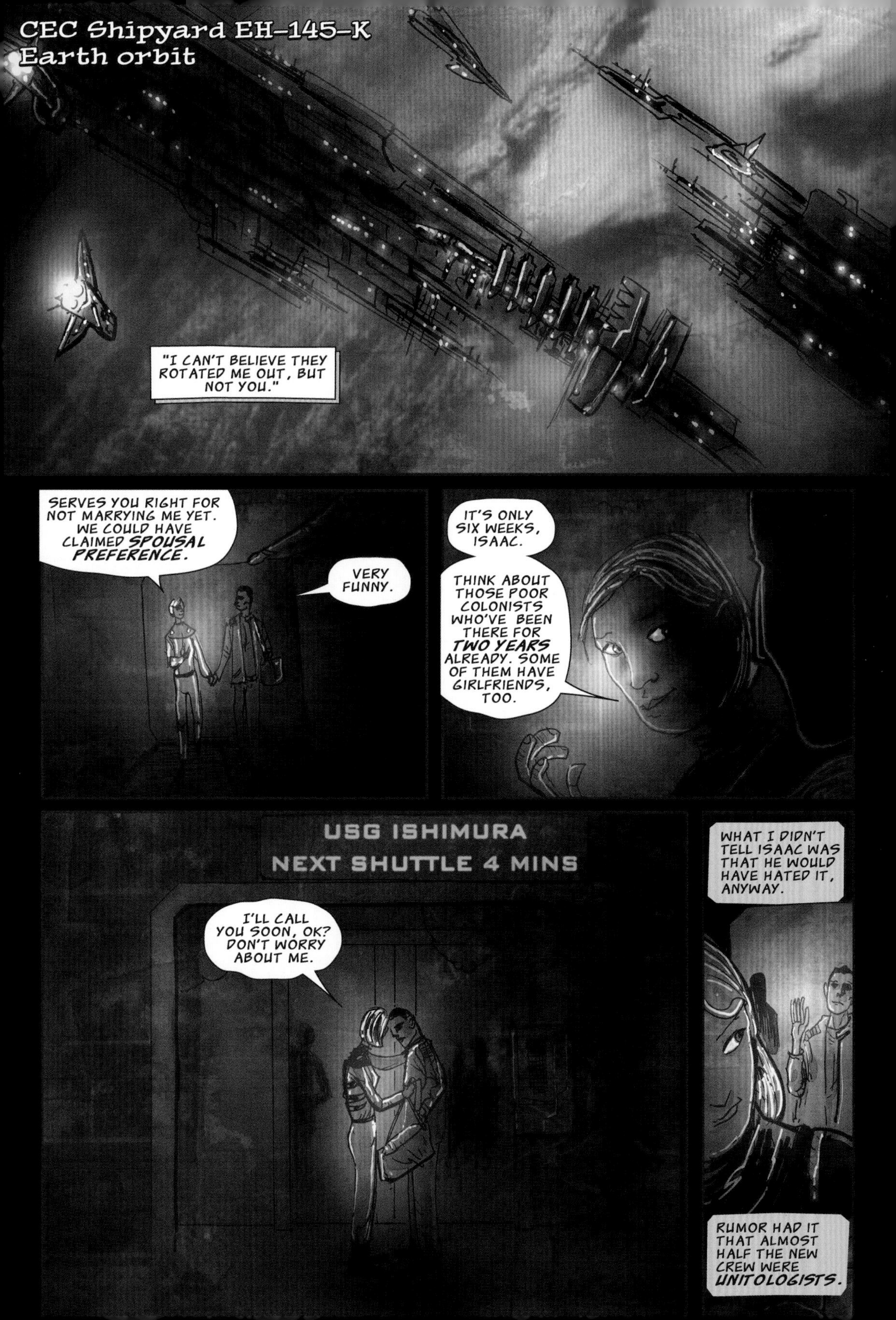

CEC Shipyard EH-145-K
Earth orbit
"I CAN'T BELIEVE THEY ROTATED ME OUT, BUT NOT YOU."
SERVES YOU RIGHT FOR NOT MARRYING ME YET. WE COULD HAVE CLAIMED ***SPOUSAL PREFERENCE***.
VERY FUNNY.
IT'S ONLY SIX WEEKS, ISAAC.
THINK ABOUT THOSE POOR COLONISTS WHO'VE BEEN THERE FOR ***TWO YEARS*** ALREADY. SOME OF THEM HAVE GIRLFRIENDS, TOO.
USG ISHIMURA
NEXT SHUTTLE 4 MINS
I'LL CALL YOU SOON, OK? DON'T WORRY ABOUT ME.
WHAT I DIDN'T TELL ISAAC WAS THAT HE WOULD HAVE HATED IT, ANYWAY.
RUMOR HAD IT THAT ALMOST HALF THE NEW CREW WERE ***UNITOLOGISTS***.

DR. NICOLE BRENNAN. SENIOR MEDICAL OFFICER.

I BET THE LINE STRETCHED ALL THE WAY OUT THE AIRLOCK ONCE THEY HEARD THE COLONISTS HAD SUPPOSEDLY FOUND A MARKER.

I DIDN'T CARE. I ONLY LOST A COUPLE OF MY REGULAR STAFF. MAYBE UNITOLOGISTS AREN'T BIG ON MEDICINE.

I KNEW ISAAC WOULD MISS ME. BUT HE'D WORKED THE *ISHIMURA* BEFORE. I COULDN'T PASS UP THE CHANCE TO HAVE IT ON MY RESUMÉ...

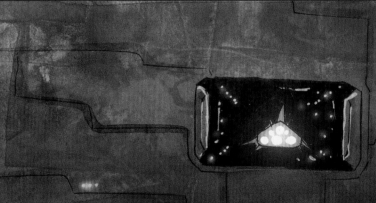

...BEFORE THE OLD GAL FINALLY WENT TO THE GREAT SHIPYARD IN THE STARS.

DOCKING IN 30 SECONDS. PLEASE SECURE ALL BELONGINGS.

WELCOME TO THE *ISHIMURA*, FOLKS

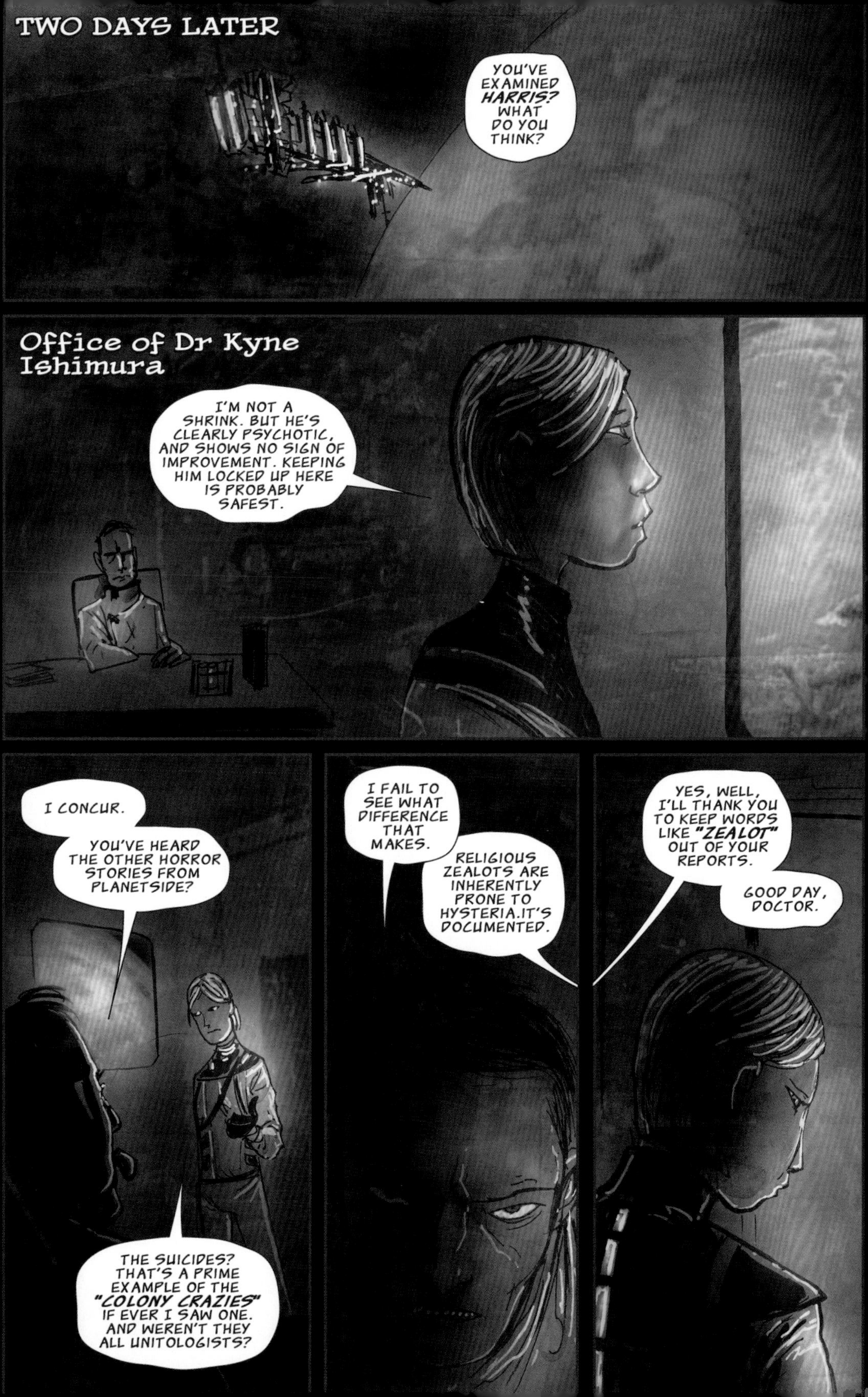
TWO DAYS LATER
YOU'VE EXAMINED HARRIS? WHAT DO YOU THINK?
Office of Dr Kyne Ishimura
I'M NOT A SHRINK. BUT HE'S CLEARLY PSYCHOTIC, AND SHOWS NO SIGN OF IMPROVEMENT. KEEPING HIM LOCKED UP HERE IS PROBABLY SAFEST.
I CONCUR.
YOU'VE HEARD THE OTHER HORROR STORIES FROM PLANETSIDE?
THE SUICIDES? THAT'S A PRIME EXAMPLE OF THE "COLONY CRAZIES" IF EVER I SAW ONE. AND WEREN'T THEY ALL UNITOLOGISTS?
I FAIL TO SEE WHAT DIFFERENCE THAT MAKES.
RELIGIOUS ZEALOTS ARE INHERENTLY PRONE TO HYSTERIA.IT'S DOCUMENTED.
YES, WELL, I'LL THANK YOU TO KEEP WORDS LIKE "ZEALOT" OUT OF YOUR REPORTS.
GOOD DAY, DOCTOR.

PLANETCRACK DAY

THIS IS GETTING BAD.

DON'T PANIC YET, PERRY. EVEN IF THE COLONY'S IN TROUBLE, WE'RE OKAY UP HERE.

UNTIL THEY START BRINGING THEIR SICK UP HERE. OH WAIT, THEY CAN'T, BECAUSE THERE'S A DAMN *NO-FLY* ORDER.

THAT NO-FLY MAY BE THE ONLY THING KEEPING US SAFE. LET'S NOT JUMP TO CONCLUSIONS.

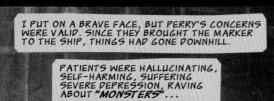

I PUT ON A BRAVE FACE, BUT PERRY'S CONCERNS WERE VALID. SINCE THEY BROUGHT THE MARKER TO THE SHIP, THINGS HAD GONE DOWNHILL.

PATIENTS WERE HALLUCINATING, SELF-HARMING, SUFFERING SEVERE DEPRESSION, RAVING ABOUT *"MONSTERS"*...

...IT WOULD TAKE MORE THAN A NO-FLY ORDER TO STOP THIS.

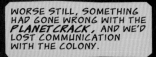

WORSE STILL, SOMETHING HAD GONE WRONG WITH THE *PLANET CRACK*, AND WE'D LOST COMMUNICATION WITH THE COLONY.

THEN WE HEARD ABOUT A COLONY SHUTTLE CRASH-LANDING ON THE FLIGHT DECK, AND A SUBSEQUENT SMALL *OUTBREAK* OF SOME KIND.

NICOLE! FLIGHT DECK CALLED. THEY'VE GOT A DOZEN INJURED THEY WANT US TO TAKE IN, SOME SERIOUS.

WHY HERE? IS THE FLIGHT DECK BAY INFECTED, TOO?

THEY DIDN'T SAY.

BEEP BEEP

HOLD ON...

DR BRENNAN SPEAKING.

THIS IS *VINCENT*, SECURITY. NEED A FAVOR, DOC. WE'VE GOT *FOUR COLONISTS* JUST SNUCK THEIR WAY ON BOARD.

SURELY THAT'S *YOUR* AREA, CHIEF.

OH, THEY'RE ALREADY IN CUSTODY. I WANT YOU TO CHECK THEM FOR INFECTION.

SEND THEM TO *QUARANTINE* ON THIS DECK.

PERRY, STAY HERE TILL THE FLIGHT DECK INJURED ARRIVE, THEN GET SOME REST. YOU LOOK LIKE YOU NEED IT

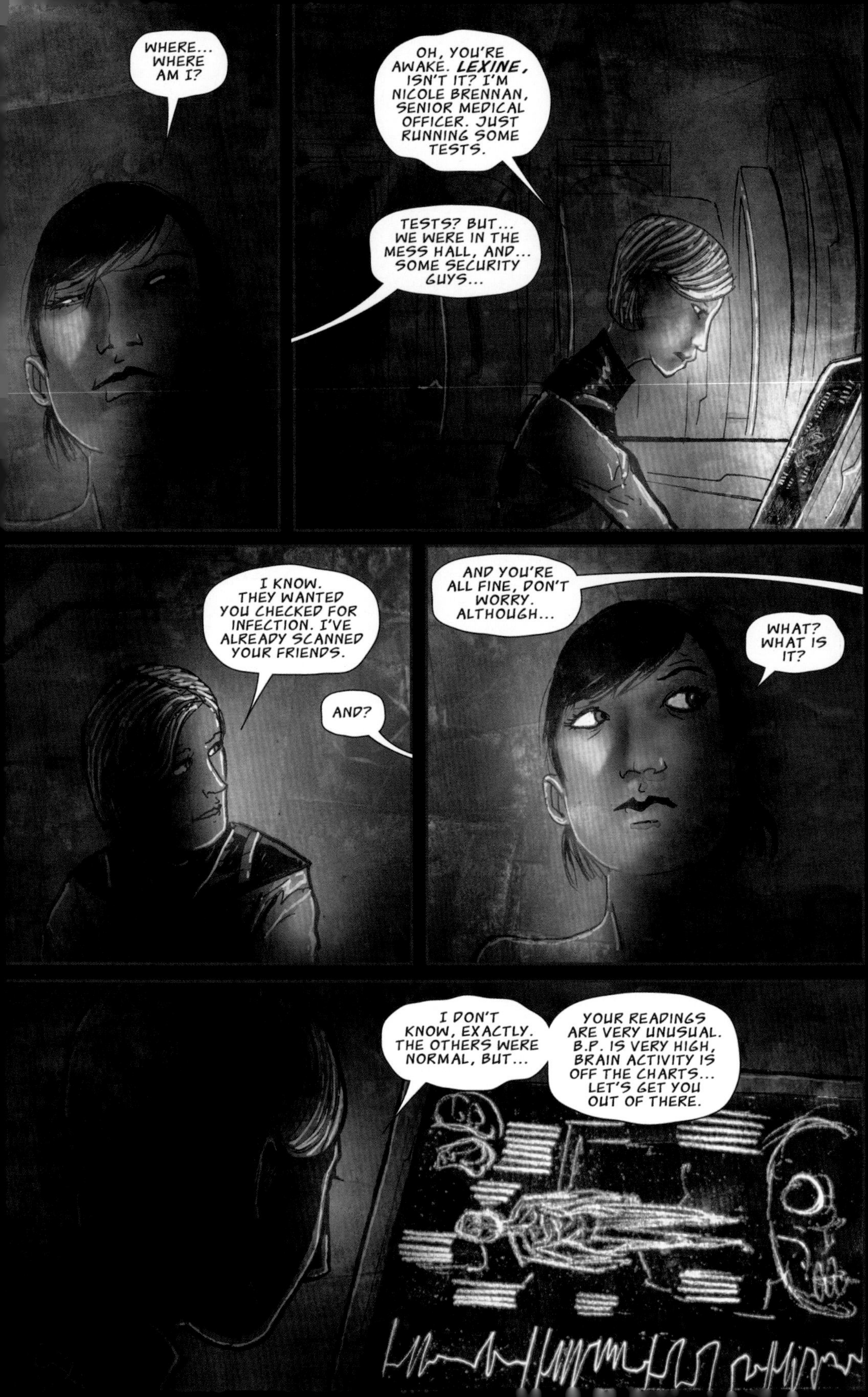
WHERE... WHERE AM I?
OH, YOU'RE AWAKE. LEXINE, ISN'T IT? I'M NICOLE BRENNAN, SENIOR MEDICAL OFFICER. JUST RUNNING SOME TESTS.
TESTS? BUT... WE WERE IN THE MESS HALL, AND... SOME SECURITY GUYS...
I KNOW. THEY WANTED YOU CHECKED FOR INFECTION. I'VE ALREADY SCANNED YOUR FRIENDS.
AND?
AND YOU'RE ALL FINE, DON'T WORRY. ALTHOUGH...
WHAT? WHAT IS IT?
I DON'T KNOW, EXACTLY. THE OTHERS WERE NORMAL, BUT...
YOUR READINGS ARE VERY UNUSUAL. B.P. IS VERY HIGH, BRAIN ACTIVITY IS OFF THE CHARTS... LET'S GET YOU OUT OF THERE.

THEY WERE AN ODD BUNCH. *MCNEILL*, A P-SEC COP; *WELLER*, A SECURITY OFFICER FROM THE ISHIMURA; AND *ECKHARDT*, A CEC EXECUTIVE.

ALL THEY HAD IN COMMON WAS THEIR ESCAPE FROM THE COLONY.

AS WE LEFT QUARANTINE, THEY TOLD ME WHAT HAD HAPPENED TO THEM ON THE SURFACE. I COULD HARDLY BELIEVE IT.

BUT THEN WE FOUND *CAPTAIN MATTHIUS'* BODY IN THE MORGUE.

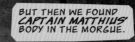

THERE HAD BEEN NO SHIP ANNOUNCEMENT, NO NOTICE THAT HE WAS DEAD. THINGS WERE A LOT WORSE THAN I'D REALIZED.

WHEN WE GOT BACK TO THE *ER*, PERRY WAS STILL THERE. HE HADN'T SLEPT IN 24 HOURS.

WE HAVE MORE PATIENTS IN THE HALLWAY. I'M GOING TO CHECK ON THEM.

SURE, I'LL BE HERE.

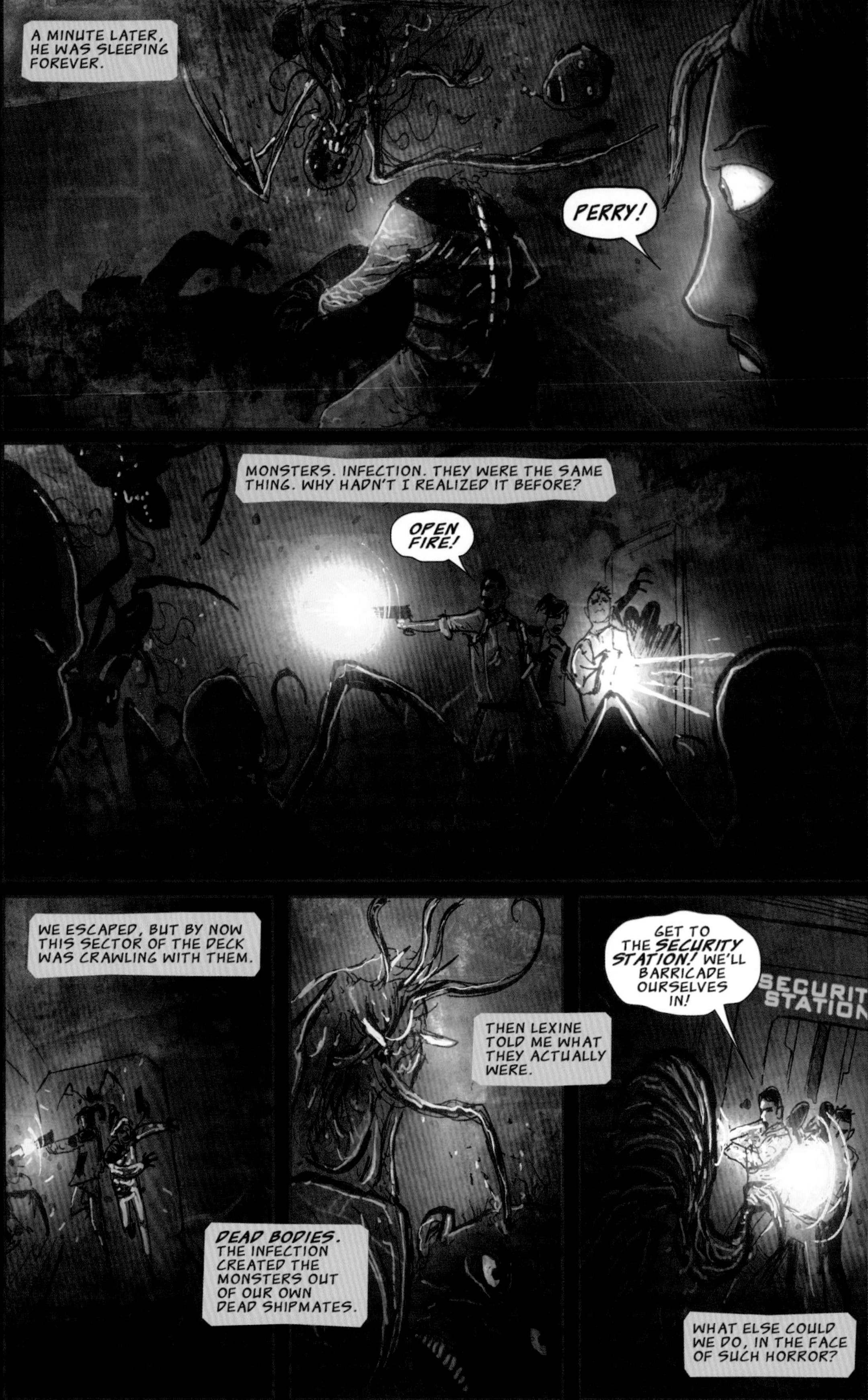
A MINUTE LATER, HE WAS SLEEPING FOREVER.
PERRY!
MONSTERS. INFECTION. THEY WERE THE SAME THING. WHY HADN'T I REALIZED IT BEFORE?
OPEN FIRE!
WE ESCAPED, BUT BY NOW THIS SECTOR OF THE DECK WAS CRAWLING WITH THEM.
THEN LEXINE TOLD ME WHAT THEY ACTUALLY WERE.
DEAD BODIES. THE INFECTION CREATED THE MONSTERS OUT OF OUR OWN DEAD SHIPMATES.
GET TO THE SECURITY STATION! WE'LL BARRICADE OURSELVES IN!
WHAT ELSE COULD WE DO, IN THE FACE OF SUCH HORROR?

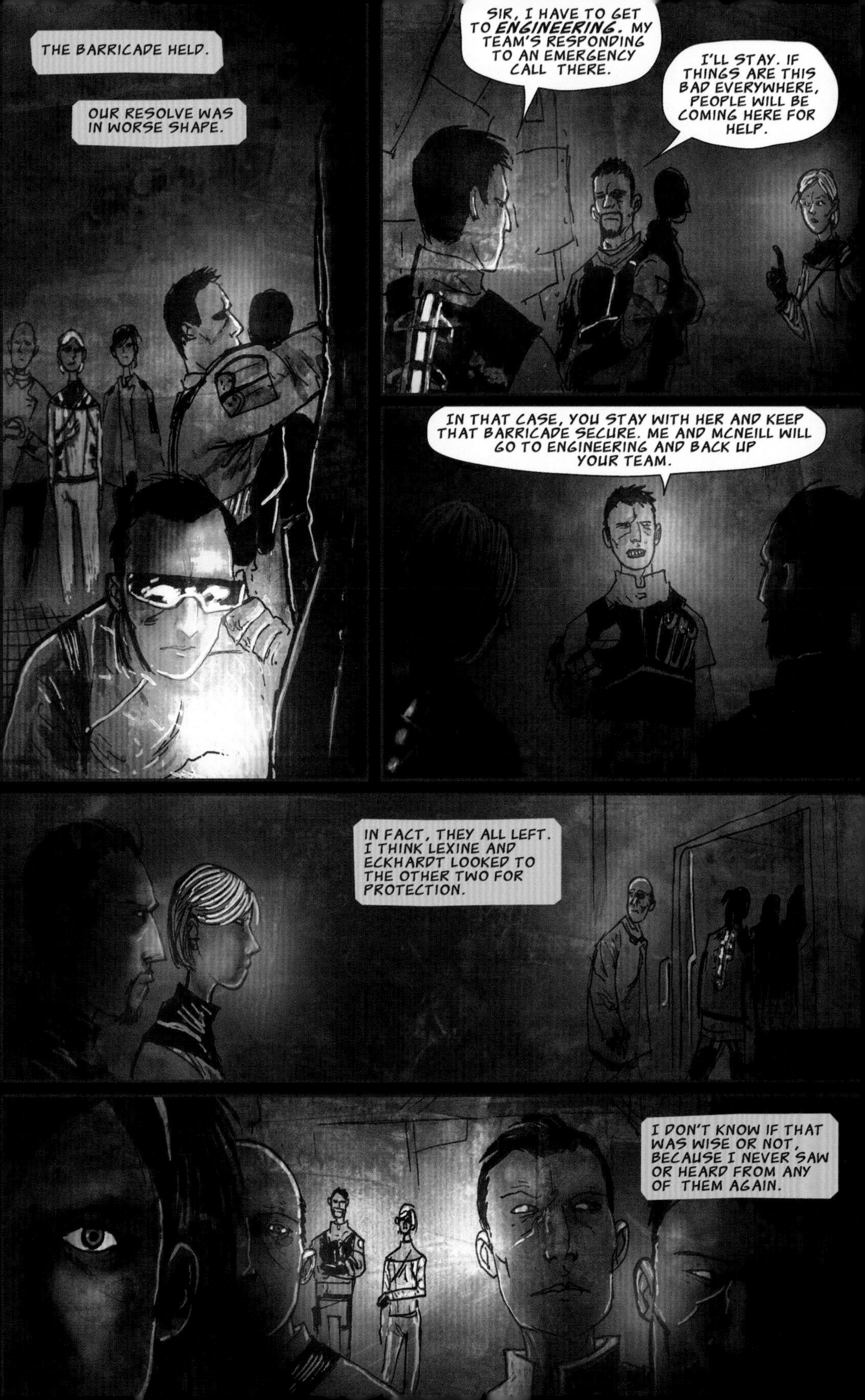
THE BARRICADE HELD.
OUR RESOLVE WAS IN WORSE SHAPE.
SIR, I HAVE TO GET TO ENGINEERING. MY TEAM'S RESPONDING TO AN EMERGENCY CALL THERE.
I'LL STAY. IF THINGS ARE THIS BAD EVERYWHERE, PEOPLE WILL BE COMING HERE FOR HELP.
IN THAT CASE, YOU STAY WITH HER AND KEEP THAT BARRICADE SECURE. ME AND MCNEILL WILL GO TO ENGINEERING AND BACK UP YOUR TEAM.
IN FACT, THEY ALL LEFT. I THINK LEXINE AND ECKHARDT LOOKED TO THE OTHER TWO FOR PROTECTION.
I DON'T KNOW IF THAT WAS WISE OR NOT, BECAUSE I NEVER SAW OR HEARD FROM ANY OF THEM AGAIN.

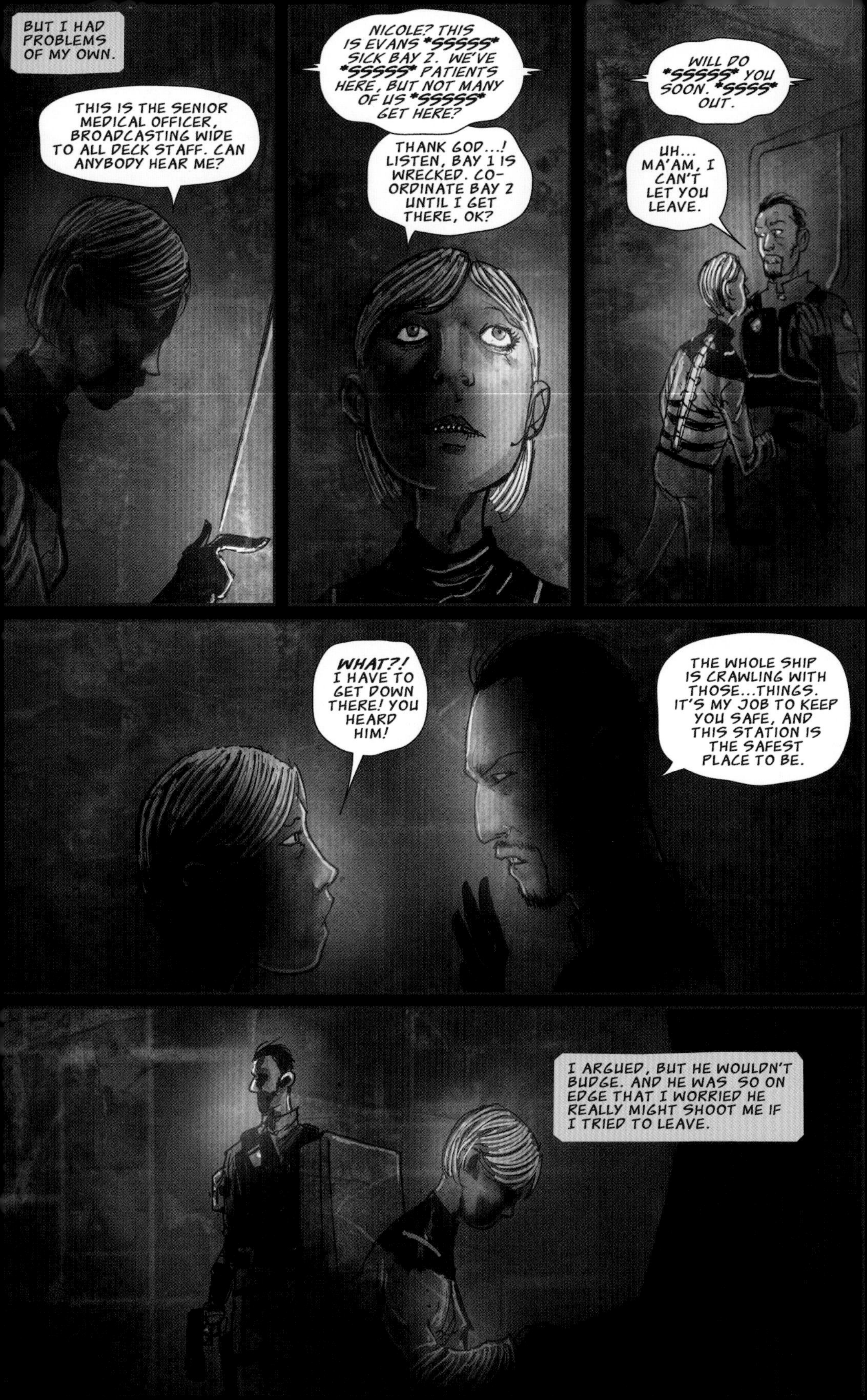
BUT I HAD PROBLEMS OF MY OWN.
THIS IS THE SENIOR MEDICAL OFFICER, BROADCASTING WIDE TO ALL DECK STAFF. CAN ANYBODY HEAR ME?
NICOLE? THIS IS EVANS *SSSSS* SICK BAY 2. WE'VE *SSSSS* PATIENTS HERE, BUT NOT MANY OF US *SSSSS* GET HERE?
THANK GOD...! LISTEN, BAY 1 IS WRECKED. CO-ORDINATE BAY 2 UNTIL I GET THERE, OK?
WILL DO *SSSSS* YOU SOON. *SSSS* OUT.
UH... MA'AM, I CAN'T LET YOU LEAVE.
WHAT?! I HAVE TO GET DOWN THERE! YOU HEARD HIM!
THE WHOLE SHIP IS CRAWLING WITH THOSE...THINGS. IT'S MY JOB TO KEEP YOU SAFE, AND THIS STATION IS THE SAFEST PLACE TO BE.
I ARGUED, BUT HE WOULDN'T BUDGE. AND HE WAS SO ON EDGE THAT I WORRIED HE REALLY MIGHT SHOOT ME IF I TRIED TO LEAVE.

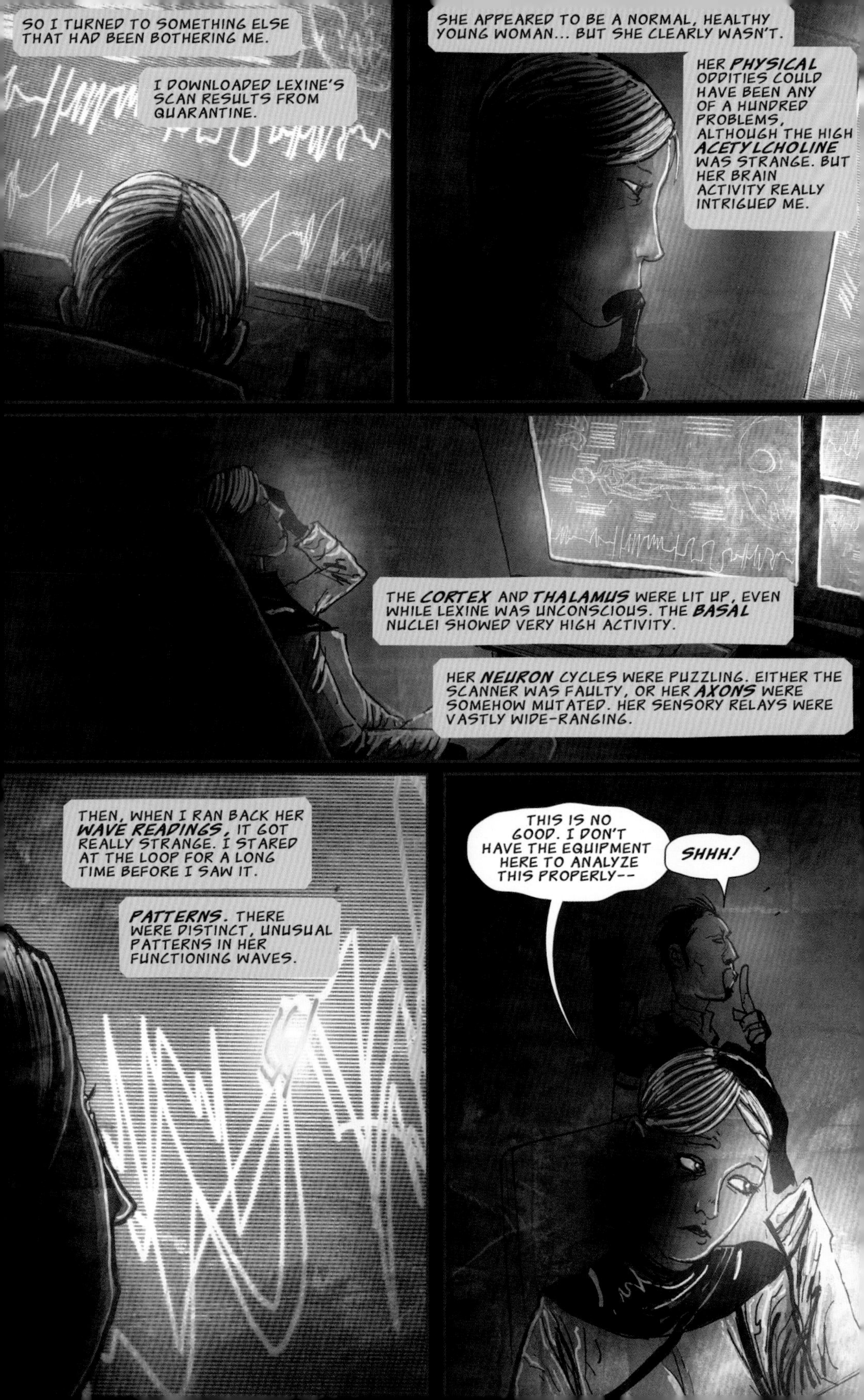
SO I TURNED TO SOMETHING ELSE THAT HAD BEEN BOTHERING ME.
I DOWNLOADED LEXINE'S SCAN RESULTS FROM QUARANTINE.
SHE APPEARED TO BE A NORMAL, HEALTHY YOUNG WOMAN... BUT SHE CLEARLY WASN'T.
HER PHYSICAL ODDITIES COULD HAVE BEEN ANY OF A HUNDRED PROBLEMS, ALTHOUGH THE HIGH ACETYLCHOLINE WAS STRANGE. BUT HER BRAIN ACTIVITY REALLY INTRIGUED ME.
THE CORTEX AND THALAMUS WERE LIT UP, EVEN WHILE LEXINE WAS UNCONSCIOUS. THE BASAL NUCLEI SHOWED VERY HIGH ACTIVITY.
HER NEURON CYCLES WERE PUZZLING. EITHER THE SCANNER WAS FAULTY, OR HER AXONS WERE SOMEHOW MUTATED. HER SENSORY RELAYS WERE VASTLY WIDE-RANGING.
THEN, WHEN I RAN BACK HER WAVE READINGS, IT GOT REALLY STRANGE. I STARED AT THE LOOP FOR A LONG TIME BEFORE I SAW IT.
PATTERNS. THERE WERE DISTINCT, UNUSUAL PATTERNS IN HER FUNCTIONING WAVES.
THIS IS NO GOOD. I DON'T HAVE THE EQUIPMENT HERE TO ANALYZE THIS PROPERLY--
SHHH!

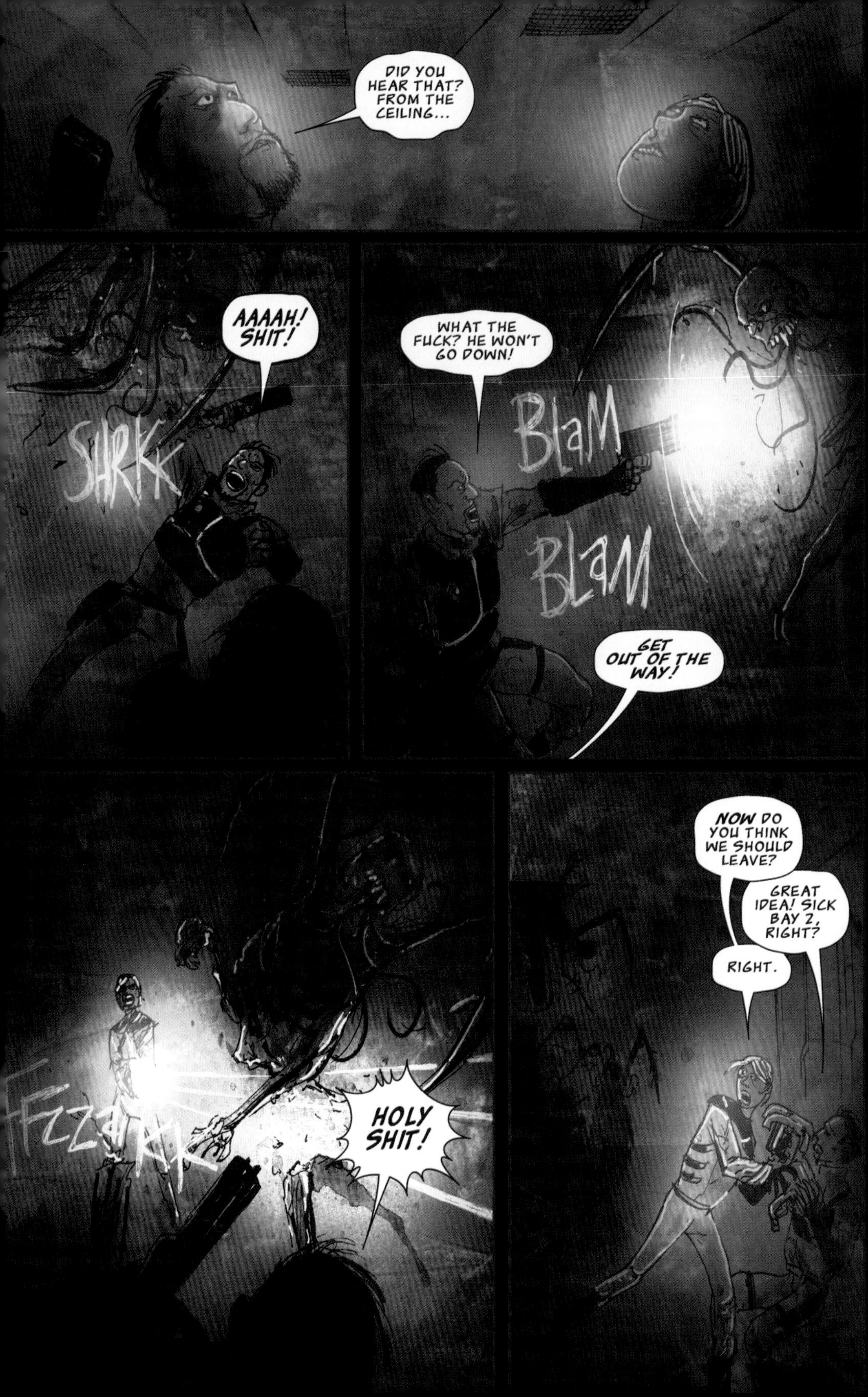
DID YOU HEAR THAT? FROM THE CEILING...
AAAAH! SHIT!
SHRKK
WHAT THE FUCK? HE WON'T GO DOWN!
BLAM
BLAM
GET OUT OF THE WAY!
FFZZAKKK
HOLY SHIT!
NOW DO YOU THINK WE SHOULD LEAVE?
GREAT IDEA! SICK BAY 2, RIGHT?
RIGHT.

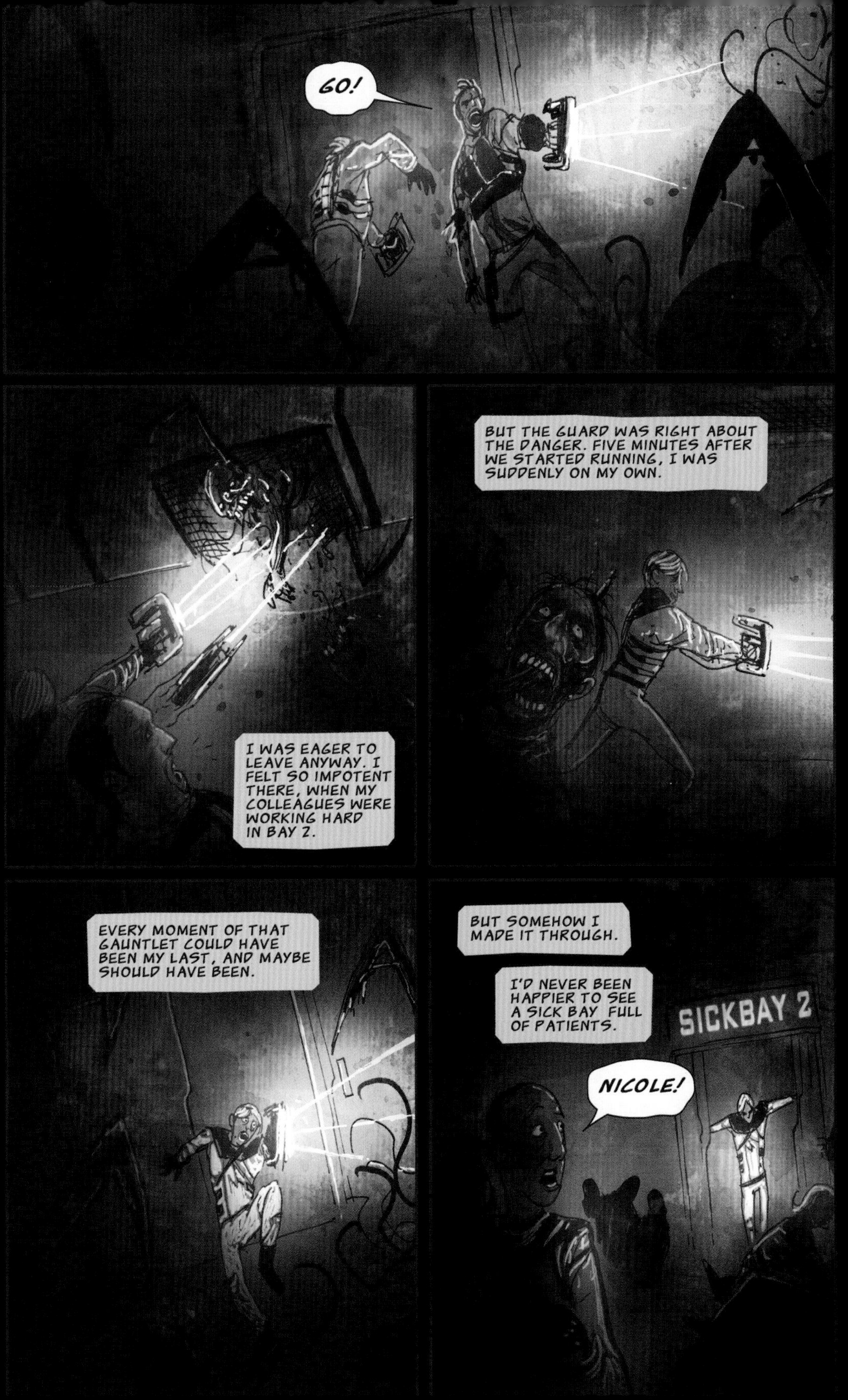
GO!
I WAS EAGER TO LEAVE ANYWAY. I FELT SO IMPOTENT THERE, WHEN MY COLLEAGUES WERE WORKING HARD IN BAY 2.
BUT THE GUARD WAS RIGHT ABOUT THE DANGER. FIVE MINUTES AFTER WE STARTED RUNNING, I WAS SUDDENLY ON MY OWN.
EVERY MOMENT OF THAT GAUNTLET COULD HAVE BEEN MY LAST, AND MAYBE SHOULD HAVE BEEN.
BUT SOMEHOW I MADE IT THROUGH.
I'D NEVER BEEN HAPPIER TO SEE A SICK BAY FULL OF PATIENTS.
SICKBAY 2
NICOLE!

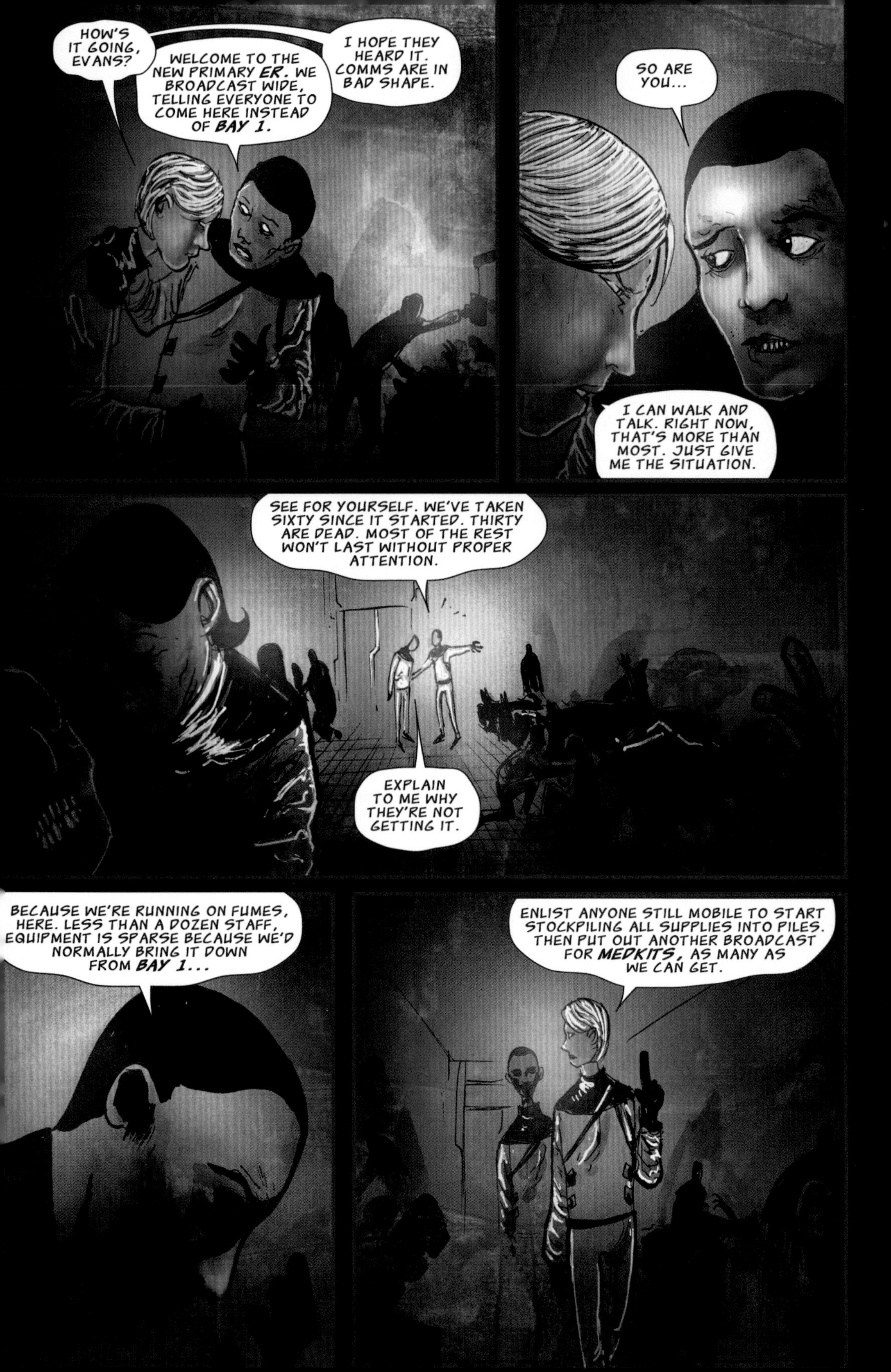
HOW'S IT GOING, EVANS?
WELCOME TO THE NEW PRIMARY ER. WE BROADCAST WIDE, TELLING EVERYONE TO COME HERE INSTEAD OF BAY 1.
I HOPE THEY HEARD IT. COMMS ARE IN BAD SHAPE.
SO ARE YOU...
I CAN WALK AND TALK. RIGHT NOW, THAT'S MORE THAN MOST. JUST GIVE ME THE SITUATION.
SEE FOR YOURSELF. WE'VE TAKEN SIXTY SINCE IT STARTED. THIRTY ARE DEAD. MOST OF THE REST WON'T LAST WITHOUT PROPER ATTENTION.
EXPLAIN TO ME WHY THEY'RE NOT GETTING IT.
BECAUSE WE'RE RUNNING ON FUMES, HERE. LESS THAN A DOZEN STAFF. EQUIPMENT IS SPARSE BECAUSE WE'D NORMALLY BRING IT DOWN FROM BAY 1...
ENLIST ANYONE STILL MOBILE TO START STOCKPILING ALL SUPPLIES INTO PILES. THEN PUT OUT ANOTHER BROADCAST FOR MEDKITS, AS MANY AS WE CAN GET.

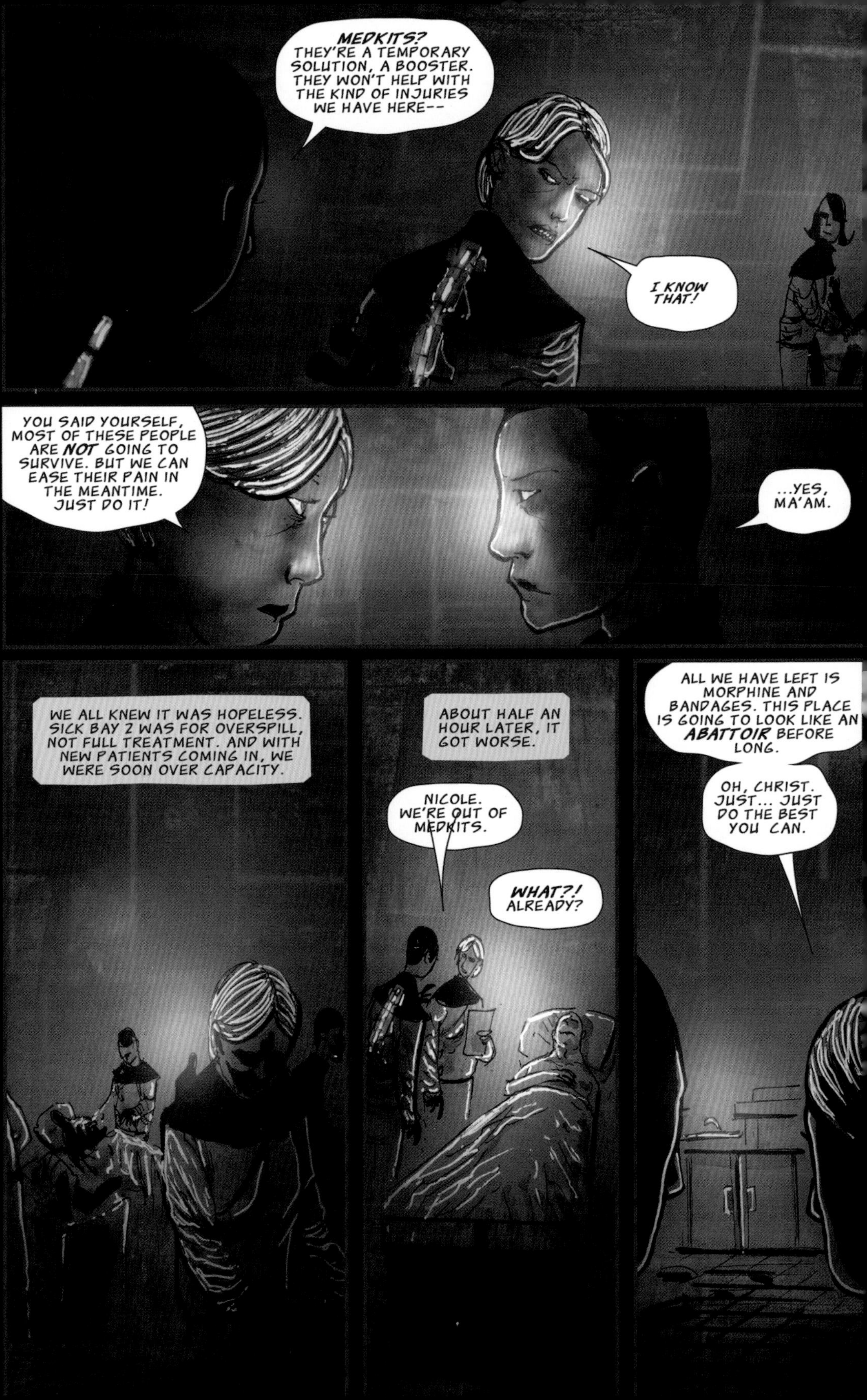
MEDKITS? THEY'RE A TEMPORARY SOLUTION, A BOOSTER. THEY WON'T HELP WITH THE KIND OF INJURIES WE HAVE HERE--
I KNOW THAT!
YOU SAID YOURSELF, MOST OF THESE PEOPLE ARE NOT GOING TO SURVIVE. BUT WE CAN EASE THEIR PAIN IN THE MEANTIME. JUST DO IT!
...YES, MA'AM.
WE ALL KNEW IT WAS HOPELESS. SICK BAY 2 WAS FOR OVERSPILL, NOT FULL TREATMENT. AND WITH NEW PATIENTS COMING IN, WE WERE SOON OVER CAPACITY.
ABOUT HALF AN HOUR LATER, IT GOT WORSE.
NICOLE. WE'RE OUT OF MEDKITS.
WHAT?! ALREADY?
ALL WE HAVE LEFT IS MORPHINE AND BANDAGES. THIS PLACE IS GOING TO LOOK LIKE AN ABATTOIR BEFORE LONG.
OH, CHRIST. JUST... JUST DO THE BEST YOU CAN.

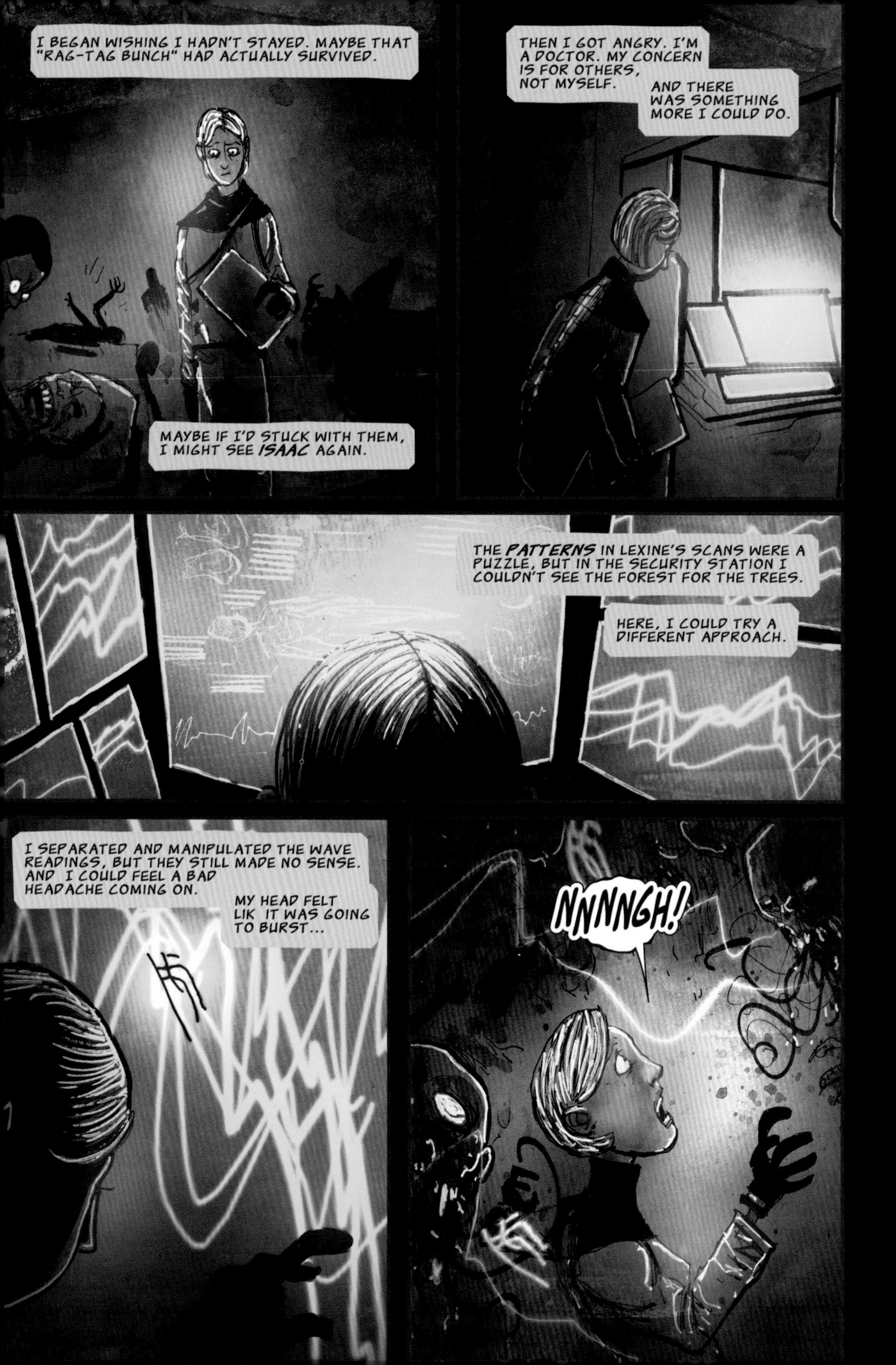
I BEGAN WISHING I HADN'T STAYED. MAYBE THAT "RAG-TAG BUNCH" HAD ACTUALLY SURVIVED.
MAYBE IF I'D STUCK WITH THEM, I MIGHT SEE ISAAC AGAIN.
THEN I GOT ANGRY. I'M A DOCTOR. MY CONCERN IS FOR OTHERS, NOT MYSELF.
AND THERE WAS SOMETHING MORE I COULD DO.
THE PATTERNS IN LEXINE'S SCANS WERE A PUZZLE, BUT IN THE SECURITY STATION I COULDN'T SEE THE FOREST FOR THE TREES.
HERE, I COULD TRY A DIFFERENT APPROACH.
I SEPARATED AND MANIPULATED THE WAVE READINGS, BUT THEY STILL MADE NO SENSE. AND I COULD FEEL A BAD HEADACHE COMING ON.
MY HEAD FELT LIK IT WAS GOING TO BURST...
NNNNGH!

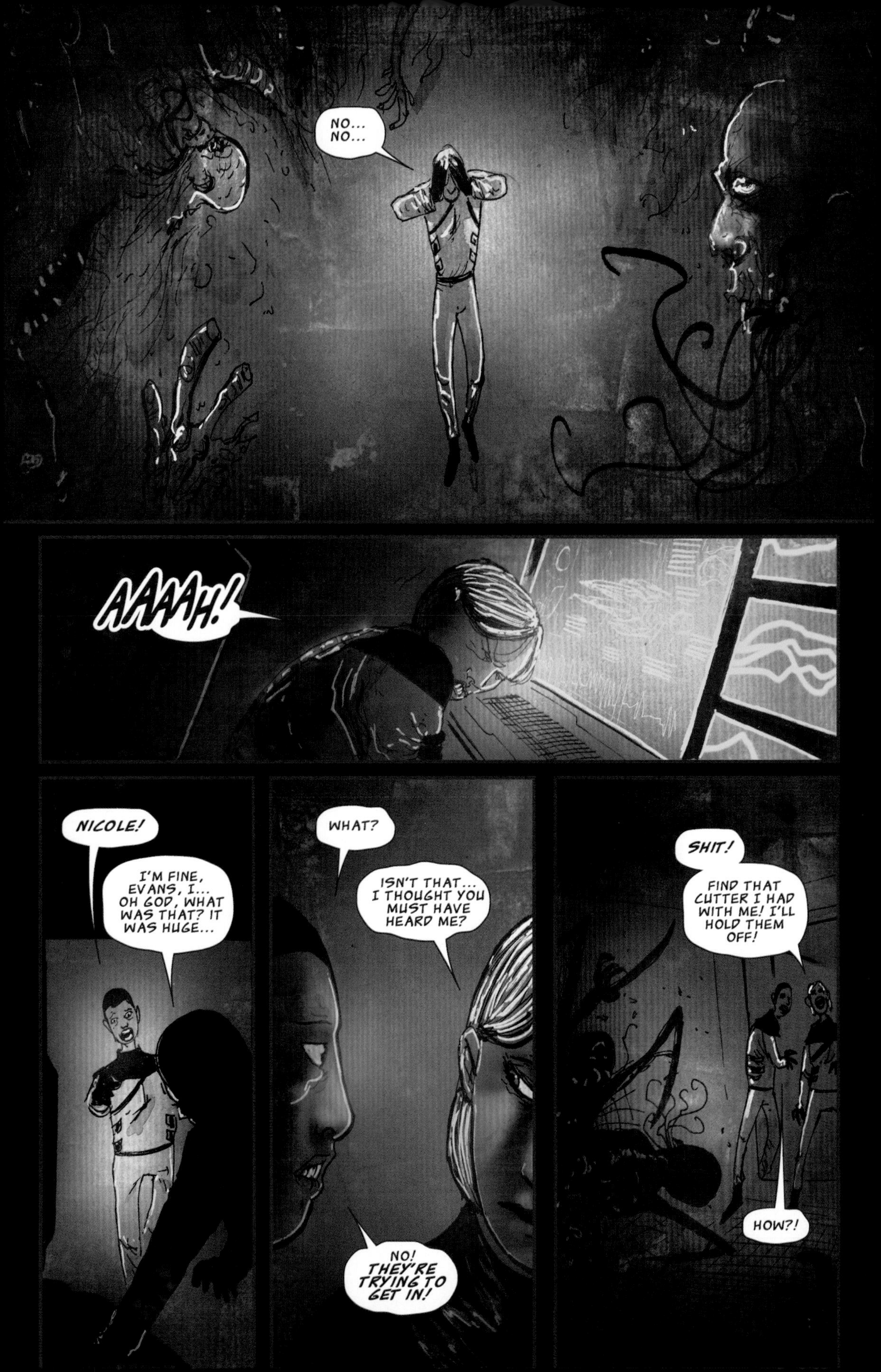
NO...
NO...
AAAAH!
NICOLE!
I'M FINE, EVANS, I... OH GOD, WHAT WAS THAT? IT WAS HUGE...
WHAT?
ISN'T THAT... I THOUGHT YOU MUST HAVE HEARD ME?
NO! THEY'RE TRYING TO GET IN!
SHIT!
FIND THAT CUTTER I HAD WITH ME! I'LL HOLD THEM OFF!
HOW?!

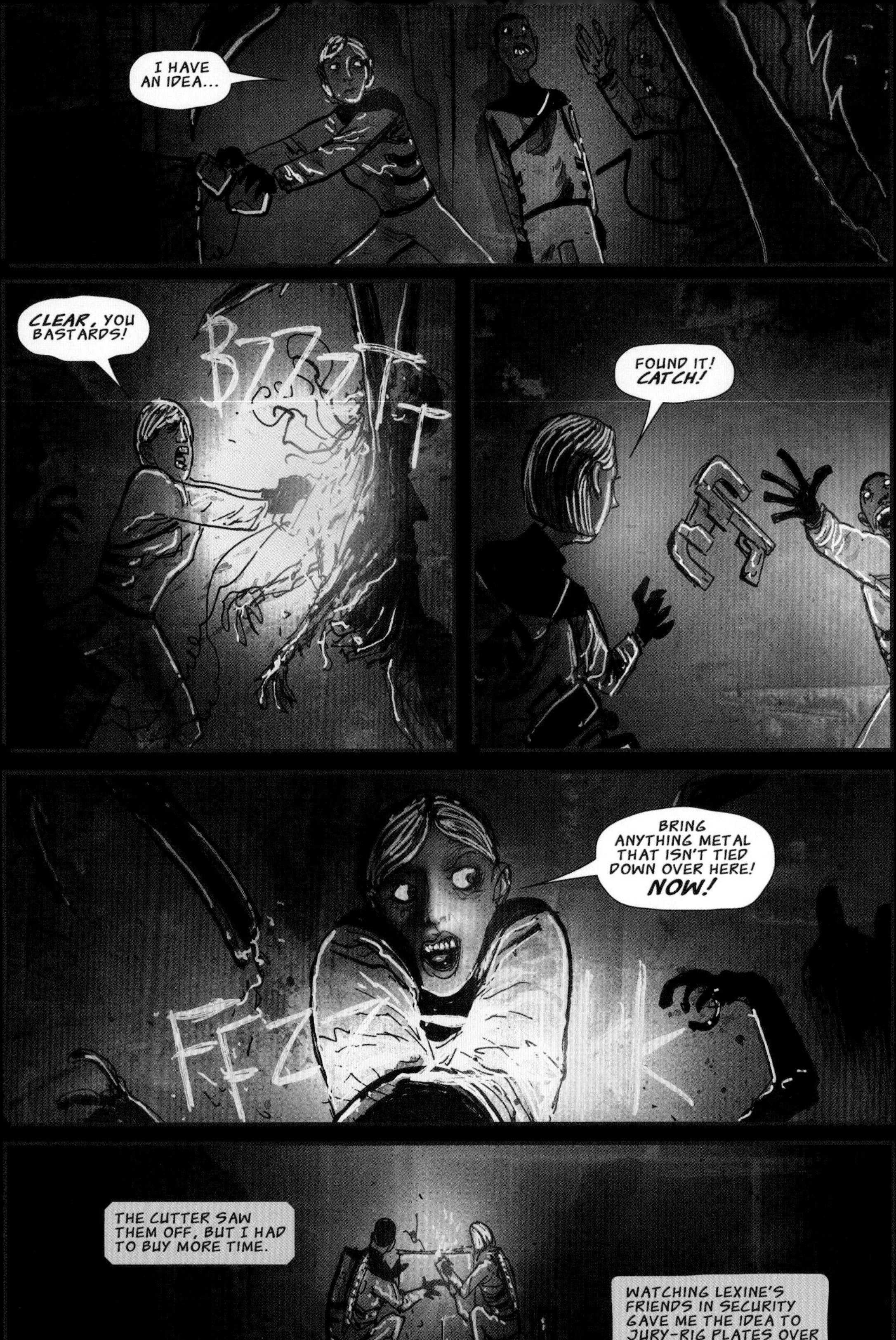
I HAVE AN IDEA...
CLEAR, YOU BASTARDS!
BZZZTT
FOUND IT! CATCH!
BRING ANYTHING METAL THAT ISN'T TIED DOWN OVER HERE! NOW!
FFZZK
THE CUTTER SAW THEM OFF, BUT I HAD TO BUY MORE TIME.
WATCHING LEXINE'S FRIENDS IN SECURITY GAVE ME THE IDEA TO JURY-RIG PLATES OVER ALL THE VENT HOLES IN THE BAY.

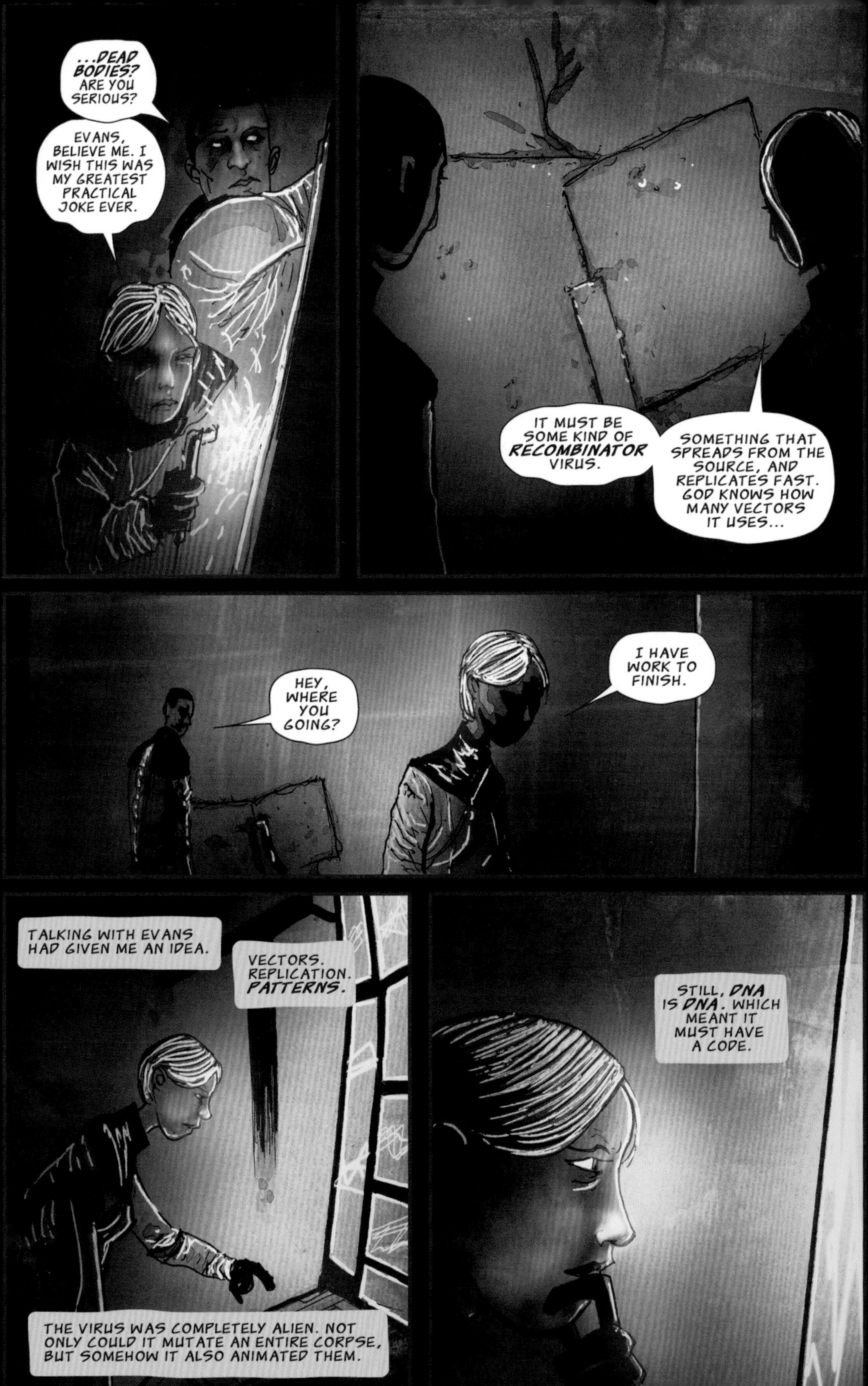
...DEAD BODIES? ARE YOU SERIOUS?
EVANS, BELIEVE ME. I WISH THIS WAS MY GREATEST PRACTICAL JOKE EVER.
IT MUST BE SOME KIND OF RECOMBINATOR VIRUS.
SOMETHING THAT SPREADS FROM THE SOURCE, AND REPLICATES FAST. GOD KNOWS HOW MANY VECTORS IT USES...
HEY, WHERE YOU GOING?
I HAVE WORK TO FINISH.
TALKING WITH EVANS HAD GIVEN ME AN IDEA.
VECTORS. REPLICATION. PATTERNS.
THE VIRUS WAS COMPLETELY ALIEN. NOT ONLY COULD IT MUTATE AN ENTIRE CORPSE, BUT SOMEHOW IT ALSO ANIMATED THEM.
STILL, DNA IS DNA. WHICH MEANT IT MUST HAVE A CODE.

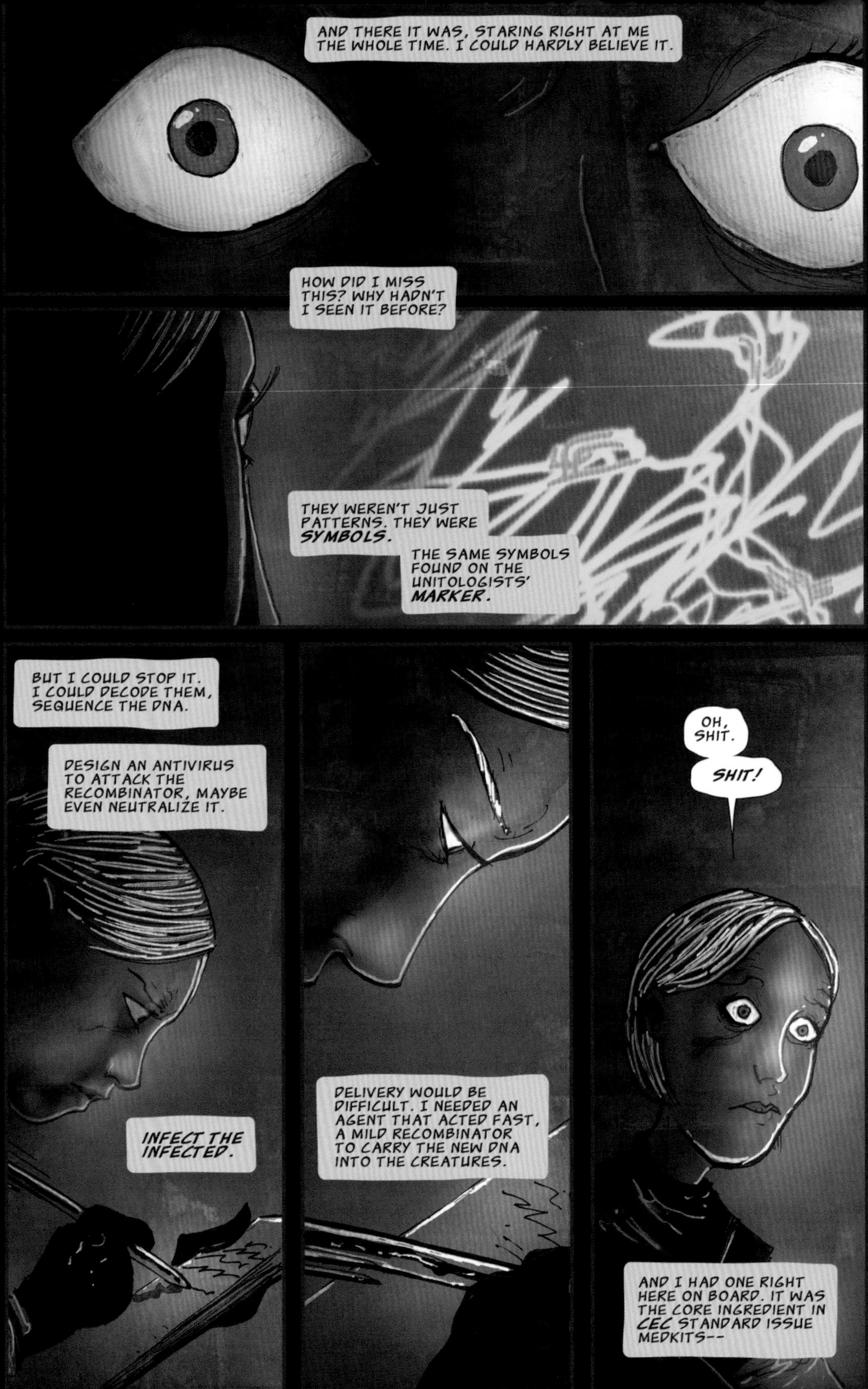
AND THERE IT WAS, STARING RIGHT AT ME THE WHOLE TIME. I COULD HARDLY BELIEVE IT.
HOW DID I MISS THIS? WHY HADN'T I SEEN IT BEFORE?
THEY WEREN'T JUST PATTERNS. THEY WERE *SYMBOLS.*
THE SAME SYMBOLS FOUND ON THE UNITOLOGISTS' *MARKER.*
BUT I COULD STOP IT. I COULD DECODE THEM, SEQUENCE THE DNA.
DESIGN AN ANTIVIRUS TO ATTACK THE RECOMBINATOR, MAYBE EVEN NEUTRALIZE IT.
INFECT THE INFECTED.
DELIVERY WOULD BE DIFFICULT. I NEEDED AN AGENT THAT ACTED FAST, A MILD RECOMBINATOR TO CARRY THE NEW DNA INTO THE CREATURES.
OH, SHIT.
SHIT!
AND I HAD ONE RIGHT HERE ON BOARD. IT WAS THE CORE INGREDIENT IN *CEC* STANDARD ISSUE MEDKITS--

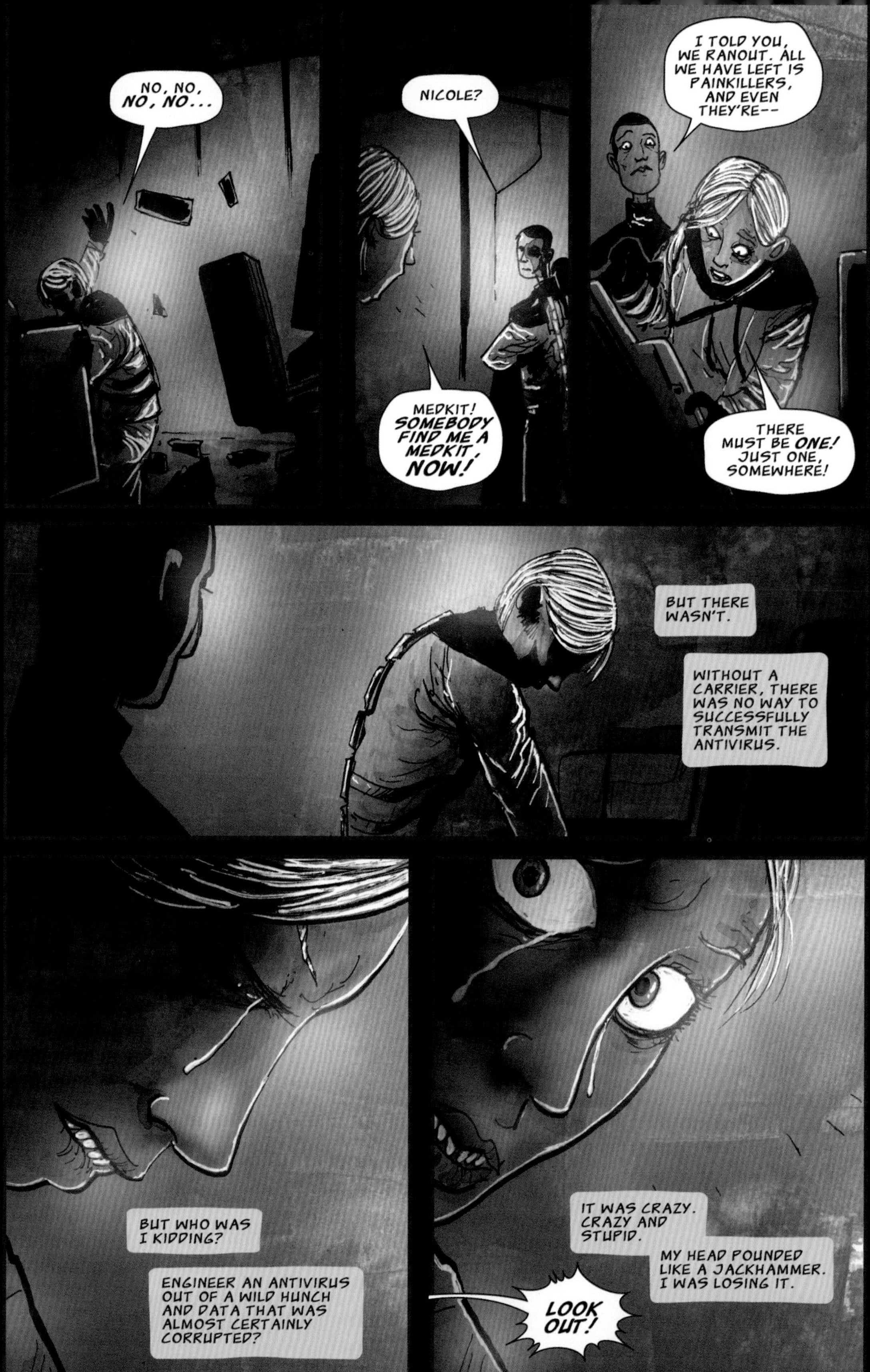
NO, NO, NO, NO...
NICOLE?
MEDKIT! SOMEBODY FIND ME A MEDKIT, NOW!
I TOLD YOU, WE RANOUT. ALL WE HAVE LEFT IS PAINKILLERS, AND EVEN THEY'RE--
THERE MUST BE ONE! JUST ONE, SOMEWHERE!
BUT THERE WASN'T.
WITHOUT A CARRIER, THERE WAS NO WAY TO SUCCESSFULLY TRANSMIT THE ANTIVIRUS.
BUT WHO WAS I KIDDING?
ENGINEER AN ANTIVIRUS OUT OF A WILD HUNCH AND DATA THAT WAS ALMOST CERTAINLY CORRUPTED?
IT WAS CRAZY. CRAZY AND STUPID.
MY HEAD POUNDED LIKE A JACKHAMMER. I WAS LOSING IT.
LOOK OUT!

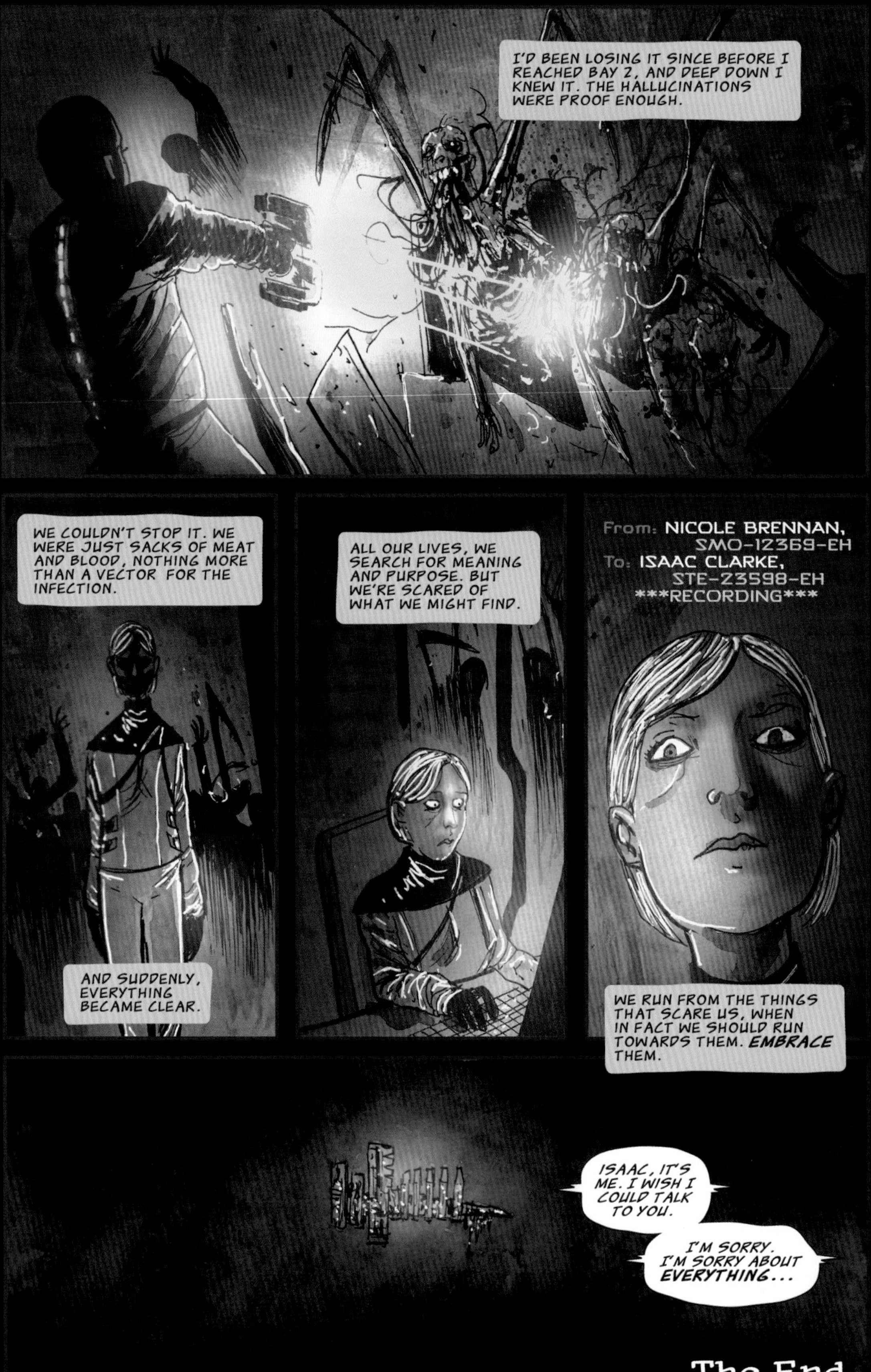
I'D BEEN LOSING IT SINCE BEFORE I REACHED BAY 2, AND DEEP DOWN I KNEW IT. THE HALLUCINATIONS WERE PROOF ENOUGH.
WE COULDN'T STOP IT. WE WERE JUST SACKS OF MEAT AND BLOOD, NOTHING MORE THAN A VECTOR FOR THE INFECTION.
AND SUDDENLY, EVERYTHING BECAME CLEAR.
ALL OUR LIVES, WE SEARCH FOR MEANING AND PURPOSE. BUT WE'RE SCARED OF WHAT WE MIGHT FIND.
From: NICOLE BRENNAN, SMO-12369-EH
To: ISAAC CLARKE, STE-23598-EH
RECORDING
WE RUN FROM THE THINGS THAT SCARE US, WHEN IN FACT WE SHOULD RUN TOWARDS THEM. EMBRACE THEM.
ISAAC, IT'S ME. I WISH I COULD TALK TO YOU.
I'M SORRY. I'M SORRY ABOUT EVERYTHING...
The End

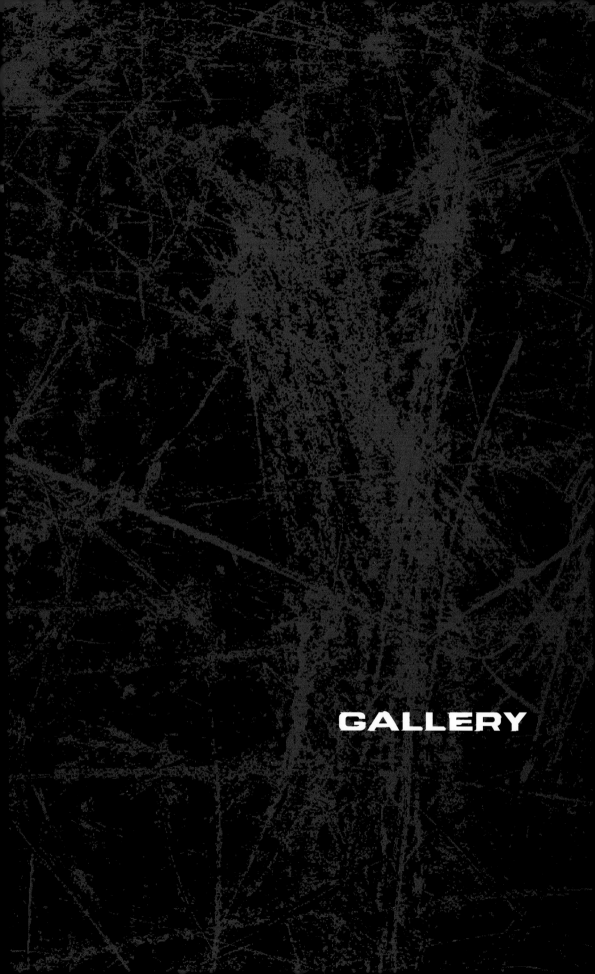

GALLERY

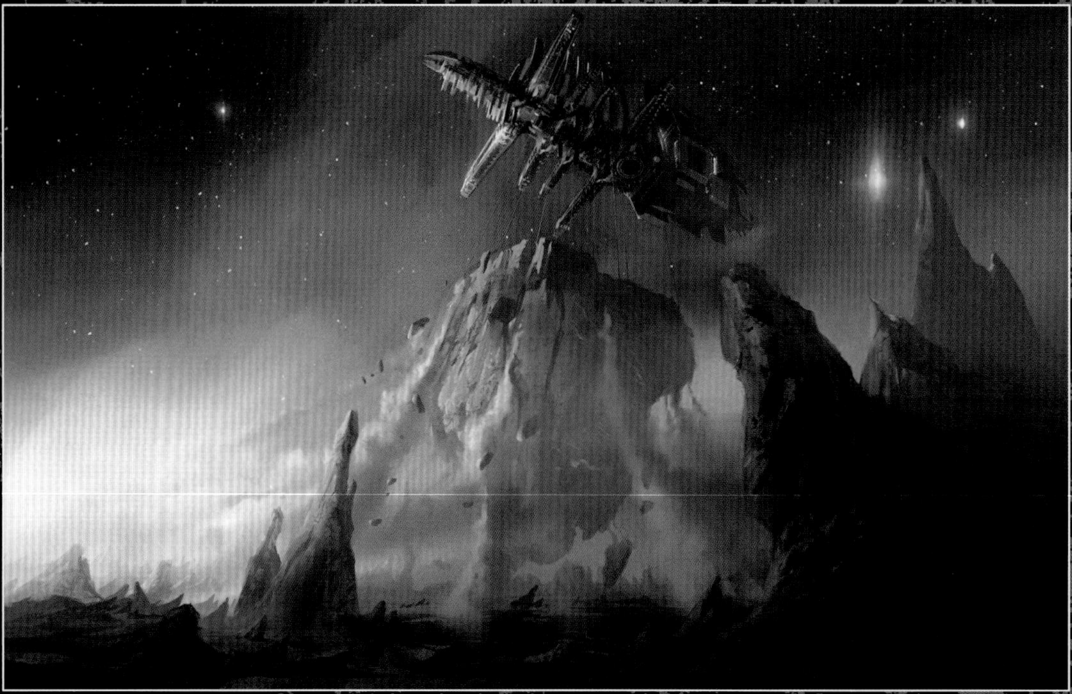

DEAD SPACE GAME CONCEPT ART

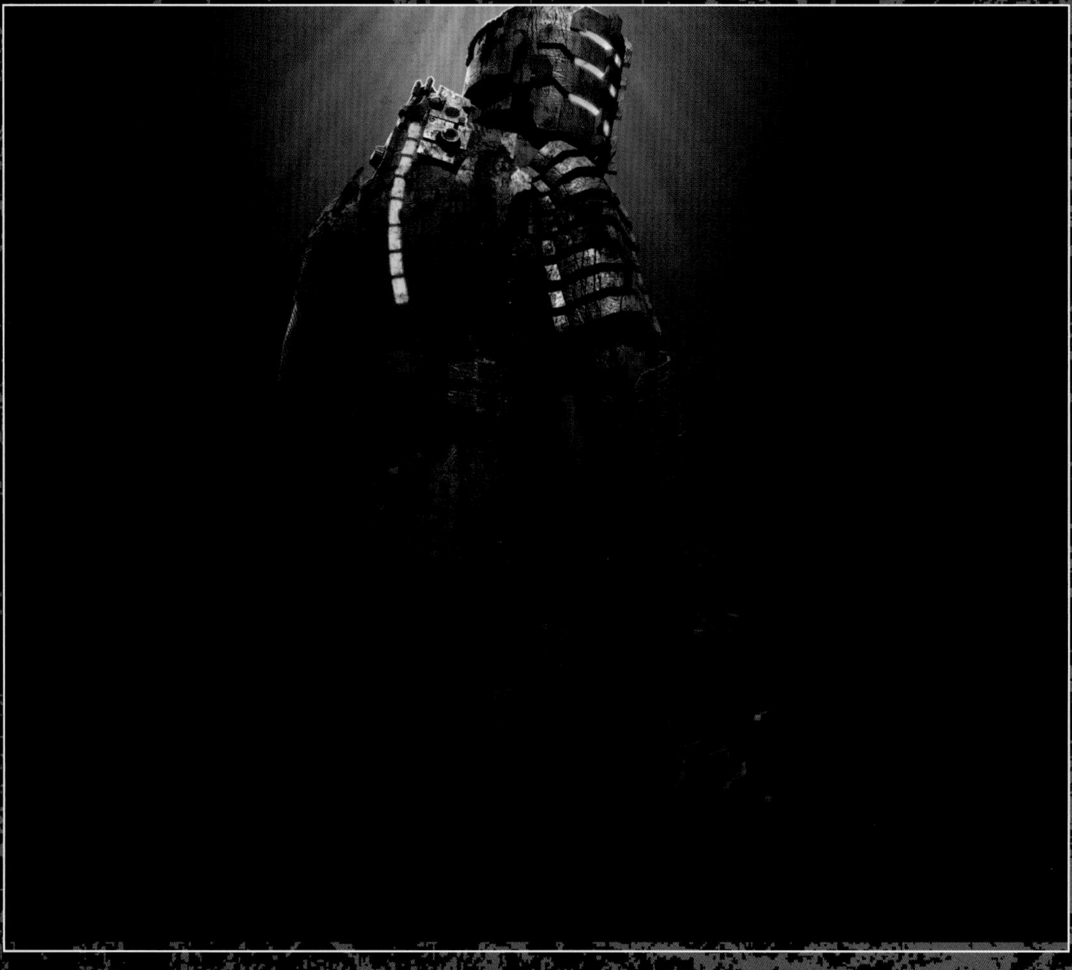

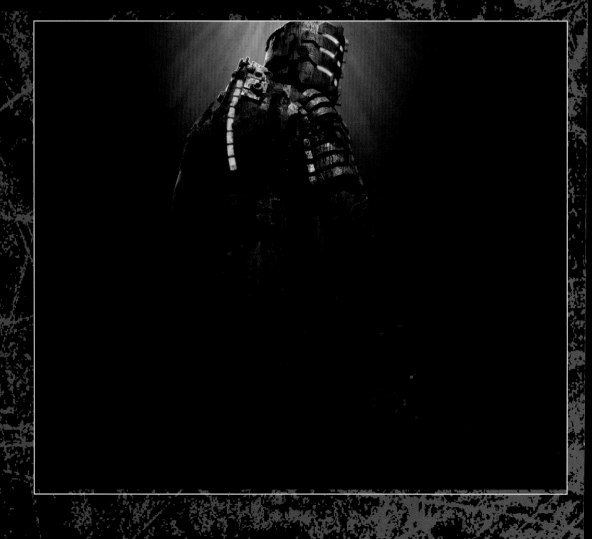

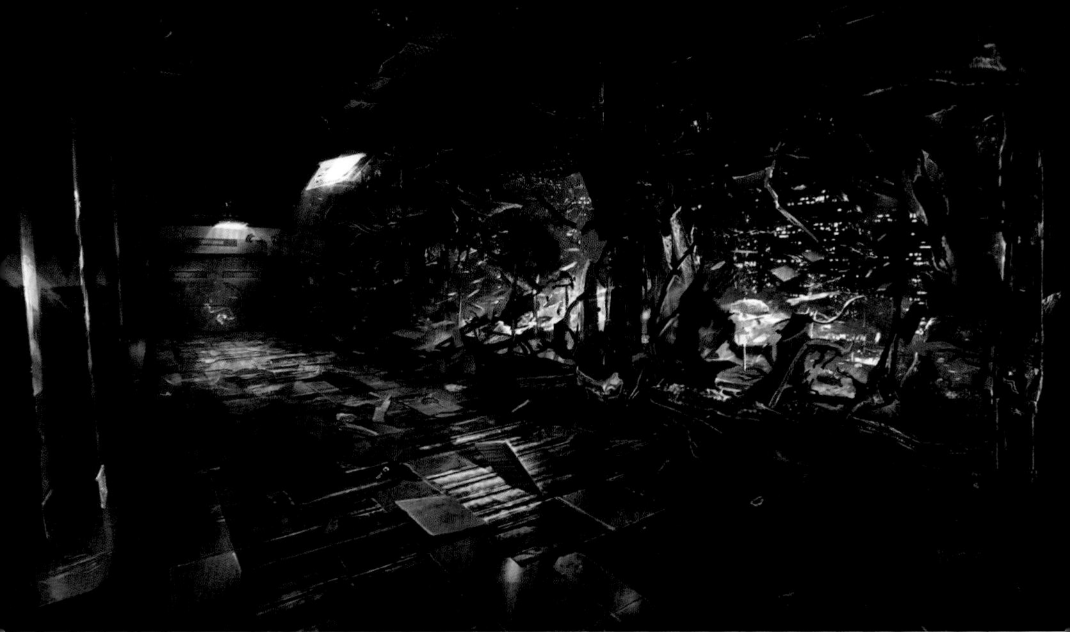

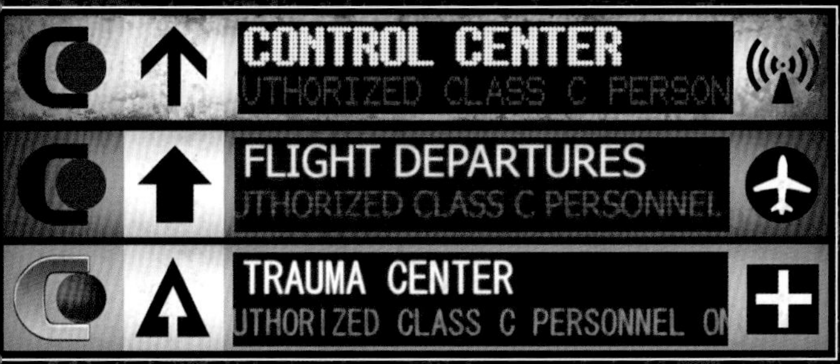
CONTROL CENTER
UTHORIZED CLASS C PERSON
FLIGHT DEPARTURES
UTHORIZED CLASS C PERSONNEL
TRAUMA CENTER
UTHORIZED CLASS C PERSONNEL ON

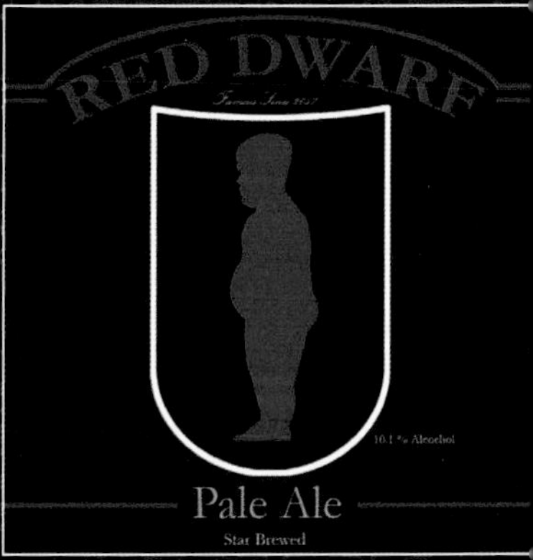
RED DWARF
Pale Ale
Star Brewed

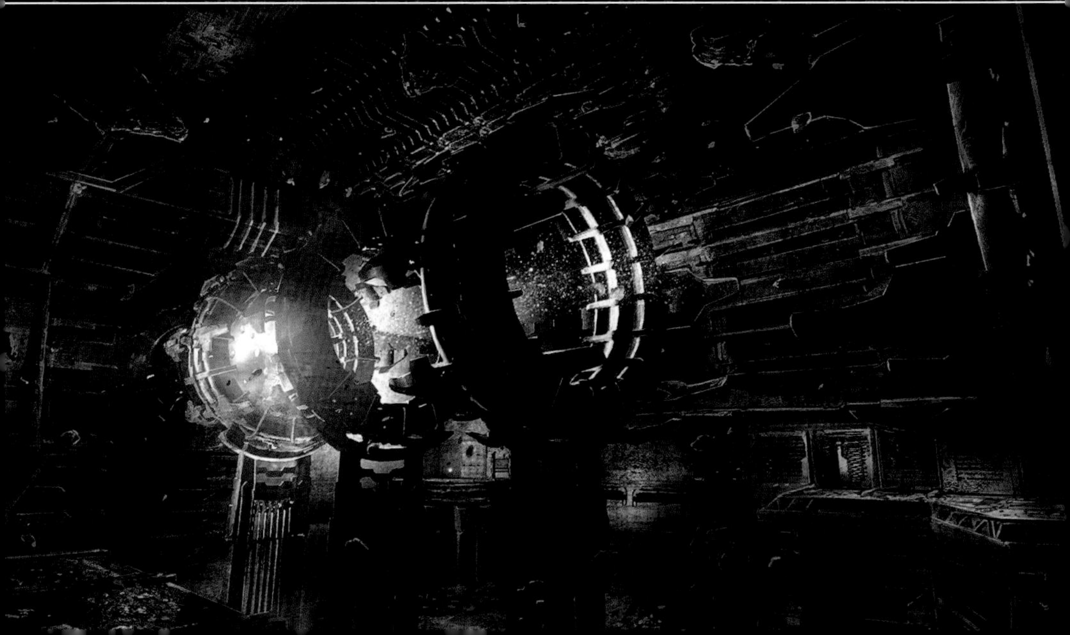

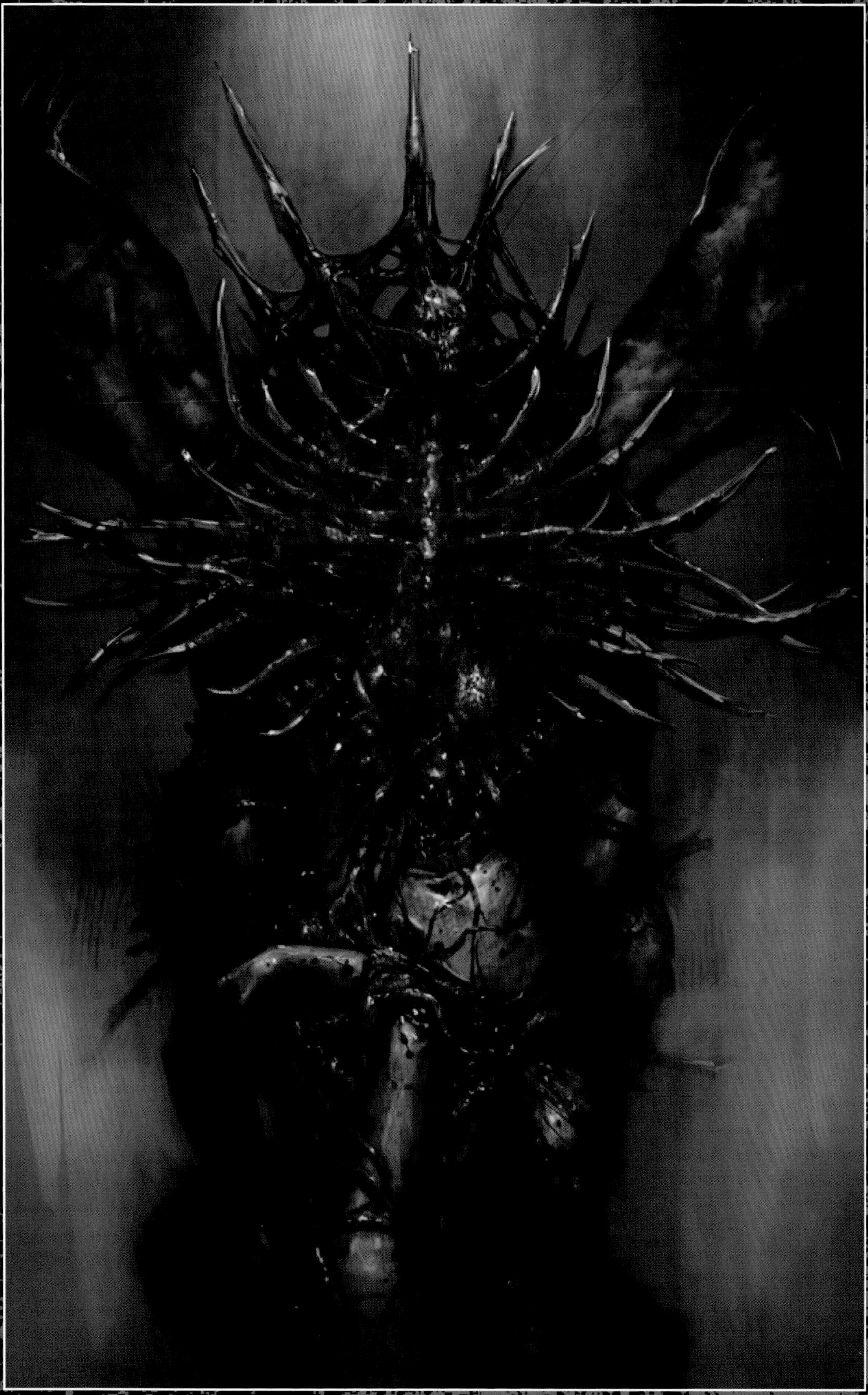

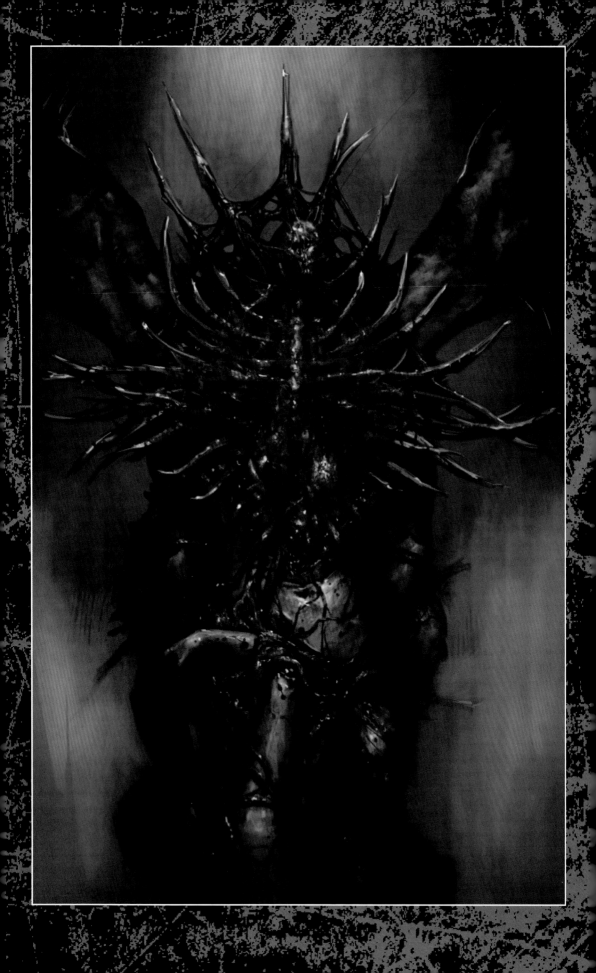

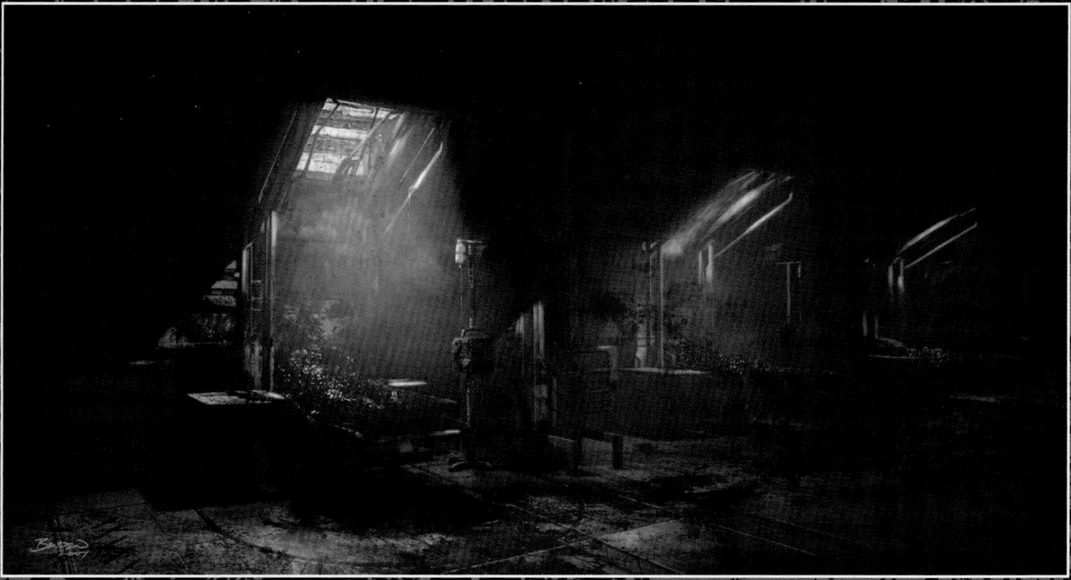

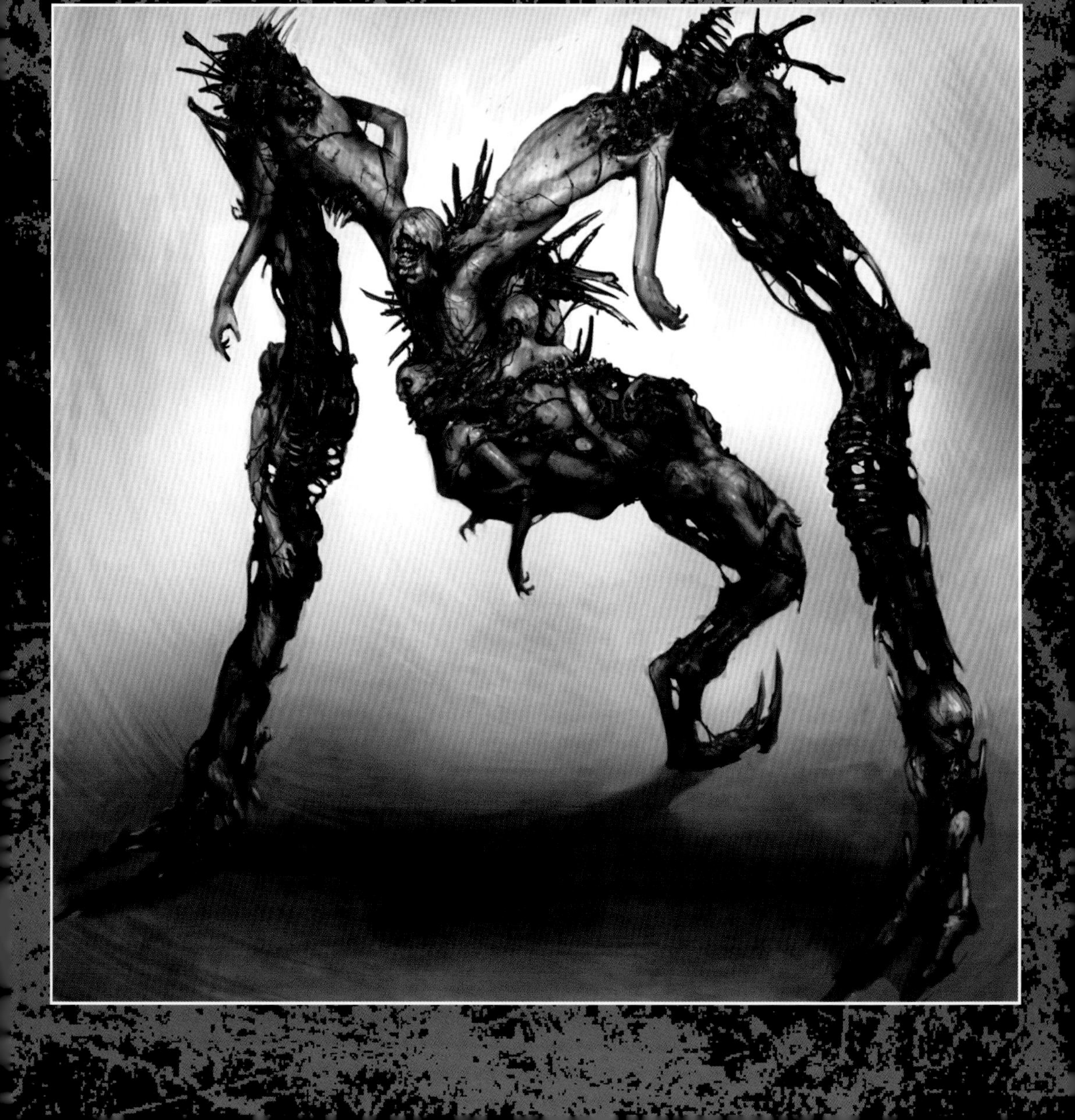

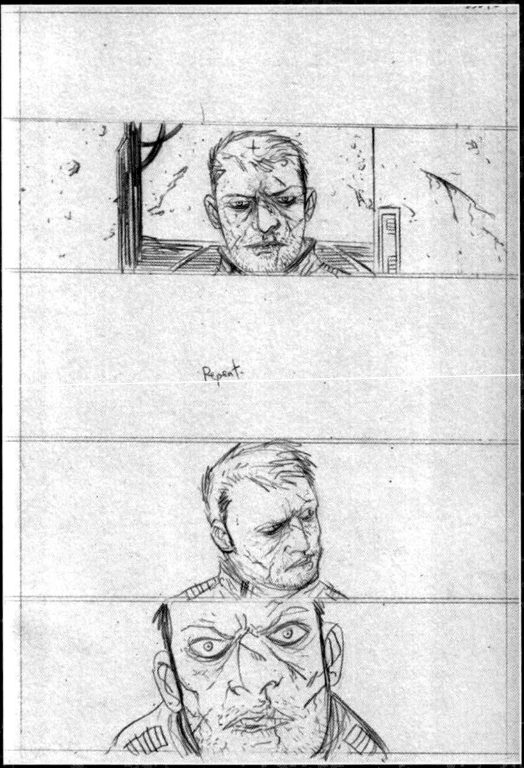
Repeat.

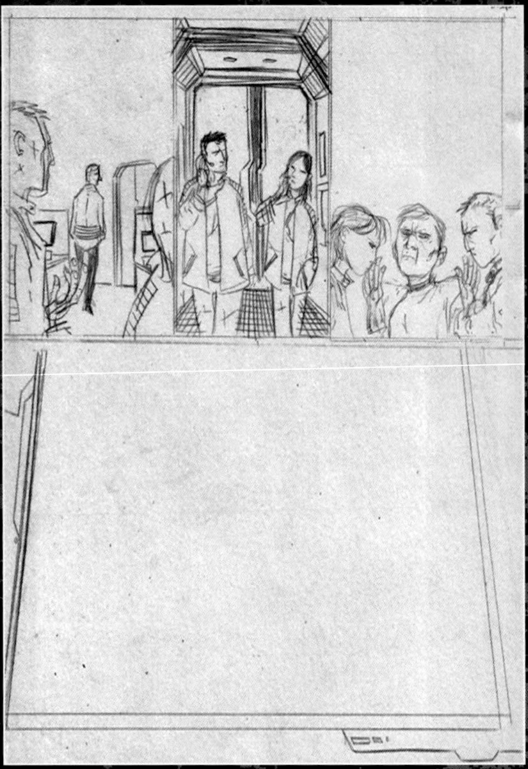

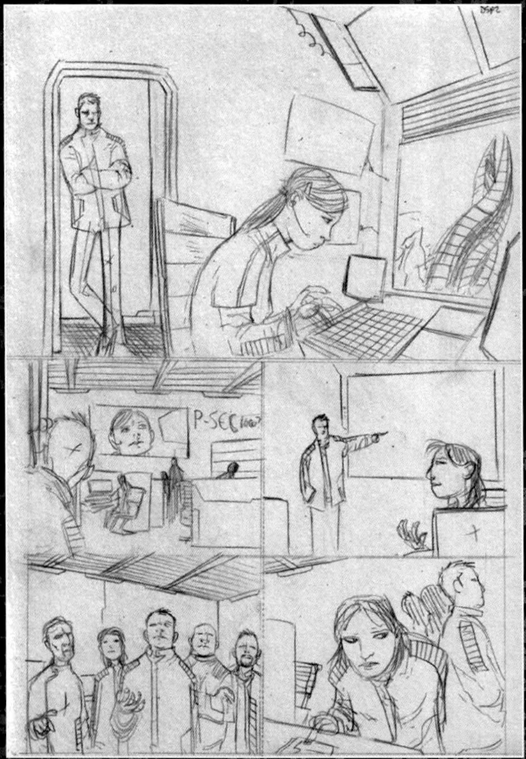
P-SEC

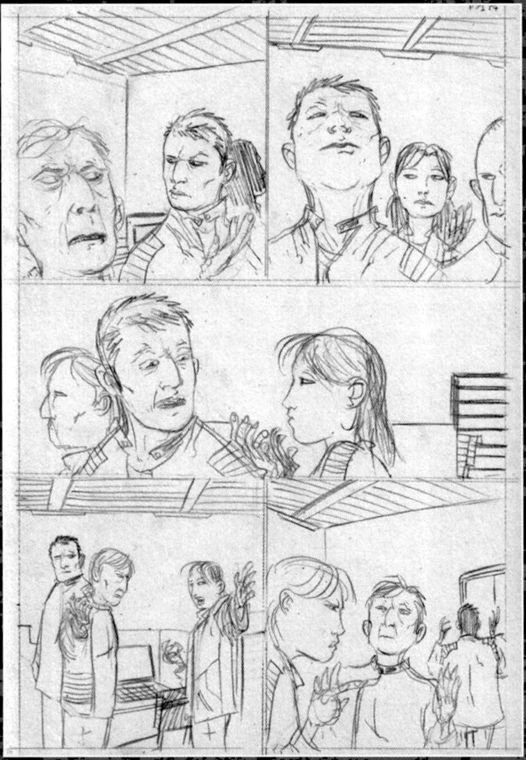

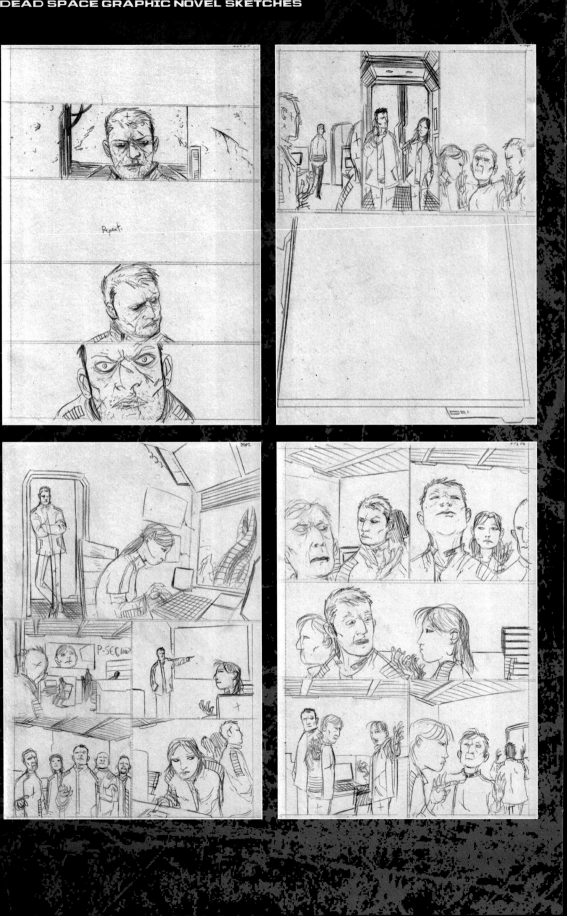

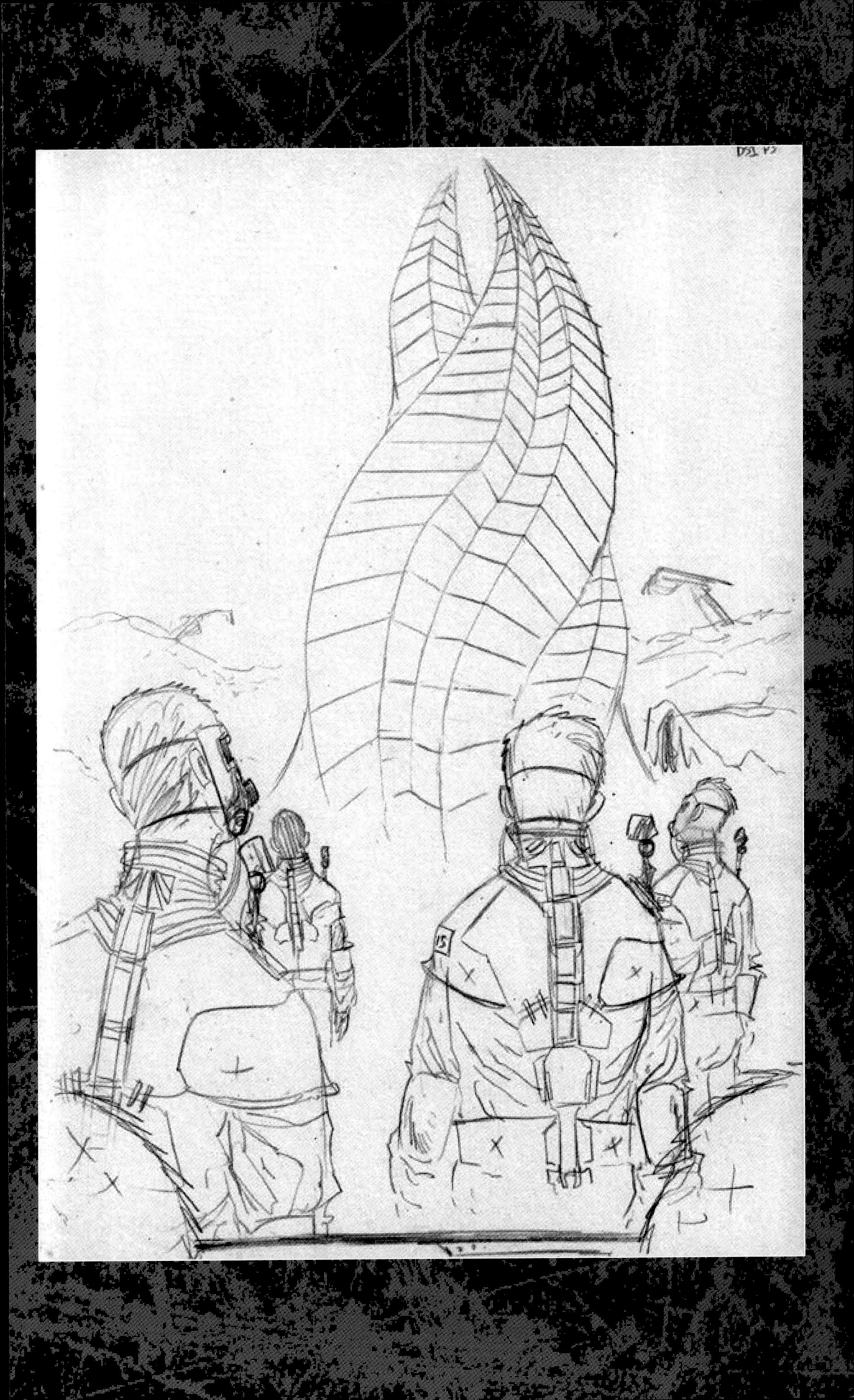

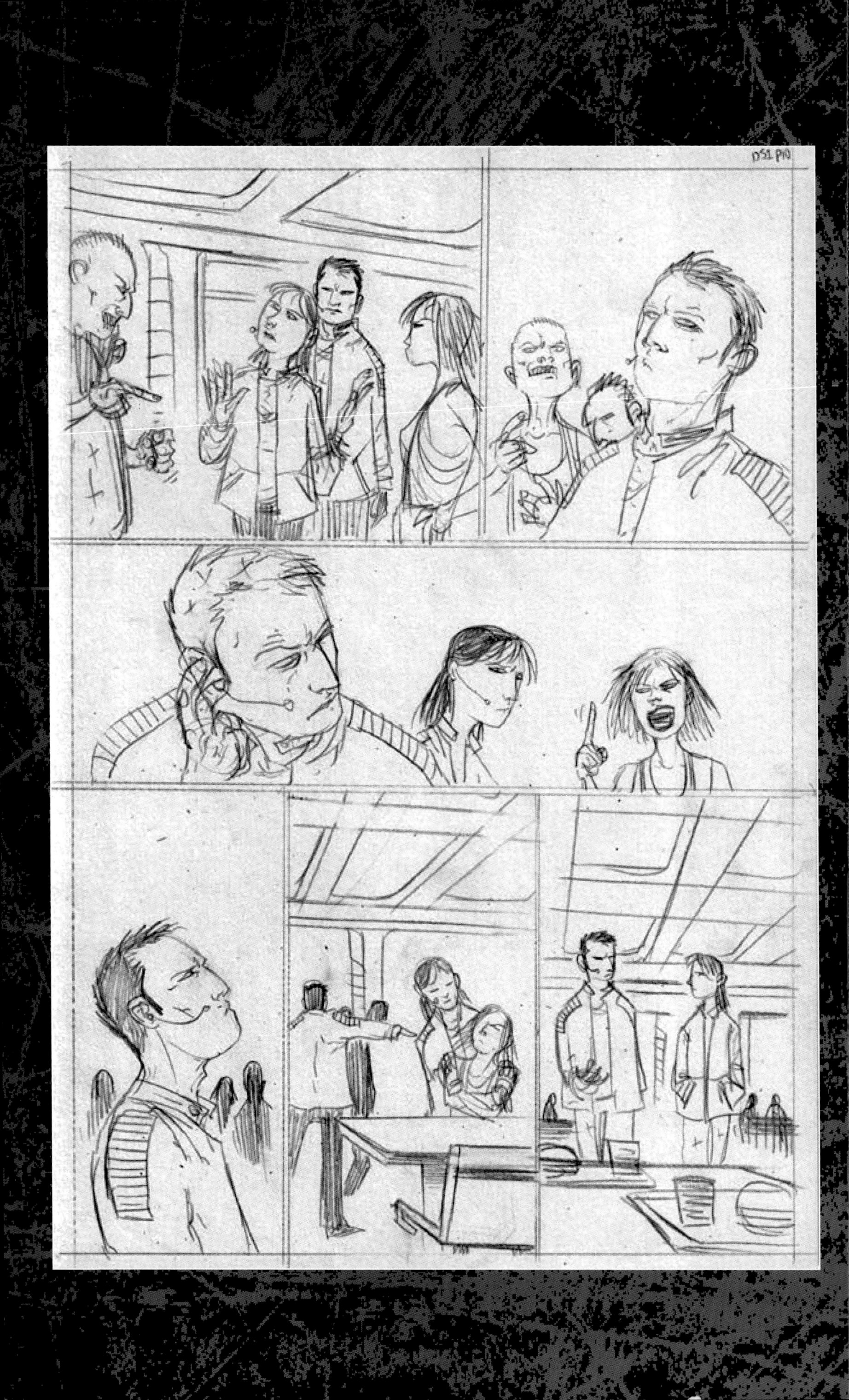
DS1 P10

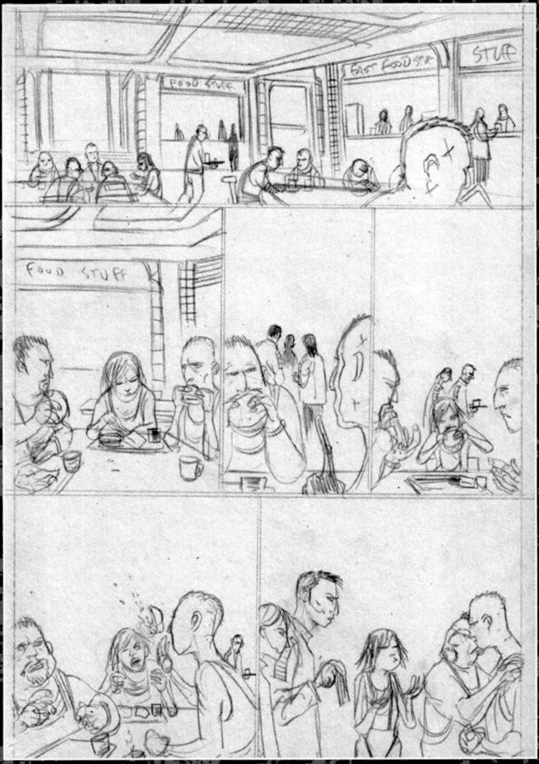
FOOD STUFF
FAST FOOD STA
STUFF
FOOD STUFF

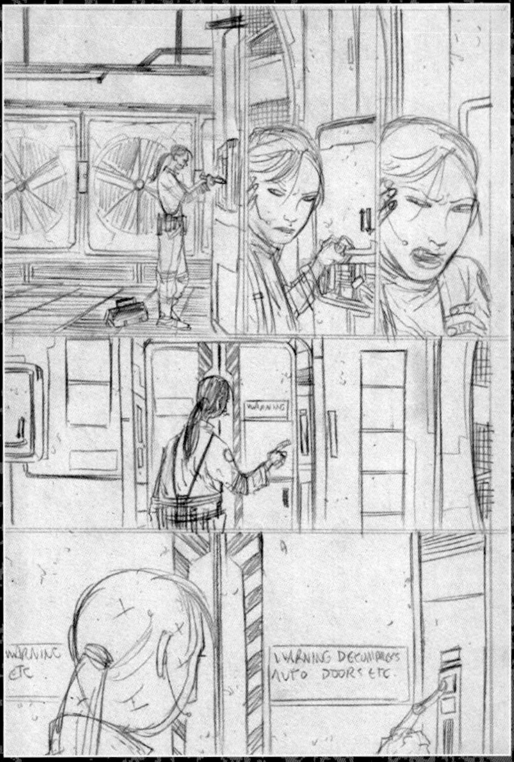
WARNING
WARNING
ETC
WARNING DECOMPRESS
AUTO DOORS ETC.

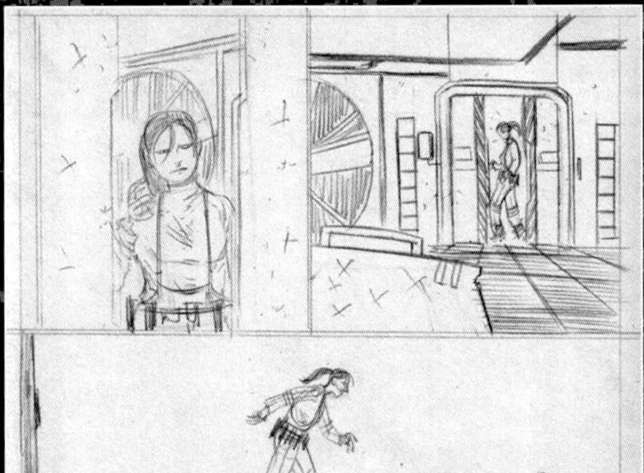

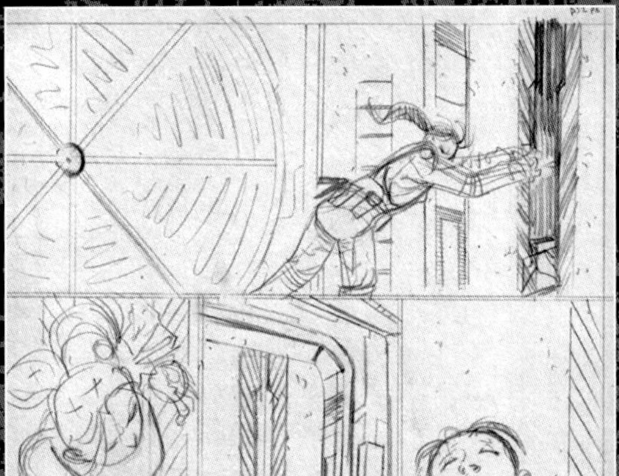

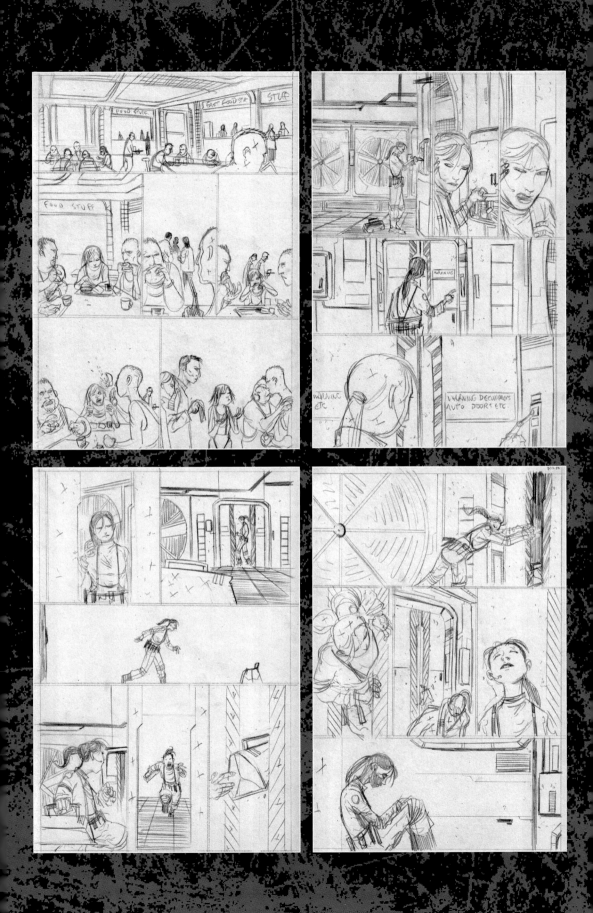

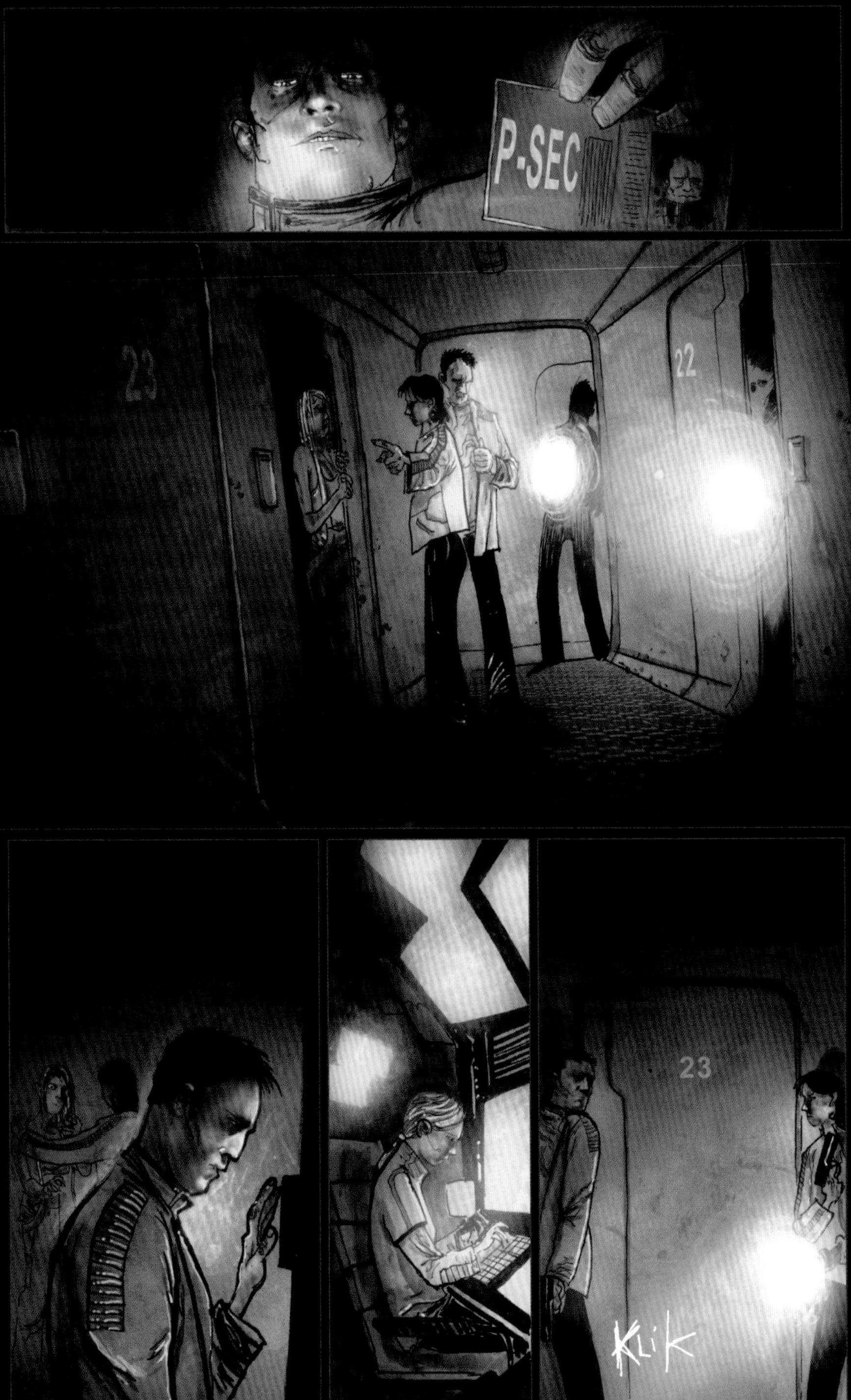
P-SEC
23
22
23
KLIK

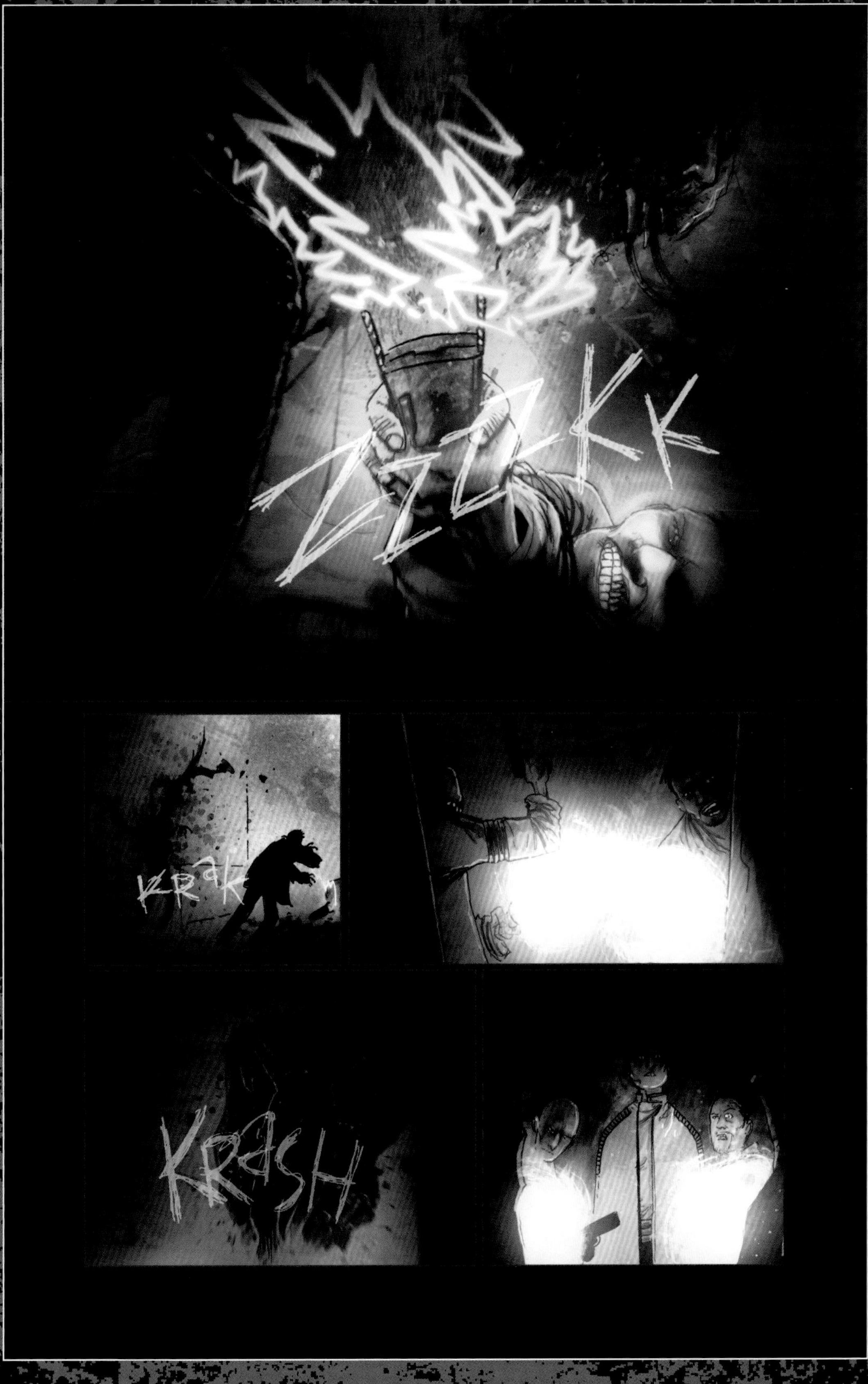
ZZZKK
KRAK
KRASH

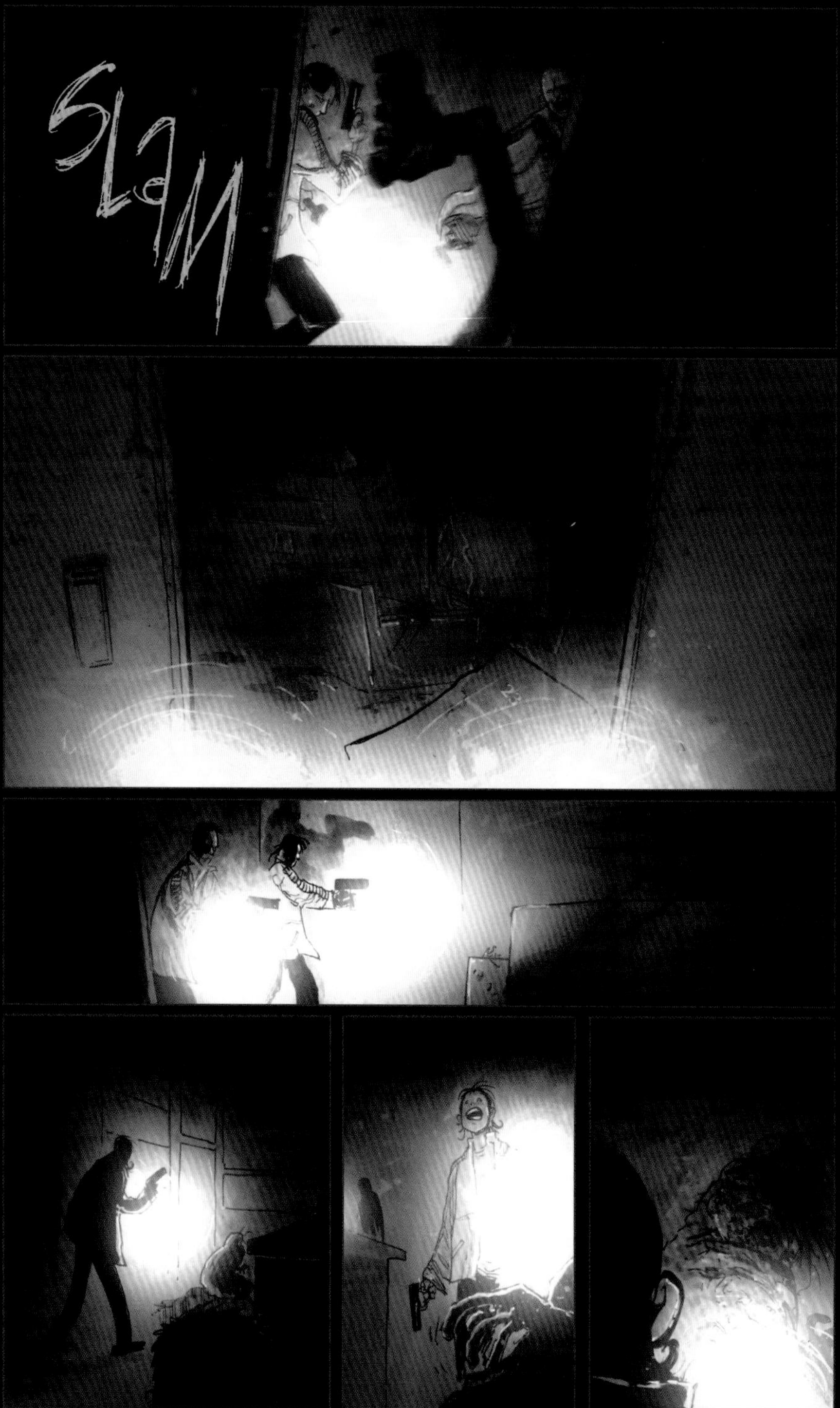
SLAM

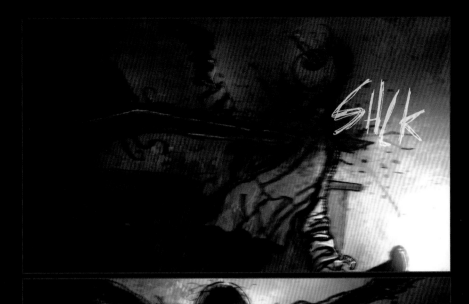

SHLK

RRRiiiiiiPPPHHHKK

BLAM
BLAM
BLAM

THUNK
THUNK
THUNK

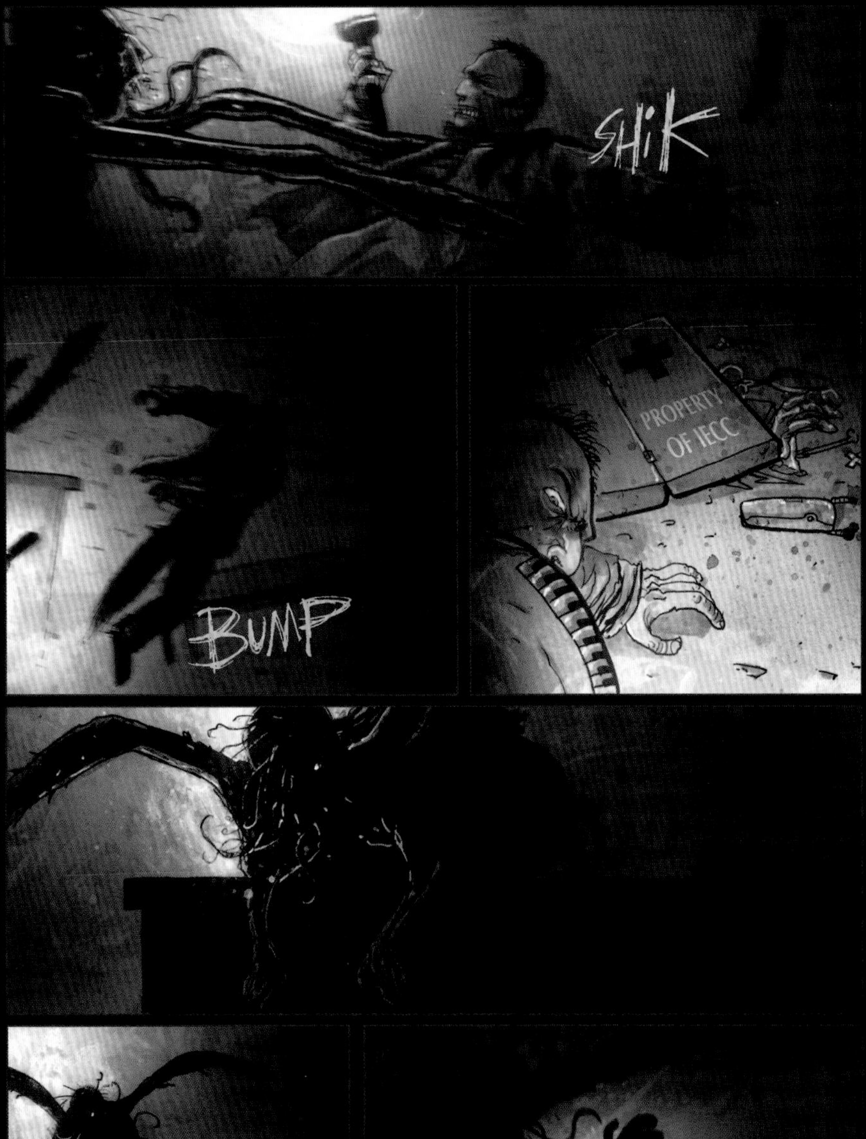
SHIK
BUMP
PROPERTY OF IECC
TZZZZZZZ

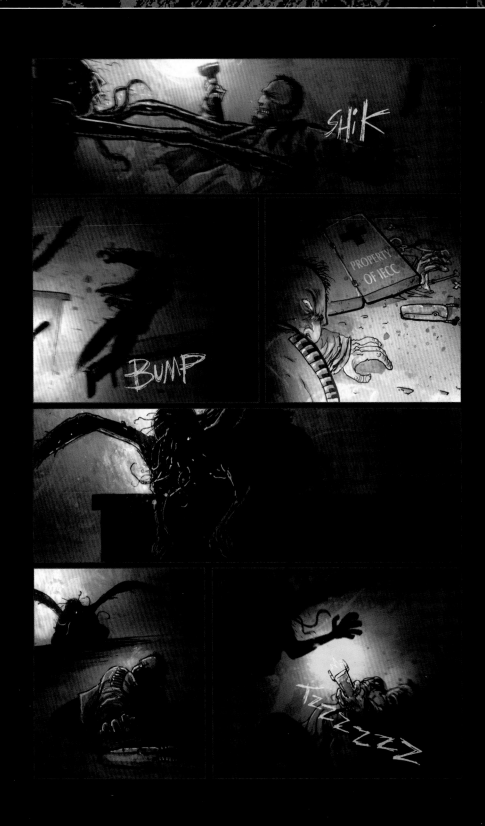

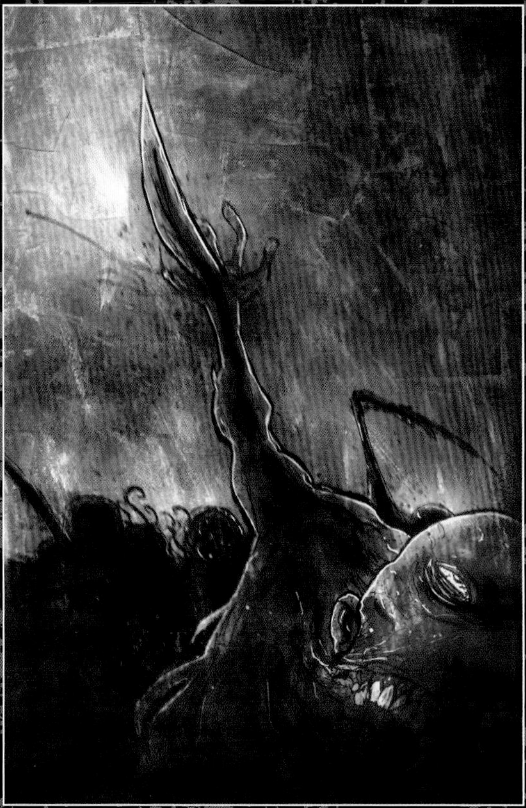

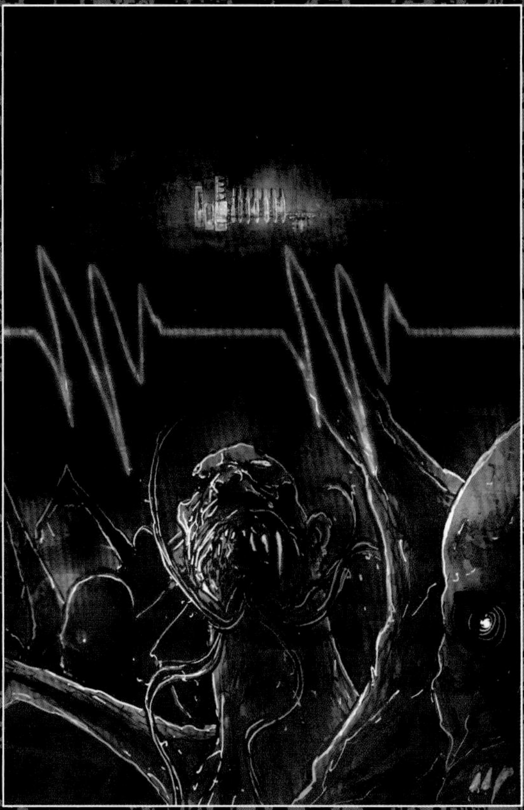

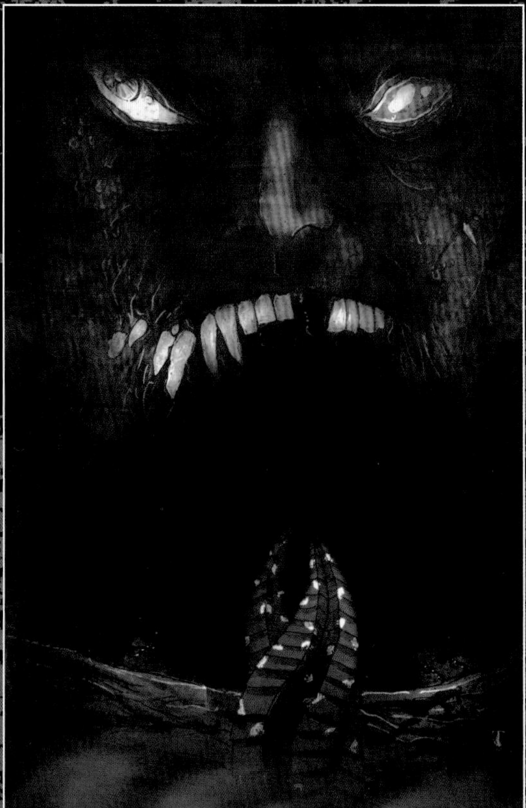

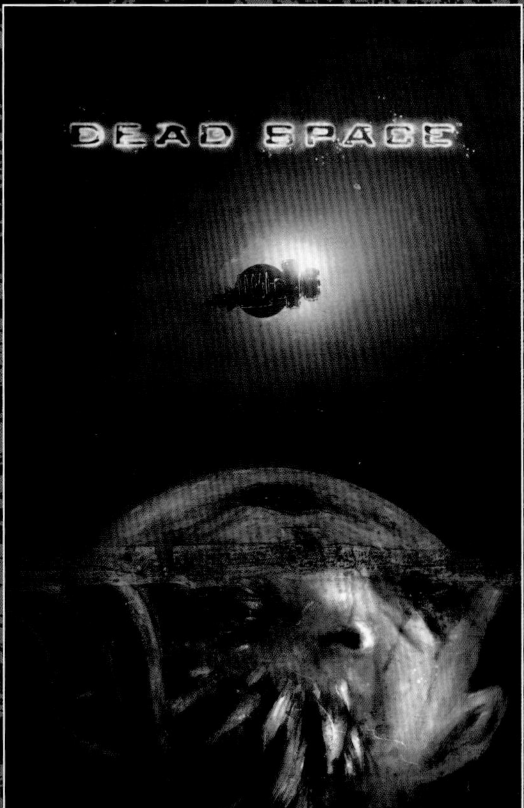
DEAD SPACE

DEAD SPACE™

Also available from Titan Books: *The Art of Dead Space*, *The Art of Dead Space* Limited Edition, graphic novels *Dead Space*, *Dead Space Salvage*, and the new *Dead Space Liberation*.

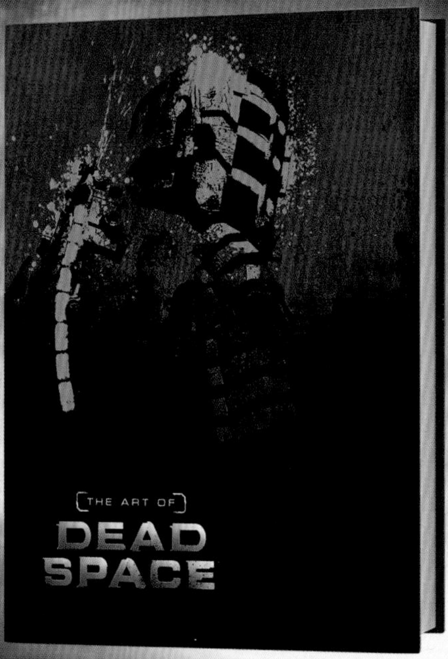
THE ART OF
DEAD SPACE

The Art of Dead Space
ISBN: 9781781164266

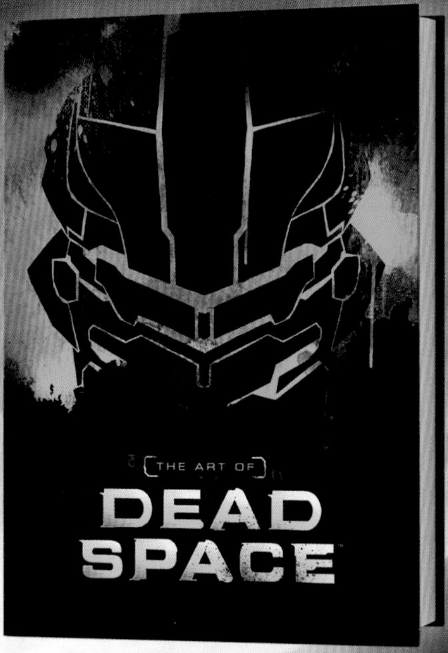
THE ART OF
DEAD SPACE™

The Art of Dead Space
Limited Slipcased Edition with signed print
ISBN: 9781781164273

GRAPHIC NOVELS

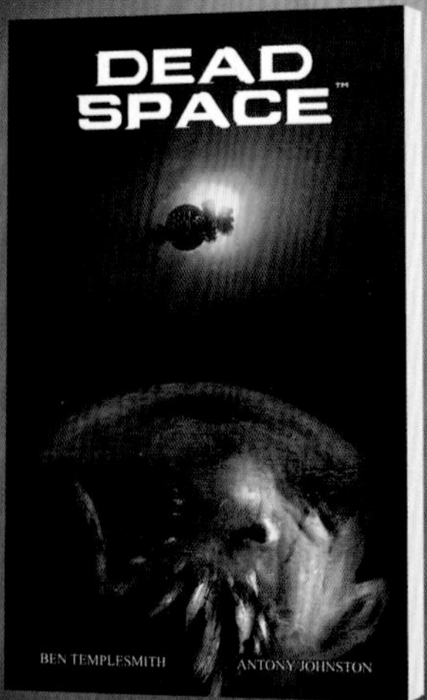
DEAD SPACE™
BEN TEMPLESMITH
ANTONY JOHNSTON

Created by
Ben Templesmith and Antony Johnston
ISBN: 9781781165515

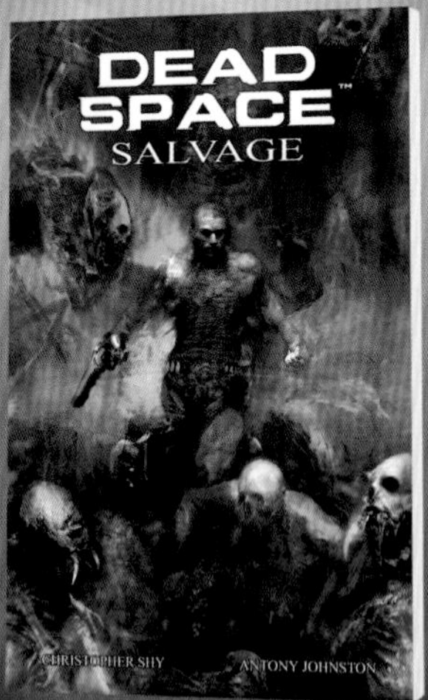
DEAD SPACE™
SALVAGE
CHRISTOPHER SHY
ANTONY JOHNSTON

Created by
Christopher Shy and Antony Johnston
ISBN: 9781781165522

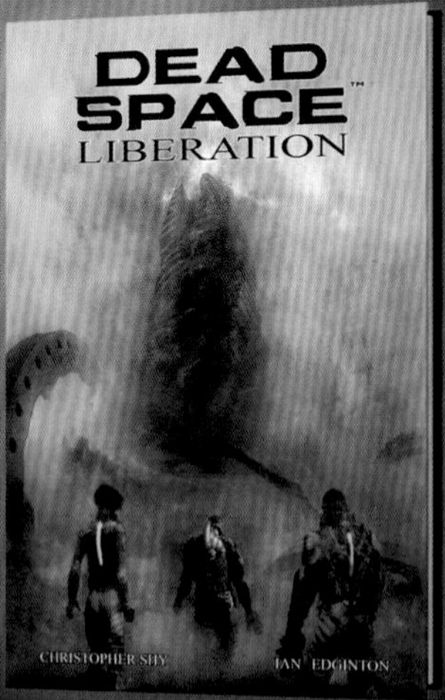
DEAD SPACE™
LIBERATION
CHRISTOPHER SHY
IAN EDGINTON

Created by
Christopher Shy and Ian Edginton
ISBN: 9781781165539